Parties and Politics in North Carolina, 1836–1865

Parties and Politics in North Carolina 1836–1865

MARC W. KRUMAN

★ ★ ★ ★ ★ ★ ★

Louisiana State University Press

Baton Rouge and London

Designer: Barbara Werden
Typeface: Linotron Aster
Typesetter: G & S Typesetters, Inc.
Printer: Thomson-Shore, Inc.

A portion of this book was originally published in somewhat different form as "Dissent in the Confederacy: The North Carolina Experience," in *Civil War History*, XXVIII, No. 4, copyright © 1982 by The Kent State University Press. It is reprinted here with the gracious permission of The Kent State University Press.

Library of Congress Cataloging in Publication Data

Kruman, Marc W.
Parties and politics in North Carolina, 1836–1865.

Bibliography: p.
Includes index.
1. Political parties—North Carolina—History.
2. North Carolina—Politics and government—1775–1865.
I. Title.
JK2295.N82K78   1983   324.2756′009   82-20364
ISBN 0-8071-1041-8
ISBN 0-8071-1061-2 (pbk.)

Publication of this book has been assisted by a grant from the Andrew W. Mellon Foundation.

For Randie

Contents

Maps and Figures

Tables

Preface

During the sixteen years between 1836 and 1852, the United States enjoyed the only truly national party system in its history. Whigs and Democrats, with relatively modern party structures, competed actively for votes in virtually every state in the Union. From the national to the state levels of the federal system, the parties differentiated themselves from one another on a variety of social, economic, and political issues. The differences reached beyond the rhetoric of the stump to the halls of Congress and the state legislatures as lawmakers voted to a remarkable degree along party lines.

In the early 1850s, the party system collapsed throughout much of the country. In the northern states the demise of the system led to unstable competition between the Democratic party and two new parties, the Americans and the Republicans. Only after several years did two-party politics return to those states, with competition now confined to Democrats and Republicans. The political upheavals of the 1850s affected the lower South differently; there, the death of the party system marked the death of competitive two-party politics. Only in North Carolina and other parts of the upper South did a competitive party system persist and retain its vitality.

As the Civil War began, party lines were muddied by the rush to support the Union and Confederate war efforts. In the northern states, after the confusion of the war's first year, two-party competition reemerged, and in the lower South politics remained in a partyless state. In most of the states of the upper South, fighting prevented the regular practice of party politics, but in North Carolina many of the forms of antebellum politics persisted.

The purpose of this book is to explain the reasons for such continuity and to delineate how the persistence of partisanship in all its nuances shaped politics and governance during the sectional era. The book will explore the various facets of party politics: structure, nominations, leadership, newspapers, ideology, rhetoric, policy making, national-state relations, and voting behavior. Party politics molded what white North Carolinians expected from government, how they democratized their political system, how they understood the sectional conflict, how they responded to the secession crisis, and how they behaved during the Confederacy's short and troubled life. On every vital matter affecting the society, party politics substantially influenced what white North Carolinians believed and how they behaved from the late 1830s to the end of the Civil War.

★

My approach to North Carolina is congruent with that suggested by Joel H. Silbey in his seminal article on the Civil War synthesis in American history. Silbey argued that historians have distorted the picture of American politics in the 1840s and 1850s by viewing it exclusively through the prism of the Civil War. By emphasizing the importance of sectional issues, they have ignored the structure of politics and a whole range of other problems that influenced the political system. I would go further to suggest that, as a result, they have also misconstrued significant aspects of the sectional conflict, including the secession crisis. Two fine recent studies by Michael F. Holt and J. Mills Thornton III have shown how important it is to view the sectional conflict in the context of the political culture of the nation and the states.*

The predominance of the Civil War synthesis has also distorted our understanding of wartime politics. Because southern political historians have concerned themselves largely with the causes of secession, they have generally ended their studies in 1861. As a result, they have rarely paid attention to the relationship between prewar and wartime politics or to the nature of political change during the war.

★

Because the federal nature of nineteenth-century American political parties made the state parties the soul of the party system, I have concentrated my work on one state. In taking such an approach, though, I have tried to be attentive to the symbiotic relationship of the state and national

---

*Joel H. Silbey, "The Civil War Synthesis in American Political History," *Civil War History*, X (1964), 130–40; Michael F. Holt, *The Political Crisis of the 1850s* (New York: John Wiley & Sons, 1978); J. Mills Thornton III, *Politics and Power in a Slave Society: Alabama, 1800–1860* (Baton Rouge: Louisiana State University Press, 1978).

parties. State parties functioned independently of their national organizations, especially when state issues were exclusively concerned. But Whigs and Democrats everywhere had political kin beyond the boundaries of their own states, and they recognized and reveled in that kinship. The state party system could only survive as part of a truly federal system with strong national and state parties. The positions of the national parties thus deeply influenced the behavior of the state parties.

My decision to study North Carolina was not based on any sense that its experience was typical of other states. Indeed, the political continuities evident in North Carolina suggest that this was not the case. Still, it is hoped that a study of a state that enjoyed such political stability may help us to understand why party systems persist or crumble. Moreover, North Carolina *was* typical in that it confronted most of the same political problems of other southern states: governmental promotion of economic development, constitutional revision, the right of southerners to take their slaves into western territories, and secession. Finally, historians have focused their attention upon the lower South and generalized from that about the southern political experience. But the politics of the upper South differed greatly from that of the lower South. A study of a state like North Carolina suggests the diversity of the antebellum and Confederate South. It particularly helps to explain the divergent paths that the upper and lower South took during the secession crisis, for their different political experiences shaped their responses to the election of Abraham Lincoln and to the momentous events that followed.

Acknowledgments

During the years that I have worked on this book, I have accumulated many debts. I completed the research for this book at the libraries of the University of North Carolina at Chapel Hill, Duke University, Yale University, Wayne State University, East Carolina University, the University of Chicago, and at the Detroit Public Library, the North Carolina State Library, and the North Carolina State Archives, and I am grateful to the staffs of each institution for their ready and able assistance. I owe special debts to Drs. Isaac Copeland, Carolyn A. Wallace, and Richard Shrader of the Southern Historical Collection of the University of North Carolina at Chapel Hill; to Dr. H. G. Jones of the North Carolina Collection of the same university; to Dr. Thornton Mitchell, Mr. Paul Hoffman, and Mr. Joe Mobley of the North Carolina Division of Archives and History; and to Dr. Mattie Russell of the Manuscripts Room of the William R. Perkins Library at Duke University. Their courteous assistance made this Yankee feel at home in North Carolina. Jeffrey Moyer carefully prepared the maps. Ginny Corbin expertly typed the final draft of the manuscript, and Margaret Fisher Dalrymple of the Louisiana State University Press edited it.

A Wayne State faculty research award enabled me to complete the research for the book, and an Andrew W. Mellon Faculty Fellowship in the Humanities at Harvard University provided me with a year to finish the writing. Dr. Richard M. Hunt of the Mellon program was enormously helpful, while William and Mary Lee Bossert, Co-Masters, and the stimulating students and tutors of Lowell House provided an ideal writing environment.

I have incurred many other obligations to historians and friends who took precious time out from their own work to talk about history and to read earlier drafts of my manuscript. Gerd Korman and Joel Silbey introduced me to the discipline of history as an undergraduate and have offered good counsel in succeeding years. Ralph A. Wooster and Thomas B. Alexander made me realize just how much we are part of an academic community. Professor Wooster shared with me his research notes on North Carolina legislators, and Professor Alexander provided me with innumerable computer print-outs in response to my unending series of questions. I have spent countless hours talking about North Carolina politics with Jeffrey Crow, Robert D. Miller, and Harry L. Watson. Early drafts of the manuscript were read by Paul G. E. Clemens, William C. Harris, Christopher H. Johnson, Howard R. Lamar, and Melvin Small. Their criticisms forced me to reconsider my arguments and undoubtedly made this book far better than it otherwise would have been. Daniel Crofts shared his thoughts about the secession crisis and presented an especially telling critique of the manuscript. David Herbert Donald offered not only warm encouragement at a crucial point in my writing but also trenchant criticism of the manuscript's early chapters.

I am even more deeply indebted to Michael F. Holt, Richard L. McCormick, and J. Mills Thornton III, who assumed obligations that far surpass those of scholars and friends. They read through the manuscript twice, and their comments improved it in every imaginable way. My greatest intellectual debt is to C. Vann Woodward, who has guided this work from its inception as a doctoral dissertation. I have learned from his advice, his criticism, and above all, from his example.

This book could not have been written without the aid and comfort of my family. I can never repay the debt that I owe to my parents, Martin and Florence Kruman, and to my brother, Henry Kruman, for their love and support over the years. My in-laws, Leon and Marjorie Schafer, offered sustenance, both physical and emotional, during several lengthy research trips in North Carolina.

The birth of my daughter Sarah delayed the completion of the manuscript, but she has made the delay most worthwhile. My greatest debt is expressed in the dedication of this book to my wife. Only Randie's constant love and encouragement, and occasional prodding, enabled me to bring this book to completion.

Abbreviations

AHR	*American Historical Review*
Duke	Duke University Library, Durham, North Carolina
HJ	*Journal of the House of Commons of North Carolina* (Raleigh: State Printer, 1841–1865).
JAH	*Journal of American History*
JSH	*Journal of Southern History*
LC	Library of Congress
MVHR	*Mississippi Valley Historical Review*
NCC	North Carolina Collection, Louis R. Wilson Library, University of North Carolina at Chapel Hill
NCDAH	North Carolina Division of Archives and History, Raleigh, North Carolina
NCHR	*North Carolina Historical Review*
SHC	Southern Historical Collection, University of North Carolina at Chapel Hill
SJ	*Journal of the Senate of North Carolina* (Raleigh: State Printer, 1841–1865)

Parties and Politics in North Carolina, 1836–1865

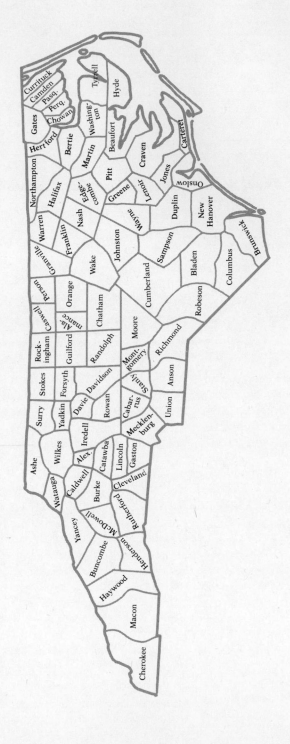

Figure 1.
North Carolina at the Beginning of 1850, Showing Approximate County Divisions within Present State Boundaries Based on a map by L. Polk Denmark in *The Formation of North Carolina Counties*. Used with the permission of the Division of Archives and History, North Carolina Department of Cultural Resources.

One   *"Contending for Political Freedom": The Creation of the Second Party System in North Carolina*

As the presidential election of 1840 approached, a worried James Owens of Wilmington, North Carolina, wrote to a friend: "It is 'sink or swim' with the Nation, & if we do not succeed in the coming elections, I believe, 'The People' will never elect another President, till we have had another Revolution." Owens' apocalyptic fears for the future were shared by Whigs and Democrats throughout North Carolina and the nation. The election, Whigs said, "must determine the great question whether we are to live as SLAVES or FREEDMEN," while Democrats argued that voters were "assuredly contending for the political freedom of themselves and their posterity."[1]

Fears that the Republic and liberty were endangered permeated the political rhetoric of 1840. Using novel political devices like conventions, mass meetings, and statewide canvassing by gubernatorial candidates, Democrats and Whigs each portrayed their presidential candidates, Martin Van Buren and William Henry Harrison respectively, as the only hope for the Republic's salvation. All political decisions and arguments, it seemed, had ramifications for the future of republican government. When President Van Buren's secretary of war, Joel Poinsett, proposed a plan for better organization of the militia, Whigs accused Van Buren of seeking to

1. James Owens to James W. Bryan, May 9, 1840, in Bryan Family Papers, SHC; Raleigh *Register*, October 9, 1840; Raleigh *North Carolina Standard*, April 1, 1840 (hereinafter referred to as Raleigh *Standard*).

establish a standing army that would rob the people of their liberties. In Van Buren's subtreasury plan, which divorced the government from the banks, Whigs saw a desire to prostrate the American economy. In his exercise of patronage appointments, they saw a wish to destroy the freedom of elections. In his northern alliances, they perceived a sympathy for abolitionists, a threat to that sine qua non of white southern liberty and equality, black slavery. And in Van Buren's White House life-style, they saw the kinds of extravagance that it was believed historically had led to corruption and the death of republics.[2]

Democrats replied in kind. They portrayed the Whigs as "federalists," aristocrats in disguise who could only obtain power by duping the people. If Harrison was elected and the Whigs obtained power, Democrats charged, they would restore that engine of oppression, the second Bank of the United States. The economic and political corruption fostered by the bank, which had been thwarted by Andrew Jackson's destruction of it, would once again threaten the Republic. Democrats also saw in Whig programs like federal aid to internal improvements the creation of a central government so strong that it would infringe on state and local rights and ultimately crush individual liberty. And like the Whigs, Democrats spied a threat to slavery, only they perceived it in Harrison's apparent ties to abolitionists.[3]

Often dismissed as a campaign in which partisan hoopla crowded out real issues, the presidential contest spoke to the deepest needs and fears of the American people. From the country's inception, Americans believed that they lived in a citadel of republicanism, with a mission to serve as an example for the world. But they also feared that their experiment was endangered: having been taught that republics were fragile entities, always under siege, Americans were sensitive to both external and internal threats. The threat from without seemed to abate with the end of the War of 1812; though the war concluded in a stalemate, Americans perceived it as a great victory for the Republic and republicanism.

Yet the internal threat remained. Citizens in the early Republic worried that their liberty would be crushed by power, usually the power of government, and they sought to protect it in the constitutional republican governments of the states and the Union. In this way they hoped to institutionalize the protection of liberty. But because governments were always susceptible to corruption and to the desires of power-hungry men, the people needed to remain vigilant.[4]

2. Raleigh *Register*, August 18, September 1, 4, 15, 28, October 10, 27, 30, November 3, 1840; Fayetteville *Observer*, February 26, June 24, July 1, 29, September 9, 1840.
3. Raleigh *Standard*, February 26, July 15, August 10, September 23, 30, October 7, 21, 1840.
4. One example of the traditional interpretation is Charles S. Sydnor, *The Development of*

In the 1830s, political parties became the people's surrogate sentinels guarding the fortress of popular liberty. Or so it seemed to partisans. As politicians established the Whig and Democratic parties throughout the country, they faced the added duty of protecting white equality, for by that time the equality of white men had become inextricably linked to the concept of liberty. Men, they said, who were not equal to others were not truly free. Throughout the life of the party system and beyond, the central mission of parties and politicians was to identify threats to republican government and to the white freedom and equality it protected, and to repel them.[5]

Although politicians in both parties sought the protection and promotion of white equality and liberty, they planned to reach those goals by following different paths. Ultimately, as Michael F. Holt has observed, these differences and the existence of a competitive political environment instilled a popular faith in the parties as defenders of republicanism. Whigs and Democrats expressed those differences most clearly when they debated the proper role of government in society, especially in the economy.[6]

Whigs viewed the government as a liberating force in the economy. In an area where capital was scarce, they believed, only government possessed the financial resources needed to build the economic substructure— transportation facilities like railroads, turnpikes, or canals. Such governmental activities would open up economic opportunities for all people and broaden economic freedoms. Always implicit and often explicit in the attitudes of Whigs were the virtues of a capitalist market economy. Whigs supported such necessary accouterments of the capitalist system as banks and limited liability for individual stockholders in corporations.

If Whigs expected good things to come from the market economy, Democrats feared it. Instead of viewing banks, railroads, and corporations

---

Southern Sectionalism, 1819–1848 (Baton Rouge: Louisiana State University Press, 1948), 320. A somewhat more balanced treatment may be found in Glyndon Van Deusen, *The Jacksonian Era, 1828–1848* (New York: Harper & Row, 1959), 141–50. Two recent books have properly reasserted the ideological significance of the contest: William R. Brock, *Parties and Political Conscience, 1840–1850* (Millwood, N.Y.: KTO Press, 1979), 4–5; and Daniel Walker Howe, *The Political Culture of the American Whigs* (Chicago: University of Chicago Press, 1979), 7–8.

On the fear for the survival of republican government, see Bernard Bailyn, *The Ideological Origins of the American Revolution* (Cambridge, Mass.: Harvard University Press, 1967); Gordon S. Wood, *The Creation of the American Republic, 1776–1787* (Chapel Hill: University of North Carolina Press, 1969); John R. Howe, "Republican Thought and the Political Violence of the 1790s," *American Quarterly*, XIV (1967), 147–65; and Roger H. Brown, *The Republic in Peril: 1812* (New York: Columbia University Press, 1964).

5. Michael F. Holt, *The Political Crisis of the 1850s* (New York: John Wiley & Sons, 1978), 17–38; J. Mills Thornton III, *Politics and Power in a Slave Society: Alabama, 1800–1860* (Baton Rouge: Louisiana State University Press, 1978), 3–58.

6. Holt, *Political Crisis*, 25–38.

as the bases of liberation, they saw them as hazards to freedom. The corporation represented unfair privileges for the few, the banks unchecked financial power. Democrats feared that state financing of internal improvements would lead to the accretion of greater and greater power in the hands of the state, which in turn threatened the liberties of the people. State financing would also place the state in debt, which, Democrats believed, would lead inevitably to corruption and the end of republican government. Democrats argued that the state should do nothing positive to promote economic growth but should simply protect the equal rights of all white men. They sought a government that freed people from outside interference; Whigs sought a government that would free people from economic dependence.[7]

★

Although the basic views of the parties were fairly consistent throughout the country, they evolved in each state in response to local circumstances. In North Carolina, the sources of political conflict were largely regional in nature. The state's geography, which stunted North Carolina's economic development, isolated North Carolinians from the outside world and from one another. The coastline, whose shifting shoals beyond the Outer Banks "render[ed] the coast of this state more dangerous to navigators than any other in the Atlantic," decreed that North Carolina would have no substantial port city. The only port of any consequence was Wilmington, the state's largest town, which sat thirty miles from the ocean at the mouth of the state's most navigable river, the Cape Fear. What foreign commerce North Carolinians engaged in left and entered through Wilmington, but the amount remained minuscule through the late antebellum decades.[8]

The state's citizens, who lived in one of the three well-defined geographic regions—the coastal plain, the Piedmont, and the mountains—were also separated from each other. The coastal plain, which enjoyed the most natural advantages, was crisscrossed by rivers that emptied into the coastal sounds. Although many were no more than sluggish streams, rivers like the Cape Fear in the south, the Neuse in the center, and the

7. For similar interpretations of Whig and Democratic attitudes toward governance, see, for examples, Lee Benson, *The Concept of Jacksonian Democracy: New York as a Test Case* (Princeton: Princeton University Press, 1961), 86–109; Herbert Ershkowitz and William Shade, "Consensus or Conflict? Political Behavior in the State Legislatures During the Jacksonian Era," *JAH*, LVIII (1971), 591–622; Holt, *Political Crisis*, 25–38; Joel H. Silbey, *The Shrine of Party: Congressional Voting Behavior, 1841–1852* (Pittsburgh: University of Pittsburgh Press, 1967); James Roger Sharp, *The Jacksonians Versus the Banks: Politics in the States After the Panic of 1837* (New York: Columbia University Press, 1970); Thornton, *Politics and Power*, 20–58.

8. J. D. B. De Bow, *The Industrial Resources, Etc., of the Southern and Western States . . .* (3 vols.; New Orleans: Office of De Bow's Review, 1852), II, 170.

Roanoke in the north were navigable well into the interior and provided transportation facilities for planters and farmers on the plain.[9]

The relatively good access that agriculturalists in the eastern part of the state enjoyed made them less receptive to internal improvements and especially to government promotion of them. Such sentiments dominated the plantation counties of the middle and western coastal plain, which stretched from Granville, Warren, and Northampton at the Virginia border to the southern counties bounded by Onslow and Robeson. In the north, the planters of Warren, Franklin, and Granville (and the neighboring Piedmont counties) grew tobacco for markets in Petersburg and Norfolk, Virginia. To the east and south lay the state's cotton region. Most of the 34,617 bales of cotton grown in the state in 1840 came from counties like Halifax and Northampton in the north to Bladen, Columbus, and Robeson in the south (and across the southern tier of the Piedmont to Mecklenburg). At the southern tip of the plain, in New Hanover and especially Brunswick, planters grew rice in abundance.[10]

These planters opposed government aid to internal improvements not merely because they already had decent transportation facilities—after all, a railroad in their region would reduce the cost of transporting their crops to market and enhance the value of their property. That is what happened when the Raleigh and Gaston and Wilmington and Weldon railroad companies completed in 1840 the construction of railroads that crossed the coastal plain in a north-south direction.[11] For many planters, opposition to internal improvements reflected a broader fear of socioeconomic and political change. Unlike their counterparts in the states of the newer South, these planters were part of a well-established elite that had long dominated their communities and the state. For them, the credit system,

9. Using the same demarcations as previous historians, I refer to the coastal plain or east as the region east of the western boundaries of the following counties: Granville, Wake, Harnett, Cumberland, and Robeson. The Piedmont refers to the region stretching westward to the western boundaries of Surry, Yadkin, Alexander, Catawba, Cleveland, Rutherford, and Polk. The mountain area, also referred to as the far west, begins west of that line. In this study, the mountain and Piedmont regions together are referred to as the west. See Joseph Carlyle Sitterson, *The Secession Movement in North Carolina* (Chapel Hill: University of North Carolina Press, 1939), 4–5. On eastern trade routes, see Hugh Talmage Lefler and Albert Ray Newsome, *North Carolina: The History of a Southern State* (3rd ed.; Chapel Hill: University of North Carolina Press, 1973), 316–17; and Harold Joseph Counihan, "North Carolina Politics, 1815–1836: State and Local Perspectives on the Age of Jackson" (Ph.D. dissertation, University of North Carolina at Chapel Hill, 1971), 122–29.

10. J. D. B. De Bow, *Statistical View of the United States . . . Being a Compendium of the Seventh Census* (Washington, D.C.: Beverly Tucker, 1854), 281, 287; Sitterson, *Secession Movement*, 6, 12.

11. William Robards to Daniel M. Barringer, April 17, 1841, in Daniel Moreau Barringer Papers, SHC.

internal improvements, and the like would necessarily bring changes that might endanger their economic, social, and political hegemony. Although they participated in the market economy, they felt threatened by it. The archetypal example of this attitude is Nathaniel Macon, an old Republican turned Jacksonian Democrat. Macon did not live an autarkic existence isolated from the capitalist economy but acquired his considerable wealth through the sale of his tobacco crop in Petersburg. Yet Macon believed that the new economy and the exercise of state power menaced the simple agrarian society in which he lived and thrived.[12]

The fear of change felt by Macon and others was not limited to the upper class. Men who lived in rural areas in the east, often near towns, feared the encroachment of the commercial world on their lives. A recent study has shown that people in the rural areas of Cumberland County in the 1830s had few ties to the market economy and little desire to enter it. They despised the world of Fayetteville, the county seat and a substantial trading town, and its commercial aspirations.[13]

Eastern opposition to the positive state grew also because the east was the wealthiest section of the state. If the state engaged in promotional activities, or built asylums, or appointed a state school superintendent, wealthier easterners would foot the bill with higher taxes. At a later date, an eastern planter and Democratic legislator, Thomas D. McDowell, summarized some of the reasons for eastern opposition to state-aided internal improvements. In a letter to a college friend who lived in the mountains, he explained: "Our people—having more advantages than you have do not so much appreciate a system of Improvements and are not willing to involve the State in too heavy a debt."[14]

The political leaders of the middle east did not speak for all of the coastal plain. Indeed, it would be appropriate to treat the counties of the northeast as a subregion different economically and politically from the rest of the east. Instead of growing staples on plantations, smaller farmers in the northeast grew grains. Instead of opposing government promotion of economic development, northeastern politicians generally endorsed such government activity. Farmers and politicians in that region, it seems, were enamored with the idea of building a canal to link Albemarle Sound with

12. Harry L. Watson, "Squire Oldway and His Friends: Opposition to Internal Improvements in Antebellum North Carolina," *NCHR*, LIV (1977), 105–19.
13. Harry L. Watson, *Jacksonian Politics and Community Conflict: The Emergence of the Second American Party System in Cumberland County, North Carolina* (Baton Rouge: Louisiana State University Press, 1981). Professor Watson kindly allowed me to read his book in manuscript.
14. Thomas D. McDowell to Walter W. Lenoir, July 8, 1854, in Lenoir Family Papers, SHC.

Chesapeake Bay and of having the government in Washington foot the bill.[15]

Farmers in the northeast and eastern men of commerce found welcome allies west of the fall line in their struggle for government aid for economic development. Transportation facilities in the Piedmont and the mountains ranged from bad to horrid, and support for government aid to improve them was strong. For example, in the state legislature mountain members consistently voted for state aid to internal improvements. Until recently, this behavior was explained simply as the expression of the desire of isolated westerners seeking to participate in the market economy. But J. Mills Thornton III has shown that in Alabama farmers living outside of or on the margins of the market economy had little desire to become enmeshed in its web. Hence the attitudes of westerners toward government promotional activity require some explanation.[16]

In fact, citizens in far western North Carolina were not always wildly enthusiastic about things like road building. The construction of a public road in Caldwell County shows the nature of popular opposition to internal improvements and how it was overcome. William A. Lenoir, a member of Caldwell County's ruling family, was one of North Carolina's leading propagandists for internal improvements and the economic development of the mountains and was actively involved in the construction and management of local roads. He spent most of February, 1851, overseeing the construction of a road from Lenoir in Caldwell County to Taylorsville in neighboring Alexander. Assigned to work on the road were about one hundred men, "most of whom," according to Lenoir, "are much opposed to the road and especially to working it. They say they blame me with it almost entirely[,] told me I would be long remembered for it. Threatined [sic] to have me whip[p]ed or killed." In the end, though, Lenoir won out.

> I worked hard among them, spoke mildly but with firmness and convinced many by various reasons of the importance of the work[,] showed them some of my correspondence with citizens in Ten. and different parts of our own State upon the subject of a Rail Road through this section—which might be promoted by first making a fine common road, about 12 out of 60 hands at the lower end appeared the first day

15. Sitterson, *Secession Movement*, 7. See also William A. Graham to James W. Bryan, November 21, 1840, in J. G. deRoulhac Hamilton and Max R. Williams (eds.), *The Papers of William Alexander Graham* (6 vols. to date; Raleigh: State Department of Archives and History, 1957–), II, 122.

16. Thomas E. Jeffrey, "Internal Improvements and Political Parties in Antebellum North Carolina," *NCHR*, LV (1978), 155; Thornton, *Politics and Power*.

to work[,] over 20 the 2nd, etc. then at the upper end where I had had more opertunities [*sic*] of exerting my influence made a tolerable turn out the first day and became much more in the spirit of working as they progressed—[17]

Lenoir's experience reveals the obvious fact that men disliked working on the public roads, but it also suggests that they saw little value in roads themselves. The threats to Lenoir showed that eighteenth-century-style deference to one's betters was dead in Caldwell, but his ultimate victory also revealed how citizens did defer to a member of the county's most powerful family. Lenoir's experience may tell us more about the wider attitudes of western North Carolinians. While many ordinary citizens may have not been wildly enthusiastic about a new road, elites in those areas who either lived in towns or were otherwise involved in the market economy were able to shape the broader political position of the region.

Farmers in the mountains had other economic reasons for supporting internal improvements. By the 1840s, many had become intimately involved in the market economy, often carrying goods to market towns either at the foot of the mountains in the state or into northern Georgia, South Carolina, or southwestern Virginia. Mountain farmers, though, often did not take crops to market; their market came to them. At the end of each fall, men herded thousands upon thousands of hogs, as well as many horses, cattle, and even ducks and turkeys, down from eastern Kentucky and Tennessee along the French Broad River through the North Carolina mountains to markets in Georgia and South Carolina. The hogs and other animals provided a ready demand for the farmers' corn, and the herdsmen demanded the goods and services of farmers, merchants, and innkeepers they encountered en route. In other words, many mountain men already participated in the market economy; hence one would not expect the resistance to the blandishments of the market economy evident elsewhere.[18]

The convergence of the interests of the west, the urban east, and the northeast ultimately provided the voting base for the Whig party in the state. The coalition was cemented further by the alliance of urban political leaders and westerners to revise the state's constitution. The sectionalism

17. William A. Lenoir Diary, February 15 and 21, 1851, in Thomas A. Lenoir, Sr., Papers, Duke.
18. Forrest McDonald and Grady McWhiney, "The Antebellum Southern Herdsman: A Reinterpretation," *JSH*, XLI (1975), 147–66; Wilma Dykeman, *The French Broad* (New York: Rinehart & Company, 1955), 137–51; Foster A. Sondley, *A History of Buncombe County, North Carolina* (2 vols.; Asheville: Advocate Printing Co., 1930), II, 619–21; De Bow, *Statistical View*, 280, 286; [?] to Calvin Wiley, May 30, 1850, in Calvin Henderson Wiley Papers, NCDAH.

encouraged by different economic needs was reinforced by the inequalities in the state constitution. As late as the 1830s, North Carolina retained unaltered its constitution of 1776, which kept power in the hands of the General Assembly and power within the General Assembly in the hands of the east.

After their experience with King George III and the royal governors, the writers of North Carolina's first state constitution severely limited the power of the state's chief executive. Elected by the state legislature for a one-year term, the governor possessed no veto power or any substantial patronage power. What influence he had lay in his ability to persuade legislators to follow a course he outlined. But without specific powers and without the cement of partisanship in the state legislature, the governorship usually proved to be little more than a ceremonial office.[19]

Like other revolutionary state constitutions, North Carolina's delegated most of the power of the state to the legislature, which elected the governor, the judiciary, and many state and local officials. The bills that the legislature passed automatically became laws because of the absence of a gubernatorial veto.

Easterners, the first settlers of colonial North Carolina, held sway during the colonial period, and they devised a state constitution that would perpetuate their power in the General Assembly. They apportioned representation according to the county system; each county received one senator and two commoners. This added considerable weight to the more numerous counties of the east. Once entrenched in the legislature, easterners limited the growth of western influence by limiting the number of new western counties. When eastern legislators permitted the establishment of a new western county, they were sure to add a new one in the east and thus perpetuate eastern domination of the assembly.

The men whom voters sent to the legislature were guaranteed to be men of means. Following the revolutionary axioms that only men of property were independent enough to act in the public interest and that the

19. On the revolutionary state constitutions generally, see Wood, *Creation of the American Republic*, 127–389. The North Carolina constitution of 1776 may be found in Francis Newton Thorpe (comp.), *The Federal and State Constitutions, Colonial Charters, and Other Organic Laws of the States, Territories, and Colonies Now or Heretofore Forming the United States* (7 vols.; Washington, D.C.: Government Printing Office, 1909), V, 2787–94.

The following discussion of constitutional change is based largely on Counihan, "North Carolina," esp. chs. 1, 5, and 6; Harold Joseph Counihan, "The North Carolina Constitutional Convention of 1835, A Study in Jacksonian Democracy" *NCHR*, XLVI (1969), 335–65; William S. Hoffmann, *Andrew Jackson and North Carolina Politics* (Chapel Hill: University of North Carolina Press, 1958), 81–89; and William A. Graham, *et al.*, "Address to the People of North Carolina, on the Subject of Amending the Constitution of the State," January, 1834, in Hamilton and Williams (eds.), *Graham Papers*, I, 285–303.

protection of liberty depended upon the protection of property, the constitution of 1776 required that senators own three hundred acres of land and
commoners one hundred, and that state senatorial electors own fifty. The
requirements also reinforced the traditional tendency of voters to defer to
the wealthy in their community. A recent study of members of the legislature in the early 1820s has shown that they were wealthy men who usually
owned far more property than was required by the constitution.[20]

Discontent with the constitution mounted in the Piedmont and mountains in the 1820s and 1830s as the western population outstripped that of
the east. The addition of a few allies from eastern urban areas unhappy
with the legislature's unwillingness to promote commercial growth enabled westerners to call for a referendum on a constitutional convention
in early 1835. With a majority of the voting population residing west of
Raleigh, the almost unanimous western counties outvoted the equally
unanimous eastern counties, so a convention was called.

Based upon prior agreement, the convention delegates, who assembled
in June, 1835, adopted several amendments that shifted some power in a
westerly direction, but even so, the amended constitution still kept it
largely in the hands of the east. By basing representation in the senate
upon taxes paid, the constitution continued to offer special protection for
property and gave disproportionate influence to the wealthier east. Western voters exercised more power in the House of Commons, though even
there the apportionment of representation was weighted in favor of the
east—the house apportionment was based upon "federal" numbers (five
slaves counted as three persons), which strengthened the slaveholding
east, but the white population of the west was so much greater than that of
the east that the western counties controlled the house. Not entirely satisfied, but happy to take what they could get, westerners provided enough
votes to ensure ratification of the amendments.[21]

The constitutional revisions still left North Carolina with a constitution of the revolutionary generation. The convention delegates democratized the basis for apportioning representation in the General Assembly,
but they continued to give disproportionate power to the east. They made
the governorship a popularly elected office but kept its occupant impotent.
They also retained property qualifications for office holding and the property requirement for senatorial electors. To soothe eastern fears that the

20. Counihan, "North Carolina," 20–22.
21. The returns for the referenda may be found in John L. Chaney, Jr. (ed.), *North Carolina
Government, 1585–1974* (Raleigh: North Carolina Department of the Secretary of State, 1975),
20–22. For the amendments adopted in 1835, see Thorpe (comp.), *Federal and State Constitutions*, V, 2794–99.

growing power of the west would undermine the stability of the slave regime, they limited the taxes placed upon slaves.

In one way, the revised constitution departed from its revolutionary heritage. Like other constitutions of the time, North Carolina abandoned annual elections and meetings of the General Assembly in favor of biennial sessions. The revolutionaries viewed annual elections as one of the few protections the citizenry had against an oppressive government. Without it, their philosophical descendants believed, the administration of government was placed "into the hands of Governors, Judges, and Corporations." In reality, though, the move to biennial sessions actually enhanced certain revolutionary beliefs, because by limiting the frequency of legislative meetings, the new amendments not only saved the government money but also helped prevent government activity and hence governmental incursions on individual liberty.[22]

The delegates to the convention hoped that their handiwork would bring an end to decades of sectional contention and political discontent, but the amended constitution actually encouraged future political battles over it. By retaining differential qualifications for senatorial electors, property requirements for officeholders, the election of judges and justices of the peace by the legislature, the unequal process of determining representation in the General Assembly, and the limit on the taxation of slaves, the new constitution provided ample grist for the future partisan mill. In addition, the popular election of the governor made conflict over future constitutional amendments almost inevitable. In a state where virtually all white adult males could vote for governor and only about 50 percent could vote for a state senator, the removal of the property requirement was an enticing political issue for gubernatorial candidates. In a state where more than 70 percent of the white families did not own slaves, the removal of limitations on the tax on slaves would also tempt the ambitious politician. And in a state where easterners still wielded an unusually large share of the power, the representation issue was still there to be exploited by western politicians.

The new amendments also ensured that, when a future politician suggested a revision, the debate over the change would be prolonged indefinitely. The constitution permitted revision by another convention, which was to be called by two-thirds of the legislature and which would certainly be opposed by easterners fearful of a further erosion of their power. Revisions could also be made by passing an amendment first with a three-

22. Bedford Brown to Weldon N. Edwards, October 8, 1842, in Katherine C. P. Conway Papers, NCDAH (author's emphasis deleted); Graham, *et al.*, "Address to the People," in Hamilton and Williams (eds.), *Graham Papers*, I, 297.

fifths majority in both houses of the General Assembly, then again two years later with a two-thirds majority, and then finally by a majority of voters in the subsequent August election. The effects of the amending process became evident when it took almost ten years to eliminate the property requirement for senatorial electors. Any constitutional changes would be a long time coming.

Given the sharply divergent interests of the east and the west, it is not surprising that, as the party system became established in the mid-1830s, there would be a close relationship between region and party loyalty—an overwhelmingly Democratic region in the middle and western coastal plain, and overwhelmingly Whig regions in the mountains, the central Piedmont, and the northeast.

★

However, there never was a perfect relationship between region and party. There were a few Democratic counties in the mountains, clusters of them in the northern and southwestern Piedmont, and several Whig counties in the western coastal plain. Obviously, other interests cut across regional lines; some of them influenced voting patterns, while others did not.

Partisan allegiance in a county apparently was somewhat related to the proportion of slaves or slaveholders in it. To the extent that there was such a relationship, it reinforced the sectional divisions in the state, because slavery was most deeply entrenched in the east and least in the mountains. The institution of slavery was fairly widespread in North Carolina—25 percent of the free families in the state owned slaves in 1850. That such a large minority of the white people had a direct economic stake in the slave economy bolstered popular support for the institution.[23]

Slaves, though, were not distributed evenly throughout the state. Slavery made little headway in the mountain economy. In 1840, slaves composed 11.3 percent of the total population of the mountain counties; by 1860, they had declined to 10.2 percent. Of the section's free families in 1860, 11.3 percent owned slaves.

To the east, in the Piedmont, the frequency of slaveholding and the density of the slave population increased. There, slaves and slaveholding were actually more widespread than previous historians have allowed. Slaves composed 25.8 percent of the total Piedmont population in 1840 and about the same proportion twenty years later. Almost one-fourth (23.5

23. Computed from data in J. G. Randall and David Donald, *The Civil War and Reconstruction* (2nd ed. rev.; Boston: D. C. Heath, 1969), 5, 28. On slaveownership throughout the South, see Otto H. Olsen, "Historians and the Extent of Slave Ownership in the Southern United States," *Civil War History*, XVIII (1972), 107–16.

percent) of the free families in the region were slaveowners. In addition, fourteen of the region's thirty-one counties in 1860 contained enough slaves to make up at least 25 percent of the county's population. In the tobacco planting counties of the northern tier and the cotton planting counties of the south, slaveholding and slaves were much more numerous than in the region as a whole.

Slavery was most deeply entrenched in the plantation counties of the coastal plain. There, slaves composed 42 percent of the total population in 1840 and 44.2 percent in 1860. Moreover, in 1860 36.2 percent of free families in the region, a substantial minority, owned slaves.[24]

Historians have assumed that the Democratic party was the premier defender of slavery and that therefore, in areas where slaveholders composed a substantial portion of the white population or where black slaves composed a large part of the total population, citizens voted Democratic. Although Whigs defended slavery with as much passion as Democrats, there was a small positive statistical relationship between presence of slavery and support for Democratic candidates. In the 1840s, the coefficient of correlation ranged from .34 to .43.[25]

Less important than the presence of slavery in determining popular voting patterns was the influence of ethnocultural and religious interests. Unlike the situation in the states of the North, North Carolina politics did not reflect ethnocultural conflict in the society. White North Carolinians were a remarkably homogeneous people in their nativity and in their religion. In 1850, only 2,525 North Carolinians had been born outside of the United States, and the bulk of them came from England, Scotland, and Ireland. Similar homogeneity was revealed in their religious preferences. Of 1,678 churches reported in the census of 1850, 1,300 (77.5 percent) were either Baptist or Methodist, and only 4 were Roman Catholic. Ten years later the story was much the same: 1,744 (76.8 percent) of the state's 2,270 churches were either Baptist or Methodist, and Roman Catholic churches numbered 7.[26]

This is not to say that religion and ethnicity played no role in shaping voting patterns. Indeed, it appears that members of several religious groups had definite party preferences. For example, one segment of the Baptist church, the Primitive Baptists, preached extreme separation of

24. Sitterson, *Secession Movement*, 2, 5, 11, 12.

25. *Ibid.*, 10–11. The correlation between percent slave in the total population and the Democratic vote in the presidential election of 1840 was .40. See Appendix A.

26. *Report of the Superintendent of the Census, 1850* (Washington, D.C.: Robert Armstrong, Printer, 1853), 32–45; *Eighth Census of the United States, 1860: Mortality and Miscellaneous Statistics* (Washington, D.C.: Government Printing Office, 1866), 435–40.

church and state and of state and society; on one occasion they protested the reading of a prayer at the opening of Congress. They found the atmosphere of the negative-state Democrats to their liking. Edgecombe County, with a large proportion of Primitive Baptists in the community, regularly polled over 90 percent of its votes for Democratic candidates. At one point, the Raleigh *Standard*, a Democratic paper, declared that the Primitive Baptists were virtually all Democrats. North Carolina's Quakers found a home in the opposition party. Areas with large concentrations of Quakers, like Guilford, Pasquotank, and Perquimans, tended to vote heavily Whig. It seems that as pacifists they were hostile to the election of a military man like Andrew Jackson to the presidency. There is also some evidence to suggest that religious prejudice helped influence voting patterns as well. In 1848, for example, Whigs claimed that their gubernatorial candidate, Episcopalian Charles Manly, lost many votes in staunchly Protestant North Carolina because Democrats in some parts of the state claimed during the campaign that Manly was a Catholic. The anti-Catholic sentiments of many North Carolinians augured well for the anti-Catholic American party in the mid-1850s. It seems evident, then, that issues of an ethnoreligious nature played a role, if a small one, in shaping the behavior of the state's electorate.[27]

The homogeneity of the North Carolina populace was enhanced because most of them lived in rural areas. Even at a time when the United States was a predominantly rural nation, the absence of urban areas in North Carolina was extraordinary. In 1840 the largest town, Wilmington, contained less than five thousand souls, and though it doubled in population over the next twenty years and remained the largest town, in 1860 its population still numbered less than ten thousand. All told, only six towns in 1860 had populations greater than two thousand, and only 2 percent of the state's residents lived in its twenty-five most populous towns. The rural nature of North Carolina is suggested further by its settlement patterns. In 1850, it had 19.3 inhabitants per square mile, the least densely populated of all the eastern states, and ten years later the density of population was roughly the same.[28]

Towns did grow, though, and conflicts emerged between townsmen and those who lived in surrounding rural areas. People in towns were ob-

27. Raleigh *Standard*, December 23, 1857, December 5, 1849; John Stafford to William A. Graham, October 19, 1848, in Hamilton and Williams (eds.), *Graham Papers*, III, 248–51. New studies are needed of the groups mentioned above, as well as of the Germans who settled in the western Piedmont, the Scots, the Scotch-Irish, and the small but important groups of Presbyterians and Episcopalians.

28. *Report of the Superintendent of the Census, 1850*, 101; *Eighth Census, 1860: Mortality and Miscellaneous Statistics*, 333.

viously attracted to the commercial aspects of Whig policy, while those nearby were often appalled by it. Harry Watson's study of Cumberland County reveals sharp urban-rural divisions between Fayetteville and the rest of the county. Similar conflict between a town and the surrounding rural area could be found throughout the state. Wilmington provided most of New Hanover County's Whig vote; Raleigh did the same for Wake and New Bern for Craven. Obviously, though, the Whigs did not depend solely on urban areas for voting support, for that would have relegated them to a small minority in rural North Carolina. Still, the fact that towns and cities tended to vote much more for the Whigs than did surrounding areas suggests that there was a relationship between Whiggery and the world of commerce.[29]

Recent studies of antebellum southern voting suggest that, despite the arrival of the democratic age, local notables, through their kin and neighborhood ties, continued to shape, if not to dictate, how the people in their community voted. This certainly seems to have been the case in antebellum North Carolina. In 1840, for example, Whig Edmund Jones of Wilkes County, a member of the powerful Lenoir family running for a seat in the Commons, wrote to a kinsman that he depended upon "our connection" in the county to secure his election. The importance of local notables and of neighborhood ties was evident too in Democrat Thomas D. McDowell's race for the Bladen and Columbus seat in the senate in 1852. After he received his party's nomination, McDowell was urged by others to conciliate N. L. Williamson, ofttimes Democratic legislator from Columbus County. One wrote:

> I would advise you to write to Williamson without delay informing him you are a candidate & at the same time hoping it might not be inconsistent with his good pleasure to give you his support & influence.— I make this suggestion as he has a strong party that are devoted to him & are rather hard to manage if they should take it into their heads to run himself (something like the old Melvin party over the river) & it is absolutely necessary to secure that interest, if possible.[30]

The significance of local notables in shaping voting patterns helps to explain, first, why the inspection of voting returns at the precinct level

29. Watson, *Jacksonian Politics*. For the other towns and counties, see precinct returns in newspapers during the weeks following the August elections. For the South as a whole, see Charles G. Sellers, Jr., "Who Were the Southern Whigs?" *AHR*, LIX (1954), 335–46.

30. Edmund Jones to Samuel F. Patterson, May 12, 1840, in Jones and Patterson Papers, SHC; K. McLeod to Thomas D. McDowell, June 18, 1852, also J. Stansell to McDowell, September 25, 1852, and James Robison to McDowell, July 10, 1852, all in Thomas D. McDowell Papers, SHC.

often reveals lopsided majorities for one party, and, second, why counties with the same socioeconomic and geographic conditions sometimes voted in opposite ways. It may also explain why, under the second party system in North Carolina, competition at the county level was often minimal, whereas interparty competition at the state level was intense. The fact that notables wielded such influence in their communities may also help explain why sectional factors were so crucial in determining broader patterns of voting in the state. These opinion-shapers, more than others, were likely to be aware of and to have a personal interest in the economic and constitutional conflicts of the day.[31]

★

Whether based upon kinship and deference, religion, urban-rural conflict, or, more likely, sectionalism, the divergent interests of the people found expression with the clear emergence of the Whig and Democratic parties in 1836. The parties themselves represented the culmination of a dozen years of conflict among political leaders in the state. The presidential election of 1824 in North Carolina, as in other states, shattered the dominant Republican party. Out of the welter of candidates, Andrew Jackson emerged victorious in the state, though in the Congress he lost the election to John Quincy Adams. During the ensuing four years, Jackson's popularity spread throughout the state. In 1828, in a two-man contest with Adams, he won North Carolina's electoral votes in a landslide, capturing more than three-fourths of the votes. He repeated that success even more convincingly four years later against Henry Clay, when he won almost 85 percent of the vote and majorities in all but one of North Carolina's sixty-four counties.[32]

Jackson's triumphs in North Carolina paralleled his massive national victories, but such a broad, heterogeneous coalition proved impossible to maintain. His policies and behavior toward the end of his first term and during his second drove many of his supporters into opposition. Politicians generally do not like to lose any supporters, but the migration out of

31. Paul F. Bourke and Donald A. DeBats, "Identifiable Voting in Nineteenth-Century America: Toward a Comparison of Britain and the United States Before the Secret Ballot," *Perspectives in American History*, X (1977–78), 259–88; Thornton, *Politics and Power*, 156–60; Thomas E. Jeffrey, "The Second Party System in North Carolina" (Ph.D. dissertation, Catholic University of America, 1976), 137–39, 198–99.

32. Albert Ray Newsome, *The Presidential Election of 1824 in North Carolina* (Chapel Hill: University of North Carolina Press, 1930); Max R. Williams, "The Foundations of the Whig Party in North Carolina," *NCHR*, XLVII (1970), 115–29; William J. Cooper, Jr., *The South and the Politics of Slavery, 1828–1856* (Baton Rouge: Louisiana State University Press, 1978), 5–22; Watson, *Jacksonian Politics*.

the Democratic party ultimately benefited it. The establishment of a national Whig organization encouraged Democrats to assume a more coherent position on political issues and thus to solidify the commitment of their remaining partisans. Now, too, party leaders could argue persuasively that party discipline and party unity must be maintained if the Democrats were to retain power.

Jackson lost some North Carolina supporters during the nullification crisis. In 1832 South Carolinians, in the midst of a recession after years of prosperity, sought to nullify the tariff act of that year partly because they blamed the tariff for their economic straits and partly because they feared that a government strong enough to enact a protective tariff that injured southern economic interests was a government strong enough to interfere with slavery. North Carolinians generally opposed the tariff but did not feel as threatened as South Carolinians did. They had not enjoyed years of prosperity, so the years of recession were a smaller shock. Although most of Jackson's supporters opposed his threat to force South Carolina to enforce the law and although some left the party on account of it, most retained their faith in Jackson's commitment to southern interests and the preservation of slavery.[33]

The president suffered more substantial losses during his "war" on the second Bank of the United States. A congressional attempt to recharter the bank in 1832, four years before its charter was to expire, met with a presidential veto. The veto itself apparently hurt Jackson little in North Carolina. But the war escalated rapidly, and in October, 1833, Jackson drove hordes of Democrats into the opposition when his secretary of the treasury ordered the removal of federal deposits from the bank. Opponents perceived the removal as an illegitimate executive usurpation of power, and they denounced as a despot the man they called King Andrew I. One North Carolinian declared that removal was "certainly the most atrocious, high handed despotick measure that ever was before assumed by the most absolute monarch." Building their organization around anger at Jackson's exercise of arbitrary power, the leadership styled their party Whig after the eighteenth-century colonial patriots who revolted against the arbitrary power of George III.[34]

---

33. On South Carolina, see William W. Freehling, *Prelude to Civil War: The Nullification Controversy in South Carolina, 1816–1836* (New York: Harper & Row, 1965); on the South generally, see Cooper, *Politics of Slavery*, 44–49; on North Carolina, see Hoffmann, *Andrew Jackson and North Carolina*, 54–68.

34. Robert Remini, *Andrew Jackson and the Bank War* (New York: W. W. Norton, 1967); Watson, *Jacksonian Politics*; Williams, "Foundations of the Whig Party," esp. p. 120; Thomas B. Littlejohn to Willie P. Mangum, January 29, 1834, in Henry T. Shanks (ed.), *The Papers of Willie Person Mangum* (6 vols.; Raleigh: State Department of Archives and History, 1950–56), II, 72.

Thus, in 1834 party lines were drawn, but the party system blossomed fully only after the state adopted the amended constitution of 1835. Some of the delegates to the convention had worried that the popular election of the governor "would result in vile political machinery, quarreling, faction, and bitterness." They were right. Popular election prompted politicians desirous of electing a governor to establish broad statewide coalitions. When North Carolina held its first popular election for governor in 1836, the second party system, pitting Whigs against Democrats, emerged throughout the state.[35]

Whig leaders established a central committee in Raleigh to coordinate the state's gubernatorial and presidential election campaigns, and the committee nominated Wilmington's Edward Dudley to run for governor against incumbent Edward Speight. For the presidency, committee members, like other southern Whigs, advocated the cause of Tennessee's Hugh Lawson White as one of the Whig party's three regional candidates, while Democrats endorsed Andrew Jackson's handpicked successor, Vice-President Martin Van Buren.

During the campaign, the Whigs drew strength from the emerging debate over slavery and from Van Buren's candidacy, against which many southern political leaders saw the need for an effective political opposition. The fear of Van Buren, a northerner, grew out of the sectional conflicts of the 1830s, when southerners were confronted by the rapid emergence of the abolitionist movement, its petition campaign to end slavery in the nation's capital, and its propaganda appeals in the South. Despite Van Buren's apparent prosouthern views, he was suspect. In 1832, a movement to substitute Philip Barbour of Virginia for Van Buren as Andrew Jackson's running mate failed, but many of the leading Barbour advocates eventually found their way into the Whig party. In 1836, southern Whigs devoted much of their campaign to questioning the devotion of Democrats to slavery and to posing as the premier defender of slavery and of southern rights. As North Carolina's Whig candidate for governor, Edward Dudley, declared: "Mr. Van Buren is not one of us. He is a Northern man . . . in soul, in principle, and in action." Thus, Van Buren's candidacy and sectional issues helped solidify the Whig opposition and hence the two-party system in North Carolina, and also showed the ways in which party competition would exacerbate sectional fears in the future.[36]

35. The quotation is from Fletcher M. Green, *Constitutional Development in the South Atlantic States, 1776–1860: A Study in the Evolution of Democracy* (Chapel Hill: University of North Carolina Press, 1930), 229.

36. Richard P. McCormick, *The Second American Party System: Party Formation in the Jacksonian Era* (Chapel Hill: University of North Carolina Press, 1966), 329; Cooper, *Politics of Slavery*, 74–97 (quotation from Raleigh *Register*, February 23, 1836, is on p. 82); Hoffmann, *Andrew Jackson and North Carolina*, 105, 108–10.

Whigs also benefited from the intensification of a debate over public land policy, which they linked to state economic development. After the Jackson administration had paid off the national debt, the flood of money from public land sales created a surplus in the federal treasury. The parties quickly took opposite sides as Jackson vetoed a Whig bill to distribute the proceeds of the sales to the states. In North Carolina in 1835, distribution became increasingly enmeshed in partisan politics as both houses of the General Assembly passed resolutions on land policy. A Whig resolution, which passed the house, demanded a permanent distribution of the land proceeds, while the Democratic senate endorsed the one-time distribution of the treasury's surplus. The houses could not reconcile their differences, but Congress did. It passed a bill authorizing the deposit in the states of federal funds, which could be withdrawn at any time. Jackson signed it reluctantly, and North Carolina soon received some $1.5 million of federal largesse. As it turned out, deposit became distribution in practice because the federal government never withdrew the funds. Nevertheless, the question of distribution had become enmeshed in partisan politics, and throughout the 1840s and 1850s Whigs advocated distribution and Democrats opposed it. In the 1830s, the distribution issue aided the Whigs because it offered North Carolinians the benefit of Whig policies without the economic costs.[37]

The campaigns brought 67 percent of those eligible to the polling place in the August gubernatorial election, but only 53 percent to November's presidential election. The parties split the elections. Whig Dudley won the gubernatorial election, but Democrat Van Buren captured the state's electoral votes; and Whigs gained a majority of two in the senate, but Democrats held the same majority in the house. Although the election results were ambiguous, they implied that if Whigs could keep turnout high in statewide elections they could win. In fact, the gubernatorial election set the basic patterns of voting in the state for many years to come.[38]

★

The ambiguity of the election results reflected the parties' somewhat indistinct ideological demarcations and their barely formed organizational structures. The final stages of party formation were completed during the depression of the late 1830s as the development of policies to combat it polarized the parties and helped prompt party leaders to develop well-defined organizations.

37. Hoffmann, *Andrew Jackson and North Carolina*, 90–101.
38. J. R. Pole, "Election Statistics in North Carolina, to 1861," *JSH*, XXIV (1958), 227; Hoffmann, *Andrew Jackson and North Carolina*, 108. The Pearson coefficient of correlation between the Democratic vote in the gubernatorial elections of 1836 and 1840 was .87.

In North Carolina, the major catalyst for partisan disagreement was the conflict over the state's relationship to two railroad companies—the Wilmington and Raleigh and the Raleigh and Gaston. The initial involvement of the state with those companies reveals the early Whig commitment to government activism and Democratic ambivalence about it. The experience with the state's investments, though, soon sharpened party differences.

In 1833 the General Assembly initiated the state's first major venture into railroad construction when it chartered a company to build a road between Wilmington and Raleigh with a capital stock of $800,000. After Raleigh's citizens proved unresponsive, the legislators amended the charter to permit the road to run from Wilmington to the Roanoke River in the northeastern part of the state and to increase the capital stock to $1,500,000. Upon obtaining subscriptions for the required portion of the stock, the company was organized in March, 1836.

Later that year, the state treasury received the federal government's deposit. The assembly determined to use the funds for internal improvements and for the establishment of a common school system, and it subscribed over $500,000 in the stock of the Wilmington and Raleigh. The vote on the state subscription is revealing. In the senate, 77.2 percent of the Whigs and 52.9 percent of the Democrats supported the subscription, and in the house, 85 percent of the Whigs gave their support, but only 51 percent of the Democrats did. Whigs, then, were relatively united in favor of state aid to railroad building, while Democrats were evenly divided. In this case, federal funding may have assuaged Democratic opposition to state aid.[39]

The company completed the road in March, 1840, with an unfunded debt of $320,000. In an effort to aid the Wilmington and Raleigh, the legislature endorsed company bonds for that amount and took a mortgage on the road as security. The endorsement of the bonds only delayed the arrival of the company's fiscal crisis. Although the company needed long-term credit, the bond issue was short term and required the company to begin paying off the principal in 1842. The Wilmington and Raleigh paid the required $50,000 of the debt that year, but its profits were too small to meet the 1843 payment. To prevent the company from defaulting, the General Assembly of 1842–1843 authorized the Literary Board (the only agency in the government with $50,000 available) to purchase the bonds. A year later, the state treasurer bought the next $50,000 in bonds with funds borrowed from the board. For a government whose general expendi-

---

39. For the Senate vote, see J. G. deRoulhac Hamilton, *Party Politics in North Carolina, 1835–1860* (Durham: Seeman Printery, 1916), 74; for the House, see Jeffrey, "Internal Improvements," 152–55.

tures averaged about $60,000 per annum, the company's failure to pay off its bonds caused significant problems.

The difficulties that arose from the financing of the Wilmington and Raleigh were compounded by those of the Raleigh and Gaston Railroad Company. Chartered in 1835 and organized in 1836 with a capital stock of $550,000, the company proposed to run a road from Raleigh to Gaston, within a few miles of the terminus of the Wilmington and Raleigh. By 1838, when the company applied for and received permission to increase its capital and a state endorsement of $500,000 of its bonds, the depression had struck and parties had become polarized over the question of state aid. The relief bill received the support of 70 percent of the Whig commoners but only 30 percent of the Democrats. When the company completed the road in 1840, a $250,000 debt remained unfunded, so the legislature of 1840–1841, voting more clearly along partisan lines, endorsed another $300,000 of the company's bonds. The bonds were secured by a first and second mortgage on the company's property and by a personal bond of the stockholders. The bond sales did not help the road because profits failed to keep up with the interest payments. This led the state to foreclose the mortgage in 1845 and to purchase the road later that year for the price of the $300,000 bond issue plus accrued interest due ($363,000).[40]

Where the parties in the legislature had behaved in a relatively similar fashion in their initial support for state aid to the railroads, the instant failure of both roads led to sharp disagreement over whether the state should seek to save them. Whigs, who had strongly supported state aid from the beginning, became even more united in their commitment to bolster the roads' finances. Democrats, who had been ambivalent about railroad building from the outset, had their doubts confirmed by the experience of the two roads and thereafter were virtually unanimous in their opposition to further state assistance. At several points, Democrats even tried to make legislative supporters of relief financially responsible if the companies defaulted on their debts. Throughout much of the 1840s, the continuing problems of the railroads perpetuated partisan divisions over state aid. As late as 1846, the Democratic gubernatorial candidate built his campaign around the state debt, and his party inserted a condemnation of it in its 1848 platform. Only the expansion of public works programs endorsed by the legislature of 1849 and the improving financial situation of the companies in the late 1840s ended the debate over railroad relief.[41]

Partisan conflict over railroad relief carried over to other proposed leg-

40. Cecil K. Brown, *A State Movement in Railroad Development: The Story of North Carolina's First Effort to Establish an East to West Trunk Line Railroad* (Chapel Hill: University of North Carolina Press, 1928), 31–38, 45–54; Jeffrey, "Internal Improvements," 152–55.
    41. See chapter 3 below; *HJ, 1840–41*, 539–41; *SJ, 1840–41*, 190–91.

islation involving state aid. In 1840–1841, for example, when 79.9 percent of senate Democrats opposed aid to the Laxton Lynch Turnpike in the mountains, 95.5 percent of the Whigs supported aid to the road. And when every Democrat voted to table a bill providing for the state-aided construction of a turnpike going west from Raleigh, 71.4 percent of the Whigs wanted to consider the measure. Ultimately, then, the conflicts of the late 1830s helped sharpen party differences, and like their fellow partisans outside of North Carolina, Whigs thereafter could generally be found in favor of government aid to internal improvements and Democrats opposed to it.[42]

Similar partisan disagreement developed over the state's banks, particularly the Bank of North Carolina and the Bank of the Cape Fear. In 1832–1833 the legislature chartered the Bank of North Carolina, in which the state would take one-half of the capital stock and choose all of the directors. Few individuals found this investment opportunity attractive, so the next legislature incorporated another Bank of North Carolina, in which private investors were to take three-fifths of the stock and compose three-fifths of the bank's directors. The incorporation of the Bank of the Cape Fear contained the same features. With the prospect of controlling the management of the banks, investors readily bought stock, and both banks were soon functioning. The parties, despite their conflict over the second Bank of the United States, ignored the state's banks until the depression and subsequent policies of the Van Buren administration turned the debate over the Bank of the United States into a debate over all banks. Van Buren blamed the depression on the speculative spirit encouraged by banks and sought to divorce the banks from the state by withdrawing federal funds from private banks and establishing an independent treasury. Afterwards, Democrats throughout the country denounced the banks. Banks, they said, benefited from special privileges denied to others. When a businessman failed to meet his financial obligations, he went out of business, but when a bank encountered the same problems, it simply suspended the payment of specie. Whigs, on the other hand, still believed banks to be a necessary part of the economic order and blamed the depression on Andrew Jackson's and Van Buren's experiments with the currency.[43]

The debate over the banks ended with different results in different states. In many western states, legislatures abolished banks entirely; other

42. *SJ, 1840–41*, 235–36, 298. For other examples, see the tables in Jeffrey, "Internal Improvements," 152–55. Jeffrey reaches conclusions from his data different from mine.

43. Hoffmann, *Andrew Jackson and North Carolina*, 69–70; Sharp, *Jacksonians Versus the Banks*; Holt, *Political Crisis*, 32–34.

states enacted reforms. In North Carolina, Whigs and Democrats disagreed sharply about the virtues of banking. Although the Democrats gained control over the legislature in 1842 and although they repeatedly denounced the banks and introduced bills like the one that stipulated a bank would lose its charter if it suspended the payment of specie for thirty days in one year, they failed to agree on one plan or even to pass a resolution denouncing the banks.[44]

The conflict over the banks echoed a broader disagreement over corporations and the state's relationship to them. The disagreement came into focus when the legislature considered whether to limit the liability of individual stockholders in a company to the amount they invested. Limited liability limited an investor's risk and hence encouraged the pooling of scarce capital. A legislator's vote against limited liability was a vote against corporations, since few investors would be willing to accept individual responsibility for a company's entire debt. Democrats attacked the limited liability clause, first, because they believed that it granted special privileges to a select few and gave the corporation unfair advantages over the small businessman who was responsible for all his business debts, and second, because they were persuaded that, by encouraging the massing of capital, the clause promoted the concentration of economic power in the hands of the corporation.

Whigs viewed the corporation as beneficent. A limited liability clause merely allowed a corporation to engage in activities that would bring prosperity to the state. Transportation corporations would enhance the wealth of the state by allowing farmers to get their crops to market and would encourage manufacturing by expanding available markets. Whatever special privileges were granted the corporation, Whigs believed, would expand the economic freedom of the people.[45]

By the early 1840s, the tendencies of both political parties had become clear. The Democrats in the legislature and on the stump revealed their party's unease with the emerging market economy. While not opposed to prosperity, they were less concerned with promoting economic growth than with preventing concentrations of power from infringing on individual freedom and equality. Any form of aid to corporations, which by their very nature were specially privileged organizations, appeared to Democrats as a triumph of special interests over popular equality. Therefore,

44. In the Senate in 1840–41, the average index of disagreement on two bank bills was 75.2 (*SJ, 1840–41*, 266–67, 270). Democratic behavior in the state legislature in 1842–43 may be traced in the Raleigh *Register* and Raleigh *Standard*, from November, 1842, to February, 1843. Also see *SJ, 1840–41*, 94–95, 253–54, 267, 276, 313–15, 322, 359; *HJ, 1840–41*, 579–80, 750–51, 942–43; and chapter 3 below.
45. Raleigh *Register*, February 10, 1843.

they opposed limited liability clauses and state financial aid. They also fought against the creation of the physical substructure of the market economy when they voted against internal improvements legislation, and they denounced the banks that were so necessary in a market economy. Their opposition to government activism extended to the realm of social policy, as they opposed state-administered insane asylums and schools for the deaf, dumb, and blind.

Whigs, while not unmindful of individual rights, looked less at the threat to freedom posed by government action and more at the benefits to be derived from that action. They perceived a need to promote the concentration of capital for investment, so they advocated limited liability for stockholders. Because they believed that transportation improvements were a necessary prerequisite for the expansion of the market economy and because private capital in the state was scarce, they advocated state aid for internal improvements. Of course, they also defended the credit system and the banks that managed it. And the social policies that Democrats opposed so vehemently, Whigs supported with a similar passion.

★

At the same time that Whigs and Democrats clarified the ideological lines dividing them, they also established modern organizational structures, and the ambiguities evident in the 1836 elections gave way to a narrow but stable Whig majority. In 1838, the newness of the party system was still evident when Democrats made little effort to run a candidate against incumbent Edward Dudley. Only a last-minute Democratic decision to run unhappy Whig leader John Branch averted a walkover by the incumbent; as it was, Dudley won handily. The experience of 1838 taught Democrats the need for a more regular organization, and as the parties geared up for the presidential contest in 1840, both adopted new techniques of party governance. The Whigs were in the forefront, as they had been in establishing a central committee. They held the first statewide party convention in North Carolina in November, 1839; the Democrats followed the next January. Both conventions, which drew delegates from around the state, nominated candidates for governor (Whig John M. Morehead and Democrat Romulus Saunders), chose delegates to the national party conventions, wrote party platforms, and appointed central committees. Morehead and Saunders set a precedent for all future gubernatorial candidates by canvassing the state and holding occasional joint debates. In these ways, political leaders completed the organizational aspects of party formation.[46]

46. Hamilton, *Party Politics*, 45–49, 55–61, 63–64; McCormick, *Second Party System*, 208–209; Clarence Clifford Norton, *The Democratic Party in Ante-Bellum North Carolina, 1835–1861*

The elections of 1840 also integrated the presidential contest into North Carolina politics. Whereas in 1836 67 percent of white male adults voted in the gubernatorial election and only 53 percent in the presidential, in 1840 the percentages were a uniformly high 84 percent in the former and 83 percent in the latter. Although politicians had long spoken of the significance of presidential contests and although the rhetoric of the campaigns of 1836 focused on national issues, the parties did not attract as many voters to the polls in November as they had in August. The elections of 1840 changed that, and in 1844 the presidential election drew just as many persons to vote as had voted in the gubernatorial election. Thereafter, though, and for the rest of the antebellum years, turnout in presidential contests began to trail off and remained consistently lower than in gubernatorial elections.[47]

Those many voters cast a substantial majority of their ballots for the Whig candidates and thus set a pattern that would last through the decade. The state gave its electoral votes to the Whig candidate in 1840, 1844, and 1848, and the Whigs won every gubernatorial election between 1836 and 1848. Although it appears that the Whigs were a colossus standing astride North Carolina politics in the 1840s, actually their majority in the state was quite small (one Democratic editor called it "a pitiful four thousand majority"). They controlled both houses in the legislature by narrow margins in 1840, 1844, and 1846, divided the General Assembly in 1848, and lost both houses to the Democrats in 1842. The Whig majority was slight, which meant that the party had little room for error. Democrats always seemed ready to snatch victory. But for the Democrats in the 1840s, victory remained elusive as a remarkably stable electorate continued to turn out Whig majorities.[48]

In the late 1840s, the political tide began to turn, and the 1850s marked a period of Democratic domination. Yet the Democratic majorities of the 1850s were as narrow as were those that Whigs had enjoyed in the 1840s. What is remarkable about voting in North Carolina was not the shift from Whig to Democratic majorities, but the absence of change. The strongest Democratic counties in the early 1840s were the strongest Democratic counties as late as 1860. Democrats continued to derive their greatest strength from the middle and western coastal plain, and Whigs gathered theirs from the northeast, the central Piedmont, and the mountains, though support in the mountains trailed off in the mid-1850s. Both parties

(Chapel Hill: University of North Carolina Press, 1930), 34, 92–100; Herbert Dale Pegg, *The Whig Party in North Carolina* (Chapel Hill: Colonial Press, [1968?]), 38–39.

47. Pole, "Election Statistics," 228; McCormick, *Second Party System*, 207–209.

48. William W. Holden to David S. Reid, December 8, 1847, in David Settle Reid Papers, NCDAH.

represented their constituents well. Whigs, perceiving the benefits and few of the dangers to be derived from governmental activism, endorsed the use of government to promote the well-being of society. Democrats only saw the danger that government activity posed to freedom.

Once a man belonged to a party, he often set aside personal, local, and regional interests and followed his party's line. Party loyalties, in other words, often came to transcend a man's other interests. In 1842, for example, the Democratic gubernatorial candidate, Louis D. Henry, persistently attacked the state's banks, though he owned stock in one of them. Four years later, another Democratic gubernatorial candidate, James B. Shepard, centered his campaign on the state's railroad investments, though he owned stock in the Raleigh and Gaston. More generally, as we have seen, when the parties voted on whether to save the two *eastern* railroads from bankruptcy, the vote was divided by party, not region. Therefore, in order to understand more fully how the party system functioned in antebellum North Carolina, it is necessary to examine the parties, their organization, their campaign techniques, and the types of men they brought to power.[49]

49. Norton, *Democratic Party*, 104–105; Jeffrey, "Internal Improvements," 134–35.

TWO *Parties, Organization, and Political Power*

Organized from the state to the local levels, North Carolina's political parties carried on campaigns that drew the vast majority of eligible voters to the polls. People who gave their allegiance to a party came back time and again to vote for the candidates of that party, and when they cast their ballots they chose their political leadership from among the state's economic elite.

The most important institution in the state party organization was the convention. Conventions usually met in Raleigh (until the mid-1850s, when new railroads made other towns more accessible) early in every even year, when gubernatorial elections were held. Party constancy in holding biennial conventions was remarkable by the standard of southern politics, especially for the Whigs. Whigs in Missouri and Alabama, for examples, held only three state conventions each between 1839 and 1854, while North Carolina Whigs met eight times during that period. Although Democrats in those other states met more frequently than did their Whig counterparts, they did not meet as regularly as North Carolina's Democrats. In states like Missouri and Alabama, huge Democratic majorities discouraged Whig efforts, which, in turn, made Democratic efforts less necessary. But in a state as competitive as North Carolina, politicians felt the need to meet regularly in convention, because attention to organizational matters might spell the difference between victory and defeat.[1]

1. Sometimes the parties met late in the preceding year, like the Whig convention of December, 1843. Raleigh *Standard*, February 2, 1848; John Vollmer Mering, *The Whig Party in Missouri* (Columbia: University of Missouri Press, 1967), 8, 49–51, 144–46, 151–53, 182, 184; J. Mills Thornton III, *Politics and Power in a Slave Society: Alabama, 1800–1860* (Baton Rouge: Louisiana State University Press, 1978), 121.

The state convention functioned as the institutional link between the state and the national party. Every four years, it chose two statewide candidates for presidential elector (the remainder were usually chosen in congressional district conventions) and appointed delegates to the national party convention. On several occasions, it advocated the claims of a presidential candidate, as in 1842, when the Whig convention formally initiated Henry Clay's drive for the presidential nomination in 1844.[2]

The convention played its most important role within the state party. It nominated a gubernatorial candidate, helped set the public image of the party by writing a platform, and established the mechanisms for the day-to-day running of the party by appointing a central committee.

The party chose its gubernatorial candidate in what appeared to be a straightforward manner, but in reality the procedure was more complex. At the convention, a committee of delegates appointed by the convention president, which usually represented each of the state's congressional districts, recommended a man for the nomination, and the delegates then approved the recommendation unanimously. However, the parties did not obtain unanimity by either magic or a few party managers clubbing dissidents into submission. The Whig nomination of William Alexander Graham in 1843 provides a good example of how the nominating process operated.

As the state legislature prepared to adjourn in January, 1843, Whig members caucused to discuss the party's gubernatorial nominee for 1844. Although the caucus reached no final decision, many participants left with a sense that it should go to Graham, who had just been turned out of the U.S. Senate by the state's Democratic legislature. His two major competitors fell by the wayside for different reasons. Charles Manly, clerk of the House of Commons when the Whigs controlled that house and longtime member of the party's central committee, declined to run. Congressman Edward Stanly, a man always ready to engage in rhetorical or physical battle with an opponent, seemed to many Whigs "too . . . rash and indiscreet" and to others "a noisy bragadocio." Moreover, they felt that the intensity of his partisanship "would bring out every Loco in the State, and cause one of the most bitter contests ever witnessed in any election."[3]

Graham, on the other hand, had attained prominence as a senator, and more than one party leader thought that his candidacy would arouse the

2. Fayetteville *Observer*, April 13, 1842.

3. Charles L. Hinton to William A. Graham, February 1, 1843, Richard Hines to Willie P. Mangum, October 18, 1843, Thomas P. Devereux to Graham, November 6, 1843, all in J. G. deRoulhac Hamilton and Max R. Williams (eds.), *The Papers of William Alexander Graham* (6 vols. to date; Raleigh: State Department of Archives and History, 1957–), II, 417, 447, 45.

least opposition in the party. While party leaders urged Graham's candidacy, support came also from local meetings. Some of those meetings were probably held, as Graham suspected, at the behest of the Raleigh leaders, but others were called by local leaders who could see the advantages of Graham's candidacy as well as those in Raleigh could. Although there was still some disagreement about the nominee when the convention met in December, 1843, most sensed that the result was a foregone conclusion. After Stanly withdrew from the race in an open letter to the convention, a committee composed of two delegates from each congressional district and appointed by the president recommended Graham, the convention delegates ratified the recommendation, and a reluctant Graham accepted the nomination.[4]

In a variety of ways, the nomination of Graham illuminates the nominating process. A man's candidacy usually received its impetus from local meetings and the state's leadership during the months before the convention. In formal meetings like the Whig caucus of 1843 or more informally through letter writing, party leaders sought to fix on one person who would ensure partisan victory. They also encouraged county leaders to call meetings to suggest nominees. Often the urging of state leaders was unnecessary because county partisans would meet anyway to nominate candidates for the state legislature and to choose delegates to the state convention. The county meetings would either endorse a candidate or, if the meeting was divided, express a willingness to abide by the convention's choice. Of some fifty Whig county meetings held in 1843 and reported in the newspapers, the largest number (twenty-one) expressed no preference and said they would endorse the party's nominee. Graham received the support of seventeen counties, three times as many counties as nominated any other candidate. In cases like Graham's, the accumulation of county endorsements snowballed and the nomination was virtually determined before the delegates assembled. In 1852, to take another example, shortly before the Whig convention met, one Whig urged the nomination of John Kerr of Caswell County because he was the best candidate and because "so many movements have now been made in his favor, that it will be difficult to concentrate on another."[5]

The unanimity with which Graham's nomination was endorsed was also typical of the nominating process. Although the meetings of the nomi-

4. William A. Graham to James Graham, November 26, 1843, in *ibid.*, II, 454; Raleigh *Register*, December 15, 1843.

5. The proceedings of Whig county meetings were located in the extant Whig newspapers. The Fayetteville *Observer* and Raleigh *Register* were most useful. William A. Graham to James W. Bryan, April 5, 1852, in Hamilton and Williams (eds.), *Graham Papers*, III, 283.

nating committee might be drawn out and acrimonious, disagreements rarely surfaced outside the committee. Once a majority in the caucus agreed upon a man, opposition ceased. In a state with as closely contested elections as North Carolina's, neither party felt it could afford public squabbling over the nominee in the convention hall. It was not coincidental that the only open convention fight over a candidate for either party came in 1858, when the Democrats faced no organized opposition. In a vote on the Democratic convention floor, delegates chose Superior Court judge John Ellis over William W. Holden, the party's leading journalist.[6]

If the procedures used to nominate Graham typified the nominating process in antebellum North Carolina, so did the choice of Graham over Stanly. The parties wanted a candidate who was well known, popular, articulate, and had aroused a minimum of personal hostility. Graham was just such a man, whereas Stanly alienated many Whigs and infuriated Democrats. In 1858, Democrats defeated William Holden for the same reason. As the party's chief ideologue and arbiter of local party disputes, Holden inspired the same kind of opposition that Stanly had. One Democratic state senator observed that "Holden has done a great deal for the Democratic party and is certainly very deserving. Still I think he would meet with stronger opposition than any man that we could start, as he is heartily despised by the other side."[7]

The choice of Graham also revealed the ways in which geographical considerations influenced the parties. With considerable popular support in each of the state's three regions, Whigs sought candidates from virtually everywhere. After Edward Dudley of Wilmington ran successfully as a Whig in 1836 and 1838, the party turned westward to nominate Greensboro's John M. Morehead. Graham became the choice of the center in 1844 and 1846. Two years later, Whigs throughout the state assumed that the nomination would go to an easterner, and only the last-minute withdrawal from the race of Hertford's Kenneth Rayner upset those plans. After nominating Raleigh's Charles Manly as a compromise choice in 1848 and again in 1850, Whigs continued their policy of spreading the nomination around geographically. They nominated candidates from different sections of the Piedmont in 1852 and 1854, only to come back finally to the east in 1860.[8]

Democrats, whose greatest strength lay on the coastal plain and whose greatest weakness lay in the mountains and the Piedmont, tried to bolster

6. Charlotte *Western Democrat*, April 20, 1858.

7. John W. Cunningham to Calvin H. Wiley, October 10, 1857, in Calvin Henderson Wiley Papers, SHC.

8. Thomas E. Jeffrey, "The Second Party System in North Carolina" (Ph.D. dissertation, Catholic University of America, 1976), 146.

their strength in the weakest areas by nominating westerners. After 1842, and except for the nomination of easterner Thomas Bragg in 1854 and 1856, Democrats turned exclusively to men living west of Raleigh.[9]

Not only did Graham's nomination exemplify the way that a candidate was chosen, but so did his reluctance to run. Often potential candidates like Graham tried to persuade their supporters that they were uninterested in the position—at times, the parties nearly had to beg for a viable candidate. In 1846 Charlotte attorney Green W. Caldwell refused the Democratic nomination, leaving an embarrassed central committee to choose a substitute. Two years later and again in 1850, Democratic leaders used all of their persuasive abilities to entice David S. Reid to accept the party's nomination. The reasons why men were reluctant to run for the governorship are readily apparent: candidates would have to engage in an arduous campaign that would last from the late spring to the August election; then, if victorious, they would have no veto power, few patronage appointments, and the task of untangling the twisted financial affairs of the state's Literary Board and Board of Internal Improvements. The job also paid poorly and, because it took a man away from his occupation, entailed substantial pecuniary sacrifices. Although the office carried great prestige, it was no wonder that Graham was reluctant to throw his hat into the ring.[10]

In addition to nominating candidates, the convention also set the political agenda for an election year when it wrote the party platform. In the early years of the party system, the platforms of North Carolina's parties dealt with national issues exclusively. Pronouncements on national concerns were interrupted only by a resolution praising the party's gubernatorial candidate. Of the eight resolutions of the Democratic state convention in January, 1840, three dealt with national economic issues and two with abolitionism, one praised Martin Van Buren, another supported a Democratic national convention, and a last one nominated Romulus Saunders for governor. The Whig platform contained a similar emphasis. That year, candidates followed the path laid out by the convention. To an unusual degree, in 1840 the party newspapers rarely even discussed the gubernatorial campaign, let alone state issues.[11]

9. In 1846 Democrats nominated Green W. Caldwell of western Mecklenberg County. After he refused the nomination, the central committee chose Raleighite James B. Shepard. See the next paragraph.

10. William A. Graham to James Graham, November 26, 1843, in Hamilton and Williams (eds.), *Graham Papers*, II, 454. Clarence Clifford Norton, *The Democratic Party in Ante-Bellum North Carolina, 1835–1861* (Chapel Hill: University of North Carolina Press, 1930), 150–62.

11. Raleigh *Standard*, January 15, 1840; Raleigh *Register*, November 16, 1839. For the campaigns, see the Raleigh *Standard*, Raleigh *Register*, Fayetteville *Observer*, and Fayetteville *North Carolinian*, January–October, 1840.

Even in 1840, though, the parties implicitly connected national and state issues. When the platforms offered contrasting views on the propriety of reestablishing a national bank, they indicated to the electorate what each party believed about the proper role of national and state government in the economy. After 1840, though the platforms continued to focus on national issues, state policies crept into gubernatorial campaigns. In 1842, Democratic candidate Louis Henry repeatedly called for an investigation of the state's banks, and four years later James Shepard, also a Democratic candidate, denounced state aid to railroad companies.[12]

Late in the decade, the platforms themselves began to change. They continued to discuss the relevant issues of slavery and the distribution of the proceeds from the sale of the public lands, and they recited the national parties' views on issues like the tariff, the national bank, and federal aid to internal improvements. But because the latter issues had been all but settled for the time being, only a rare Whig still advocated the reestablishment of a national bank or a protective tariff. In the prosperous late 1840s, such measures seemed unnecessary. That did not mean that national issues were entirely irrelevant appendages to the platforms, for they evoked the traditional ties that voters had to their parties.

Politicians may have recognized the diminishing salience of such national issues for voters because the platforms they wrote increasingly emphasized state issues. This change in emphasis became evident in 1848, when Democratic gubernatorial candidate David S. Reid advocated the removal of the fifty-acre property requirement for senatorial electors. The "equal suffrage" proposal touched off a ten-year debate and kept constitutional revision as a crucial political issue for most of the decade. Soon after Reid's first try for the governorship, in an unrelated action, the General Assembly of 1848–1849 initiated a campaign of government aid to internal improvements. This new government activism intensified the partisan debate over the propriety of government's assisting projects of internal improvement and precipitated conflict over how government should raise the money to aid them. Thus, where the state party platforms of the early 1840s dealt mostly with national issues, the platforms of the mid-1850s dealt mostly with issues of constitutional reform, internal improvements, and taxation.

★

The state convention did more than define the party's position on the issues; it also established the machinery that would carry on party opera-

12. The Democratic gubernatorial nominee Romulus B. Saunders, hitherto a leading supporter of governmental promotion of economic development, backed away from that position

tions between conventions. Both parties placed day-to-day operations in the hands of a central committee, usually appointed by the president of the convention, which was controlled by party leaders living in or near Raleigh. Although the convention appointed men from all over the state to serve on the committee, North Carolina's poor transportation network and its large size made it virtually impossible for those members living far from Raleigh to attend committee meetings. Taking these circumstances into consideration, the convention always appointed to the committee enough men, usually the same men, from the Raleigh area to compose a quorum. As a result, the central committee became not only the central organizational arm of the party but a committee run by men from the central part of the state.[13]

The committee ran the party organization on a day-to-day basis. It was the chief fund-raising arm of the party; it helped finance many of the party's newspapers; it arranged mass rallies and provided speakers for them; it coordinated its gubernatorial candidate's campaign and the state campaign of its presidential candidate; and it ensured that there were ample party tickets available on the election grounds. It also called the convention into session and arranged for its smooth operation. Among its members was the editor of the Raleigh *Standard* (if Democratic) or the Raleigh *Register* (if Whig), so it had the influential voice of the party's organ to speak its views.[14]

At times, the central committee's power looked stronger on paper than it was in reality. Just after the gubernatorial election of 1844, which the Whig candidate won by a narrow margin, the chairman of the Democratic committee complained "that the Central Committee did not receive a dozen letters during the campaign." He asked county leaders to do better for the presidential campaign and to report weekly to the committee "on the subject of the Election of President and the politics of your County." How well local leaders responded to the committee's new appeal is not clear, but their behavior during the gubernatorial campaign revealed how rudimentary party organizations still were in the 1840s.[15]

Nevertheless, the central committee did wield considerable power,

when he accepted the nomination. Raleigh *Standard*, January 15, 1840, January 19, 1842; Fayetteville *Observer*, April 8, 1840; Raleigh *Register*, June 19, July 14, 1840, April 8, 1842.

13. Raleigh *Register*, January 16, 1846, February 26, 1848; Raleigh *Standard*, January 14, 1846, April 19, 1848.

14. T. L. Hybart, Democratic Central Committee circular, July, 1842, in David Settle Reid Papers, NCDAH; Richard H. Hines, Whig Central Committee circular, [1844], in John H. Bryan Papers, NCDAH. The central committees in North Carolina were more powerful than in states like Alabama. Compare Thornton, *Politics and Power*, 131.

15. Louis D. Henry to Dear Sir, August 15, 1844, Confidential Printed Circular, in Reid Papers.

which sometimes aroused the hostility of party members who were injured by the committee's decisions. In 1846, after the Democratic party failed to convince its gubernatorial nominee, Green Caldwell, to run, the central committee chose the party's candidate. The committee nominated one of its own members, James B. Shepard, even though another candidate, Walter Leak, had entered the race and embarked on the campaign trail. For a while, Leak continued his campaign against Shepard and the "Raleigh dictators." After party leaders devised a face-saving plan, Leak withdrew and supported Shepard, but his backers in the southeastern part of the state, where he resided, rebuked the party by staying away from the polls.[16]

The state party organizations of the 1840s, then, were not quite the well-oiled partisan machines that historians have contended they were. Such a notion exaggerates their efficiency and power. The weaknesses displayed in the organizations reflected the unease that citizens and politicians often felt about the legitimacy of parties. In the 1840s, the parties were barely out of their infancies. Although they matured rapidly and established many of the norms of modern party organization, they did not precipitate the instantaneous demise of long-held antiparty sentiments. People's beliefs, while certainly adaptable, accommodate themselves slowly to rapid changes, and the triumph of the second party system represented a rapid transformation in the way that American politics was conducted. Under such circumstances, many Americans gave only grudging acceptance to the idea of parties. Throughout the life of the second party system and beyond, a strong undercurrent of antiparty sentiment, or at least a skepticism about the value of parties, persisted and helped shape party politics.[17]

A recent study of Cumberland County politics reveals that in the 1820s antiparty beliefs pervaded the political culture and were adhered to by both future Whigs and future Democrats. Those findings seem to contradict the conclusions of other historians, who have contended that in other states the Whigs were the only transmitters of the antiparty tradition. These two views can be reconciled when one takes into account the chro-

16. Richard A. Rhodes to Drs. McDowell and Robeson, March 28, 1846, in Thomas D. McDowell Papers, SHC; Norton, *Democratic Party*, 149–52; Raleigh *Standard*, January 14 and 28, March 11, April 29, May 27, 1846; Harry L. Watson, *Jacksonian Politics and Community Conflict: The Emergence of the Second American Party System in Cumberland County, North Carolina* (Baton Rouge: Louisiana State University Press, 1981).

17. On the state party as a machine, see William R. Brock, *Parties and Political Conscience, 1840–1850* (Millwood, N.Y.: KTO Press, 1979), 31; on antiparty sentiment, see Richard Hofstadter, *The Idea of a Party System: The Rise of Legitimate Opposition in the United States, 1780–1840* (Berkeley: University of California Press, 1969).

nology of party formation. The Jacksonians had established their dominance in state politics in 1828 and maintained it virtually unopposed for eight years. They created a semblance of party organization and a sense of member loyalty to Jackson and the party. Almost out of necessity, the Whig party emerged as an antiparty party. They feared what they supposed to be Jackson's corrupt use of patronage and his interference with the conduct of free elections. It seemed to Whigs that Jackson's partisanship might be used to threaten the survival of republican government. As we have seen, in 1840 Whigs worried privately and publicly whether the Republic could survive a national Democratic victory.[18]

The appeal to antiparty sentiment also served a practical partisan purpose for Whigs. In the 1830s, they were seeking to remove from power a party with a substantial majority. In order to win elections, they would have to loosen whatever ties men had to the Democratic party. Antiparty appeals answered this purpose well. Therefore, for pragmatic and ideological reasons, the Whig party remained the chief, though not the sole, repository of antiparty beliefs.

As the Whig party became better established, the needs of party organization blunted but did not destroy the Whig antiparty commitment. In 1846, for example, the editor of the Whig Raleigh *Register* lamented the disappearance of the independent politician. "A Statesman, belonging to either of the great political parties of the day," the editor remarked sadly, "is expected madly and blindly to folly [*sic*] the mercenary behests of party discipline." He continued: "So profound and startling is the astonishment occasioned by a Politician daring to *think* and *act* for himself, in contradistinction from party trammels, that the whole community is aroused, and instead of being applauded by all for such a display of manly independence and moral courage—by some, the most ignoble, detestable and base motives are attributed for his action in the matter." The editor blamed the organizations themselves. "By the craftiness of demagogues and designing men, a web of deception and falsehood has been thrown around the People, in the shape of party rules, and party bias, which sometimes misleads them from the paths of propriety to the performance of unworthy actions."[19]

Whigs also contrasted their attitudes toward parties with those of their opponents. After arguing that parties were useful insofar as they propa-

18. Watson, *Jacksonian Politics*; Ronald Formisano, "Political Character, Antipartyism, and the Second Party System," *American Quarterly*, XXI (1969), 683–709; Daniel Walker Howe, *The Political Culture of the American Whigs* (Chicago: University of Chicago Press, 1979), 51–54; Lynn L. Marshall, "The Strange Stillbirth of the Whig Party," *AHR*, LXXII (1967), 445–68; Hofstadter, *Idea*, 267.

19. Raleigh *Register*, August 7, 1846.

gated "principles or measures of Government," one Whig editor contended that "where the party abandons the principles for which it was organized, the individual members of it are released from all obligation to go with it." This view, he claimed, contrasted sharply with that of the Democrats. "Locofocoism teaches that there is something sacred in the name of organization, which it is treason to question or oppose."[20]

Whig antipartyism also surfaced in the 1848 presidential campaign. At the national level, Zachary Taylor's portrayal of himself as a man above party represented a broad attempt to restructure the Whig party around him. Because by that time North Carolina Whigs held a solid majority in the state, many were unenthusiastic about a 'no party' campaign, but even so, they, like Whigs elsewhere, pictured Taylor as a kind of nonpartisan Whig. The linchpin in their contention that a Taylor victory would represent a triumph over partisanship was his future patronage policy. Unlike his Democratic predecessors who only permitted fellow party members to hold office, Taylor, Whigs claimed, would never proscribe a man "for opinion's sake"—that is, he would never remove a faithful officer merely because he was a Democrat. The Whig attack on Democratic proscription of Whigs had long been a staple of party rhetoric. In its crudest form, it stemmed from the Whig party's inability to obtain offices when the Democrats controlled the federal government, which was most of the time. But Whig opposition to proscription also revealed a distrust of the accepted method by which parties held themselves together—the partisan distribution of patronage. By calling into question the legitimacy of the powers that parties exercised, Whigs raised questions about the legitimacy of parties themselves.[21]

After Taylor won the election, Whigs clamored for offices despite their antiparty protestations, and when Taylor gave jobs to his personal supporters rather than to loyal Whig party workers, local politicians let out bloody screams of betrayal. The Democrats looked upon all of this with bemused detachment. They chided the Whigs for demanding that patronage be distributed on a partisan basis after swearing that they would never drink from the dirty trough of partisanship. All along, the Democrats had expected to be turned out of office if a Whig won. That was the way of parties. Whigs, they said, ought not to be so hypocritical about the whole matter. Rather than hypocrisy, the episode indicates the deep ambivalence of Whigs toward the very idea of party. They hoped for an end to

20. *Ibid.*, November 30, 1853.

21. Michael F. Holt, *The Political Crisis of the 1850s* (New York: John Wiley & Sons, 1978), 62, 72–75; Edward J. Hale to Daniel M. Barringer, April 7 and May 5, 1848, in Daniel Moreau Barringer Papers, SHC; Greensboro *Patriot*, July 1, 1848.

partisanship, yet they were politicians who wanted to reap the material benefits that a political career offered. The Whig party was a party of ideas, as Daniel Walker Howe has recently suggested, but it was also a party of men seeking pelf and power.[22]

The same tug toward party regularity and resistance to it were evident below the state level. Just as the state's competitive party system influenced the decisions of the state's organization, so too did the extent of local competitiveness shape the contours of local decision making. Alfred Dockery's congressional races illustrate this point.

Dockery, a wealthy Whig planter from southern Richmond County, sought the Whig nomination for Congress in 1845 in his predominantly Whig district, but the convention nominated Randolph's Jonathan Worth. Dockery then ran an independent campaign in which he denounced conventions and party machinery, and in the election he defeated Worth decisively.[23]

The redistricting of the state in 1847 placed Dockery's Richmond in the same district with another incumbent Whig, Daniel M. Barringer. After considering a run for reelection, Dockery decided against it and gave his support to Barringer. Two years later, after Barringer vacated his congressional seat to become minister to Spain, Dockery announced his candidacy. He was soon joined by two Whigs and one Democrat. Aware that if more than one Whig ran, the district would surely elect the Democrat, the three Whigs submitted to the decision of a convention, which nominated a fourth man, former congressman Edmund Deberry. Dockery accepted the decision. The difference between Dockery's behavior in 1845 and in 1849 reflected the difference in the extent of interparty competition in the two districts. His independent candidacy in 1845 did not jeopardize a Whig victory, but if he had run again as an independent in 1849, a Democrat probably would have won. In 1851, Dockery was rewarded for his patience. He was the only Whig candidate that year, and he won the election.[24]

22. Holt, *Political Crisis*, 75–76; J. Winslow to Daniel M. Barringer, March 21, 1849, in Barringer Papers; Calvin H. Wiley to Griffith J. McRee, March 28, 1849, in Griffith J. McRee Papers, SHC; Raleigh *Standard*, April 18, May 16, 1849; Raleigh *Standard*, n.d., quoted in Durward T. Stokes, "Charles Napoleon Bonaparte and the *Milton Chronicle*," *NCHR*, XLVI (1969), 256; Daniel Walker Howe, *Political Culture of the American Whigs*, 51–54, 280.

23. Richard L. Zuber, *Jonathan Worth: Biography of a Southern Unionist* (Chapel Hill: University of North Carolina Press, 1965), 60–64.

24. Alfred Dockery to Edmund Deberry, February 4, 1847, in Edmund Deberry Papers, SHC; Daniel M. Barringer to Alfred Dockery (draft), February 2, 1849, in Barringer Papers. The 1849 campaign may be followed in James W. Osborne to Barringer, January 12, 1849, J. L. Badger to Barringer, March 2, 1849, Samuel A. Walkup to Barringer, March 2, 1849, all in Barringer Papers. Also see Charlotte *Journal*, March 23 and 30, April 6 and 13, May 4 and 18, 1849; Raleigh *Register*, May 26, July 14, 1849. On the election of 1851, see James W. Osborne to William A. Graham, June 13, 1851, in Hamilton and Williams (eds.), *Graham Papers*, IV, 120–22.

Below the congressional district level in the senatorial districts and in the counties, the nature of interparty competition and local custom determined party practices. Democrats in Cumberland County, for instance, stopped holding local nominating conventions in 1846, after a duel between two candidates for the state senatorial nomination ended in one's death. In highly competitive counties like Orange, the parties regularly held conventions to nominate candidates, and independent candidates were almost unknown. But in counties where one party won with large majorities, the majority party was often subjected to internal schism. For example, in 1840 in Wilkes County, where Whigs predominated, dissident Whigs opposed the party's nominee and, with Democratic support, defeated him.[25]

★

The effort to elect state legislators was part of larger state campaigns to control the General Assembly and to win the governorship and the state's electoral votes. Campaigns at the local level were often well organized. Whether a local party held a large majority or a small minority in its county, it actively pursued voters. The intense competition at the state level for gubernatorial and presidential elections made organizational activity at the county level imperative, regardless of the competitive situation in a particular county. That explains why Democrats in Caswell County, who could normally expect about 75 percent of the popular vote, established in 1844 "a Democratic Association" in every militia district and "appointed committees of Vigilance . . . to aid our great and good cause."[26]

Such local organizations arranged mass meetings to ratify their party's gubernatorial and presidential nominations and to promote the candidacies of those nominees and of local legislative aspirants. The meetings, which were held at times when citizens were brought together for tax gatherings, militia drills, or court sessions, usually featured a speech by a local notable. In 1844, William W. Cherry, a Whig from coastal Bertie County whose name was frequently mentioned as a possible gubernatorial candidate, spoke all over his congressional district, twice in each county. On October 19, he reported that he had given fourteen speeches during the previous ten days.[27]

25. Watson, *Jacksonian Politics*; Priestly H. Mangum to William A. Graham, May 30, 1842, in Hamilton and Williams (eds.), *Graham Papers*, II, 316–17; Edward W. Jones to Samuel F. Patterson, May 12, September 6, 1840, Patterson to John T. Jones, August 6, 1840, all in Jones and Patterson Papers, SHC.

26. Barzillai Graves to David S. Reid, May 16, 1844, in Reid Papers.

27. William W. Cherry to John M. Morehead, October 19, 1844, in Governors' Papers, NCDAH.

At the meetings, the mood of those attending was improved by the smell and taste of a barbecue and freely flowing liquor. Because the meetings brought people together for the kind of social occasions often lacking in rural North Carolina, they made political participation a pleasurable experience. Popular enjoyment was enhanced by politicians who entertained the audiences with hours and hours of political speeches. Although today the prospect of listening to endless speeches seems insufferable, at that time good oratory was appreciated as great entertainment.[28]

The most significant local meetings involved gubernatorial candidates. After 1840, when the practice began, any man who wanted to run for the governorship had to be willing to stump the state. The candidates, whose campaigns usually ran from May to August, divided their time between speech making on their own and joint debates. Although many potential candidates withdrew their names from consideration because they refused to canvass the state and although the young Democratic candidate in 1844, Michael Hoke, died soon after a grueling campaign, the practice continued unabated through the antebellum period. In as competitive a state as North Carolina, parties could not allow the opposition an edge by refusing to participate in the canvass.[29]

The gubernatorial campaign aided the future governor because, as one newspaper editor asserted, "it reminds the officer of the source of his powers—makes him acquainted with the State, its people and their wants and necessities." Even the most widely traveled men had rarely seen more than a portion of the state. The canvass also enabled citizens to become better acquainted with the candidates. John M. Morehead initiated the tradition in 1840 because his opponent, Romulus Saunders, was much better known than he. Beyond introducing the candidates and the citizenry to one another, the canvass aroused great popular interest in the campaigns as thousands flocked to hear the candidates. The speeches and debates also provided a means by which politicians educated the electorate. Although the debates occasionally degenerated to personal insults, they usually dealt with the issues. Despite North Carolina's high illiteracy rate, the candidates helped educate its citizens politically.[30]

28. Richard P. McCormick, *The Second American Party System: Party Formation in the Jacksonian Era* (Chapel Hill: University of North Carolina Press, 1966), 350; Don E. Fehrenbacher, *Prelude to Greatness: Lincoln in the 1850s* (Stanford: Stanford University Press, 1962), 15. For a vivid description of a Whig party meeting in Orange County, see Walter W. Lenoir to Rufus T. Lenoir, October 15, 1844, in Lenoir Family Papers, SHC.
29. On opposition to canvassing, see Walter F. Leak to William Lander, in Raleigh *Standard*, March 22, 1848; James W. Bryan to William A. Graham, January 21, 1848, in James W. Bryan Letterbooks, Bryan Family Papers, SHC.
30. Fayetteville *North Carolina Argus*, quoted in Raleigh *Register*, April 15, 1848; John M. Morehead to James W. Bryan, January 25, 1840, in Bryan Family Papers.

Literate citizens also obtained their party's views and general political information from the party press, so the effectiveness of electoral campaigns depended on the quality and quantity of the party newspapers. In antebellum North Carolina, as elsewhere, all but a few newspapers attached themselves to a party, which often funded them. Because the Whigs had the overwhelming majority of the state's newspapers, twenty-nine to the Democrats' ten, they were able to send their message into more homes throughout the state.[31]

Each party was fortunate to have at the capital an effective party organ, the main cog in the partisan press machinery. The Democratic Raleigh *North Carolina Standard* and the Whig Raleigh *Register* were crucial to their party's success. The editor of each organ helped decide the party's position on issues or on questions involving party organization, and then the paper disseminated it to the other party papers in the state, which often reprinted it. In this way, the editor acted as a spokesman for the party and helped resolve intraparty disputes.

Joseph Gales, a member of the family that established the famous *National Intelligencer* in Washington, D.C., began to publish the *Register* in 1799 as a Jeffersonian Republican and later as a Whig paper. His son Weston maintained the quality of the paper through the 1840s, when it began to deteriorate badly under the direction of his grandson Seaton.[32]

Philo White established the *Standard* in 1834 as a Democratic paper but soon sold out to Thomas Loring, who edited it until 1843. Loring, a lukewarm partisan, gave halfhearted support to Democratic positions on the state bank and on the tariff. The Democratic central committee forced him out and found a more steadfast and energetic editor for the *Standard* in William W. Holden, who had recently converted from Whiggery to the Democratic faith and proved to be an outstanding political editor. His editorials presented the Democratic position effectively, and his maneuvering within the party helped it to attain the majorities of the 1850s.[33]

★

Because so few votes separated victor and loser, the parties were more concerned with drawing out the party faithful than in winning new converts. The chairman of the Whig central committee in 1844 captured this strategy in a circular to local Whig leaders: "First, To attend the Polls in

31. Norton, *Democratic Party*, 12; Pegg, *Whig Party*, 26.
32. Robert N. Elliott, Jr., *The Raleigh Register, 1799–1863* (Chapel Hill: University of North Carolina Press, 1955).
33. Edgar Estes Folk, "W. W. Holden and the *North Carolina Standard*, 1843–1848," *NCHR*, XIX (1942), 22–47.

TABLE 1
Democratic Percentage of the State Vote for President and Governor, 1840–1854

	Governor	President
1840	44.6	42.3
1842	46.9	
1844	48.1	47.8
1846	45.0	
1848	49.5	44.8
1850	51.6	
1852	53.0	50.5
1854	51.1	

SOURCE: Inter-University Consortium for Political and Social Research, Ann Arbor, Michigan.

their Precinct, and see that every Whig is brought forward to vote. Secondly, To see the people of the Precinct before the day of the Election, urging upon them the duty of attending and voting, and gain their promise to do so." Both Whigs and Democrats were successful in bringing out the vote. Although turnout in statewide elections reached 80 percent only in two elections after the extraordinary rates of participation of 1840, it dropped below 70 percent just twice.[34]

In this competitive atmosphere, Whigs emerged with a narrow majority that they maintained through the 1840s. In 1850, Democrats reversed the roles and assumed the mantle of power, though again holding it by a narrow margin (see table 1). Not only did the parties remain extremely competitive during the early 1840s, but they continued to draw their support from the same areas. The strongest Whig counties of 1840 remained the strongest Whig counties twelve or fourteen years later (see table 2).

The purpose of getting voters to the polls, of course, was to elect the party's candidates to office. For a party's candidate to win the presidency would bring enormous political benefits to the party and would allow state party leaders to enjoy considerable control over federal patronage in the state. The state party would have a major say in the appointment of postal and customs officials and the director of the mint in Charlotte, in the assignment of federal government printing contracts, and even in the appointment of a U.S. district judge in the state.[35]

A party obtained fewer tangible benefits when its gubernatorial candidate won. The governor appointed a handful of men to serve on the Literary Board or on the Board of Internal Improvements, but until the state

34. Richard H. Hines, *et al.*, Central Committee Circular [1844], in John H. Bryan Papers.
35. On patronage see, for examples, James W. Osborne to Daniel M. Barringer, December 18, 1848, A. Graham to Barringer, February 24, 1849, both in Barringer Papers; William S. Ashe to James Buchanan, January 13, 1858, in James Buchanan Papers, Duke.

TABLE 2

Democratic Vote for President (P) and Governor (G), 1840–1854: Pearson Correlations

	1840G	1842G	1844P	1844G	1846G	1848P	1848G	1850G	1852P	1852G	1854G
1840P	.99	.97	.97	.97	.91	.97	.93	.92	.95	.92	.94
1840G		.97	.96	.96	.93	.96	.95	.92	.96	.94	.95
1842G			.95	.97	.91	.95	.91	.90	.94	.91	.93
1844P				.98	.93	.96	.94	.94	.96	.94	.95
1844G					.95	.96	.95	.93	.96	.95	.95
1846G						.95	.96	.93	.93	.92	.93
1848P							.97	.93	.98	.96	.97
1848G								.96	.97	.97	.96
1850G									.97	.98	.96
1852P										.98	.99

Source: Inter-University Consortium for Political and Social Research, Ann Arbor, Michigan.

became a stockholder in a variety of economic development projects, the governor enjoyed little patronage power.

A governor's power was further weakened by the poor timing of his messages to the General Assembly. He made his inaugural address on January 1st of each odd-numbered year. Usually the assembly had been in session for at least a month, so its agenda was essentially set, and since the address was generally a brief one without specific recommendations, it usually had little effect on the legislative process. The next time that the governor addressed the General Assembly was during December of the second year of his term. Then, as long as he had won reelection (and all but one governor in the antebellum period did), he could deliver a message that carried some clout. The force of his next message was limited, though, because he was a lame duck.[36]

Then why did the parties make such a fuss about the governorship? Much of its importance was symbolic. In the minds of state politicians, a gubernatorial election determined whether North Carolina was a Whig or a Democratic state, and this was the benchmark by which a party measured its success. The gubernatorial election was also important for local politicians and candidates. The excitement of the gubernatorial race was bound to carry over to local contests, and popular candidates for the governorship would help draw votes for legislative candidates. Winning the governorship also gave the party the only official statewide political pulpit for preaching party doctrine. In his campaign and in his messages, the governor articulated his party's position on a variety of issues. William A. Graham's cogent analysis of the state's railroads and economy in 1848 and his proposals for state aid to economic development shaped subsequent legislation that provided state aid to internal improvement projects. The governor also could influence his party's position on particular issues. For example, David Reid's advocacy of the end to the freehold requirement for senatorial electors brought the Democratic party to support the measure and ultimately helped to pass it.

★

Still, the real power in the state rested in the General Assembly. The legislature of North Carolina was almost omnipotent in the state government. It elected all of the state's executive officers except the governor and all of the state's judiciary. In the realm of legislation, it reigned supreme because the governor had no veto power. In effect, the legislature was the state government. It influenced the machinery of local government, too, by electing the justices of the peace.[37]

36. Jeffrey, "Second Party System," 100.
37. Francis Newton Thorpe (comp.), *The Federal and State Constitutions, Colonial Charters,*

Therefore, it is important to understand who the men were who wielded political power in the state. A typical legislature was that of 1850–1851, with 65 Democrats and 53 Whigs in the House of Commons and 28 Democrats and 22 Whigs in the Senate.[38] As befit the legislature of a state that attracted few immigrants, most members of the General Assembly were born and raised in North Carolina; over 90 percent of the members in 1850 were natives of the state. Most of them were in their thirties and forties; their median age was thirty-eight. The majority of legislators (56.8 percent) identified themselves as farmers in the 1850 census; the only other occupation represented in substantial numbers was the law (see table 3). Slightly more than one-fourth of the legislators were attorneys, far out of proportion to their numbers in the state. The lawyer's activities and skills made him an ideal politician and legislator: traveling his circuit, the attorney made acquaintances with prominent men along the way; in order to be successful, he had to develop his skills in speech, debate, and negotiation, all of which would stand him in good stead on the stump and in the legislature. Then too, the legislature attracted lawyers who desired to wield power and to further their legal careers. The contacts and reputation that a young attorney would acquire in the legislature would enhance his standing in the profession.[39]

The census officials in 1850 also recorded two measures of wealth: the number of slaves people owned and the value of their real estate. In a slave society like North Carolina, one of the better measures of economic

---

and Other Organic Laws of the States, Territories, and Colonies Now or Heretofore Forming the United States (7 vols.; Washington, D.C.: Government Printing Office, 1909), V, 2787–99.

38. The major sources for this collective biography of North Carolina's legislators are Schedule No. 1, Free Inhabitants, and Schedule No. 2, Slave Inhabitants, of the Seventh Census of the United States, 1850. I used copies of the schedules in NCDAH and microfilm copies available at the Detroit Public Library, Detroit, Michigan. I have located information for 136 of 170 legislators—42 of 50 senators, and 94 of 120 commoners. Professor Ralph A. Wooster kindly shared with me his research notes on North Carolina legislators. However, because I discovered that Professor Wooster's findings understated the proportion of slaveowners in the legislature in 1850, I undertook my own examination of the census. *Cf.* Ralph A. Wooster, *Politicians, Planters, and Plain Folk: Courthouse and Statehouse in the Upper South: 1850–1860* (Knoxville: University of Tennessee Press, 1975), 40.

It is possible that Professor Wooster's studies contain errors for other states similar to the ones for North Carolina that I discovered. However, this appears to be unlikely. An examination of his tables for the lower and upper South reveals that only for North Carolina was there a substantial discrepancy in the proportion of slaveowners among legislators in 1850 and in 1860. Even if his data are accurate, however, his decisions to include all legislators not located in the census as nonslaveowners leads him to overstate the numbers of nonslaveowners. On this point, see Thornton, *Politics and Power*, 297n. In any case, because his data are the only materials available for other southern states (except Alabama), I decided to use his data for the purpose of making a rough comparison between North Carolina and the rest of the South.

39. Leander B. Carmichael to Ed. Bryan, October 26, 1848, in Bryan and Leventhorpe Papers, SHC.

TABLE 3
Legislators' Occupations, by Party, 1850

	Whig	Democrat	All
Farmer	46.6	63.5	56.8
Attorney	31.0	21.6	25.8
Other	22.4	14.9	17.4

TABLE 4
Percentage of Slaveowners and Planters, by Party, 1850

	Whig	Democrat	Legislature
Slaveowners	83.9	80.8	81.2
Planters	37.5	35.9	36.1

and social status was the number of slaves a man possessed. Since slave-owning represented a tangible interest in the slave system, a distinction should be made between the nonslaveholder and slaveholder. The most convenient measure of high economic status is the generally accepted designation of men owning twenty or more slaves as planters. In 1850, about 25.6 percent of North Carolina's white families owned slaves, though only 3.1 percent belonged to the planter class.[40]

Despite composing only slightly more than one-fourth of the state's white populace, slaveowners dominated the state legislature (see table 4). More than 81 percent of the members owned slaves; often they owned substantial numbers of slaves—planters composed 36.1 percent of the legislature's members. The median number of slaves owned by legislators was twelve. Given the massive representation of slaveowners, one could be sure of the legislators' commitment to the preservation of slavery. That these men were well-to-do is suggested further by their ownership of valuable real estate. Legislators owned a median of $5,000 worth of real property.

When the figures derived above are broken down by party, the results are revealing. No difference between the parties existed in terms of nativity or age. Almost all legislators were born in the state, and the median age was thirty-eight for Whigs and forty for Democrats. The age similarities are significant because contemporaries then, and historians since, fre-

40. Ulrich Bonnell Phillips, *Life and Labor in the Old South* (1929; reprint ed., Boston: Little, Brown, 1963), 339. The number of white families and slaves was taken from data in J. G. Randall and David Donald, *The Civil War and Reconstruction* (2nd ed. rev.; Boston: D. C. Heath, 1969), 5, 68; the number of planters was computed from data in J. D. B. De Bow, *Statistical View of the United States . . . Being a Compendium of the Seventh Census* (Washington, D.C.: Beverly Tucker, 1854), 95.

quently argued that young, ambitious politicians entered the Democratic party in the late 1840s because that party's leadership was more open than that of the Whigs. That the median age of Democratic legislators was slightly higher than the median age for the legislature as a whole belies this contention.

There were, however, important occupational differences that separated the legislators. Democrats were much more involved in agriculture, whereas Whigs were more frequently found in the legal profession. These facts seem to suggest further the agrarian ties of the Democrats and the commercial ties of the Whigs.

To say that Democrats were more often farmers than Whigs were is not to suggest that Democrats represented slaveowners and Whigs nonslaveowners. Whigs and Democrats actually owned about the same number of slaves. Moreover, Whigs were just as likely to be slaveowners or to come from the planter class as Democrats were. This is what one would expect when there was little correlation between county party affiliation and the extent of slaveowning. These figures may be broken down further by the two houses of the legislature. Here we see that slaveowning was more common among senators than commoners and that the typical senator was a member of the planter class. There was, however, no difference between the parties within each house. Hence, one can conclude that partisans were little divided by their economic interest in slavery (see table 5).

Our understanding of North Carolina's political elite is elucidated further by a comparison of it with the elites of other southern states. In 1850, the percentage of North Carolina legislators who owned slaves was sub-

TABLE 5
Slaveownership and Planters, by Party, House and Senate, 1850

	Whig	*Democrat*	*Total*
MEDIAN SLAVEOWNERSHIP			
House	10	11	10.5
Senate	28	24	24.5
PERCENTAGE OF SLAVEOWNERS			
House	79.1	77.4	78.1
Senate	94.1	96.0	95.2
PERCENTAGE OF PLANTERS			
House	27.9	28.3	28.1
Senate	58.8	56.0	57.1

TABLE 6
Slaveownership Among Southern White Families and Legislators, 1850

	Percentage of White Families Owning Slaves	Percentage of Slaveowners, Legislature
N. Carolina	25.6	81.2
S. Carolina	46.6	80.5
Georgia	36.9	69.7
Florida	37.3	—
Alabama	34.2	66.4
Mississippi	39.1	42.6
Louisiana	41.5	38.8
Virginia	30.8	67.1
Arkansas	18.5	53.6
Tennessee	22.3	41.0
Texas	25.1	—

SOURCES: For slaveownership among white families, see J. D. B. DeBow, *Statistical View of the United States . . . Being a Compendium of the Seventh Census* (Washington, D.C.: Beverly Tucker, 1854), 45, 95. For slaveownership among legislators, see Ralph A. Wooster, *The People in Power: Courthouse and Statehouse in the Lower South, 1850–1860* (Knoxville: University of Tennessee Press, 1969), 41; Wooster, *Politicians*, 40.

stantially greater than that of any other southern legislature but South Carolina. While over 80 percent of the legislators in those two states owned slaves, in no other state in the South did slaveowners compose even 70 percent of its legislators. The difference between North Carolina and the rest of the South was magnified by the somewhat smaller proportion of the white families in North Carolina who owned slaves (see table 6).

Not only did a larger percentage of North Carolina's legislators own slaves, but a larger percentage of them were planters than were the legislators in all the rest of the South but South Carolina. The high percentage of planters among North Carolina's legislators is remarkable because of the relatively small number of planters in the state (see table 7).

Slaveowners in North Carolina clearly wielded power far disproportionate to their numbers. They represented in the legislature not only the large slaveholding regions of the state but the areas where whites owned few slaves. In a state where less than one-third of the white families owned slaves, more than 80 percent of its legislators owned them. And in a state where 3 percent of the white families belonged to the planter class, planters composed more than one-third of the General Assembly's members.

That a slaveholding elite wielded such power in North Carolina requires some explanation, especially because historians have often viewed the state as "Southern more in terms of yeoman democracy than in terms of slaveholding aristocracy." The prominence of wealthy slaveowners in the state's politics in 1850 represented the persistence of much older pat-

TABLE 7
Percentage of Planters Among Southern White Families and Legislators, 1850

	Percentage of White Families Owning 20 or More Slaves	Percentage of Legislators Owning 20 or More Slaves
N. Carolina	3.1	36.1
S. Carolina	8.5	53.5
Georgia	5.7	29.8
Florida	5.1	—
Alabama	5.5	33.6
Mississippi	6.9	30.3
Louisiana	5.5	19.8
Texas	1.5	5.5
Virginia	3.2	22.9
Arkansas	1.6	10.3
Tennessee	1.6	7.0

SOURCES: See sources for Table 6.

terns of political leadership in the state. Studies of the delegates to the two conventions held to ratify the United States Constitution revealed that roughly the same proportion of slaveholders and planters were represented there as in the General Assembly of 1850. Harold Counihan's study of state legislators in the 1820s, although not directly comparable to the present study, reveals that they were men of considerable wealth, so the wealth of legislators in 1850 was part of a continuing pattern and not simply a phenomenon of the late antebellum period.[41]

The persistence of the power of slaveholders was the logical culmination of the state's representational system. Because the lines for senatorial districts were drawn according to taxes paid, the wealthy slaveowning counties were more fully represented than were the poor counties. A similar bias shaped the membership in the House of Commons, where representation was determined on the federal basis (five slaves counted as three persons). As a result, counties with more slaves held more power. In those areas, it was obviously more likely that partisans would turn to well-to-do slaveowners as their candidates.

Such a tendency was reinforced by constitutionally mandated property-holding requirements for legislators. Commoners were required to own one hundred acres of land and senators three hundred. Although most of the legislators probably owned more than the required property, the requirements did exclude most citizens from the legislature. In that way, the

41. Emory M. Thomas, *The Confederate Nation* (New York: Harper & Row, 1978), 86; Harold Joseph Counihan, "North Carolina Politics, 1815–1836: State and Local Perspectives on the Age of Jackson" (Ph.D. dissertation, University of North Carolina at Chapel Hill, 1971), 20–22.

rules helped create an atmosphere that encouraged upper-class dominance of the political process.[42]

Although wealthy slaveowners were numerous in the legislature, they
did not simply impose their political will on the state's citizens. The campaign of Walter L. Steele for a seat in the House of Commons in 1846 provides a good example. Steele, a Whig member of a prominent family in
Richmond, a cotton-planting county on the South Carolina border, reported to David Lowry Swain, president of the University of North Carolina, that he was "busily engaged in proving to the people, the soundness
of my political faith, and the purity of my personal character & playing the
fool to a considerable extent, as you know, all candidates are obliged to
do." He added condescendingly, "A 'candied (would that it were can*did*)
tongue' is absolutely necessary to a politician, but I shall endeavor to play
the hypocrite as little as possible." Steele expected to win easily, but he did
fear that he would lose some votes because he supported a "yes" vote on
the forthcoming referendum on the establishment of a state penitentiary
while his constituents opposed one. As a result, he said, he would "advocate the 'right and binding force of instructions[,] in respect to that particular case."[43]

Steele's letter might be dismissed as the hypocritical whining of an
"aristocrat" out to deceive the people. He was obviously averse to what
he considered pandering to the masses. But the important lesson to be
learned from Steele's letter is that in the end he pandered. By speaking
with a "candied tongue," he acted the way that voters expected a candidate to act. And his commitment to abide by the people's verdict on the
penitentiary question revealed a willingness, however grudging, to accept
the popular will. Steele's behavior is even more striking because he faced
little opposition. Rather than showing the persistence of aristocratic beliefs among North Carolina's political elite, this letter suggests just how
deeply democratic notions had penetrated the political culture.

The power of slaveholders was limited further by the high turnover in
the General Assembly's membership. Unlike the situation in the early decades of the century when legislators would be returned to office year after
year, under the second party system high turnover characterized the General Assembly. More than 60 percent of the members of the legislature
from 1836 to 1850 served only one term; an additional one-fourth of the
members served two terms. Between 1844 and 1860, an average of about
39 percent of the senators and 33 percent of the commoners in a given ses-

42. Thorpe (comp.), *Federal and State Constitutions*, V, 2790.
43. Walter L. Steele to David L. Swain, May 19, 1846, in David Lowry Swain Papers,
NCDAH.

sion served in their respective houses during the previous session. Most of the men who came to Raleigh to serve in the legislature had not served before and would not serve again. So while many slaveholders served in the General Assembly, they did not compose a stable elite.[44]

In the legislature, the behavior of these unpracticed lawmakers was governed less by their membership in a class than by their membership in a political party. Because of their inexperience, they frequently relied for patronage and policy decisions upon other fellow partisans who knew their way around the capital. The case of Samuel Finley Patterson, state senator from Caldwell County in 1846, is instructive. Although he had not served before in the General Assembly, Patterson had been a member of the Whig central committee and president of the Raleigh and Gaston Railroad. Legislators from each of the congressional districts made committee assignments (a novel method that weakened the power of the speaker), and mountain-district legislators chose Patterson to serve on the Internal Improvements and Finance committees, the two most important committees in the senate. Patterson was appointed chairman of both, though he declined the chairmanship of the Finance Committee. Later in the session, he chaired a joint committee to devise a means to pay off the state debt. After the session was well under way, Patterson reported that "almost the whole of the business devolves on a few individuals, and of that number I have rather more than my share." Hard work, though, had its own rewards because, of the various bills requesting state aid for internal improvement projects, the only one to become law provided for construction of a turnpike in Patterson's Caldwell County.[45]

Party leaders like Patterson also wielded power over patronage in the party caucus. When members arrived in Raleigh, they went into a party caucus almost immediately in order to choose candidates for speakers of the houses and for other legislative offices. Clearly, men of experience helped shape the decisions of new members. Once a caucus reached a decision, the party vote in the legislature was virtually unanimous; it would be hard to find more than an occasional renegade who abandoned his party to vote for an opposition candidate for either speakership.

The parties were only a bit less successful in getting legislators to vote for the caucus' choices for the U.S. Senate. Twice the Democratic majority could not get enough votes to elect their caucus choice. In 1842 and again in 1852, Romulus Saunders, a longtime leader of the party, ran against the

44. Wooster, *Politicians, Planters, and Plain Folk*, 43. The persistence of senators and commoners from one term to the next was calculated from Robert Diggs Wimberly Connor, *A Manual of North Carolina, 1913* (Raleigh: N.C. Historical Commission, 1913).

45. Samuel F. Patterson to wife, November 27, 1846, in Jones and Patterson Papers; Patterson to Thomas I. Lenoir, December 14, 1846, in Lenoir Family Papers; Raleigh *Register*, February 2, 1847.

caucus nominee. The first time he forced the caucus to choose a third man; the second time he prevented the election of any candidate, so North Carolina was without a senator in 1853 and 1854. The Whigs also had some trouble. In 1848, when the parties in the legislature were closely balanced, a few opponents delayed George E. Badger's reelection to the Senate. One eventually gave up and provided Badger with the vote he needed to be elected.[46]

Those three episodes were atypical. Usually, no matter how divided a party might be in caucus, it rallied around the majority's choice. In 1840, for example, the Whig majority in the legislature had the opportunity to elect two senators because of the resignation of Democrat Robert Strange. They nominated for the full term Willie P. Mangum, who had served in the Senate for a number of years and had played a major role in founding the Whig party. Much more contention arose over the choice for filling the short two-year term. At one party meeting, legislators discussed eight men for the job, but when the caucus decided upon William A. Graham, Whig legislators fell into line and elected him with a unanimous vote.[47]

The unity of the parties in their major patronage votes was replicated in their votes on many matters of policy. Much of what legislators voted on, like the myriad private laws they passed, concerned the parties not at all. But the parties were more united on state and national issues. Remarkable unity existed, as might be expected, on resolutions on national issues such as a national bank, the tariff, public land policy, or territorial expansion. On state issues, partisanship was less intense but was nevertheless present. The vast majority of men of either party would be found voting for their party's position on state banking, internal improvements, individual liability of corporate stockholders, an insane asylum, or the appointment of a state superintendent of the common schools.

An examination of these issues reveals how party politics shaped what North Carolinians expected from government (and did not expect), how it helped democratize the political process, and how it influenced the ways that North Carolinians perceived the world beyond the state's borders. Partisanship, whether in the precinct meeting or the county convention, the state party convention or the legislative caucus, the ballot box or the legislative roll call vote, shaped the contours of the state's political cul-

46. Brian G. Walton, "Elections to the United States Senate in North Carolina, 1835–1861," *NCHR*, LIII (1976), 168–92; Raleigh *Register*, October 28, November 22 and 25, December 16 and 20, 1848; Thomas L. Clingman, *Address of T. L. Clingman on the Recent Senatorial Election* (n.p., [1849]), in NCC; Raleigh *Standard*, November 24, December 29, 1852, January 5 and 12, 1853.
47. See William A. Graham to James Graham, November 21, 1840, in Hamilton and Williams (eds.), *Graham Papers*, II, 121–22; *HJ, 1840–41*, 372–73; *SJ, 1840–41*, 44–45; Walton, "Elections," 177.

ture. As Whig congressman David Outlaw remarked in 1852, "party ties are among the strongest associations which bind men together. . . . The very name of party has a talismanic power on the passions and prejudices of the people."[48]

48. *Congressional Globe*, 32nd Cong., 1st Sess., Appendix, 678, quoted in David M. Potter, *The Impending Crisis, 1848–1861*, completed and edited by Don E. Fehrenbacher (New York: Harper & Row, 1976), 225n.

Three   *"Perfectly Infatuated with Her Mad Schemes of 'Improvement'": Parties and Governance, 1840–1855*

Partisanship in North Carolina shaped what politicians said on the stump and how they acted in the state legislature. Party conflict, especially over the proper role of government in the society, prompted the parties to develop divergent policies. As we have seen, Whigs believed that government should foster economic development and social institutions like insane asylums, whereas Democrats ardently opposed such activities. Of course, antebellum parties, like American parties since, were not monolithic institutions, and they rarely attained the unanimity that often characterizes party voting under parliamentary systems of government. There were some Democrats who endorsed state activism and some Whigs who opposed it, but given the limited sanctions that parties had over their supporters, it is remarkable how united the parties actually were.

The interparty differences of the mid-1840s became the interparty consensus of the mid-1850s. Where Whigs in the 1840s had endorsed the positive state and Democrats opposed it, by the mid-1850s Democrats increasingly came to accept Whig premises and policies. This dramatic departure reflected no marked shift in popular voting patterns, since they remained stable, but rather represented a response to changed economic circumstances and the dynamics of interparty competition in the late 1840s and early 1850s. In the crucible of those years, North Carolina's

Democrats joined the emerging nineteenth-century American consensus that accepted government as a legitimate promoter of economic freedom.

The differences between the two parties in the 1840s were most clearly expressed in early 1843 in the majority and minority reports of the Senate Committee on Internal Improvements. The Democratic majority issued a searing condemnation of corporations and of government aid to them. It complained that in recent years "the Legislature has . . . granted away, to . . . corporations the Rivers of North Carolina, and now the People cannot carry a boatload to market, without paying tribute money to Navigation Corporations." Future incorporations of transportation companies would only offer citizens the opportunity to pay "tribute to these Corporations." And that would be the result only if a corporation were successful—if unsuccessful, the corporation would come scurrying to the legislature to be rescued, and ultimately, the people would be saddled with high taxes to pay the corporation's debts. According to the Democrats, state assistance to corporations would only lead to the impoverishment of the state, oppressive taxation, and the increasing influence of private interests in the state.

The Whig minority, though it challenged the Democrats on the specifics of their argument, devoted much of its report to an attack upon the Democrats' general position. While the Democrats tried to protect citizens against profligate, corrupt, and exploitative corporations, the Whigs emphasized the practical benefits to be derived from internal improvements. They complained accurately that the majority tried "to draw into discredit and disrepute the works of Internal Improvement already established in the State, and to prejudice the public mind against all and every improvement, which may be now contemplated or devised." Whereas the Democrats denounced tolls on the rivers as tribute, the Whigs defended the tolls on the Roanoke River on the grounds that members of a joint-stock company had invested over $400,000 to open the river and deserved some return on their investment. Conceding for the sake of argument that the state's railroad investments had proved "a bad investment of capital," the Whigs did not conclude from that experience, as the Democrats had, that the state should never support internal-improvement ventures. Rather, they were determined to push on with other projects. Although the railroads had returned no direct profit to the government, Whigs contended, "much the greater portion of it has been diffused and distributed more equally among the people, and has gone into the pockets of those who have furnished supplies of provisions, materials, and labor, for constructing the Roads, and still remains in the State to benefit and bless hundreds and

TABLE 8
Index of Party Disagreement in the North Carolina General Assembly, 1840–1849:
Economic Issues

	Senate	*N**	*House*	*N**
RAILROAD RELIEF				
1840–41	77.9	2	63.5	9
1842–43	67.4	3	55.3	1
1844–45	91.4	3	94.6	4
1846–47	75.0	3	69.5	1
1848–49	—		46.1	1
INDIVIDUAL STOCKHOLDER'S LIABILITY FOR CORPORATION'S DEBTS				
1840–41	60.0	3	60.4	5
1844–45	97.0	3	95.6	2
1846–47	83.8	4	59.3	1
1848–49	—		54.6	2
SUPPORT FOR INTERNAL IMPROVEMENTS				
1840–41	72.9	2	59.8	9
1842–43	55.0	2	51.5	6
1844–45	72.4	9	64.6	7
1846–47	47.7	4	57.8	6
1848–49	50.4	9	41.8	6
SUPPORT FOR STATE'S BANKS				
1840–41	75.2	2	69.7	1
1842–43	74.0	8	69.4	2

* N = Number of Roll-Call Votes
SOURCES: *SJ, 1840–41*, 190–91, 194, 235–36, 254–55, 266–67, 270, 274–75, 294–95, 298; *HJ, 1840–41*, 528, 539–42, 547–49, 575–78, 581–83, 593–94, 600–601, 611–13, 661–62, 672–73, 675–76, 701–703, 706–709, 711, 717–18; *SJ, 1842–43*, 94–95, 119–20, 191–92, 228, 247–48, 253–54, 267–69, 297–98, 313–15, 322, 333–34, 340–41, 359; *HJ, 1842–43*, 553–54, 562–64, 579–80, 692–93, 721–22, 750–51, 754–55, 847–49, 942–43; *SJ, 1844–45*, 95, 154–55, 163–65, 178, 206–207, 237–38, 245–46, 259, 273–74, 292–93, 309, 318–19, 329, 335–36; *HJ, 1844–45*, 610–13, 627–29, 638–41, 648–49, 680–82, 732–33, 754–55; *SJ, 1846–47*, 78–79, 128–29, 159, 183–84, 187–90, 201, 214; *HJ, 1846–47*, 354, 419, 476–78, 547–50; *SJ, 1848–49*, 171–72, 207, 236–37, 260, 284, 285–86, 295, 298, 302; *HJ, 1848–49*, 484–85, 634, 672, 695–96, 706, 709–10, 715, 718–19, 744–45, 752–53, 799.

thousands." Moreover, the railroads provided regular and cheaper transportation of crops to market, thereby widely diffusing their benefits.[1]

Party disagreement, as we have seen, had been sparked by the state's unsuccessful ventures into railroad building. Throughout the early 1840s, Democrats opposed relief for the ailing corporations. Even Democrats

1. Raleigh *Register*, February 10, 1843.

TABLE 9
Percentage Affirmative Votes in the North Carolina General Assembly, 1840–1849, by Party:
Economic Issues

	Senate		House	
	Democrats	*Whigs*	*Democrats*	*Whigs*
RAILROAD RELIEF				
1840–41	10.6	89.4	14.2	78.0
1842–43	28.8	96.1	42.7	97.7
1844–45	8.4	100.0	2.1	97.7
1846–47	16.7	91.6	25.5	95.0
1848–49	—	—	28.9	75.0
INDIVIDUAL STOCKHOLDER'S LIABILITY FOR CORPORATION'S DEBTS				
1840–41	81.1	17.8	79.5	19.0
1844–45	100.0	3.0	98.0	1.6
1846–47	89.7	5.9	73.0	13.7
1848–49	—	—	84.1	29.5
SUPPORT FOR INTERNAL IMPROVEMENTS				
1840–41	10.6	83.5	19.7	79.5
1842–43	10.0	65.0	23.9	75.4
1844–45	10.7	81.9	5.8	82.6
1846–47	19.6	50.0	12.7	78.5
1848–49	31.5	82.0	37.4	79.3
SUPPORT FOR STATE'S BANKS				
1840–41	11.1	86.3	16.7	86.4
1842–43	19.4	93.3	27.5	96.9

SOURCES: See Table 8.

who were advocates of state aid denounced relief on the grounds that Whigs had placed the state in debt for poorly planned projects or that the railroads only benefited a small section of the state. Whigs, meanwhile, continued to stand firmly behind the roads (see tables 8 and 9).[2]

The parties' positions found expression not only in votes over the relief of the Wilmington and Raleigh and the Raleigh and Gaston, but also on more general votes on questions of government aid. Tables 8 and 9 reveal that on measure after measure the legislators tended to vote along divergent party lines, Whigs tending largely to support state aid and Democrats overwhelmingly voting against it.

On social issues, as on economic ones, Whigs saw the need for a pater-

2. John W. Ellis, "Raleigh and Gaston Railroad Speech, Delivered in the House of Commons," December 26, 1844, in Noble J. Tolbert (ed.), *The Papers of John Willis Ellis* (2 vols.; Raleigh: State Department of Archives and History, 1964), I, 3–18.

nal state to pursue activities that they believed individuals could not undertake. Democrats saw in state activity only the threat of higher taxes and greater incursions of the government on individual freedom. The differences between the parties were revealed by their response to a public-school system. The distribution of federal funds to the state in 1836 provided North Carolina with the money it needed to establish state-supported common schools. A Whig legislature in 1838–1839 passed a bill that encouraged the creation of primary schools in districts throughout the state, whereby state funds would be used to match funds raised from special county taxes. Each county retained the option to accept or reject common schools, but in August, 1839, only seven turned down the opportunity, and they fell into line over the next several years.

The parties disagreed less about the creation of the school system than about the appointment of a state superintendent of the common schools and over whether to require counties to raise $20 to match the state's $40 contribution to each district. Despite an optimistic beginning, the schools foundered because of a lack of coordination among districts and counties and because of an inadequate financial base.[3] Throughout the 1840s, Whigs tried to remedy this situation by advocating the appointment of a state education official, but Democrats, who just as adamantly opposed it, defeated the proposal. When the state Senate in 1848–1849 debated a new requirement for county taxes to support local schools, 69.6 percent of the Whigs voted for such legislation, while 80.0 percent of the Democrats opposed it (see tables 10 and 11).

The parties also differed over whether to erect and support schools for the deaf, dumb, and blind, and an insane asylum (see tables 10 and 11). In 1844–1845, for example, a Whig proposal in favor of a state-run school for the deaf and dumb succeeded despite the opposition of Democrats. Two years after the bill had passed, though, Democrats did vote for appropriations for the school. In 1848–1849, the legislature voted to build an insane asylum in Raleigh and to name it Dix Hills, after the crusader Dorothea Dix, who had come to Raleigh to lobby for such an asylum. The story of the passage of the bill by the House of Commons reads like a soap opera. During her stay in Raleigh, Dix befriended Mrs. James C. Dobbin, who was mortally ill. On her deathbed, Mrs. Dobbin asked her husband, a powerful Democratic member of the House, to support the asylum bill. After she died, he gave an impassioned speech that broke down partisan barriers and led to a virtually unanimous vote in favor of the insane asylum. The action of the legislators, though, obscured the extent to which the insane-

3. Guion Griffis Johnson, *Ante-Bellum North Carolina: A Social History* (Chapel Hill: University of North Carolina Press, 1937), 271–77.

TABLE 10
Index of Party Disagreement in the North Carolina General Assembly, 1840–1849:
Social Issues

	Senate	N*	House	N*
EDUCATION				
Loans to Private				
Institutions				
1840–41	46.1	2	—	
1842–43	—		38.6	1
1844–45	72.2	1	—	
Appointment of a				
Superintendent of the				
Common Schools				
1844–45	91.5	1	—	
1846–47	—		42.2	1
1848–49	66.4	1	—	
SCHOOL FOR THE				
DEAF & DUMB/				
INSANE ASYLUM				
1844–45	79.4	2	48.7	2
1846–47	—		22.8	1
1848–49	76.9	1	—	
MEDICAL BOARD				
1848–49	—	—	29.2	1

SOURCES: *SJ, 1840–41*, 247–48, 256; *HJ, 1842–43*, 835–36; *SJ, 1844–45*, 299, 332–33, 343, 348–49; *HJ, 1844–45*, 585–87, 762–63; *HJ, 1846–47*, 474, 583–84; *SJ, 1848–49*, 155, 215; *HJ, 1848–49*, 620.
*N = Number of Roll-Call Votes

asylum bill had been a partisan Whig measure. After the Commons acted on it, it passed in the Senate on a party-line vote: 90.5 percent of the Whigs supported it and 86.4 percent of the Democrats opposed it.[4]

Until 1848, though, little major legislation enlarging the state's role was passed into law by the General Assembly. When one considers that the Whigs were reputedly all-powerful during this period, the lack of governmental activity is somewhat puzzling. First, it should be noted that the party rarely had a lopsided majority in the state legislature. Although the Whigs controlled the governorship, their grasp on the legislature was more tenuous. They did hold a substantial majority in 1840, but they lost both houses to the Democrats in 1842. Whigs regained control of the legislature in 1844, widened their margins in 1846, but fell back into a virtual tie with the Democrats in both houses in 1848. Throughout the decade, partisan

4. *Ibid.*, 711–15; Margaret C. McCulloch, "Founding the North Carolina Asylum for the Insane," *NCHR*, XIII (1936), 185–201; Samuel F. Patterson to Walter W. Lenoir, December 27, 1848, in Lenoir Family Papers, SHC.

TABLE 11
Percentage Affirmative Votes in the North Carolina General Assembly, 1840–1849,
by Party: Social Issues

	Senate		House	
	Democrats	*Whigs*	*Democrats*	*Whigs*
EDUCATION				
Loans to Private				
Institutions				
1840–41	29.6	75.6	—	—
1842–43	—	—	59.0	97.6
1844–45	22.2	94.4	—	—
Appointment of a				
Superintendent of the				
Common Schools				
1844–45	4.2	95.7	—	—
1846–47	—	—	1.9	55.9
1848–49	13.6	90.5	—	—
SCHOOL FOR THE				
DEAF & DUMB/				
INSANE ASYLUM				
1844–45	13.9	90.3	35.9	84.5
1846–47	—	—	72.5	95.3
1848–49	13.6	90.5	—	—
MEDICAL BOARD				
1848–49	—	—	41.7	70.9

SOURCES: See Table 10.

TABLE 12
Partisan Division in the North Carolina General Assembly, 1840–1849

	Senate		House	
	Democrats	*Whigs*	*Democrats*	*Whigs*
1840–41	22	28	45	75
1842–43	29	21	69	51
1844–45	25	25	50	70
1846–47	23	27	54	65
1848–49	25	25	59	61

balance in the Senate was especially close. Under these circumstances, only a few Whigs needed to abandon a measure for it to be defeated by the united Democratic opposition (see table 12).

An even more significant influence on legislative behavior was the prolonged depression. During hard times, legislators found it difficult to vote for increased state spending and a heavier tax burden on their constituents. The reluctance that the depression created was deepened by the state's unsuccessful ventures in its support of railroads. Throughout the first half of the decade, only frequent infusions of state aid kept the Wilmington and Raleigh and the Raleigh and Gaston out of bankruptcy. Even then, the Raleigh and Gaston could not survive, and in 1845 the legislature authorized the governor to take it over. Repeated Democratic attacks on what they deemed Whig profligacy in aiding the railroads made even avid supporters of state activism reluctant to endorse substantial new state initiatives.[5]

The effects of the depression and of Democratic attacks on the Whigs were evident in the annual gubernatorial messages of John M. Morehead and William A. Graham. Morehead, North Carolina's leading advocate of state-aided improvements, told the General Assembly in 1844 that certain new transportation facilities would help the state, but he hastened to add that he offered his suggestions only in the hope that they would "attract public attention and elicit public enquiry." Similarly, in his 1846 gubernatorial message, Graham lamented that "the State is not in possession of the means for the construction of" a major railroad. Therefore, he suggested that the assembly pass laws incorporating several railroad companies that asked for no state aid.[6]

Indicative of the general reluctance to support any major new state initiatives was the way that legislators dealt with the question of a state penitentiary in 1844–1845. In a bipartisan legislative decision, the General Assembly decided to hold a popular referendum on whether the state should construct a penitentiary. The press of both parties seemed favorably inclined to a penitentiary, but neither gave it active support. One leading eastern Whig warned Governor Graham not to take a stand on the penitentiary in his reelection campaign. "I am satisfied that a determined opposition to the measure exists in the minds of the people, and that the better course for the Whig party will be to make no issue about it and to suffer none to be made." His prediction was borne out in the referendum. In all but a few counties, voters overwhelmingly rejected the institution.[7]

The gubernatorial campaign of that year also suggested that Whigs had temporarily softened their endorsement of state promotional activities. In the campaign, Democratic challenger James B. Shepard planned

5. Fayetteville *Observer*, August 17, 1842, October 2, 1844; Hugh Waddell to William A. Graham, June 8, 1842, in J. G. deRoulhac Hamilton and Max R. Williams (eds.), *The Papers of William Alexander Graham* (6 vols. to date; Raleigh: State Department of Archives and History, 1957–), II, 338; William H. Washington to James Bryan, December 9, 1844, in Bryan Family Papers, SHC.

6. Raleigh *Standard*, December 4, 1844, November 17, 1846; Fayetteville *Observer*, December 4, 1844.

7. Johnson, *Ante-Bellum North Carolina*, 672–73; Robert B. Gilliam to William A. Graham, March 29, 1846, in Hamilton and Williams (eds.), *Graham Papers*, III, 109–10.

to "attack Gov. G[raham] in the East and in the West upon the Rail Road debts." In joint debates held througout the state, Shepard criticized Graham and the Whig party for contracting the debt and for paying too much for the state's purchase of the Raleigh and Gaston Railroad in 1845. In reply, Graham might have argued, as Whig legislators had in 1843, that despite the monetary losses the investments were justified because they gave many citizens easier access to markets. Avoiding this line of argument, the governor tried to spread the political blame for the investments by charging that Democrats were also responsible for the state's railroad ventures.[8]

From the foregoing, it might be surmised that the parties simply endorsed an activist role for the state during prosperous times and opposed it during economic slumps. To a limited extent, this was the case; the government did tend to be more active in the 1830s and 1850s and much less so in the 1840s. Nevertheless, it is apparent from tables 9 and 11 (see pp. 58, 61) that Whigs, even during hard times, voted for a positive state role in society. They did not support a penitentiary nor did they vote for major ventures like the construction of a new railroad, but they did establish a school for the deaf and dumb and voted in favor of aid to numerous local transportation projects.

★

The depression of the 1840s may have augured ill for those who wished the state to encourage economic growth and promote education and social welfare. They either sought solace in continued Whig legislative support for internal improvements or were dismayed by the party's rhetorical retreat on the subject and by the persistence of Democratic opposition to activity. Yet within a decade, a broad political consensus emerged in favor of the positive state. Ironically, while state activism was initiated under a Whig aegis, it was carried out by the Democrats, who controlled the legislature for most of the decade of the 1850s. Democratic endorsement of the positive state in the late 1840s and early 1850s symbolized the broad bipartisan acceptance of Whiggish notions of government and society. The best way to examine this transformation is to look at the question of state aid to internal improvements because that was the issue that politicians discussed most fully and that aroused the most popular interest.

North Carolina was pushed toward accepting state promotion of economic development by her neighbors, South Carolina and Virginia. In 1847, the South Carolina legislature chartered a railroad from Camden, South Carolina, to Charlotte, North Carolina, and the Virginia legislature

8. William W. Holden to David S. Reid, March 20, 1846, in David Settle Reid Papers, NCDAH; Raleigh *Register*, May 19, 1846.

chartered one from Richmond to Danville. As North Carolinians recognized, some people would inevitably seek to connect Charlotte and Danville with a north-south road through North Carolina. The trade of the southwestern part of the state would be lost to Charleston, while the northwestern trade would go to Richmond. Without the improvement of transportation facilities between eastern and western North Carolina, it would be impossible for eastern Carolina to compete in the future for the west's trade.[9]

Eastern North Carolina had always had difficulty attracting much of the trade of the western part of the state. Charleston and the towns of northern South Carolina and Georgia lured most of the trade of the mountains and the southern Piedmont, while Virginia provided the most convenient outlet for the northern Piedmont's commerce. Those facts had often been lamented by the commercially oriented citizens of eastern North Carolina towns. In 1846, the editor of the Fayetteville *Observer* asked its readers: "Now are we forever to be a tributary to Virginia on one side and South Carolina on the other?" North Carolina could remedy this situation by building turnpikes and railroads that gave western Carolinians markets in the eastern portion of the state.[10]

Although leaders in the eastern towns recognized that they had been losing potential trade to their neighbors, the impending construction of a connection between Danville and Charlotte made the threat to their towns' economic survival imminent. It also threatened to make the state's tributary status permanent. Samuel Finley Patterson, a manufacturer and a Whig state senator from Appalachian Caldwell County, warned: "If something is not done at the present session, she [North Carolina] will be irretrievably ruined. We are being tapped on both sides by our Sister States, and before another session comes round, the process will be carried to such an extent by them that we can never recover from its effects."[11]

Western demands for a charter for the Charlotte-Danville connection also made the project difficult for easterners to resist. Support from some North Carolina investors plus infusions of money from South Carolinians and Virginians would enable a company to construct the road without state aid. Legislators opposed to the project would find it hard to vote against simple incorporation. To do so, it appeared to some westerners, would threaten the statewide coalitions of the two parties. John W. Osborne, a Charlotte Whig, warned William Graham: "A refusal to grant a Charter . . . will utterly destroy the Whig party—indeed the organization of parties as it now exists—and divide us into sectional factions, which

9. Raleigh *Register*, October 27, 1847.
10. Fayetteville *Observer*, September 4, 1844, September 29, 1846.
11. Samuel F. Patterson to Walter W. Lenoir, December 27, 1848, in Lenoir Family Papers.

will embarrass our legislature, destroy our harmony for years to come." Osborne's threat was certainly overstated, yet the road plan left many politicians with the urgent sense that they must take some steps to meet western demands.[12]

The further deterioration of the Raleigh and Gaston heightened the pressure on the legislature to do something about internal improvements. In his message to the General Assembly, Governor Graham recommended that the legislature help finance the construction of a railroad from Charlotte to Raleigh, where it would be connected with the Raleigh and Gaston. This plan, the governor hoped, would revitalize the Raleigh and Gaston and would give western Carolina a trade outlet. Moreover, the proposed Danville connection would probably cut enough into the business of the Raleigh and Gaston to kill that road. Because the death of the state-owned road would cost the state hundreds of thousands of dollars, its plight demanded immediate legislative attention.[13]

Although Whigs like Governor Graham constituted the vast majority of state-aid advocates, in 1848 they received assistance from an unexpected source, William Holden, editor of the Democratic Raleigh *Standard*. The Democratic platform that year denounced the Whigs for placing the state in debt, but during the gubernatorial campaign Holden alluded briefly to the state's need for an internal-improvement system. Once that election and the presidential election passed, he came out vigorously for liberal state support for internal improvements. On November 8, he argued that, if North Carolina did not invest in improvements, her economic condition, already bad, would deteriorate so much that the trend would be irreversible. When the legislature assembled a month later, Holden appealed for a general system of improvements in the state and painted a bleak picture of North Carolina's future without it.

> Our young men are leaving us, by fifties and by hundreds, to seek their fortunes and to win distinction in other and distant lands; our Commerce languishes, and our Farmers and Planters, as a general rule, scarcely realize enough to keep their estate together; and with the exception of a few localities, . . . the whole State labors under a weight and encounters disadvantages, which nothing but a bold, a general, and a vigorous system of Internal Improvements can remove.[14]

The transformation of Holden's position did not represent a change in the whole party's attitudes toward internal improvements, but rather ex-

12. James W. Osborne to William A. Graham, October 11, 1848, in Hamilton and Williams (eds.), *Graham Papers*, III, 247.
13. Governor's Message, November 27, 1848, in Raleigh *Register*, November 29, 1848.
14. Raleigh *Standard*, December 6, 1848.

pressed the attitudes of an increasingly influential group of urban Democrats like James C. Dobbin of Fayetteville and William S. Ashe of Wilmington, who could see as well as eastern Whigs the threat posed by the Danville connection. As editor of the party's central organ, Holden helped legitimize the idea of state aid within the ranks of the Democratic party. Democrats desiring to support aid for improvements but not firmly committed to such a vote must have found it difficult to cast an affirmative vote when they believed it would violate Democratic principles. Holden made it easier for such legislators to follow their personal wishes by arguing that a vote for state aid would breach no party principle.

Advocates of state aid fostered support for their cause, too, with a renewed propaganda offensive. The state's population had increased only slightly since 1830 because large numbers of citizens migrated from the state. Supporters of state aid, like the Whig Raleigh *Register*, blamed the state's inadequate transportation facilities for the massive migration. The *Register* believed "that this emigration is caused by the laggard policy of our people on the subject of Internal Improvement." While the state was losing so many native sons and daughters, it was attracting few of the many European immigrants who came to the United States in the 1840s. "It is to be lamented," the *Register*'s editor wrote, "that there is no inducement for hardy, industrious and intelligent freemen to emigrate to North Carolina." Since immigrants were still arriving in unprecedented numbers, North Carolina had time to encourage their settlement in the state. "An extensive system of Internal Improvement might give employment to many immigrants, and induce them to come among us."[15] Propagandists thus argued that improved transportation facilities would make North Carolina so prosperous that it could halt emigration and promote immigration.

The impetus toward the adoption of state-aid legislation received further encouragement from the political balance in the General Assembly of 1848–1849. The Senate had an equal number of Democrats and Whigs, while the Whigs had a majority of two in the House of Commons. The near-equal strength of the parties delayed the organization of the assembly for six days, and the difficulty that the assembly had electing a senator further postponed its work. Indeed, the legislature took almost a month to elect its own officers and other public officials.[16]

Although such a balance in the legislature had made the election of men to offices difficult, it had the paradoxical effect of making possible

15. Raleigh *Register*, December 27, 1848.
16. See chapter 6 below.

some state support for improvements. The Whigs remained advocates of state aid, but they accepted little responsibility for the condition of the state's railroad investments; the Democrats continued to oppose all state aid. Since the legislature had not yet funded the debts incurred by the earlier railroad investments, no party wanted to assume sole responsibility for any further financial aid to railroads or other improvements. As the Raleigh *Register* argued, "in matters of grave moment, involving the interests, affecting the condition, and appropriating the money of the people, neither party, hitherto, in North Carolina, has *dared* to assume the *sole* responsibility."[17] Since no party in the General Assembly of 1848–1849 could pass a bill without the support of members of the opposition, it seemed to many Whigs and Democrats that no party would have to assume complete responsibility for any improvements supported by the state.

The actual votes cast by the legislators—though affected by the close party balance, pro-improvements propaganda, the condition of the Raleigh and Gaston, the new position of William Holden, and the proposed Danville connection—were influenced as well by logrolling. The roundabout routing of the central road from Charlotte through Salisbury, Greensboro, Hillsboro, and Raleigh to Goldsboro was obviously intended to maximize voting support for the road. But supporters of the central road also needed the votes of members who supported other projects like the improvement of the Cape Fear and Deep rivers (aiding the Cape Fear region) or the building of a turnpike from Salisbury to the Georgia border (aiding the southwest). The passage of the central road bill also depended on the votes of men who demanded aid for projects of more local interest. Legislators who traded votes and passed bills aiding the construction of the central road and other improvements prompted one legislator to dub the General Assembly "the Log-rolling session of NC."[18]

Despite these pressures, promotional legislation passed only by the narrowest of margins. The legislative centerpiece, the North Carolina Railroad (for which the state would pay two million of the anticipated three-million-dollar cost of construction), passed the House by only eight votes and succeeded in the Senate only after Calvin Graves, Democratic Speaker of the Senate, cast the deciding vote in favor of the road. An analysis of the vote on the road's charter reveals that although some things had changed, the attitudes of members of the political parties in the legislature remained much the same. Seventy-five percent of the Whig commoners and 78 percent of the Whig senators voted for the bill; 68 percent of the

17. Raleigh *Register*, February 3, 1849.
18. J. H. White to Daniel M. Barringer, January 27, 1849, in Daniel Moreau Barringer Papers, SHC.

Democratic commoners and 77 percent of the Democratic senators voted against the bill. The strong Whig support for the measure and the equally strong Democratic opposition to it suggests that Democrats and Whigs remained divided on the question of government involvement in the economy. Although a Democrat, William S. Ashe of Wilmington, had written the charter, and another Democrat, Calvin Graves of Caswell County, cast the deciding vote in the Senate in favor of it, the North Carolina Railroad charter was essentially a Whig measure.[19] The same partisan divisions were evident too on votes on other projects (see tables 8 and 9, pp. 57, 58).

★

Nevertheless, the changes that had taken place in the Democratic party should not be ignored. Not only did the *Standard* support the legislature's work, but so did eight of the state's eleven Democratic papers. Such press support, though significant, did not indicate that the Democratic party had shifted overnight from support of a negative state to the advocacy of a positive one. The *Standard* and other Democratic papers failed to convince many of their readers at either the leadership or the rank-and-file levels that their state government should become active in the economy, and for much of the next decade Democrats debated the virtues and vices of an activist government.[20]

In 1849, the pro-improvement stance of a number of Democrats wrought much dissension in the party. One Democrat, writing under the pseudonym "Anti State Debt," expressed his party's traditional hostility to state aid and fear of state debt. He complained bitterly that the last legislature had been elected to pay off the state debt but instead had augmented it, and he contended further that private financing of improvements would make the projects cheaper and more profitable than those constructed with state assistance. Financed by the state, the North Carolina Railroad would cost the taxpayers a fortune and be unprofitable for the state government. The complaints of men like "Anti State Debt" and the anger expressed by its readers led the Hillsboro *Democrat* to conclude that the actions of the recent legislature had "met with considerable opposition from the people at large."[21]

Indicative of popular Democratic opposition to the new promotional activities of the state was the fate of three Democrats who supported the central road. Calvin Graves, who cast the deciding vote in the Senate, be-

19. Cecil K. Brown, *A State Movement in Railroad Development: The Story of North Carolina's First Effort to Establish an East and West Trunk Line Railroad* (Chapel Hill: University of North Carolina Press, 1928), 69.

20. Raleigh *Standard*, February 14, 1849.

21. *Ibid.*; Hillsboro *Democrat*, n.d., quoted in *ibid.*

lieved that "the intelligent and well-informed" supported the various acts of the legislature but that they were "opposed by most of the unenlightened part of the Community." The unenlightened evidently held sway in Caswell politics, for Graves, a long-time legislator, never again returned to the legislature. A similar fate awaited George W. Thompson of Wake County, who reluctantly supported the central road. His vote, a Whig editor reported, "has killed him . . . but by his political death, we have been enabled to *live* in *hope*."[22]

One of the bill's authors, William S. Ashe of Wilmington, fared better than Thompson and Graves. After completing his term in the Senate, Ashe sought the party nomination for the seat of the retiring congressman from the Cape Fear district. The Democratic convention nominated Ashe, but only after James Fulton, editor of the Wilmington *Journal*, convinced the delegates that "every other prominent Democrat in the District . . . were [*sic*] equally pledged to that policy." The conflict aroused by Ashe's role in the chartering of the railroad caused Fulton to fear that the improvement issue would injure the party. He contended that "even in this District although the *mind* of the party accede [*sic*] to the policy, the masses are opposed to it." This would, he feared, make Democratic voters apathetic in the next election. They would vote for Democratic candidates, "*but they wont* [*sic*] *go it strong*." If pro-improvement Democrats wanted to change their party's position, they would have to do so gradually.[23]

Pro-improvement Democrats argued that the question of internal improvements had nothing to do with party politics. Parties differed over interpretations of the federal Constitution, not over state policies. Since men of both parties disagreed with members of their own parties over state policies, the introduction of an issue like the chartering of the North Carolina Railroad into the partisan debates would shatter both parties. Romulus Saunders, former gubernatorial candidate and long-time advocate of state aid to improvements, declared that the railroad charter "was a State matter, and should not be mixed up with party politics. It was . . . above all party questions, and he should be sorry to see it brought within the party conflicts of the day." Democrats could preserve harmony only by agreeing to disagree on the question. While trying to legitimize Democratic support for state aid, Saunders was also arguing that men with different economic and geographic constituencies should represent their constituent's best interests, regardless of party.[24]

22. Calvin Graves to Samuel F. Patterson, March 1, 1849, in Jones and Patterson Papers, SHC; Charles C. Raboteau to David F. Caldwell, August 18, 1849, in David F. Caldwell Papers, SHC.
23. James Fulton to John W. Ellis, June 25, 1849, in Tolbert (ed.), *Ellis Papers*, I, 86–87.
24. Raleigh *Standard*, April 17, 1850.

The intraparty conflict aroused by the legislation of the General Assembly of 1848–1849 and the way proponents and opponents of state aid dealt with the question is best illustrated by the behavior of the Democratic party of Wake County, home of the state capital. The chartering of the North Carolina Railroad, though it was to pass through Wake, divided Raleigh's Democrats from their rural neighbors. The factions first clashed over the nomination of candidates to represent the county in the 1850–1851 legislature. In mid-April, an anonymous Democrat called for a convention to nominate candidates despite the fact that "there is not an entire unanimity of feeling existing in our ranks on the subject of Internal Improvement." In mid-May, Wake Democrats held a convention to debate the improvements issue and to nominate candidates. At the meeting, James B. Shepard, the party's gubernatorial candidate in 1846, introduced a resolution requiring candidates to pledge their opposition to further aid to improvements and to any increase in the state's share of the North Carolina Railroad, without instructions from their constituents. State-aid proponents, which included most of the Raleigh leadership, defeated Shepard's proposal and adopted a resolution claiming "that it was inexpedient to discuss the Central Road and that Democrats should make no party tests for state and local issues." The convention also nominated four pro-improvement Democrats as candidates for the state legislature.[25]

The actions of the convention aroused the ire of anti-improvement Democrats in the county. William Hearstfield, from Wake Forest, attacked what he called the "Democratic Rail Road Convention" for adopting Whig doctrines. He contended that "Democratic doctrine has always been low taxes and an economical expenditure of the public money, but these Rail Road Democrats are for extravagant expenditures, which will certainly lead to high taxes." Hearstfield warned that anti-improvement Democrats would not accept the nominations: "The *Standard* has been sending out some very bitter pills for the last eighteen months, and they were very bad to take, . . . but this last Rail Road pill is so large, and looks so bad, that we think it dangerous; and therefore we cannot take it, neither will we try."[26]

Refusing to swallow the "Rail Road pill," about two hundred anti-improvement Democrats gathered at Rolesville precinct to determine a course of action. They decided that if the regular nominees did not reverse their positions on internal improvements and agree to oppose new state-aid bills, they would nominate their own candidates. The pro-improvement

25. *Ibid.*; Raleigh *Register*, June 5, May 25 and 29, 1850.
26. William Hearstfield to Editor, May 23, 1850, in Raleigh *Standard*, May 29, 1850.

candidates, aware that their attempt to divorce the improvements issue from the party had failed, capitulated. Romulus Saunders, then running for a seat in the House of Commons, wrote that because the present projects were experiments, he would oppose aid to new transportation projects until the results of the present ones were known. After the other Democratic candidates made similar replies, the Rolesville meeting reconvened and approved the candidates' responses. The Democratic leadership had retreated temporarily in order to prevent a possibly irreparable split in the party's ranks.[27]

They met with more success at the state level, where they continued to portray the issue as separate from party politics and to conciliate the anti-improvement wing without allowing that faction to force the party into an official anti-improvement stance. At the state Democratic convention, Asa Biggs from Martin County on the coastal plain, the party's most vocal opponent of state aid, introduced a resolution advocating a constitutional amendment that would effectively prevent any further aid to improvements. Pro-improvement Democrats defeated Biggs's proposal but did not attempt to pass a pro-improvements resolution. They were satisfied when the convention ignored the question entirely in its platform. This strategy was consonant with the pro-improvement Democratic position that the party should take no stance on the issue and that it should not alienate those opposed to further state aid. By ignoring the question, the convention tacitly permitted members to follow their own course on questions of state aid without fear of contradicting the party's position. That was exactly what the pro-improvement men desired.[28]

The problems faced by the party on the improvements issue and the strategy of the pro-improvement faction were also evident in the nomination of a gubernatorial candidate in 1850. The candidate in 1848, David S. Reid, had lost a close race to Charles Manly. Reid had based much of his campaign on the need to liberalize the state constitution so that all adult white male taxpayers could vote for state senators as well as commoners. A popular issue, it had instilled energy into the Democratic party's organization and had weakened the enthusiasm of some Whigs for their party's cause. Since he had lost by less than one thousand votes, Reid seemed to be the party's logical nominee in 1850.[29]

However, David Reid opposed state aid to internal improvements in general and the charter of the North Carolina Railroad in particular. He accepted the charter as a *fait accompli* but opposed further appropriations

27. *Ibid.*, June 30, July 10, 1850.
28. *Ibid.*, June 19, 1850.
29. See chapter 4 below.

TABLE 13
Percentage Affirmative Votes in the North Carolina General Assembly, by Party, 1850–1855:
Economic Issues

	Senate			House		
	Democrats	Whigs	N*	Democrats	Whigs	N*
INTERNAL IMPROVEMENTS						
1850–51	31.3	90.1	6	38.4	76.3	2
1852	34.3	73.0	6	49.0	59.0	3
1854–55	63.0	77.2	11	51.8	76.7	9
BANK INCORPORATIONS						
1850–51	32.0	87.8	4	—	—	—
1852	30.4	74.1	10	78.0	67.9	1
1854–55	54.3	68.3	2	—	—	2
UNLIMITED STOCKHOLDER LIABILITY						
1850–51	59.3	0	1	—	—	—

*N = Number of Roll-Call Votes.
SOURCES: SJ, 1850–51, 106, 130, 184, 272–73, 286–87, 331–32, 340–42, 365, 404; HJ, 1850–51, 546–47, 621, 861; SJ, 1852, 160, 166–67, 192–93, 205–206, 215, 239–40, 278, 304, 313, 322, 333, 365–67; HJ, 1852, 232–33, 283, 407–408; SJ, 1854–55, 209, 214, 220–22, 277–78, 287, 291, 305–306, 316, 343–44; HJ, 1854–55, 306, 327, 361–62, 392, 405–406, 410, 415, 425, 491.

for improvements in the state. Believing that much of the party disagreed with him on the issue, Reid declined to run again. William Holden's reply to Reid's declination provides a good example of the strategy of the pro-improvement men. Holden insisted that "it would be madness to make . . . the Central Road a test." Although the party had to permit its members to disagree on the question, all agreed that the state had gone far enough for the time being. Therefore, Holden wrote, "your election . . . could not injure the Rail Road Democrats, who have nothing more to ask in the way of appropriation." Indeed, "Rail Road Democrats" were satisfied with Reid's position that the North Carolina Railroad's charter ought not be repealed. Holden also told Reid that his identification with the antirailroad men would aid the party. Reid's candidacy, Holden wrote, "would give confidence to the anti-Rail Road Democrats because they could trust you on the subject." Over Reid's protestations, the convention nominated him and eventually convinced him to run. In August, he won the election.[30]

Popular opposition to the new policies of Holden and others temporarily halted the party's drift away for its traditional ideological moorings. Not only had Reid won election, but when the new General Assembly met, only one-third of the Democratic members supported the new state-aid

30. Raleigh Standard, June 12, 1850; William W. Holden to David S. Reid, June 1, 1850, in Reid Papers.

legislation (see table 13). Nevertheless, over the next several years the position of Reid and most Democratic legislators evolved toward an endorsement of the positive state.

During the campaign of 1850, Reid repeatedly told audiences that he would have voted against the charter of the North Carolina Railroad if he had been a member of the General Assembly, but the debate over the virtues and vices of the charter was now moot. The state had committed itself to the charter; therefore, the state's honor demanded that it carry out its obligation.[31]

Elevated to the governorship, David Reid delivered his first message to the General Assembly in October, 1852. Like governors before him, he discussed the state of internal improvements and made recommendations on the subject to the legislature. Men who had followed Reid's career or had heard him speak during the campaign of 1850 must have been surprised to read the governor's claim that "a judicious system of Internal Improvements by the State, has ever been regarded as a subject of great importance, and entitled to the favorable consideration of the General Assembly." More in keeping with his earlier thoughts on the subject was Reid's reminder that all internal improvements "involve a large expenditure" and that the taxpayers' money should be spent carefully. He concluded by cautioning the legislature that "a wise and prudent system all should approve: a wild and extravagant scheme all should deprecate."

In his second message two years later, Reid repeated his theme. North Carolina's system of transportation was "still far from affording facilities adequate to the wants of the people," and the state was obliged to improve it. But because the construction of improvements would take "time and a large expenditure of money," he warned lawmakers to proceed cautiously. An opponent of state aid in the 1840s, by 1854 David Reid had become committed to the construction of a widespread system of internal improvements with state financial assistance. He warned that such a system would take time to complete, but this warning indicated that he believed the state was ultimately responsible for its completion.[32]

The General Assembly, acting as if the building of a system of internal improvements could be accomplished overnight, enacted numerous bills appropriating money for internal improvements. In order to understand why this Democratic-dominated legislature acted in the way that it did and why David Reid's stance on the question had changed, we must examine the increasing public pressures on the state government to aid improvement projects.

The commercial possibilities created by the chartering of the North

31. Raleigh *Standard*, July 6, 1850.
32. Governor's Messages, in Raleigh *Standard*, October 20, 1852, November 29, 1854.

Carolina Railroad whetted the appetite of many North Carolinians for a more extensive system of internal improvements. Those not immediately affected by the road often were initially angered by the charter, but within a short time they began to see how the charter might set a precedent for aid to their own area. This transition occurred most strikingly in New Bern, colonial capital of North Carolina. Once flourishing, by 1850 New Bern's economy was in decline. The passage of the North Carolina Railroad charter outraged the town's citizens. One prominent resident, James W. Bryan, wrote William A. Graham in August, 1849, that "our people are highly incensed at what is deemed by our considerate men, the pernicious legislation of our last general assembly. We shall be satisfied with nothing short of the repeal of the Central Rail Road bill & the loan of $2,000,000 & the new Revenue law." [33]

Within a few months, New Bern's mood reversed itself as some citizens revived the idea of a central road from the Tennessee border through Greensboro, Raleigh, and New Bern to Beaufort harbor. They thought such a road would enable the state to tap the trade of the Mississippi Valley and would give the state's farmers a port within the state from which to export their crops. The idea of extending the North Carolina Railroad eastward evidently caught hold in New Bern. In February, 1850, Bryan informed a friend that "the Rail road excitement seems to swallow up all other matters & our people are now canvassing with great spirit the project of a rail road from Goldsboro [the eastern terminus of the North Carolina Railroad] to Newbern." The movement for the extension even disrupted the normally competitive two-party system in Craven County, where New Bern was located. County politicians ran a bipartisan railroad-extension slate of candidates for the legislature. In less than a year and a half, public opinion had thus been transformed. [34]

In 1850, too, Whig governor Charles Manly felt the fury of a county scorned. The previous legislature's authorization of state funds to aid in the construction of a turnpike from Salisbury to the Georgia border had left the precise route up to commissioners appointed by the governor. Citizens of both Rutherfordton in Rutherford County and Morganton in Burke vied for the road to pass through their town. Any choice of commissioners was bound to injure one town, and when Manly appointed his commissioners, he angered the people of Rutherford. James Graham, a Whig leader in the county, reported that "Gov. Manly is much censured in Rutherford, Lincoln, and Cleveland for the appointment of the Com-

33. James W. Bryan to William A. Graham, August 20, 1849, in James W. Bryan Letterbooks, Bryan Family Papers.

34. James W. Bryan to Reuben Knox, February 16, 1850, in *ibid.*; Raleigh *Register*, August 14, 1850; S. F. Adams to David S. Reid, July 4, 1850, in Reid Papers.

missioners whom he has designated to lay off the Turnpike, the Road. The people say that, by appointment, the Gov. *has himself located* the road through Statesville & Morganton." In August, 1850, the voters of Rutherford, who regularly cast more than 70 percent of their votes for the Whig gubernatorial candidate (74 percent for Manly in 1848), repudiated the governor by giving him only 35 percent in 1850.[35]

The behavior of the citizens of Rutherford and New Bern reflected the growing appeal of transportation improvements. By the early 1850s, North Carolina had emerged from a prolonged depression and was enjoying a taste of prosperity. Towns like Charlotte, which had recently been connected by rail to Columbia, South Carolina, grew rapidly, and the long-unprofitable Wilmington and Weldon (formerly the Wilmington and Raleigh) and Raleigh and Gaston railroads began to turn a profit. Many who had resisted the charms of the market economy now succumbed to them. Men of commerce demanded better transportation and banking facilities. For them and others, especially townsmen, the lure of improvements that would supposedly bring great wealth to the state proved irresistible.[36]

From the outset, those who planned the North Carolina Railroad envisioned extensions east and west. As contractors made rapid strides toward completing the central road, popular pressure to extend the road grew as well. Demands that the legislature charter extensions led to a full discussion of the question during the 1852–1853 session and to the passage of a bill that provided money for surveys of both extensions and reserved for the state the right to purchase two-thirds of the stock in both companies in 1854.[37]

The bill's passage raised eastern and western hopes for state aid to the extension of the North Carolina Railroad. This in turn placed pressure on politicians to take a firm stand in favor of the extensions and of aid to other improvements. In late 1853, William H. Thomas, the Democratic leader in the extreme western counties, warned the governor that western Whigs were supporting a westerner "as their candidate for Governor, with a view of riding into the Governors palace upon the extension of the western Rail Road." The extension question, Thomas claimed, was "a subject which it is supposed will at the next election absorb all others in this part

35. James Graham to William A. Graham, August 1, 1849, in Hamilton and Williams (eds.), *Graham Papers*, III, 309–10. Also see James Graham to William A. Graham, April 21, 1850, in *ibid.*, III, 319–22; S. F. Adams to David S. Reid, July 11, 1850, and William W. Holden to Reid, July 7, 1850, both in Reid Papers; Edward Stanly to David F. Caldwell, March 1, 1850 (typescript), in Caldwell Papers; Rutherfordton *Mountain Banner*, April 9, 1850.

36. Cecil K. Brown, *State Movement*, 40, 59–60. On Charlotte, see William A. Graham to James W. Bryan, August 4, 1853, in Hamilton and Williams (eds.), *Graham Papers*, IV, 501; T. S. W. Mott to Samuel F. Patterson, January 3, 1852, in Samuel Finley Patterson Papers, Duke; Fayetteville *Observer*, December 14, 1852.

37. See note 13 above; Cecil K. Brown, *State Movement*, 98–99.

of the state which is quite probable." In 1854, political leaders from the far eastern and western regions of the state intensified their efforts to convince the political parties to endorse a liberal system of state aid to internal improvements. Marcus Erwin, an attorney and Democrat from Asheville, reported to David Reid that "the Democracy in the West are in fine spirits & confident of success if the Convention will only lay down some acceptable ground on the subject of Internal Improvements. This question overrides every other in the Counties West of Asheville, & no candidate who stands upon a platform worse in this respect than that of the Whigs can in my opinion poll the full strength of his party vote."[38]

The Whig platform that Erwin referred to was adopted at the party's state convention in February, 1854, where the delegates passed a strong resolution in favor of state aid for the development of the state's transportation facilities. In particular, it recommended that the next General Assembly aid the eastern and western extensions of the North Carolina Railroad.[39]

The Whig resolution forced the hand of the Democratic party. Since 1848 the Democrats had equivocated on the improvements issue, but with growing public support for a system of improvements and the Whig endorsement of such a system, Democrats felt compelled to take a stand on the issue. They decided upon a resolution that would appear strong enough in favor of government aid to satisfy the pro-improvement men in the party, but not so strong that it would alienate anti-improvement Democrats. In its eighth resolution, the convention declared that "it would . . . be politic and proper for the Legislature, from time to time, to extend such further aid in the completion of the works already taken, and the extension of the same, as a just regard for the interest of the people may require, and the means and resources of the State will prudently allow." Pro-improvement Democrats could argue that the "interest of the people" required further railroad building and that the state had the financial ability to support such a system. The anti-improvement men could just as easily claim that the people needed no further improvements, and even if they did, the state did not have the financial resources to warrant further expenditures.[40]

Although the resolution could be interpreted freely, it represented a major shift in the official position of the party. Democrats abandoned their policy of avoiding the question and unmistakably sanctioned state finan-

38. William H. Thomas to David S. Reid, December 28, 1853, in Governors' Papers, NCDAH; Marcus Erwin to David S. Reid, March 31, 1854, in Reid Papers.
39. Raleigh *Register*, February 25, 1854.
40. Raleigh *Standard*, April 26, 1854.

cial aid for the development of a transportation system—an idea that had been unacceptable to a large portion of the party in the late 1840s. Thus, in its 1854 platform the Democratic party had advanced toward an acceptance of the need for a positive state. The ensuing gubernatorial campaign pushed the party to take another step in that direction.

The election campaign of 1854 soon evolved into a dispute over which party was a better friend of internal improvements. Democrats claimed that their resolution on improvements evidenced stronger support for the extensions than did the policy of the Whigs, who only "recommended" them to the favorable consideration of the legislature. Whigs defended their own position and charged that the Democratic platform was equivocal because it enabled Democratic candidates to be anti-improvement men in areas opposed to state aid and pro-improvement men in areas supporting state aid.[41]

In the campaign, Whig Alfred Dockery faced Democrat Thomas Bragg. Bragg, a little-known attorney from Northampton County on the Virginia border, had been active in party affairs for many years, represented his county in the House of Commons in 1842, and served on the Board of Internal Improvements during the Reid administration. Though a member of the board, Bragg had been an early opponent of state aid for improvements. Dockery, a wealthy planter from the southern Piedmont county of Richmond on the South Carolina border, had been a member of the state constitutional convention of 1835 and had served two terms in Congress. For a number of years he had advocated the need for the state to provide financial support for improvements.[42]

In late April, the two candidates began the traditional series of debates throughout the state. From the first, Dockery attacked Bragg's position on internal improvements. He charged that in their first discussion Bragg refused to say whether he thought the state ought to borrow money to extend the North Carolina Railroad. Dockery's charges were probably untrue, but they compelled Bragg to assume an increasingly firm position in favor of improvements and the extensions. On May 10, in Fayetteville—a hotbed of improvement sentiment—Bragg claimed that he favored state aid to improvements and was willing to give as much aid "as the means of the State would prudently justify." Soon after, in a debate at Raleigh, Bragg, apparently prompted by the city's political leaders, announced his support for state aid for both extensions. As the campaign moved westward, Dockery and the Whig press still attacked him for being unreliable

41. *Ibid.*, May 24, 1854; Raleigh *Register*, April 26, May 10, 1854.
42. Fayetteville *Observer*, July 31, May 15, 1854.

on the question, but Bragg repeatedly reaffirmed his and his party's support for appropriations to aid improvements. The competition engendered by a closely contested political campaign pushed Bragg and the Democratic party into a firmer commitment to state aid.[43]

Before the candidates arrived in the far west, local politicians discussed the improvements question. One Macon County Whig wrote to a friend that "the main hinge upon which the votes of the western counties . . . will turn is the position the two Candidates take respecting Internal Improvements and especially the Central Road's extension west." As of July 4, the date of the letter, he claimed that all agreed that "Dockery shows 'the cleanest bill of health.'" The writer went on to claim that "if Bragg takes position against the extension I beleive [*sic*] even strong Democrats will vote for Dockery."[44]

Bragg certainly tried to convince the writer and others that he was "sound" on the extension question. Whether or not he succeeded is unclear, but western Democratic newspapers attributed Dockery's substantial majority in the mountains to his successful attempt to cast doubt on Bragg's position on internal improvements. The Democratic Asheville *News* argued that Bragg would have carried the mountain congressional district "had it not been for the unscrupulous and unremitting efforts of our opponents to place him in an attitude of hostility to works of Internal Improvement, and especially to the extension of the Central Rail Road." Although he may not have convinced voters of his support for the extension, Bragg's repeated affirmations of that support cemented his party's position in favor of the extension and other improvements. As the Charlotte *Western Democrat* remarked about the election campaign, "the subject of Internal Improvement was fully discussed; and both parties are committed to a liberal policy."[45]

While the gubernatorial campaign helped shape a consensus on what activities the state government should undertake, it also highlighted party disagreement about how to pay for government's new role. Between 1852 and 1853, government expenses had jumped by 37.7 percent and would certainly go far higher if the legislature supported the extensions of the North Carolina Railroad. Dockery charged that Bragg and the Democrats would force the people to pay onerous taxes in order to meet the state's greater financial obligations. In place of higher taxes, he offered the longtime Whig nostrum, the distribution of the proceeds from the sale of the federal public lands. Distribution, the origins of which lay in Henry Clay's

43. *Ibid.*, May 15, June 12, 1854; Robert T. Paine to John C. Badham, *et al.*, (draft), June 27, 1854, in Robert Treat Paine Papers, SHC.

44. R. B. to William L. Scott, July 4, 1854, in William Lafayette Scott Papers, Duke.

45. Asheville *News*, September 6, 1854; Charlotte *Western Democrat*, August 18, 1854.

American system, offered a kind of modern politician's manna by which he could obtain for his constituents turnpikes and railroads that would not cost them a penny.[46]

Whigs, who had been aided by their support for distribution in the 1830s and had continued to reiterate regularly their desire for it, began to place new emphasis on the idea in 1852 and 1853 as a means of paying off the newly acquired and the anticipated state debt. The more parochial concerns of North Carolinians meshed well with the broader efforts of national lawmakers to create a more coherent public-lands policy. Many northern congressmen and a few southerners advocated a homestead law that would give federal lands to settlers. North Carolina Whigs and Democrats opposed it because they believed that rapid settlement of the territories would bring antislavery states into the Union and cheat North Carolina out of its fair share of the lands. Both parties wanted the public lands to be sold, not given, to settlers. Democrats wanted to use the money to cover the expenses of the federal government because they feared that the loss of federal revenue occasioned by distribution would allow Whigs to urge the adoption of a protective tariff. Whigs dismissed the idea that they would seek a tariff increase. They argued that westerners were receiving all the benefits from the federal lands and little of the land-sale proceeds ever went into the federal treasury. So if North Carolinians wanted to gain their fair share of the lands, they had to fight for distribution now.[47]

The call for distribution elicited a positive response not only from the expected Whigs but also from some Democrats. In 1853, distribution Democrats ran against regular party nominees in three predominantly Democratic congressional districts. This assault from within was quelled after the regulars won easily in two districts and a Whig defeated the divided Democrats in the third. Despite some grumbling, Democrats presented in 1854 a united front against distribution. At a time when Democrats were endorsing much of the Whig economic program, distribution enabled Whigs to distinguish themselves from their opponents on a crucial issue. However, the continued disagreement over the means of financing the state's ventures in the construction of transportation facilities did not obscure the agreement about the state's activities.[48]

The consensus reached in the debates of the gubernatorial candidates

46. Hershal L. Macon, "A Fiscal History of North Carolina, 1776–1860" (Ph.D. dissertation, University of North Carolina, 1932), 347; Raleigh *Standard*, April 12, 1854.

47. For the Democratic view, see Raleigh *Standard*, June 22 and 29, July 6, 16, and 20, 1853, April 12, May 17, 1854; Tarboro *Southerner*, March 4, 1854; for the Whig view, see Fayetteville *Observer*, May 25, 1852, March 21, May 14, August 1, September 26, 1853, February 6, 1854; Raleigh *Register*, January 14, 1854.

48. Raleigh *Standard*, July 20, 1853, April 26, 1854; Walter F. Leak to Lawrence O'Bryan Branch, March 27, 1854, in Lawrence O'Bryan Branch Papers, Duke.

and of candidates for the legislature led a diverse group of politicians to see the coming session of the General Assembly as one that would embark forthrightly on a major system of internal improvements. Take, for example, the views of Thomas D. McDowell, a wealthy planter, businessman, and attorney, and a Democratic state senator from Bladen County, in the Cape Fear region. In the General Assembly of 1852–1853, McDowell was one of only six senators to oppose the appropriations for the surveys of the eastern and western extensions. In the summer of 1854, he wrote to a former college classmate, a Whig from the western part of the state, that although easterners had hitherto opposed increasing the state debt in order to build transportation facilities, "a great change has taken place in public sentiment; and I am satisfied that this section of the State will justify their Representatives in the next Assembly in voting for a liberal s[c]heme of Improvements. . . . The difficulty will be—not where we will begin but where we will stop." [49]

McDowell accurately predicted the actions of the legislature. It authorized the state to provide millions of dollars of aid to various projects of improvement. It also passed charters providing assistance for the Atlantic and North Carolina Railroad (extending the central road from Goldsboro to New Bern and Beaufort), the Western and North Carolina Railroad (with one terminus at Salisbury and the other on the Tennessee border), and the Wilmington, Charlotte, and Rutherfordton Railroad (traversing the southern part of the state). The legislature also chartered numerous plank roads (providing financial aid for some) and appropriated funds for several river improvements. [50]

The citizens of forty-three of North Carolina's eighty-five counties were immediately interested in one or more of the three major railroad charters. If one adds to this list of potential supporters of improvement legislation those legislators who sought the passage of projects of more local interest and who were willing to trade votes to attain that goal, it is obvious that a large majority of potential pro-improvements votes existed in the General Assembly, regardless of party. It should have surprised no one that so many bills passed during the session. [51]

49. Thomas D. McDowell to Walter W. Lenoir, July 8, 1854, in Lenoir Family Papers. For the similar views of an eastern Whig, see Walter L. Steele to Samuel F. Patterson, July 22, 1854, in Jones and Patterson Papers. On the improvements issue in local races, see, for Lincoln County, Henry Cansler to David S. Reid, May 18, 1854, and John F. Hoke to Reid, May 19, 1854, both in Governors' Papers; for Caldwell County, see Samuel F. Patterson to Rufus L. Patterson, July 11, 1854, in Patterson Papers; for Mecklenburg County, see Charlotte *Western Democrat*, June 23, 1854.

50. Raleigh *Standard*, February 21, 1855.

51. This figure was arrived at by adding the counties through which the railroads would pass to the counties through which the North Carolina Railroad passed. The North Carolina Railroad would obviously benefit from the eastern and western extensions.

Much of the internal-improvements legislation that passed enjoyed bipartisan support. Senate votes on the major bills—the extensions and the Wilmington, Charlotte, and Rutherfordton road—revealed that majorities in both parties supported the legislation. In the Commons, both parties voted for the extensions, though no vote was recorded for the Wilmington road. Although Whigs provided larger majorities than the Democrats, voting on state aid to internal improvements had lost its partisan dimension (see tables 13–15). Men now voted on the basis of local, rather than partisan, interest.

J. C. Badham, a member of the House from Chowan County, described the logrolling process to his brother: "Railroads & Banks appear to pass as a matter of course. They do not so much as provoke discussion. Combination puts all through. No one will vote against his neighbor's proposition, lest his neighbor will do the same thing for some object he has at heart. Thus, almost every Bill travels through unobstructed." John W. Cunningham, a state senator from Person County who in the past had consistently opposed state aid, described similar legislative maneuvering to his constituents in a speech delivered after the adjournment of the General Assembly. He told them that he had unsuccessfully tried to get a charter for the Dan River and Yadkin Railroad, which would pass through Person. "Of course," he went on to explain, "I could do nothing for our measure unless I assisted in passing others—for you well know that these things are always done by clubbing different interests & different roads together, or in other words by a system of barter called log-rolling."[52]

Logrolling and the official Democratic advocacy of state aid to improvements led the Democratic-controlled legislature to aid numerous improvement projects. Senator John Gray Bynum described the legislature in late January, 1855: "Internal improvements is at full heat." An amazed Lawrence O'Bryan Branch, president of the Raleigh & Gaston Railroad, wrote: "The Legislature is running wild about Rail Roads. No scheme, however wild or even pernicious, meets with any serious opposition. Federal politics have been completely lost sight of, and all parties are vying with each other in the Internal Improvement race."[53]

★

It seemed to some observers outside the legislative halls that North Carolina had become "perfectly infatuated with her mad schemes of 'im-

52. J. C. Badham to William Badham, January 9, 1855, in William Badham Papers, Duke; speech by John Cunningham, ghost-written by Calvin H. Wiley [Spring, 1855], in John W. Cunningham Papers, SHC.

53. John Gray Bynum to David S. Reid, January 25, 1855, and Lawrence O'Bryan Branch to David S. Reid, January 27, 1855, both in Reid Papers. Also see Joseph B. Cherry to Calvin H. Wiley, February 6, 1855, in Calvin Henderson Wiley Papers, NCDAH.

TABLE 14

Percentage Affirmative Votes in the North Carolina General Assembly, 1854–1855, by Party:
Railroad Legislation

	Democrats	Whigs
SENATE		
Atlantic & NCRR/		
NC & Western RR	67.9	83.3
NC & Western RR	57.1	83.0
Wilmington, Charlotte,		
& Rutherfordton RR	63.0	70.6
HOUSE		
NC & Western RR	52.0	82.2
Atlantic & NCRR	68.5	91.8
Wilmington, Charlotte,		
& Rutherfordton RR	48.3	72.0

SOURCES: *SJ, 1854–55*, 214, 277–78; *HJ, 1854–55*, 306, 327, 410

TABLE 15

Index of Party Disagreement in the North Carolina General Assembly, 1850–1855:
Economic Issues

	Senate	N*	House	N*
INTERNAL IMPROVEMENTS				
1850–51	58.8	6	37.9	2
1852	42.5	6	10.0	3
1854–55	19.3	11	24.0	9
BANK INCORPORATIONS				
1850–51	55.8	4	—	—
1852	43.7	10	10.1	1
1854–55	16.7	2	21.6	2
UNLIMITED STOCKHOLDER				
LIABILITY				
1850–51	59.3	1	—	—

*N = Number of Roll-Call Votes.
SOURCES: See Table 13.

provement.'" By 1854, lawmakers had established asylums for the insane
and schools for the deaf, dumb, and blind. By 1860, the legislature had put
the state nine million dollars into debt to finance the construction of 891
miles of railroad track, 641 miles of which were laid between 1849 and
1860. It incorporated, and often aided, scores of companies involved in improving navigation on the state's rivers and in building turnpikes and
plank roads. Banks spread all over the state. Before 1848, they were limited to the Bank of the State and the Bank of the Cape Fear and their
branches, but between 1848 and 1855 the General Assembly incorporated

TABLE 16
Index of Party Disagreement in the North Carolina General Assembly, 1850–1855:
Social Issues (Education)

	Senate	N*	House	N*
EDUCATIONAL LOANS				
1854–55	21.5	2	—	—
APPOINTMENT OF A STATE SUPERINTENDENT OF COMMON SCHOOLS				
1852	56.0	2	22.7	1

*N = Number of Roll-Call Votes.
SOURCES: *SJ, 1852*, 200–202, 206; *HJ, 1852*, 202–203; *SJ, 1854–55*, 171–72.

TABLE 17
Percentage Affirmative Votes in the North Carolina General Assembly, by Party, 1850–1855:
Social Issues (Education)

	Senate		House	
	Democrats	Whigs	Democrats	Whigs
EDUCATIONAL LOANS				
1854–55	45.1	66.6	—	—
APPOINTMENT OF A STATE SUPERINTENDENT OF COMMON SCHOOLS				
1852	39.3	95.2	45.1	67.8

SOURCES: See Table 16.

thirteen new banks, and by 1860 there were thirty banks in the state. In 1852, the General Assembly created the office of state superintendent of the common schools. Virtually unanimous Whigs were joined by a large minority of Democrats to pass the bill in the Senate, while majorities of both parties voted for it in the Commons (see tables 13, 15, 16, and 17).[54]

At the beginning, these state actions had largely been Whig ventures, but by 1854 the Whigs had been joined by a majority of Democrats. Figures 2 and 3 summarize the changing relationship of partisanship and policy making between 1840 and 1855. They reveal the Whigs' constancy in support of government aid for transportation projects, the Democrats' gradual acceptance of the Whig position, and more generally, the emergence of a bipartisan consensus endorsing active state involvement in the economy.

Although Whigs had muted their voices in favor of the positive state during the early 1840s, the return of prosperity led them to support an ag-

54. Tarboro *Press*, December 17, 1850; Macon, "Fiscal History," 318, 327–28, 344.

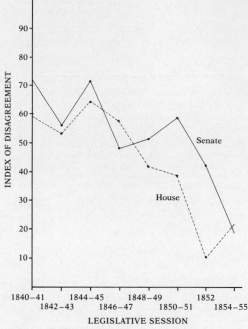

FIGURE 2.
Index of Partisan Disagreement
over Government Aid to Internal
Improvements, 1840–1855

SOURCES: See Tables 8 and 15.

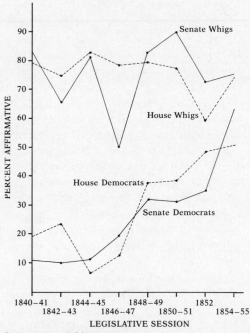

FIGURE 3.
Partisan Support for Government
Aid to Internal Improvements,
1840–1855

SOURCES: See Tables 9 and 13.

gressive policy of state aid and bank chartering. But as they asserted themselves more forcefully, they were gradually losing power, so the success of their programs depended on some Democratic support. They received the minimum opposition support needed for victory in 1848–1849, for a minority of Democrats were as impressed as Whigs by the outside threats of railroad building in neighboring states. Those threats especially influenced urban Democratic leaders, who had often been sympathetic to the positive state in the past.

The return of prosperity also encouraged some people previously hostile to the positive state. The older roads began to make money for the first time and to return to the state some of its investment, and the construction of the North Carolina Railroad generated dreams of economic greatness in towns and elsewhere in the state. In a sense, much of the opposition to the positive state in North Carolina dissipated in the prosperous 1850s.

Partisanship also played a crucial role in generating a political consensus. The effective gradualist strategy of pro-state-aid Democrats like William Holden had promoted a change in their party's position. Pressure to endorse government promotional activities came also from the opposition. Whig support for the extension of the central road drove Democrats fearful of being left behind on a popular issue to endorse the principle of state aid. The Bragg-Dockery campaign clearly solidified that stance.

Not everyone welcomed the involvement of government in the market economy, but those who resisted it were steadily diminishing in number. Legislative activisim in 1854 and 1855 elicited none of the popular protest that had followed the incorporation of the North Carolina Railroad in 1849. In 1850, the rural resistance to state aid expressed by Democrats at Rolesville precinct had endangered party unity in Wake County; in 1855, the people of Rolesville were quiet. Much of the continued resistance to the positive state was expressed in wealthier eastern counties, since road-building in the west meant substantially higher taxes in the east.[55]

Both Democrats and Whigs in North Carolina had come to accept Whiggish notions of the relationship of government and society. In so doing, they joined other southern states as they abandoned the vestiges of Jacksonian beliefs. They joined, too, a broader emerging American consensus that government should be used as a tool, in the words of James Willard Hurst, "to release the pent up economic energies of the people."[56]

55. Marc Wayne Kruman, "Parties and Politics in North Carolina, 1846–1865" (Ph.D. dissertation, Yale University, 1978), 107–12.
56. James Willard Hurst, *Law and the Conditions of Freedom in the Nineteenth-Century United States* (Madison: University of Wisconsin Press, 1956), 3–32; Richard L. McCormick, "The Party Period and Public Policy: An Exploratory Hypothesis," *JAH*, LXVI (1979), 279–98.

Four *Parties and Constitutional Revision, 1848–1855*

The emergence of a political consensus on the role of government in society was part of a broader acceptance of the idea of a positive liberal state. White North Carolinians expected not only that government would create economic opportunities for them but that government would be democratic as well. Although this may seem a truism in contemporary America, it was not so in North Carolina in the 1840s. Then, the state had anything but a democratic polity, with property requirements for some officeholders and voters and with a system of representation in the legislature that was weighted heavily in favor of wealthier counties. Just as questions of governmental policy rent the Democratic party into factions, questions of constitutional revision rent the Whigs. And just as Democrats came to endorse the positive state, Whigs came to support the democratization of the state constitution.

As the gubernatorial campaign of 1848 began, Democratic prospects seemed dim. Party organization was in disarray; only two years earlier, the party had failed to convince its nominee to accept the gubernatorial nomination. In 1848, it again had trouble finding someone to run for governor. The convention nominated David S. Reid, a Rockingham County resident who had left Congress in 1847 after a redistricting of the state had placed his county in a Whig district. For a while it appeared that the party would be embarrassed again by the rejection of another proffered nomination, but Reid ultimately accepted.[1]

1. William W. Holden to David S. Reid, December 22, 1880, in David Settle Reid Papers, NCDAH; William K. Boyd (ed.), *Memoirs of W. W. Holden* (Durham: Seeman Printery, 1911), 5; John W. Carr, Jr., "The Manhood Suffrage Movement in North Carolina," Trinity College Historical Society *Historical Papers*, Ser. IV (1915), 50.

At the first stop on the campaign trail, in a debate at New Bern in May with opponent Charles Manly, Reid introduced a new issue into North Carolina politics—the elimination of the fifty-acre property requirement for state senatorial electors, which he called "equal suffrage." The next day, Manly attacked Reid's proposal. If Manly had supported Reid's idea, he might have defused a potentially explosive issue—after all, equal suffrage was bound to be popular, since the fifty-acre requirement prevented more than half of the state's voters from participating in state senatorial elections.[2] But given the intensity of party conflict in the 1840s, such a decision was unlikely. Parties instinctively opposed anything that their opponents suggested, so Manly followed his instincts and committed his party to opposition to equal suffrage. But Manly's opposition arose out of more than merely a desire to be different. It represented the conflicting views that Democrats and Whigs held about white freedom and equality.

In their defense of suffrage reform, Democratic newspapers reaffirmed their commitment to white equality. When they used the term "equal suffrage," Democrats conveyed their belief in the equality of all white men and their desire to make the state constitution reflect that equality. Reid declared that "equality in the exercise of suffrage among free white men who are citizens of our State, is one of the first principles of Democracy." The Wilmington *Journal* argued that equal suffrage would remove "an artificial distinction between men who are, in fact, equal" and would restore whites "to that natural equality to which they are entitled under a republican form of government, irrespective of their riches or their poverty." The New Bern *Republican* made the same point when it wrote: "We hold that all men are free and equal, that each man possesses an equal share of political liberty, and that any distinction between one citizen and another . . . is a variation from this spirit of political liberty and equality."[3]

Whigs contended that equal suffrage smacked of radicalism and represented the first step toward tearing down the pillars of conservative society. They charged that equal suffrage struck "at the Conservative principle of our Constitution" and that once all white adult citizens were allowed to vote for state senators, the floodgates of radicalism would open. Landholders would be the first to suffer, for without the protection of the freehold requirement, they would be forced to pay high, oppressive taxes. The end of protection for the rights of landholders would lead eventually to the removal of constitutional protections for the rights of other individuals. The Wilmington *Commercial* declared that Democrats "intended to minis-

2. Raleigh *Standard*, May 17, 1848; Richard P. McCormick, "Suffrage Classes and Party Alignments: A Study in Voter Behavior," *MVHR*, XLVI (1959), 399–400.

3. Raleigh *Standard*, May 24, 1848; Wilmington *Journal*, n.d., quoted in *ibid.*, July 6, 1850; New Bern *Republican*, n.d., quoted in *ibid.*, May 24, 1848.

ter to the lawless desire for levelling all the bulwarks which are raised for the protection of individual rights." If equal suffrage became part of the constitution, the Fayetteville *North Carolina Argus* argued, Democrats soon "may advocate an equal distribution of all the property in the state, the right of free negroes to serve on juries, or the abrogation of the laws regarding matrimony." In a similar vein, the *Commercial* contended that equal suffrage would be followed by "desecration of the Bible and abolition of Matrimony."[4]

The reaction of Whig newspapers to the equal suffrage issue harkened back to the republicanism of eighteenth-century America. Then, individual property owning provided the base for American republicanism. Only a man of property could be economically independent of others, it was believed, and only an independent man, not beholden to representatives of special interests, could be entrusted with decision-making powers. By owning land, this independent man also showed that he had a permanent stake in the welfare of his society. The freeholder, one Whig correspondent declared, "has given bond and security to the community in which he resides to exercise this right [of suffrage] properly." Because he had a permanent personal interest in society, his self-interest prompted him to act in ways that would benefit the community as a whole.[5]

The Whigs' revolutionary forebears had nevertheless accepted some participation by nonlandowners in the political process when they allowd all taxpayers to vote for members of the House of Commons. Yet the authors of the state constitution had kept power firmly in the hands of the landowners by limiting the vote for state senators to men owning fifty acres of land and by requiring commoners to own one hundred acres and senators three hundred. It was this conservative inheritance that the Whigs of 1848 defended. With power in the hands of the propertied, liberty was protected. Equal suffrage would take away some of that power and therefore threatened to destroy liberty and the very fabric of society.[6]

Political circumstances, though, quickly made untenable the Whig defense of the status quo upon anti-egalitarian grounds. Whigs simply had to

4. Raleigh *Register*, May 20, 1848; Wilmington *Commercial*, n.d., quoted in *ibid.*, July 1, 1848; Fayetteville *North Carolina Argus*, n.d., quoted in *ibid.*, July 5, 1848; Wilmington *Commercial*, n.d., quoted in *ibid.*

5. Raleigh *Register*, July 22 and 15, 1848; Fayetteville *Observer*, June 11, 1850; Chilton Williamson, *American Suffrage: From Property to Democracy, 1760–1860* (Princeton: Princeton University Press, 1960), 76–116; Bernard Bailyn, *The Ideological Origins of the American Revolution* (Cambridge, Mass.: Harvard University Press, 1967); Gordon S. Wood, *The Creation of the American Republic, 1776–1787* (Chapel Hill: University of North Carolina Press, 1969), 169–70.

6. Francis Newton Thorpe (comp.), *The Federal and State Constitutions, Colonial Charters, and Other Organic Laws of the States, Territories, and Colonies Now or Heretofore Forming the United States* (7 vols.; Washington, D.C.: Government Printing Office, 1909), V, 2790, 2796.

face the reality that the half of the electorate who did not enjoy the senatorial franchise did vote for commoners, governor, and president. In addition, Whigs may have realized that they did not fare any better than Democrats did among voters owning fifty or more acres of land. Certainly no Whig stated in his correspondence or speeches that he thought that his party received a disproportionate share of the votes of those landowners.[7] Therefore, Whigs felt compelled to alter their argument and denounce equal suffrage in the name of white democracy rather than as a threat to conservative, property-oriented society. Any other defense would likely drive some of the disfranchised out of the party's narrow majority coalition and relegate the Whigs to a minority position in the state. Politicians wishing to win elections quickly realized that they would have to advocate the equality of white men, not the rights of the propertied, and so Whigs discarded their conservative argument. As Democrats pressed the issue of suffrage reform and denounced Whig opposition to it as a manifestation of Whiggery's "aristocratic" beliefs, Whigs were forced to assert ever more vehemently their defense of white equality.

They did so by shifting the issue from equal rights to equal power. Equal suffrage, they argued, would not equalize the power of white men in the society. They told easterners that the logic of suffrage reform—"that all White men should have equal priviledges [*sic*] without regard to property"—would lead to the apportionment of legislative representation according to white population and would therefore diminish eastern power. In the west, Whigs made precisely the opposite argument—that equal suffrage offered some of the forms of white equality but not its substance. Equal suffrage, they contended, was an empty shell because western white men still would not exercise power equal to that enjoyed by their eastern counterparts.[8]

Whigs also argued that the Democrats had brought up the issue "for purposes of political capital," not to expand the rights of white men, and they warned Democrats "that the people of North Carolina are not to be humbugged by any such specious or newfangled clap-trap." Reid had "foisted" upon "the people" an issue that they cared little about, and because the people had not demanded equal suffrage, it was undemocratic for Reid to advocate it. The Greensboro *Patriot* remarked sarcastically that Democrats had discovered "that the dear people are laboring under a tyranny and oppression which they had not the sense to discover!"[9]

Despite Whig opposition, equal suffrage was an enormously popular is-

7. McCormick, "Suffrage Classes."
8. Raleigh *Register*, July 22, 1848.
9. *Ibid.*, May 20, June 7, and May 27, 1848; Greensboro *Patriot*, May 27, 1848.

sue. It offered Democrats, after years of defeat, a sense that victory was within their grasp. During the campaign, William Holden informed Reid that "the enthusiasm is all on our side," while another Democrat declared that "the Suffrage question . . . will opperate [*sic*] in your favor everywhere." Even the Whig Greensboro *Patriot* acknowledged that the issue "increased the zeal of multitudes of the Democratic party." The enthusiasm of the Democrats was matched by the equal-suffrage-induced apathy of the Whigs. As the *Patriot* observed, many Whigs "declined to vote under the impression, . . . that to vote for Mr. Manly would commit them *against* the principle of equal suffrage." [10]

The suffrage issue, which provided most of the fuel for the partisan debate during the 1848 gubernatorial campaign, helped bring Reid within a hairbreadth of winning. He received 49.5 percent of the votes cast, only 854 votes shy of victory. The Democrats, though defeated, had fared better than in any previous gubernatorial election and looked forward to the next contest. The Whigs, though victorious, regarded the election as a defeat and were uncertain about how to rid themselves of this vexing issue. [11]

By the time the legislature assembled in December, support for equal suffrage had become an article of Democratic faith. The party could choose between two methods of obtaining its adoption. One way was to call a new constitutional convention, but this appealed little to Democrats, who either thought it would be too expensive to make just one amendment or who feared that a convention would change the constitution in other ways that they opposed. So they opted for the more complicated legislative method: first, each house would have to pass the amendment with support of three-fifths of its members, then the houses of the succeeding legislature needed to pass it with majorities of at least two-thirds, and finally a majority of voters would have to approve the amendment in a popular referendum. If an amendment failed to meet the requirements anywhere along the way, the process had to begin again. [12]

Democrats in the Senate and House overwhelmingly supported the amendment, but Whigs were divided. Although most Whig senators opposed the bill, a small majority of the party's commoners supported it. Whig senators, whose constituents, by definition, met the landholding qualification, faced little constituent pressure to endorse equal suffrage and therefore found it easier to follow the party's position. Even so, the

10. William W. Holden to David S. Reid, August 23, 1848, James C. Dobbin to Reid, June 16, 1848, Walter F. Leak to Reid, July 18, 1848, L. Mastrie to Reid, June 30, 1848, all in Reid Papers; Greensboro *Patriot*, August 5, 1848.

11. Raleigh *Register*, August 12, 1848.

12. Thorpe (comp.), *Federal and State Constitutions*, V, 2798.

TABLE 18
Index of Party Disagreement in the North Carolina General Assembly,
1848–1855: Constitutional Revision

	Senate	N*	House	N*
ALL QUESTIONS RELATING TO CONSTITUTIONAL REVISION				
1848–49	59.6	2	43.9	5
1850–51	70.4	11	60.5	4
1852	70.7	2	52.1	2
1854–55	79.8	10	60.1	4
EQUAL SUFFRAGE AMENDMENT				
1848–49	51.0	1	33.4	1
1850–51	76.7	2	61.1	2
1852**	69.9	1	36.1	1
1852***	71.4	1	68.1	1
1854–55	72.6	4	37.8	1
CONSTITUTIONAL CONVENTION				
1848–49	—	—	82.4	1
1850–51	77.9	2	69.9	1
1854–55	94.4	1	47.4	1

*N = Number of Roll-Call Votes.
**Before the Democratic Senate Speaker's negative vote caused the amendment's defeat.
***After the Speaker's vote.
SOURCES: SJ, 1848–49, 266–67, 269; HJ, 1848–49, 493–94, 651–57, 661; SJ, 1850–51, 298–303, 323, 327–28, 336–39, 370–71; HJ, 1850–51, 733–35, 741–42, 821, 850–51, 928; SJ, 1852, 207–208, 230; HJ, 1852, 175–76, 211–12, 335; SJ, 1854–55, 99, 107, 149, 182, 185.

broad appeal of the measure was evident, since one-third of them supported the bill anyway. Whig commoners, even if they wanted to retain the requirement, must have found it difficult to refuse the extension of the franchise privileges of roughly half of their constituents. That accounts for the relatively low level of party disagreement on the issue. Although the bill passed in the House of Commons, it did not get through the evenly divided Senate, so Democrats would have to renew their effort in the next assembly (see table 18).

★

As the elections of 1850 approached, Whigs decided to oppose the suffrage issue, but upon egalitarian grounds. Whigs from the west pushed the party to go beyond limited change in the suffrage laws to the adoption of the white basis for apportioning representation in the legislature and in the distribution of the common-school fund and to the elimination of property requirements for members of the state legislature. In order to make those changes, some Whigs called for the assembling of a constitutional convention. Easterners agreed to go along with any reform but those involving a change to the white basis.[13]

At the party's convention in June, after renominating Manly, delegates ignored the convention question. Instead, they declared that, because many people had indicated their support for the equal-suffrage amendment and because "it is a fundamental principle of popular government . . . that all political power is vested in and derived from the People only," there ought to be a referendum on the amendment. The party also recommended a referendum on making judicial and executive offices elective. By supporting a referendum, Whigs hoped to eliminate the troublesome issues of constitutional reform from the political arena.[14]

The Democrats, whose convention met soon after the Whigs', stayed with their successful combination of 1848. They renominated Reid and declared themselves in favor of equal suffrage and of the popular election of judges.[15]

During the campaign, both parties portrayed themselves as the best defenders of democracy. The Democratic Raleigh *Standard*, comparing the parties' platforms, asserted that the Democratic party supported constitutional reforms "as *rights*," whereas "the Whigs . . . have merely consented that the people may have them if they insist upon them!" Whigs argued that they, not the Democrats, were the true advocates of white democracy. The Fayetteville *Observer* declared that "the majority of the people have a right to make their Constitution what they please, to keep it as it is or to change it. If the people don't want it, then it is anti-republican to try to foist it upon them."[16]

The Whig acceptance of a referendum on equal suffrage proved unsatisfactory to many of its supporters. Just after Reid defeated Manly and the Democrats captured the Commons and Senate, the Whig Greensboro *Patriot* explained that Reid had an advantage because equal suffrage was "a simple, distinct proposition, directly enlisting the popular favor." On the other hand, "Whigs, though not unfavorable to the proposition *per se*, manifested a reluctance to mixing up questions of *constitutional reform* with *party politics*; and this reluctance was too apt to be taken for opposition to free suffrage itself." The Whigs had hoped to remove a damaging issue from the political arena but had failed.[17]

13. Greensboro *Patriot*, June 1 and April 3, 1850.
14. Raleigh *Register*, June 15, 1850.
15. Raleigh *Standard*, June 19, 1850.
16. *Ibid.*; Fayetteville *Observer*, June 25, 1850.
17. Greensboro *Patriot*, August 16, 1850.

During the campaign, Governor Manly tried to show voters that equal suffrage would not bring equality to anyone. He had used this argument in 1848, but two years later he made the point more forcefully. He argued that if the property qualification for senatorial electors was removed, then "it would be unjust to retain the taxation feature in regard to representation." Logically, he said, the state ought to apportion representation according to the white population of the state, rather than according to the "federal population" and to taxes paid. A switch to the white basis would alter the geography of power in the state, since people in the wealthier slaveholding areas would lose power to westerners. When Manly made those remarks, he was trying to argue that neither of those changes ought to be made, but Democrats claimed he was advocating a change to the white basis. When Reid informed William Holden that "Manly had come out against the black [federal] basis," Holden replied that, "if the people of the East, Centre, and South, are convinced of the fact, Manly must lose thousands." The *Standard* and other Democratic papers tried their hardest to convince voters of that fact.[18]

The Democrats also turned Manly's supposed support for the change into a Whig attempt to undermine slavery and southern rights. Congress was then considering compromise measures designed to resolve the sectional conflict over slavery and its expansion into newly acquired territories. With the South under sectional attack, Democrats could easily construe an attack on the federal basis in North Carolina as a threat to southern power in the House of Representatives, which rested upon the same method of apportionment. Since a shift to the white basis in the state would, it was claimed, weaken the power of slaveholders, Democrats charged that Whigs were placing "vital interests . . . in jeopardy." Democrats were therefore able to portray themselves as the defenders of southern rights and of the rights of white men, while Whigs staggered on the defensive.[19]

The Democratic attempt to capitalize on the representation issue revealed the limits of their commitment to white equality. A change in the basis would reapportion power in the state, reducing the representation of the areas controlled by the Democrats; nothing of the sort would happen if the state adopted the suffrage amendment. It was probably apparent to voters that those who owned less than fifty acres of land voted little dif-

18. Fayetteville *Observer*, July 9, 1850; William W. Holden to David S. Reid, July 7, 1850, in Reid Papers; Charles L. Hinton to William A. Graham, August 22, 1850, in J. G. de Roulhac Hamilton and Max R. Williams (eds.), *The Papers of William Alexander Graham* (6 vols. to date; Raleigh: State Department of Archives and History, 1957–), III, 365; Raleigh *Standard*, July 10, 17, and 24, 1850.

19. Raleigh *Standard*, July 10, 1850. Also see William J. Cooper, Jr., *The South and the Politics of Slavery, 1828–1856* (Baton Rouge: Louisiana State University Press, 1978), 311–12.

ferently from those who owned fifty acres. In addition, the constitutional requirements that legislators own substantial amounts of land assured landowners that they would lose little power from the adoption of the equal-suffrage amendment. Because equal suffrage threatened no entrenched interests and enhanced the equality of white men, it appealed to adherents of both parties throughout the state.[20]

Democratic support for equal suffrage and hostility to the white basis reflected the state's political and constitutional realities. It was much easier to establish the white basis in Alabama, for example, when that state was formed in 1819, since no constitution had to be changed and no particular group would *lose* power because of the alteration of a constitution. The situation in North Carolina was different. The state constitution of 1776, still intact despite modifications made in 1835, skewed power in favor of the wealthier east, so any attempt to change the basis of representation would meet with hostility from easterners who benefited from the status quo. Since the heart of Democratic strength lay in the east, only suicidal impulses would have led the party to support a change in the basis, and the Democrats were not suicidal. They and most Whigs realized that any attempt to provide greater political equality among whites would have to tread lightly on vested interests. Equal suffrage met that test; it provided equality without changing power relationships in the state. That fact helps to explain why Democrats were so united in support of equal suffrage.

In the General Assembly, the Democrats, who controlled both houses for the first time since 1842, pressed hard for the adoption of the equal-suffrage amendment. Whigs continued to seek a course that would allow them to portray themselves as egalitarians and still to oppose equal suffrage. They abandoned the idea of a referendum on the amendment and, under pressure from western members, supported a referendum on a constitutional convention. Westerners wanted a convention because it might enable them to obtain the white basis. The referendum also appealed to the conservative proclivities of many Whigs. A convention would settle at once all outstanding quarrels about constitutional changes, whereas the legislative method, at its quickest, would take almost five years. And then, of course, politicians might suggest a new amendment that would again enmesh the constitution in partisan politics and destroy its utility. A united Whig party supported a convention referendum, but the equally united majority Democrats easily defeated the bill. That rejection apparently galvanized Whig opposition to equal suffrage. Although the amend-

20. McCormick, "Suffrage Classes," 397–410; Thomas E. Jeffrey, "The Second Party System in North Carolina" (Ph.D. dissertation, Catholic University of America, 1976), 416; Thorpe (comp.), *Federal and State Constitutions*, V, 2790, 2796.

TABLE 19
Percent Affirmative Votes in the North Carolina General Assembly by Party,
1848–1855: Constitutional Revision

	Senate		House	
	Democrats	*Whigs*	*Democrats*	*Whigs*
EQUAL SUFFRAGE AMENDMENT				
1848–49	82.6	31.6	90.0	56.8
1850–51	100.0	23.3	91.4	30.4
1852*	100.0	27.5	96.1	60.0
1852**	—	—	98.0	29.9
1854–55	96.7	30.4	100.0	62.2
CONSTITUTIONAL CONVENTION				
1848–49	—	—	3.8	86.2
1850–51	1.9	79.7	11.1	80.0
1854–55	0	94.4	16.4	63.8

*Before the Democratic Senate Speaker's negative vote caused the amendment's defeat.
**After the Speaker's vote.
SOURCES: See Table 18.

ment passed with the needed three-fifths majority, it did so despite the overwhelming opposition of Whigs in both houses (see table 19).[21]

Unsatisfied with only the suffrage amendment, western Whig legislators pursued their goals after the session ended. In a major address, thirty-seven of them declared themselves in favor of an open constitutional convention and a change in the basis of representation. Mountain Whigs carried the campaign further as they held meetings in Watauga, Henderson, and Buncombe counties in March and April, 1851, and a western convention in the late spring. All of the meetings issued resolutions demanding dramatic changes in the constitution. In Watauga, for example, they called for the white basis, the abolition of property requirements for officeholding, and limitations on the tenure of state judges. The Asheville *News* even went so far as to advocate the organization of a Constitutional Reform party. The Greensboro *Patriot*, which supported major constitutional changes, warned that "if any man is afraid to trust the fundamental law of the State freely to the councils of the whole people of the State, he must confess one of two things—either that he thinks the people are not fit to govern themselves, or that he hugs to his bosom the tyrannous doctrine of favor and security to the Few at the expense of the Many." Whigs in much of the west argued for the establishment of a truly democratic political system—a system that would go further than Democrats and eastern Whigs were willing to concede.[22]

21. *SJ, 1850–51*, 300–303, 336–39; *HJ, 1850–51*, 733–35, 821, 850–51, 928.
22. Raleigh *Register*, March 22 and April 19, 1851; Asheville *News*, n.d., quoted in Greensboro *Patriot*, March 22, 1851; Greensboro *Patriot*, March 22 and January 11, 1851.

The Whig party leadership in the central and eastern parts of the state recognized the threat that western demands posed to the party. Although the Whig party was especially strong in the mountains, it depended for electoral success upon substantial support in wealthy slaveholding counties—whose citizens would lose power if western demands were acceded to. Even the west itself was not united. Before the constitution was revised in 1835, the wealthier Piedmont counties with many slaveholders were as aggrieved by the county basis of representation as were the poor counties of the west. Then, the coastal plain controlled the legislature by keeping western counties large and by limiting their number. The revisions of 1835 gave greater weight to wealth and slaves in apportioning representation, and therefore wealthy, slaveowning Piedmont counties like Mecklenburg and Anson in the south and Caswell and Rockingham in the north would likely lose power with a change in the basis. Whereas before 1835 all of the west had united behind the demands for constitutional change, now many western counties would stand to lose if the white basis were adopted, so westerners desirous of change would face an enormous uphill struggle, even in their own section. In order to keep the party coalition intact, leaders made numerous concessions to western demands but without going so far as to alienate others in the party.

★

As the party convention of 1852 drew near, some western Whigs pledged themselves not to vote for the party's nominee if he did not support an open constitutional convention, while some eastern Whigs threatened to bolt the party if it endorsed a constitutional convention. With good reason Whig leaders feared that the party would "be split to pieces & defeated, by the introduction of the Convention question into the Whig Convention," and so they agreed that "there must be some compromise of the ultra views on both sides."[23]

When the convention assembled on April 26, delegates from the extreme east and extreme west were absent. Transportation difficulties, as usual, had prevented their attendance. Their absence enabled the delegates to reach a compromise that followed the course of Whig behavior in the previous legislature. The resolution called for a referendum on "whether . . . a Convention shall be called or not, for the purposes of mak-

23. Greensboro *Patriot*, March 13, 1852; Charles C. Raboteau to David F. Caldwell, March 27, 1852, in David F. Caldwell papers, SHC; proceedings of the Chowan County Whig meeting in Fayetteville *Observer*, April 13, 1852; Henry Miller to William A. Graham, March 20, 1852, in Hamilton and Williams (eds.), *Graham Papers*, IV, 261. Also see John H. Bryan to Graham, April 5, 1852, James W. Osborne to Graham, March 25, 1852, and James W. Bryan to Graham, March 24, 1852, all in Hamilton and Williams (eds.), *Graham Papers*, IV, 281, 268, 265.

ing amendments to our Constitution." The plank held out to the west the possibility of gaining a convention, while it offered the east an opportunity to avoid any changes in the constitution. Also, a referendum would rid the party of the vexing issues of constitutional revision. By assuming no position on whether they thought a convention should be held, the delegates avoided alienating either faction. The call for a referendum also represented a significant shift in the party's views about constitutional change. In four years, Whigs had moved far toward support for the democratization of the state constitution. In 1848 they had denounced the Democratic proposal as part of a "levelling" doctrine; by 1850 they had endorsed a referendum on equal suffrage; and in 1852 they accepted the possibility of truly dramatic changes in the constitution through a state convention.[24]

The party chose as its gubernatorial candidate John Kerr of Caswell, a man who gave only slight support to constitutional reform. Kerr was not the man western Whigs hoped for, but most supported him. As the Whig editor of the Raleigh *Times*, Charles Raboteau, explained to Greensboro Whig leader David F. Caldwell: "I see no reason for going against the nominee of the Whig party, especially as we look to that very party principally in the West, for the votes which are to carry the Convention measure."[25]

Democrats, meanwhile, were content to sit back and enjoy the Whigs' discomfort. Editor William Holden wrote happily to Congressman Abraham W. Venable that "the Whig division on the Convention business may be patched up, *but cannot be cured*. The Feds will enter the campaign disorganized, and this will cripple them." Unlike the Whigs, Democrats were united on a gubernatorial nominee (Governor Reid was the obvious choice) and on constitutional reform (for equal suffrage and the popular election of judges and against a constitutional convention).[26]

The first problem the Whigs faced during the campaign involved their proposal for reform. Whigs supposed that if a majority of the people voted in favor of a convention, a convention would be held. But immediately Democrats charged that Whig plans threatened minority rights. Constitutions protected the rights of minorities; to adopt the Whig plan would mean the acceptance of majoritarianism, not republicanism, and to accept simple majoritarianism threatened the liberties of the people. The *Standard* declared that "if the Constitution may be broken down in one respect it may in another; and if broken at all, there can be no safety thence forth to the people's rights and liberties." Later in the campaign, the *Standard* warned Democrats: "Every vote cast for Kerr will be a vote in favor of his 'higher law' or 'moral power' doctrine of majorities, as against the ves-

24. *Raleigh* Register, May 1, 1852.
25. Charles C. Raboteau to David F. Caldwell, March 27, 1852, in Caldwell Papers.
26. William W. Holden to Abraham W. Venable, March 26, 1852, in Abraham Watkins Vena-

ted rights of minorities and the plain language of the State Constitution."
As in 1850, Democrats were trying to link in the voters' minds the principles of North Carolina Whigs with the "higher law" beliefs of northern
abolitionists.

Democrats also attacked the Whig proposal as an elaborate device designed to defeat equal suffrage. They pointed out that many Whigs, including Kerr, who had initially opposed any change in the constitution, now
supported the Whig party's convention resolution. This contradiction
proved to the satisfaction of Democrats that at heart the Whigs opposed
any constitutional change.[27]

Whigs replied by clothing themselves in the garb of white equality.
When Democrats attacked the convention proposal, the *Register* retorted:
"Just as we expected, the locofoco Press of the State are assailing the sacred cause of Popular Rights." The party's candidate, Kerr, had been opposed to equal suffrage, Whigs said, only because Democrats had introduced it as a partisan measure, but he now accepted it and "goes forth
before the people as the advocate and defender of popular liberty and representative government." Because David Reid rejected the idea of a popular referendum, he proved himself to be a man "with love for the people on
his lips, with contempt for them in his heart." Although the Whigs had developed a somewhat similar argument in 1848, their portrayal of themselves as the premier advocates of white rights and equality represented a
substantial change in their approach to the question of constitutional
reform.[28]

The most important problem of Kerr's candidacy involved the basis of
representation and the distribution of the public-school fund according to
federal population. In the east, where Kerr began his campaign, he apparently satisfied his audiences by opposing any changes in the basis for representation or for the distribution of the school fund. As Kerr remarked to
William Graham, "Our friends in this region care nothing about the State
issues, I have satisfied them on that subject." But Kerr soon ran into problems. Democrats placed him on the defensive when they contended that,
as he moved to the west, he came out in favor of a change to the white
basis. Repeatedly, Whig papers, worried about their eastern flank, denied
that Kerr had ever altered his position. "In this respect," the Raleigh *Register* declared, "there is no difference of opinion between him and his com-

ble Papers, SHC; Raleigh *Standard*, May 19, 1852.

27. Goldsboro *Republican and Patriot*, n.d., quoted in Raleigh *Standard*, May 19, 1852;
Raleigh *Standard*, June 18, July 28, and April 14, 1852; Samuel J. Person to Thomas D.
McDowell, July 6, 1852, in Thomas D. McDowell Papers, SHC.

28. Raleigh *Register*, May 8 and 22, June 26, 1852.

petitor"—both opposed a change. But each time Kerr and the Whig press denied Democratic charges, they reminded western Whigs that Kerr opposed western interests. And western Whig voters did learn Kerr's position by reading the dissident Whig paper, the Asheville *News*, which attacked Kerr repeatedly for his opposition to western interests, particularly his hostility to a change in the basis. The recently established Whig paper, the Asheville *Messenger*, replied by arguing that Kerr's positions on representation and the school fund were irrelevant. If the Whig position was accepted, westerners would have an opportunity to get a convention and obtain the constitutional reforms they desired, regardless of what Kerr thought. Despite the arguments of the *Messenger*, western Whigs were still left with a gubernatorial candidate who opposed their interests. This led Whig David Swain, president of the University of North Carolina, to declare that Kerr's "opposition . . . to any change in the basis of representation, and his advocacy of the principle of distribution of the common school fund (according to the federal population), will, I fear, cost him many votes in the extreme West." Buncombe Whig Zebulon Vance asserted that "Kerr is a dead weight upon the necks of his friends." [29]

Vance and Swain were correct. The disorganization in the Whig party caused by the defection of some mountain Whigs over the issue of constitutional reform injured the party. Whigs still carried the mountains with a substantial majority of 57.8 percent, but this was a good bit less than they had ever received in that region since the inception of the party system. In the state as a whole, Kerr also fared badly. Reid carried the election with 53 percent of the vote.

The Whigs' ambivalence on the issue of constitutional revision also hurt them in another way, since it once again appeared that the party was evading the issue of equal suffrage. As the Greensboro *Patriot* pointed out, the party's position was so unclear that it had to spend much of the campaign explaining it, which left many voters with the impression that the Whigs continued to oppose equal suffrage. [30]

Although the Whigs had lost the gubernatorial election and the Senate, they captured a narrow majority in the Commons. The suffrage amendment sailed through the Commons with the support of virtually all Democrats and a substantial majority of Whigs. In the Senate, though, the measure's success hung on the vote of the Senate Speaker, Weldon N. Edwards.

29. John Kerr to William A. Graham, May 22, 1852, David L. Swain to Graham, July 6, 1852, both in Hamilton and Williams (eds.), *Graham Papers*, IV, 301, 341; Raleigh *Standard*, July 7, 1852; Asheville *News*, n.d., quoted in Raleigh *Standard*, July 7, 1852; Raleigh *Register*, June 9, July 10, 17, 21, 1852; Asheville *Messenger*, May 22, 1852, quoted in Raleigh *Standard*, June 9, 1852; Asheville *Messenger*, n.d., quoted in Raleigh *Standard*, July 7, 1852.

30. Greensboro *Patriot*, August 14, 1852.

Edwards, one of a small minority of "old Republican" Democrats who were determined to preserve all constitutional devices designed to protect property, voted no. Although Whigs had provided almost every other negative vote on the amendment in the Senate, the publicity surrounding Edwards' vote placed the onus for the amendment's failure on the Democrats. Now Whigs could argue more persuasively that Democrats really did not want to pass the amendment but planned only to use it as a political "hobby" to "ride" into office. All they wanted was continual strife over the issue. Democrats, Whigs charged, would not democratize the constitution but would only agitate constitutional issues endlessly. So when Democrats in the Commons began the amendment process again, a united Whig opposition prevented it from getting the required three-fifths of the votes (see tables 18 and 19, pp. 91, 95).[31]

★

Whig leaders knew that in 1854 Democrats would again press for the adoption of the equal-suffrage amendment and that western Whigs would press for an open constitutional convention. The Whig party would again have to formulate responses. Instead of allowing the constitution to be subjected to continual political discussion, Whigs said, a constitutional convention should be called to discuss all constitutional reforms except a change in the basis of representation in the state legislature. Since 1850, the party had sought to appease western demands for reform without driving off easterners. They hoped that open support for a convention would placate the west and that proposed limits on the convention would satisfy the east. At the state convention in February, 1854, the party resolved that "the people of North Carolina desire a change in the Constitution of the State" and that such changes should be made through a convention; therefore, it called for a convention that would "preserve the present basis of representation in the Legislature."[32]

The plank on constitutional reform alienated many westerners. The Greensboro *Patriot* declared: "We can never, with our republican notions of popular rights, swallow such logic as this!" Whigs in Henderson, a mountain county, met in April to repudiate the party's limitations on what a convention might do. After a while, however, the hostility began to subside, and in late July the *Patriot* declared: "Hurra for Dockery, a convention to amend the Constitution, Free Suffrage, Free Schools and a Free People—Internal Improvements and Distribution of the Public Lands."[33]

31. Weldon N. Edwards, *Address of Weldon N. Edwards to His Constituents, the Freemen of Warren County* (n.p., [1853]), in NCC; Raleigh *Register*, January 8, 1853.

32. Raleigh *Register*, February 25, March 1, 1854.

33. Greensboro *Patriot*, quoted in Raleigh *Standard*, April 19, 1854; proceedings of Henderson County meeting, in Raleigh *Standard*, April 19, 1854; Greensboro *Patriot*, July 22, 1854.

Whigs, like the editor of the *Patriot*, came to accept the Whig platform because it did actually benefit westerners in some ways. The white basis would have given greater power to the west and enabled westerners to obtain legislation beneficial to their region, especially state aid to internal improvements. The party advocated liberal state aid to internal improvements and specifically supported the state-aided construction of a western extension of the North Carolina Railroad to the Tennessee border, a project especially dear to westerners. As we have seen, gubernatorial candidate Alfred Dockery based much of his campaign on his support for western and eastern extensions.[34]

Western Whig acceptance of the party platform may also have reflected a pragmatic acknowledgment that it was the best they could get. At least the Whig party offered them a convention; the Democrats offered them little more than equal suffrage. They may also have realized that if the platform endorsed an open convention, the Whig party would lose many votes in the eastern and Piedmont counties and gain few in other parts of the west. Despite the Whigs' losses in the late 1840s and early 1850s, mountain voters in 1852 still cast almost 58 percent of their votes for the Whig candidate. It would be difficult for them to get a much higher percentage of the vote. As Whig candidate Alfred Dockery explained to white-basis advocate David F. Caldwell: "If we go into the campaign with a change of the basis upon our banner we shall lose thousands of votes over the Eastern and middle counties and what shall we gain in the West—scarcely a vote." Dockery also reminded Caldwell that western Whigs who wanted a convention had little choice but to support the Whig party. "In the event of our quarreling among ourselves and thereby continuing the democrats in power," he wrote, "what will our friends who think with you gain, certainly not an open convention."[35]

Dockery also satisfied those who were unhappy about the party's equivocation on equal suffrage. He declared himself in favor of the measure: "They who bear their full quota of the burdens of the Government and contribute their proportion to its defence, should not . . . be deprived . . . of the right of choosing their own representatives—a privilege dear to freemen and formidable to tyrants only."[36]

The election returns showed clearly that the Whigs had halted their statewide electoral decline. Dockery won 48.9 percent of the vote. Despite the issue of equal suffrage and the split in the party over a constitutional convention, the Whigs still came near victory in 1854. The legislative elections, though, relegated them to a minority position in both houses.

34. See chapter 3.
35. Alfred Dockery to David F. Caldwell, March 10, 1854, in Caldwell Papers.
36. Charlotte *Western Democrat*, March 24, 1854.

The majority Democrats, despite the debacle of the Edwards vote in 1852, rallied around the equal-suffrage amendment. The pattern of voting was by then familiar. United Senate Democrats passed the amendment over the opposition of two-thirds of the Whigs, while in the Commons unanimous Democrats joined about 60 percent of the Whigs to pass the measure. But the persistence of older voting patterns belied significant changes that had taken place. Senate Whigs still largely opposed equal suffrage, but in its place they pressed for a constitutional convention that would undoubtedly democratize the constitution further than would the suffrage amendment. And although House Whigs continued to give a small but solid majority for the amendment, they too sought more than equal suffrage (see tables 18 and 19, pp. 91, 95).

In the next meeting of the General Assembly in 1856, the suffrage amendment itself easily obtained the required two-thirds majority when the Whig party's successor, the American party, assumed no position on questions of constitutional revision and joined the Democrats in voting for equal suffrage. On the next election day, in August, 1857, voters overwhelmingly ratified the amendment.[37]

★

In 1848 Democrats found a remarkably effective issue in the proposed equal suffrage amendment. It was a simple, direct issue that enabled them to portray themselves as the defenders of the equal rights of white men. Because Whigs opposed the amendment, and initially opposed it on antiegalitarian grounds, Democrats created an effective image of the Whigs as aristocratic opponents of popular rights.

Whigs were not the aristocrats of Democratic myth, but they did cling to the older republican belief that requirements for the franchise offered property its only defense against oppressive taxation. Under pressure from Democratic competition, Whigs found it impossible to maintain this position and win elections. The peculiar constitutional structure of North Carolina shaped their ultimate response. The white adult males who could not vote for state senator could vote in other elections, and since they composed about half the electorate, their support was necessary for partisan success. The Democratic proposal for broadening their franchise privileges obviously appealed to them, so Whigs could not blatantly oppose it without endangering victory. As a result, the Whig party drifted further and further in a democratic direction. They were pushed even further by western Whigs who wanted to equalize the power of white men, not just

37. Raleigh *Register*, April 16, 1856.

their rights, by changing the method of apportioning representation in the legislature. So the party moved from outright opposition to the suffrage amendment, to favoring a referendum on it, to favoring a referendum on a convention, to a demand for a convention. By 1854 they had gone well beyond Democratic proposals for the democratization of the constitution. Yet Whigs still maintained the support of their more conservative members. A referendum on a convention or a convention itself appealed to many conservatives who feared that piecemeal changes in the constitution would destroy the conservative balance of that instrument.

While the Whig party might go as far as endorsing the holding of a convention, because both parties relied upon the votes of easterners, neither could afford to endorse a change in the basis of representation. The greater significance of the far west in the Whig coalition forced that party closer to supporting western demands, but neither party would take a position that threatened its survival.

In the end, North Carolina adopted the equal suffrage amendment. Equal suffrage did not fully democratize the state's political structure. In 1860, the senators elected by the newly enfranchised voters were wealthier than senators had been before the amendment was adopted. Legislators still were required to be substantial landowners, and the east still wielded power out of proportion to the size of its white population. But the partisan debate over constitutional revision nevertheless helped create a more egalitarian political culture in North Carolina.

Five   *Parties, Slavery, and Union*
1840–1854

In the 1850s, contemporaries recognized that party loyalties played a crucial role in shaping the contours of the sectional conflict. They saw in the existence of two national parties a bulwark of American nationalism, or an arrangement that prevented a politician from fully asserting his section's rights, since parties gave men ties that bound them to others outside of their town, county, and state.[1]

Those contemporaries were correct, at least in that parties did help moderate the sectional views of southerners and northerners. However, the relationship between the parties and the conflict over slavery was more complex than that. The party system was a federal system, but state parties did not follow in lockstep the lead of the national organizations. Indeed, much of the popular perception of the sectional crisis came not from the divisions between or within the national parties but from party conflict within the states.

Partly out of an instinct to present distinct views to their constituents and partly as an expression of ideological differences, the political parties assumed sharply contrasting positions on a whole range of issues. In this respect, the issues of slavery and its expansion were no different from questions involving constitutional reform and governance. Although Whigs and Democrats, indeed virtually all the white North Carolinians, agreed that slavery in the state must be protected from outside interference, partisans disagreed about how to protect it. And when, in the late 1840s, the question of protecting slavery became a question of protecting the right of

1. Speech of David Outlaw in *Congressional Globe*, 32nd Cong., 1st Sess., Appendix, p. 678.

southerners to take their slaves into the territories, the parties also disagreed about the best way to do that.

In this way, state party loyalty made united action virtually impossible. At the same time, partisans vied with one another to prove that they
and their party were the only reliable defenders of southern rights, and by
harping on that theme in their rhetoric, they heightened popular fears
that slavery and southern rights were endangered. Because of party competition within the states, the threat from the North seemed imminent.
While raising the level of popular anxiety, politicians offered to save voters
from those perils; elect us, they claimed, and the South may rest easy.

The overwhelming majority of white North Carolinians were deeply
committed to the preservation of the institution of slavery, although in the
last antebellum decades there were still some antislavery advocates, often
Quakers, to be found in the state. One Guilford County Quaker, for instance, condemned slavery as "a great moral and political evil" and hoped
for its abolition. The north-central Piedmont region, where Guilford is located, also provided a fertile field for abolitionist preachers to plow. From
1848 to 1850, Wesleyan Methodist ministers preached abolition in different
parts of Guilford. In neighboring Alamance County in 1848, a small group
of antislavery men gathered together to establish a presidential ticket for
Martin Van Buren, whose Free-Soil party opposed the further expansion of
slavery. However, these and other instances of antislavery thought and action added up only to a small ripple in the large lake of positive support
for slavery.[2]

Even those North Carolinians who criticized slavery as an evil argued
that outsiders should not interfere with it. Congressman David Outlaw, a
large slaveowner, believed that there were many "evils . . . attendant upon
the institution of slavery," and he did not expect to convince people of its
goodness: "To expect men to agree that slavery is a blessing, social, moral
and political, when many of those who have all their lives been accus-
tomed to it, do not believe it and so far from believing it, believe exactly
the reverse, is absurd." Though slavery was an evil, Outlaw believed,
southerners should be left alone with it. "It is sufficient to deal with it as an
existing fact," he wrote, "one for which we are not responsible, and which
we must treat as practical men." From Outlaw's point of view, practical
obstacles were enough to prevent the abolition of slavery.[3]

Most white people supported slavery without reservation. One of the

2. Jesse Wheeler to Benjamin S. Hedrick, August 20, 1859, in Benjamin Sherwood Hedrick
Papers, Duke; Raleigh *Standard*, January 22, May 22, 1850, June 4, August 6, 1851, October 18,
1848.
3. David Outlaw to Emily Outlaw, December 10, 1849, and July [n.d.], 1848, both in David

most striking signs of their commitment was the virtual absence of any intellectual defense of slavery in the political press between 1840 and 1860. Editors wrote often and extensively about the need and the best ways to protect slavery, but they rarely bothered to undertake a defense of it on moral and economic grounds—the peculiar institution was so much a part of the warp and woof of North Carolina society that few saw any need to defend it. That the absence of a proslavery argument in the state press expressed a broad consensus within the state in favor of protecting slavery is suggested further by the speeches that North Carolina's congressmen delivered in Washington on the slavery question during the 1840s and 1850s. In most of those speeches, the congressmen offered numerous arguments to prove that slavery was a good institution. Unlike the situation in their home state, where the virtues of slavery were assumed and required no articulation, in Washington the slave system was challenged often, so North Carolina congressmen felt obliged to defend it explicitly.[4]

There were several reasons for the broad consensus that existed in North Carolina on the slavery question. One basic reason was economic. White North Carolinians had as deep an economic stake in the preservation of slavery as did people in the states of the lower South. More than 25 percent of the white families in the state in 1850 owned slaves, more than in Texas and not much less than in Alabama and Georgia (see table 6, p. 00). For slaveowners, the protection of slavery obviously meant the protection of their economic interests. As David Outlaw put it: "People are not going to give up their property to a sickly, morbid sentiment of philanthropy." Slaveownership also was the mark of high social status in the community and, as we have seen, paved the way for political preferment. Since slavery offered significant benefits for such a substantial minority of the population, its broad popular acceptance is better understood.[5]

The nonslaveholder also had economic reasons for defending slavery. He always dreamed that he too might own slaves, and the large number of white families that owned slaves made this dream realistic. The likelihood of obtaining slaves was even greater in the eastern and central parts of the state, where slavery was much more widespread than in the mountains. Also, whereas slavery may have injured the economic position of nonslaveholders, those whites who were prosperous or satisfied with their eco-

Outlaw Papers, SHC. Also see Francis E. Shober to Mary Wheat Shober, April 15, 1853, in Wheat-Shober Papers, SHC.

4. *Cf.* Eugene Genovese, *The World the Slaveholders Made: Two Essays in Interpretation* (New York: Pantheon Books, 1969), pt. 2.

5. Otto Olsen, "Historians and the Extent of Slave Ownership in the Southern United States," *Civil War History*, XVIII (1972), 107–16; David Outlaw to Emily Outlaw, February 27, 1850, in Outlaw Papers.

nomic condition would likely have supported the system within which they prospered.[6]

Slaveholders and nonslaveholders also defended slavery for other than tangible reasons. Among the most important was the inertia that pervades most societies at most times. North Carolinians were born into a slave society and lived their entire lives in it, and, like people in other times and other places, they did not question the beneficence of the institutions of their society. When they reacted angrily to northern attacks on slavery, they were not just defending slavery, but their society and their way of life.[7]

White North Carolinians, slaveholders and nonslaveholders alike, also saw slavery and the subordination of blacks as the foundation of white equality and freedom in the South, and they accepted without question Congressman Thomas Clingman's declaration that the black man "is in respects different from the white man and inferior." Because the basis for determining superiority and inferiority was racial, it implied that all members of the superior white race were equal. As the Raleigh *Standard* argued: "No negroes are born free and upon equality with white men, but all white men are entitled, at the proper age, to the privileges of citizenship, and are all equal." The realities of politics did not always comport with this notion of white equality, for the suffrage was somewhat limited and only men of property could serve in the legislature or as governor. Nevertheless, the pervasiveness of the belief in white equality was starkly revealed in the dispute over the equal-suffrage amendment. And all white adult male North Carolina citizens could vote for president, governor, members of the House of Commons, and, after 1857, members of the state senate. They were full members of the society and had a voice, no matter how weak or ineffectual, in the way society was run. With some qualifications, it may be said that white North Carolinians lived in what Pierre L. van den Berghe has called a "*herrenvolk* democracy"—one that was "democratic for the master race but tyrannical for the subordinate groups." Because whites believed that the subordination of blacks was a precondition of white equality, they tenaciously defended slavery.[8]

★

In a state where white people were so committed to the preservation of slavery, in order for politicians to win elections they had to prove again

6. James D. B. De Bow, *The Interest in Slavery of the Southern Non-slaveholder* (Charleston: Evans and Cogswell, 1860).

7. George M. Fredrickson, *The Black Image in the White Mind: The Debate on Afro-American Character and Destiny, 1817–1914* (New York: Harper & Row, 1971), 48.

8. *Speech of T. L. Clingman of North Carolina on the Political Aspect of the Slave Question,*

and again their devotion to the peculiar institution and to southern rights within the nation. From the beginning of the second party system in North Carolina, Whigs and Democrats each contended that they alone were the best defenders of the South's institutions and that their opponents' credentials as defenders of slavery and southern rights were somehow suspect.

In 1836, Whigs had built much of their campaign around the fact that they were running for president a southerner, one who could be depended upon to defend southern interests, while Democrats were running a northerner whose views on that subject were at least suspect. North Carolina Democrats that year were so unnerved by the Whig attack that a group of them wrote a public letter to Martin Van Buren asking him to clarify his position on slavery.[9]

Four years later, the slavery issue played a significant, if not decisive, role in the presidential and gubernatorial campaigns. Now that both candidates for the presidency were northerners, each party was left trying to show its candidate as the sounder of the two on the slavery question. Whigs charged that Van Buren worked in collusion with the abolitionists in order to get votes, and Democrats made the same accusations against Harrison. In the state contest, the party press dredged up actions taken in the 1820s and early 1830s by the two gubernatorial candidates to prove that they were abolitionist sympathizers.[10]

The slavery question assumed even greater significance in 1844 as the parties debated a specific issue, the annexation of Texas. President John Tyler, estranged from the Whig party almost from the time he became president after William Henry Harrison's death, sought in Texas' annexation an issue that would enable him to seek reelection as an independent or perhaps a Democrat, and both he and his secretary of state, John C. Calhoun, perceived annexation as a means of protecting slavery and of expanding the political power of the slave states. Annexation itself need not have been cast in terms of slavery's protection, but Calhoun forced the

Delivered in the House of Representatives, December 22, 1847 (n.p., n.d.); Raleigh *Standard*, October 20, 1847; Pierre L. van den Berghe, *Race and Racism: A Comparative Perspective* (New York: Wiley, 1967), 17–18; Fredrickson, *Black Image*, 61–70.

9. William J. Cooper, Jr., *The South and the Politics of Slavery, 1828–1856* (Baton Rouge: Louisiana State University Press, 1978), 81–96; William S. Hoffmann, *Andrew Jackson and North Carolina Politics* (Chapel Hill: University of North Carolina Press, 1958), 108–10; "Letter from North Carolina Citizens to Martin Van Buren," February 23, 1836, and "Martin Van Buren's Reply," March 6, 1836, both in Joel H. Silbey, "Election of 1836," in Arthur M. Schlesinger, Jr. (ed.), *History of American Presidential Elections, 1789–1968* (4 vols.; New York: Chelsea House, 1971), I, 601–606.

10. Fayetteville *Observer*, January 29, February 5, March 4, April 15, September 2, 1840; Raleigh *Register*, June 30, July 3, 1840; Raleigh *Standard*, January 1, February 12, 19, and 26, March 25, April 1, 1840; Bedford Brown to Weldon N. Edwards, June 21, 1840, in Katherine C. P. Conway Papers, NCDAH.

question into precisely those terms in two letters to Robert Pakenham, England's minister to the United States. In them, Calhoun denounced what he believed to be England's desire to rule Texas, destroy slavery there, and then use Texas as a springboard to overthrow slavery in the United States.

Calhoun's letters came to light soon after the public became aware that Tyler had submitted a treaty of annexation to the Senate.[11] Once the treaty became public knowledge, the leading candidates for the presidency, Democrat Martin Van Buren and Whig Henry Clay, felt compelled to take a stand on Texas; both opposed immediate annexation.

For North Carolina's Whigs, Clay's position melded nicely with their own. From the beginning of Tyler's propaganda campaign for Texas, Whigs had been unenthusiastic about the acquisition of the newly independent republic. The state's Democrats faced a more painful problem. From the first, they had been wildly excited about Texas: in early April, one Democratic editor declared that "Texas seems to be absorbing every other question. The whole South is for annexation"; another Democrat claimed that "the people are generally in favour of the annexation of" Texas and Oregon. So when the Democrats learned that Van Buren opposed immediate annexation, they were filled, as one said, with "a feeling of despondency." He and others would continue to support Van Buren's candidacy, but with "no enthusiasm."

Enthusiastic or not about Van Buren, Democrats quickly began to retreat from their earlier vigorous support of annexation. Although displeased with his stand on Texas, Democrats believed that Van Buren would be their standard-bearer that year, so it would not do to snipe at him. After reading Van Buren's letter, the editor of the Raleigh *Standard*, the state party organ, declared that he still favored annexation. However, if the Texas issue threatened to "break up and destroy the democratic party" or injure the Union, then he would wish "Texas had been smitten by the hand of Providence into a barren and neglected desert." What was most striking about the *Standard*'s attitude was the extent to which partisans in the state were willing to bend for the sake of national party unity. But if before their national convention North Carolina's Democrats restrained their enthusiasm for Texas, they were unleashed by the party's nomination of James K. Polk on a platform favoring the annexation of Texas and Oregon. With Henry Clay's easy nomination as the Whig candidate, the party fight over Texas was clearly joined.[12]

11. Cooper, *Politics of Slavery*, 182–92; Frederick Merk, *Slavery and the Annexation of Texas* (New York: Alfred A. Knopf, 1972), Chs. 1–3; Frederick Merk, *Fruits of Propaganda in the Tyler Administration* (Cambridge: Harvard University Press, 1971).

12. Cooper, *Politics of Slavery*, 198–99, 207; Raleigh *Standard*, April 3, May 8, 1844; A. J. Totger to David S. Reid, April 2, 1844, John T. Garland to Reid, May 12, 1844, both in David Settle Reid Papers, NCDAH.

Annexation involved two discrete but intermingled issues: the protection of slavery and of southern rights and the expansion of the nation. Because of Calhoun's letter and because slavery flourished in cotton-growing Texas, the question inevitably became wrapped up in what William J. Cooper, Jr., has called the politics of slavery. Both parties needed to defend their position on the grounds that annexation would either strengthen or weaken slavery and southern rights.[13]

Democrats readily picked up Calhoun's argument that the South needed Texas as protection against English abolitionism. They argued that if Texas did not become a part of the United States, it would fall under the sway of Great Britain, and the English, committed to the worldwide abolition of slavery, would then incite the slaves of the South to rebellion. Anxieties about English intentions expressed a broader fear that English involvement in Texas threatened not only slavery but the general security of the South and Southwest. One Democrat predicted that if the United States did not annex Texas, England would take it over, encourage Indian attacks in the Southwest, "incite our slaves . . . to rebellion," and then launch from Canada an invasion of a weakened United States.

The second part of the Democratic proslavery argument in favor of annexation was political. Texas would add at least one slave state to the Union, and since most people expected that the large republic would be divided into several states, annexation might add three to five new slave states. As one Democrat put it, the expansion of the power of the slaveowning states, one of the "principal reasons" for annexation, would "serve as a check to the villainous proceedings of the Abolitionists."[14]

Whigs countered with a different proslavery argument to oppose annexation. Whereas Democrats argued that England would use Texas to launch an antislavery attack on the South, Whigs accepted British disclaimers of interest in Texas. Whigs also contended that the acquisition of Texas would provide ruinous competition to cotton planters in the Southeast, including North Carolina. They warned, too, that the attraction of Texas land would turn the steady loss of population in older states into a massive exodus. When Democrats argued that Texas would add several slave states to the Union, Whigs replied that if four or five states were made out of Texas, as many as three would be free cattle-grazing states. Texas, then, would not benefit the South in any way. In fact, Whigs contended, annexation would weaken slavery by arousing sectional tensions.

Whigs perceived in the cry for Texas a desire not to protect slavery but

13. Cooper, *Politics of Slavery*.
14. Raleigh *Standard*, April 17, 1844; speech of James B. Shepard, in *ibid.*, December 25, 1844.

rather a desire to antagonize the North and South and hence promote the idea of disunion. The Charlotte *Journal* declared that the Democratic position on annexation reflected "a disposition on the part of the Loco Foco party to join the malcontents of South Carolina in overthrowing our present government and establishing a Southern Confederacy with Mr. Calhoun at its head." Just before the election, the Whig central committee urged local party workers to bring Whigs to the polls because a united Democratic party would try "to carry this State for Texas and Disunion." For the sake of the Union and slavery, Whigs argued, Texas should not be annexed.[15]

Just as no party could afford to be perceived as a less-than-ardent defender of slavery, so, too, no party could afford to be perceived as a lukewarm defender of the Union. As David Potter has observed, Americans in the 1840s possessed all the traits of a nation—a common language, a common ethnic background (except black Americans), a common religion, a common territory (drawn closer together by an improved transportation and communication network), a common belief in democracy, and what North Carolina Whig Thomas Clingman called "historic associations and recollections of common ancestral struggles and triumphs." Moreover, North Carolinians and other Americans perceived the Union as "the temple of our liberties," and they ardently defended the temple. Therefore, Whig charges that Democrats wanted Texas in order to promote disunion drove Democrats to reassert the primacy of the Union in their pantheon of political beliefs.

Democrats agreed that if annexation would "impair the value or terminate the existence of the Union itself," then Texas should not be annexed, but they concluded that annexation would not endanger the Union. In response to Whig claims that the Democrats supported disunion, the Democratic central committee published a letter declaring that the party was "for the UNION AND TEXAS—TEXAS AND THE UNION—but for the Union, TEXAS OR NO TEXAS."[16]

The debate over Texas was not only about the preservation of slavery

15. Charlotte *Journal*, May 3, June 7, July 19, 1844; David F. Caldwell to Daniel M. Barringer, April 10, May 2, 11, 20, June 12, 1844, all in Daniel Moreau Barringer Papers, SHC; Raleigh *Register*, July 9, 1844; Richard Hines, *et al.*, Whig Central Committee Circular, [1844], in John H. Bryan Papers, NCDAH.

16. David M. Potter, *The Impending Crisis, 1848–1861*, completed and edited by Don E. Fehrenbacher (New York: Harper and Row, 1976), 1–14; Thomas L. Clingman, *Speech of T. L. Clingman of North Carolina: Defense of the South Against the Aggressive Movement of the North* (n.p., 1851); Raleigh *Register*, March 20, 1850, quoted in Joseph Carlyle Sitterson, *The Secession Movement in North Carolina* (Chapel Hill: University of North Carolina Press, 1939), 62; Raleigh *Standard*, May 8, 1844, Democratic Central Committee letter, September 10, 1844, in Wilmington *Journal*, September 21, 1844.

and the Union but also about the nature of the Union. Both Whigs and Democrats spoke often and glowingly about the virtues of American republicanism and believed that the United States had a mission to spread republicanism and freedom throughout the world. However, they intended to reach those goals in very different ways. Democrats expected to expand freedom by expanding the boundaries of the United States; they wanted to "extend the blessings of our free institutions over the valley of the Mississippi." North Carolina Whigs also hoped that America would spread freedom, not by physically transplanting it elsewhere as the Democrats desired, but rather by improving the United States so much that other people would emulate it. For this reason, Whigs had consistently sought the *internal* improvement of the country—from schools to railroads—because such improvements would showcase the virtues of a free government for all the world to see. The United States, Whigs argued, should confine itself to its already large boundaries and instead "be for this continent, the *mother of Republics*."[17]

Given the depth of partisan differences over Texas, it was hardly surprising that those divisions continued on beyond the election, in which Clay carried the state and Polk the nation. When the state legislature assembled later in the year, the partisan dimension to the slavery issue became clear. In the House of Commons, a united Whig majority tabled a Democratic resolution praising the annexation of Texas. The partisanship evident in the campaign and during the roll-call vote suggests that southerners were not as united in favor of the acquisition of Texas as recent historians have claimed.[18]

★

The debate over expansion persisted and deepened as war broke out with Mexico in 1846. North Carolina partisans, at home and in Congress, viewed the war as they had the annexation of Texas. Democrats applauded President Polk, justified the war on the grounds that it was necessary for the preservation of national honor, and called for the cession of Mexican land to the United States as repayment for the supposed damage that Mexico had inflicted on the nation. Whigs, while advocating full support for the soldiers in the field, denounced the war as a Democratic imperialist ven-

17. Democratic Central Committee letter, October 1, 1844, in Wilmington *Journal*, October 11, 1844; Raleigh *Register*, May 21, 1844; Major L. Wilson, *Space, Time and Freedom: The Quest for Nationality and the Irrepressible Conflict, 1815–1861* (Westport, Conn.: Greenwood Press, 1974), 94–119.

18. Eighty-eight percent of the Whig commoners voted to table the proannexation resolution; all of the Democrats opposed it. *HJ, 1844–45*, 538–39.

ture and opposed the acquisition of new territory. Whigs reminded voters that in 1844 they had warned that the annexation of Texas would inevitably lead to war with Mexico and that subsequent events had borne them out. When the Whig legislature appropriated $10,000 to clothe and equip the state's troops in Mexico, it added a preamble that declared that the United States was at war "by the action of the Executive and the subsequent sanction of Congress."[19]

Even after David Wilmot introduced his proviso, which would exclude slaves from any territory acquired from Mexico, the parties in North Carolina still continued to perceive the territorial issue as not only a sectional question but one of expansion versus no expansion. Whigs contended that if the country took no territory from Mexico in what their party deemed an unjust war, then southerners would not suffer the slights and dishonor of the proviso. Whig congressman James Graham declared: "We want no more new foreign country with Abolition Prohibitions and restriction upon southern people." As late as October, 1848—months after Mexico ceded the modern Southwest to the United States—a Whig meeting in Cabarrus County declared itself opposed to the acquisition because it was "not required by our people for any purposes whatever, [was] inconsistent with the objects of our free institutions, and . . . [would be] a fruitful and interminable source of sectional jealousies and prejudices between the slave and non-slaveholding States of the Union." In November, the Whig Charlotte *Journal* claimed that the Whig candidate, Zachary Taylor, was "one who does not go for the miscalled extension of the area of freedom, but who is for preserving intact, inviolate, the liberties we have heretofore enjoyed. One who would rather preserve this Union entire, than to see patches of foreign soil annexed at the risk of its dismemberment."[20]

However, by the time the *Journal* editor wrote and Cabarrus Whigs assembled, the political question was no longer one of whether the country should expand but of whether slavery would be permitted into the newly acquired territories. Although Whigs never tired of reminding Democrats that, if Henry Clay's views on Texas had been adopted, sectional strife over slavery in the territories would have been avoided, the actual acquisition of new territory deprived Whigs of the anti-expansion issue.

The end of the war compelled politicians to address the question of slavery in the territories directly. The northern effort to exclude slaves

19. Joel H. Silbey, *The Shrine of Party: Congressional Voting Behavior, 1841–1852* (Pittsburgh: University of Pittsburgh Press, 1967), 186; Clarence Clifford Norton, *The Democratic Party in Ante-Bellum North Carolina* (Chapel Hill: University of North Carolina Press, 1930), 112.

20. James Graham to Samuel F. Patterson, January 17, 1847, in Jones and Patterson Papers, SHC; Charlotte *Journal*, September 6, November 10, 1848.

alarmed North Carolinians because they viewed it, first, as the initial step in the drive toward the abolition of slavery in the states and, second, as a deprivation of southern rights in the nation and hence a denial of southern equality. Democrats occasionally argued (though Whigs never did) that the pressures of a growing slave population and of the slave economy required the acquisition of new slave territory, but this was a minor theme in their rhetorical assault on the Wilmot Proviso. More often, Democrats viewed any effort to exclude slavery from the territories as the first attempt of northerners to destroy slavery where it already existed. Accepting a nineteenth-century version of the "domino theory," they argued that if the South permitted Congress to exclude slaves from the territories, the North would then press for the abolition of slavery in the District of Columbia, for the destruction of the interstate slave trade, and ultimately for the abolition of slavery in the states. Southerners could not permit that first step to be taken by Congress, or else disaster would ensue. "A small leak will, in time, sink a ship," the Raleigh *Standard* declared, "and these attacks upon rights and property, no matter what the purpose apparently may be, must ultimately, if continued, result in our ruin here at home." Another writer put it more succinctly: "One aggression will follow another and another, until the sunny fields of the South will be given up to the curse of Northern fanaticism."[21]

Whigs also denounced the Wilmot Proviso as unjust and feared that it was only the beginning of a comprehensive northern attack on slavery and southern rights, but they were willing to give northerners another chance to prove their good will. That chance would come when and if politicians debated the status of slavery in the District of Columbia. Whigs and Democrats alike agreed that if northerners continued their attack on slavery, they would do it over the question of abolition in the District. On that question, Whigs said, they would take their stand. If northerners in Congress sought to abolish slavery in the District—in a place where it already existed—they would prove once and for all that they intended ultimately to destroy slavery in the states. The *Register* argued that abolition in the District would signal "the beginning of a regular and systematic attempt to interfere with the *Institution* of Slavery in the States" and warned that it "would as surely be followed by a dissolution of the Union, as the explosion of a powder magazine would take effect from the lighted match of the incendiary."[22] Both parties, then, were determined to protect slavery, and

21. Raleigh *Standard*, December 27, 1848, May 23, 1849; Charlotte *Hornet's Nest*, n.d., quoted in Raleigh *Standard*, October 3, 1849. Also see Raleigh *Standard*, June 20, July 1, August 31, and October 17, 1849.
22. Raleigh *Register*, October 24, September 10, and January 2, 1850.

both believed that continued northern aggression would destroy the Union, but they differed about what action would constitute an imminent threat to slavery.

However, the conflict over the territorial issue was more than a dispute over slavery in the territories or even in the states. Throughout the debate on slavery, southerners and northerners defended their own freedom and equality and the constitutional Union that protected them. Just as politicians advocated constitutional reforms and defended slavery on the grounds that they promoted white freedom and equality, so did they defend the right of slaveholders to take their slaves into the territories.

North Carolina Democrats believed that the exclusion of slavery from the territories denied southerners their equality and threatened their liberty. If northerners could deny slaveholders the right to take their slaves into territories, they would mark southerners as inferior partners in the nation and would also deprive slaveholders of the right to carry their property with them—a denial of one of the basic rights of all citizens. The nation had been dedicated to the principle of equality and freedom for all whites, yet now northerners threatened those principles. By excluding slavery from the territories, the Raleigh *Standard* complained, "the South shall be debarred from an equal participation in territory belonging to all the States and common property of the Union" and this would "destroy the great principle of equality between the States, which lies at the foundation of the Constitution, and ultimately break up the Confederacy itself." White southerners were free men and would not allow northerners to abrogate their rights or treat them as inferiors. A meeting in coastal Beaufort County in March, 1850, declared that "they [*i.e.*, southerners] will maintain their Constitutional rights at all hazards, no matter who may preach submission." To submit to violations of those rights would make white southerners no more than slaves: "They are not yet prepared for political slavery, or for the horrors that would result from that condition." The same month, a Democratic editor asserted that North Carolinians "are determined to maintain the honor of their State, and to defend, if necessary, their threatened liberties."[23]

Whigs also demanded that southerners be treated as they deserved—as the equals of northern whites. By excluding slavery from the territories, northerners would declare southerners their inferiors. If northerners refused to treat southerners as equals, the Union would not survive. As one Whig editor asserted, "even in private associations for trade, where the object is mere gain, men of spirit will not endure allusions to the inequality

23. Raleigh *Standard*, October 6, 1847, April 3, 1850, March 27, 1850.

of advantages amongst the partners, but rather separate at any pecuniary sacrifice." Southerners would rather leave the Union than accept a political status in it that seemed little better than slavery.[24]

Although politicians concurred that the Wilmot Proviso posed a threat to slavery and to southern rights, they disagreed about whether the proviso was unconstitutional or simply unjust. Democrats contended that it was unconstitutional. Adopting the arguments of John C. Calhoun, they contended that the territories were the common property of all the states and that therefore the federal government did not have the power to prevent all citizens of any of the states from taking their property, including slaves, into them.[25]

Whigs generally accepted the constitutionality of the proviso but denounced it as unjust. They argued that because the Constitution gave the federal government the right to make "all needful rules and regulations" for the territories, the federal government had the power either to establish or to exclude slavery from the territories. Whigs said that the South should simply accept that fact and defend its right to bring slaves into the territories on the grounds of justice. They argued that the proviso, though constitutional, was "most grossly unjust" and wanted to defeat it "by uniting the whole South upon the grounds of its injustice, waiving the Constitutional view of the question."[26]

The dispute became heated as each party accused the other of undermining southern unity. If only their opponents would accept a proper constitutional view of the matter, partisans thought, then a united South could repel the northern threat. The seriousness with which they approached these constitutional questions was derived from two sources, one political, the other ideological. Politicians always need to distinguish themselves from their opponents in order to convey to voters the idea that there is a reason to go to the polls to vote for a particular man and party. For southern politicians to be successful, they needed not only prove themselves ardent defenders of southern rights but to gain the sole political credit for defending the South. Whigs were willing to defend the South only on their own terms and Democrats only on theirs. The different constitutional interpretations also expressed the broader differences of opinion about the constitutional powers of the federal government. As we have seen, on a host of issues, including the tariff, aid to internal improvements,

24. Raleigh *Register*, March 12, 1847.

25. Raleigh *Standard*, October 6, 1847, April 3, March 27, and February 6, 1850.

26. Raleigh *Register*, February 6, 1850, March 12, 1847. Also see the statement of U.S. Senator Willie P. Mangum, quoted in Joseph Carlyle Sitterson, *The Secession Movement in North Carolina* (Chapel Hill: University of North Carolina Press, 1939), 67.

and a national bank, Whigs were much more willing than Democrats to see the central government exercise substantial positive power.

★

Soon the introduction of congressional bills to organize the newly acquired territories forced state politicians to translate their fears and their constitutional theories into actions, and their behavior revealed how the structure of state and national politics shaped North Carolina's response to the territorial crisis. The initial confrontation about the territorial issue came not over the Mexican Cession, however, but over the Oregon Territory, a most unlikely place.

In 1846, a bill to organize the territory of Oregon was introduced in Congress and immediately became part of the congressional debate over slavery in the territories. Nobody expected slaveowners to move to Oregon, but southerners objected on principle to that part of the bill which excluded slavery from the territory. Under prodding from President James K. Polk, some southern Democrats voted for the bill on the grounds that Oregon lay north of the 36° 30' Missouri Compromise line. Ultimately, enough of them voted for it to pass it in 1848.

The enactment of the Oregon bill with its clause excluding slavery hurt southern interests. The bill was one of the few bargaining chips that southerners had in their negotiations with northerners about the territories, and if they had further delayed its passage, they would have been in a position to demand greater concessions from the North than they received in 1850. The Oregon bill was also the first skirmish in the conflict over the exclusion of slavery from the Mexican Cession. Whig Congressman David Outlaw wrote to his wife that the bill was "important as manifesting the determination of the Northern States, to appropriate the whole of our late acquisitions for themselves."[27]

The existence of party competition in the state tended to heighten the negative response of North Carolinians to the Oregon bill. When Democratic President Polk signed the bill, North Carolina Whigs, seeing an opportunity to gain an edge on their Democratic competitors, attacked the bill as hostile to southern interests. By signing the bill, Polk "thereby surrendered the hold which the South had, to force the North into a fair compromise in reference to all the Territories."[28]

Polk's signing of the bill and the support for it that he received from North Carolina Democrats reinforced the feeling that Whigs had had all

27. Potter, *Impending Crisis*, 65–67, 75–76; David Outlaw to Emily Outlaw, August 1, 1848, in Outlaw Papers.
28. Raleigh *Register*, August 23, 1848.

along that only they were true to southern interests and that Democrats would abandon the South for the sake of their party. The Whig party, its supporters said, admitted that Congress had the power to exclude slavery from the territories, but it was "opposed to the exercise of this power." Their opposition to the exercise of that power, they claimed, proved the fidelity of their commitment to the South. Democrats, though, had claimed congressional exclusion unconstitutional, yet that power "*was exercised* by a locofoco President."[29]

Throughout the debate over Oregon, Whigs portrayed themselves as the only true defenders of slavery and Democrats as abettors of the abolitionists and free-soilers. Despite their reputation for moderation on national questions, Whigs assumed a more extreme position in this instance and, in so doing, heightened popular awareness of the apparent injustices that northerners were perpetrating on the South.

There was another side to the Oregon story—one that reveals the ways that parties mitigated sectional tensions. While interparty competition within a state often tended to increase southern sensitivity on the slavery question, the ties of the state organizations to national parties served to moderate the views of the state parties. For example, the state Democratic organ, the Raleigh *Standard*—despite its deserved reputation as one of the state's most outspoken defenders of southern rights—softened its rhetoric on the Oregon question. Since the national party had taken a stand on the issue and the Democratic president had supported the bill and then signed it, for the *Standard* to attack the bill would be for it to attack the party— something it was loathe to do. As a result, the newspaper used a number of specious arguments to defend the bill. First, it contended that the Oregon bill was of no practical importance to the South because no slaveholder would ever contemplate settling there. Even if a slaveholder wanted to take his slaves to Oregon, residents there were adamantly opposed to slavery. Second, the newspaper said, southern congressmen who supported the bill were merely adhering to the Missouri Compromise. The *Standard* repeatedly pointed out that Oregon sat far north of the 36° 30' compromise line.[30]

There were many inconsistencies in the *Standard*'s argument. Less than six weeks before, it had argued that "the first step is, to yield the power [to exclude slavery from the territories] to Congress, . . . and the next is, *to cease* to question the expediency of its exercise." By supporting the Oregon bill, North Carolina Democrats accepted implicitly, just as Whigs charged, the constitutionality of congressional authority over slavery in the federal territories and the actual exercise of that authority. The

29. *Ibid.*, August 29, 1849.
30. Raleigh *Standard*, August 30, 1848.

Standard's argument that Oregon should be free because it lay north of the 36° 30' parallel was irrelevant because the compromise line applied only to the territory that comprised the Louisiana Purchase and therefore had nothing to do with the exclusion of slavery from Oregon.[31]

The *Standard*'s inconsistencies were important, not because they proved that Democrats were two-faced, but rather because they illustrated how state organizations treated issues over which they disagreed with the national party. If the *Standard*'s editor, William W. Holden, had had no ties to the national party, he undoubtedly would have attacked the Oregon bill as an unconstitutional exercise of power by Congress. But his position as editor of the Democratic party's organ in Raleigh forbade such a course. Since his success was bound up in the success of his party, any criticism he would have to offer of the national party would have to be muted, or else party unity and party victory would be imperiled.

★

The Oregon issue, though significant, was overshadowed in 1848 by the presidential election campaign, which again disclosed how state party competition exacerbated sectional tensions, while national party ties mitigated them. No southern politician would, or could afford to, support a presidential candidate openly committed to the Wilmot Proviso, but both parties found candidates whom they could defend in the South.

The Whig candidate, Zachary Taylor, had not been the first choice of the North Carolina Whigs. At the national party convention, the state's delegation gave more support to Henry Clay, the traditional Whig standard-bearer, than did any southern state delegation but Kentucky and Maryland. North Carolina Whigs had built a majority in the state around traditional issues and saw no need for an apolitical war hero as the party's candidate. Nevertheless, Taylor suited them well. As a military hero, he had a broad national appeal, and as a Louisiana planter, he attracted support in the South. North Carolina's Whigs could argue cogently that a southern planter would never permit the disgraceful Wilmot Proviso to become law.

Democrats, too, portrayed their candidate, Lewis Cass, as a defender of southern rights and as an opponent of the Wilmot Proviso. They also had something more—Cass's Nicholson letter, which argued that Congress should not deal with the question of slavery in the territories but should leave it to the people living there to decide whether they wanted slavery.[32] Democrats contended that Cass, a man of principle, would veto the Wilmot Proviso and give the South what it desired, "repose and non-interference," but that Taylor, sharing the traditional Whig hostility to the presidential

31. *Ibid.*, July 12, 1848.
32. Cooper, *Politics of Slavery*, 244–58.

veto, would sign the proviso. Taylor's election, Democrats argued, threatened the destruction of slavery, whereas Cass's election promised the South peace.[33]

Throughout the campaign, as Democrats proclaimed Cass the better southern-rights candidate, the northern wing of the party asserted that he was the better free-soil man. North Carolina Democrats were aware of the northern strategy, but they willingly averted their eyes for the sake of political victory. An excellent example of how Democrats rationalized their party's ambiguous stand on the territorial issue is the case of James C. Dobbin, Democratic leader from Fayetteville and later secretary of the navy under Franklin Pierce. In a letter to Georgia Democrat Howell Cobb, Dobbin wrote that he "struggled hard to prove Cass orthodox on the slavery question, and I would not have done [so] had I suspected him." He believed that Cass's Nicholson letter was "certainly liberal and magnanimous for a Northern man" and interpreted the letter to mean that the people of a territory could not legislate on slavery until they had applied for statehood—a delay that would give slaveowners a chance to move to those territories and establish slavery there. To allow the first territorial legislature to rule on the slavery question would inevitably lead to slavery's exclusion because the first settlers would be nonslaveholders. Dobbin was satisfied simply because Cass had *not contradicted* his own interpretation: "I do not think Cass has *publicly*—certainly not in his Nicholson letter—expressed any opinion contravening my position. . . . He does not say that he thinks the Territorial Legislature can prohibit it. I hope he will not say so. Because it may never in all probability become a practical question on which he as President could act. Yet the expression of such an opinion would prejudice him in the south with many, very many." Dobbin and virtually every other partisan were willing to go far to accommodate their northern brethren.[34]

Although Whigs knew that their fellow northern partisans were playing with the same two-faced game, they had less to rationalize (or so it seemed). After all, Taylor was a southerner, and Whigs grabbed every opportunity to remind voters that Taylor was a Louisiana planter and Cass a northerner. The Raleigh *Register* asked voters: "Can Gen. TAYLOR, a Southern . . . prove recreant to the institutions of those among whom he has lived, sacrifice his own and *your* interests? . . . Or is it safer to trust Gen.

33. Raleigh *Standard*, October 18, 1848; also see issue of August 30, 1848.

34. James C. Dobbin to Howell Cobb, June 15, 1848, in Ulrich B. Phillips (ed.), *The Correspondence of Robert Toombs, Alexander H. Stephens, and Howell Cobb,* in *Annual Report of the American Historical Association for the Year 1911* (2 vols.; Washington, D.C.: Government Printing Office, 1913), II, 108–109.

CASS—who is a northern man, with Northern ideas about the matter—who is proclaimed by his neighbors the uncompromising advocate of free soil—who once expressed a desire to VOTE *for the Wilmot Proviso?*" To Whigs, Taylor was the candidate for southern rights and Cass the candidate for northern aggression.

To Democrats, the roles of the candidates were reversed, but some Democrats in North Carolina were apparently convinced by the Whig argument, because many refused to go to the polls. Only a few months earlier, the gubernatorial candidates had finished in a nearly dead heat; now, Taylor won 55.2 percent of the state's vote. The Democratic vote had dropped 5,910 since August, while the Whig vote increased by 1,518.[35] After Taylor captured the state and the election, North Carolina Democrats attributed his state victory to his southern ties.

★

After North Carolina Whigs had helped elect a southern Whig to the presidency, they felt assured that southern rights would be protected, and they acted accordingly over the next several years. Their faith in Taylor's ability to resolve the sectional conflict was challenged quickly in late 1848 by John C. Calhoun, who once again sought to unite southerners in a coalition that transcended partisanship. However, whereas North Carolina Democrats had earlier worried little about Oregon because they had a southern Democratic president, now North Carolina Whigs felt secure with a southern Whig about to move into the White House. This circumstance doomed Calhoun's plan to failure. Most Whigs stayed away from the meeting and then denounced the Southern Address that it produced. In the end, the address became a southern Democratic manifesto. As David Potter has observed, Calhoun's effort for southern unity foundered "because the southern Whigs had no incentive to support it. . . . In their hour of victory they saw no reason to join their vanquished opponents." In addition, since from the first the meeting had been dominated by Democrats, for Whigs to support it would make them appear as secondary players on the political stage—an obviously intolerable situation for any politician seeking office. This is not to say that North Carolina Whigs were insensible to the apparently dangerous threats of the North; rather, Whigs retained their campaign-expressed faith that Taylor was good for the South and would protect southern interests.[36]

At about the same time that Calhoun was maneuvering in Washington,

35. Raleigh *Register*, October 21, 1848.
36. Potter, *Impending Crisis*, 85; Joel H. Silbey, "John C. Calhoun and the Limits of Southern Congressional Unity, 1841–1850," *Historian*, XXX (1967), 58–71.

North Carolina's legislators were also debating the territorial issue. Walter L. Steele, one of a few leading Whigs then setting out on a road that would soon lead them into the Democratic party, introduced a series of resolutions on the territorial issue. Reiterating Calhoun's arguments, the resolutions stated "that the Territories of the United States belong to the several States composing this Union, and are held by them as their joint and common property." Therefore, "Congress had no right to . . . do any act whatever, . . . by which any of them shall be deprived of its full and equal right in any Territory of the United States." Any attempt by Congress to "deprive the citizens of any of the States, from emigrating with their property" to the territories "would . . . be a violation of the Constitution . . . and would tend directly to subvert the Union itself." On a party-line vote, Whigs, with a narrow majority in the House, referred the resolutions to a special four-member committee composed of two Democrats and two Whigs.[37]

Later in the session, the committee reported new resolutions that received virtually unanimous approval. They declared "that the citizens of each state are entitled to equal rights," that the U.S. Constitution contained distinct and ample guarantees of the rights of slaveholders, and "that we view with a deep concern and alarm, the constant aggressions on the rights of the slaveholder, by certain reckless politicians of the North." The resolutions also denounced any future attempt to exclude slavery from the territories or to abolish it in the District of Columbia as "not only an act of gross injustice and wrong, but [representing] the exercise of power contrary to the true meaning and spirit of the Constitution"; and they declared that the extension of the Missouri Compromise line to the Pacific Ocean would be a suitable compromise and that "the people of North Carolina of all parties, are devotedly attached to the Union of these States."[38]

For the most part, the resolutions were simply statements about southern rights to which virtually all southerners agreed. On two of the resolutions, though, there was sharp partisan disagreement that expressed itself in the preliminary voting. Conflict over the fourth resolution focused on the constitutionality of congressional efforts to exclude slavery from the territories. A few Whigs joined a unanimous Democratic party to defeat a Whig effort to delete the clause and state that such congressional action would be unjust. The vote expressed the continuing partisan differences over the constitutionality of the Wilmot Proviso. In the end, Whigs were

37. *HJ*, *1848–49*, 355–56.
38. *Ibid.*, 727–32; *SJ*, *1848–49*, 211–12.

able to vote for the clause because, unlike the Steele resolutions that explicitly called the Proviso unconstitutional, it fudged the constitutional question. In addition, once the series of resolutions was finally presented for a vote, Whigs could do little but vote for it, whatever their misgivings, lest they appear to be abandoning southern interests.[39]

Democrats faced a similar problem on the last resolution, which vigorously asserted the citizenry's deep commitment to the Union. Added to the committee's report by Whig efforts, the resolution made many Democrats uneasy because it seemed to vitiate the impact of the other resolutions. Although most Democrats opposed it in a preliminary vote in the House, a majority supported it on the final vote, and only three Senate Democrats opposed it in that body. Like the Whigs who found it difficult to appear to vote against southern rights, Democrats found it equally difficult to appear to vote against the Union.[40]

These resolutions expressed the popular belief that northern actions endangered the South. Whigs and Democrats alike insisted that partisanship be ignored in the united struggle for southern rights. Whigs declared themselves in favor of "elevating this question of Southern rights above the struggles of the party." Democrats, too, said that the defense of the South had nothing to do with parties.

Despite their disclaimers, however, North Carolina's politicians continued to view the territorial crisis through the prism of partisanship. Democrats perceived themselves as the simple exponents of southern rights and the Whigs as partisan schemers willing to abandon those rights for the spoils of office under the Taylor administration. Whigs, too, perceived themselves as the only true devotees of the South's rights. They claimed that if the Democrats would only unite on the Whig platform's view of the Wilmot Proviso, the South would be safe, but Whigs believed that Democrats were not truly interested in defending the South, only in exacerbating sectional tensions in order to tear down Zachary Taylor and the Whig party.[41]

Whigs and Democrats continued their battle to prove each other faithless to the South as the congressional elections of 1849 approached. Elsewhere, the position of southern Whigs was shaken by Democrats who charged Taylor with undermining southern interests, but in North Carolina Whigs remained firm in their support for him. The constancy of North Carolina Whigs was partly a function of their continued success at a time

39. Eighty-seven percent of the Whig commoners voted to delete the clause on the constitutionality of the Wilmot Proviso. *HJ, 1848–49*, 649, 729–30; *SJ, 1848–49*, 221–24.

40. *HJ, 1848–49*, 725–26, 731–32; *SJ, 1848–49*, 262.

41. Raleigh *Standard*, July 11, 1849; Raleigh *Register*, June 27, 1849.

when their party was losing elections throughout the rest of the region. In much of the South, Whigs suffered serious setbacks in the elections and blamed their defeats on the president's policies, but North Carolina's Whig delegation remained strong. In 1847, a Whig legislature had redistricted the state to ensure a substantial Whig majority in the state's congressional delegation, so in 1849 Whigs won six of the state's nine seats. Therefore, the state's Whigs shared none of the sense of impending doom felt by other southern Whigs. A month after the August election, the Raleigh *Register* denounced southern Democrats for "laboring in their dirty vocation, abetting our common enemy, and zealously doing their part to paralyze the arm of a Southern President and render him powerless to protect our rights."[42]

Zachary Taylor announced his plan for the territories in his December message to Congress. In a brief paragraph buried in the middle of the document, he informed Congress that he expected Californians and New Mexicans to apply for admission to the Union as states; assuming that the new state constitutions would provide for republican governments, he said he would urge Congress to admit them. Thus, the crisis over the territories would be resolved by skipping the territorial stage entirely.[43]

Taylor's plan might have resolved the territorial issue; in fact, a number of southern Whigs had endorsed it earlier in the year. However, a combination of Taylor's patronage policy, which provided offices for Taylor supporters at the expense of regular Whigs, and the losses in southern congressional elections had left many southern Whigs unhappy with the administration. Michael F. Holt has recently argued that these Whigs, needing an alternative policy with which to contest Taylor's hegemony in the party, rallied around Henry Clay's more general compromise plan. Holt has pointed out that Clay's plan was not far different from Taylor's; it, too, had a decided free-soil slant. Clay proposed that California be admitted as a free state; that the rest of the Mexican Cession be organized without reference to slavery; that a new, stronger fugitive-slave law be enacted; that Texas concede New Mexico's claim in their boundary dispute, and that in return the U.S. government would assume the bonded debt Texas had accumulated as an independent country. He also provided that slave depots in Washington, D.C., then used for the interstate slave trade, be banned, but that Congress forbid by statute the abolition of slavery in the District

42. *Cf.* Cooper, *Politics of Slavery*, 278; Clarence Clifford Norton, *The Democratic Party in Ante-Bellum North Carolina, 1835–1861* (Chapel Hill: University of North Carolina Press, 1930), 145–47; Raleigh *Register*, September 8, 1849.

43. James D. Richardson (comp.), *A Compilation of the Messages and Papers of the Presidents, 1789–1897* (10 vols.; Washington, D.C.: Government Printing Office, 1896–99), V, 18–19.

without the consent of Maryland and District citizens and without com-
pensation for slaveholders. On one point, Whigs criticized Clay's proposal.
His initial plan for the territories, though it eliminated the Wilmot Proviso, would have had the same result as the Proviso because it assumed
that Mexico's earlier abolition of slavery applied to those territories. But
despite the plan's free-soil slant, North Carolina Whigs blithely assumed
that the Mexican prohibition would be eliminated. Although Clay's and
Taylor's plans had much in common, the absence in Clay's proposal of the
Wilmot Proviso or of any other explicit prohibition of slavery in the new
territories, and the provision for a tougher fugitive-slave law, offered concessions to the South that were lacking in the Taylor plan.[44]

In North Carolina, politicians of both parties demanded that the North
yield and threatened dire consequences if it did not. The Whig editor of the
Fayetteville *Observer* declared that because he was a staunch Unionist he
had "a right to tell our Northern Brethren that 'THE UNION IS IN PERIL'. And
further, that they reckon without their host when they suppose that there
will be any division in the South on this question, if the South be driven to
extremities by the injustice of the North." The Raleigh *Register* asserted
that "the South will never submit to a state of vassalage." Democrats also
raised the specter of disunion. While Congress debated the compromise
proposals in March, 1850, the Raleigh *Standard* defiantly declared that if
the South wanted to separate from the Union, there was nothing that the
North could do about it: "No power which the North could muster . . .
could subdue millions of brave men, fighting on their own soil in defense
of their social and political rights, and for the preservation and security of
eighteen hundred millions worth of slave property."[45]

Although Whigs spoke with as much vehemence as the Democrats in
demanding concessions from the North, during the months of debate over
the compromise they acted more moderately than their opponents. To
some extent this was due to the greater conservatism of the Whig party.
Earlier in the 1840s, their opposition to territorial expansion as a means of
easing sectional strife was clearly a less potentially disruptive policy than
that of Democratic expansionism. Yet that apparent conservatism had not
restrained their sectional appeals for Taylor's candidacy or their denunciations of the Oregon territorial bill. The most significant moderating force
was the tie of the state Whig party to the national party and the national
administration.

44. Michael F. Holt, *The Political Crisis of the 1850s* (New York: John Wiley & Sons, 1978),
73–84.
45. Fayetteville *Observer*, December 24, 1849; Raleigh *Register*, February 6, 1850; Raleigh
Standard, January 16, 1850.

Whigs had just regained the White House, and they did not want to see their party rent by factionalism as it had been under John Tyler's administration. So the state's Whig press went to great lengths to avoid conflict with the new administration. Many Whigs supported the admission of California as a free state on the noninterventionist grounds that the people of a state had a right to decide whether or not they wanted slavery in their state. The Greensboro *Patriot* believed Taylor's message "will commend itself to . . . *the American people*." When Henry Clay offered his plan of compromise, Whigs saw it not so much as an alternative to Taylor's plan as an expansion of it. Hence, they could easily continue to support Clay's plan *and* the president. Even after Clay openly broke with the president on May 21, 1850, and congressional Whigs became aware that Taylor might veto Clay's plan if it passed in Congress, North Carolina's Whigs continued to see the two men's plans as eminently reconcilable. As late as mid-June, the party's state convention adopted resolutions praising Clay's compromise proposals and reaffirming their faith in President Taylor. Perhaps the actual veto of compromise measures by Taylor would have driven off North Carolina Whigs, but up to the moment of Taylor's death on July 9 they acknowledged no split in the party. Whig congressman David Outlaw might write to his wife: "The South has no influence with the Cabinet, or with the Administration. It is in the hands of the North." But Whigs back home recognized no such occurrence. Historians have not generally recognized that the split between Taylor and Clay was very much a split in the congressional party and had little effect in the South. North Carolina Whigs acknowledged the crisis of 1850, but they assumed that a Whig president and Whig congressional leaders would resolve it.[46]

North Carolina Democrats, not bound by a national party position on the crisis or enamored with Clay's plan, which they considered a *Whig* plan and one which offered the South too little, sought a southern Democratic solution to the dispute. They denounced Clay's proposals and demanded that the South act if it could obtain no substantial concessions from the North. Therefore, they, along with other southern Democrats, supported the Mississippi legislature's call for a southern convention to meet in Nashville in June. Of the convention, the *Standard* wrote: "This is no party question. It comes home to us all—to our firesides, to our dearest rights, and to our highest interests with a force which we could not des-

46. Raleigh *Register*, February 27, 1850; Greensboro *Patriot*, January 5, 1850; Potter, *Impending Crisis*, 103–104; Raleigh *Register*, February 27, 1850; David Outlaw to Emily Outlaw, June 24, 1850, in Outlaw Papers. Also see circular of James M. Edney for the Asheville *Messenger*, June 1, 1850, enclosed in Henry W. Miller to Griffith J. McRee, July 2, 1850, in Griffith J. McRee Papers, SHC. For other southern states, see Cooper, *Politics of Slavery*, 286.

regard—if we would." But only a few months later the *Standard* was accusing the Whigs of opposing the convention for partisan purposes, "relying upon the party prejudices of the Whig masses to bear them out."[47]

Whigs did view the Nashville Convention as a party question. Although they affirmed their commitment to the preservation of southern rights, Whigs saw no need for southerners to meet in convention. With one of their party in the White House and another leading the compromise effort in Congress, they expected that a suitable settlement would emerge. Therefore, they deemed a convention unnecessary and concluded that the only motive Democrats could have for advocating it was a desire to destroy the Union. One Whig likened the Nashville Convention to the Hartford Convention of 1814 and asserted that the organizers of the meeting were plotting disunion. Such charges destroyed Democratic hopes that North Carolina would send a bipartisan delegation to Nashville; few Whigs were interested. It should be remembered that the parties in 1850 remained deeply divided over questions of state constitutional reform and the proper role of government in the society. They could hardly be expected to agree with one another on the proper course of action during the crisis.[48]

Whig criticism of the convention also placed the Democrats on the defensive and forced them to reaffirm their loyalty to the Union. Democrats asserted that they supported the convention "for the sake of the Union and of Southern rights." In this way, Whig opposition kept Democrats from assuming a more extreme position on southern rights. Whigs successfully changed the issue from a debate over the proper way to unite the South in defense of southern rights to a debate over whether the ultimate goal of the convention was disunion. On those new grounds, Democrats were bound to lose, since Unionist sentiment, even among the more extreme southern-rights Democrats, remained strong in North Carolina. As the convention became tainted with disloyalty, state Democratic efforts to obtain the selection of delegates to Nashville flagged, and as prospects for a compromise improved in the late spring, Democrats withdrew their support from the convention. In the end, North Carolina did not even send a delegation to the meeting. Much of the credit or blame for the decision of North Carolina's Democrats must be given to the state's two-party system. The Whigs' national party ties had solidified their faith that a compromise would be reached, and conflict between the parties at the state level prevented united state action.[49]

47. Raleigh *Standard*, January 16, March 27, 1850.
48. Raleigh *Register*, February 23, 1850; Sitterson, *Secession Movement*, 61–62.
49. Raleigh *Standard*, February 6, 1850.

As interest in the Nashville Convention waned, Democrats began to back off from their earlier hard-line opposition to the compromise proposals. Whigs rejoiced. In late May, the *Standard* declared that although it abhorred many of the provisions of the compromise, it would accept the plan as a final settlement of the slavery question: "Though the South loses by these measures, she may gain repose." As long as the South would be left alone by the North, the Democrats would tolerate the arrangement. The final compromise, which passed in September as separate bills and was quickly signed into law by the new president, Millard Fillmore, was a bit more to the Democrats' liking because the territorial bills included the Democratic plan of popular sovereignty. Moreover, the Texas bill held out for southerners the possibility that Texas might ultimtely be divided into as many as five slave states. But for North Carolinians the compromise still bore a Whig imprint; Democrats accepted it grudgingly, while Whigs were delighted. The Greensboro *Patriot* asserted that "the great conservative mass of the people enjoy a deep feeling of satisfaction at the settlement of questions which have so long disturbed the quiet and threatened the integrity of the Union."[50]

Of all the provisions of the compromise, southerners were most concerned about the enforcement of the fugitive-slave law. This concern was to be expressed in the so-called "Georgia Platform," by which the Georgia state convention had acquiesced in the terms of the compromise. Although the platform demanded that all parts of the compromise be carried out, it was especially adamant that the fugitive law be strictly enforced and warned that any northern repeal of that law would result in disunion. The feelings expressed by Georgians were representative of sentiments throughout much of the South, including North Carolina.

Historians have often acknowledged that southerners perceived the enforcement of the fugitive-slave law as vital to their interests, but they have been less successful in explaining why this was so. Slaves were not actually running away in large enough numbers to cause a significant financial drain, especially in those states not bordering the North, nor were southerners merely drawing an imaginary line and warning northerners not to cross it. Rather, southern concerns were basically constitutional in nature. The fugitive-slave law rested squarely upon Article IV, Section II of the Constitution, which provided that persons bound to service who ran away across state lines had to be returned to their masters. For norther-

50. *Ibid.*, May 22, September 25, 1850; Holt, *Political Crisis*, 85–86; Greensboro *Patriot*, September 21, 1850. On these points, I have benefited from the suggestions of Professors Michael F. Holt and J. Mills Thornton III.

ners to disregard the fugitive-slave law would be for them to ignore the Constitution. And if northerners could trample on the Constitution in this instance, what would prevent them from doing the same to other of its provisions and from eventually destroying the rights of southerners? The end result would be the untrammeled domination of the country by a northern majority and the enslavement of southerners to the will of the North. So when, in the weeks after the passage of the compromise, northerners spoke loudly about resisting the law or repealing it, Whigs and Democrats alike were infuriated. The Whig Fayetteville *Observer* declared: "Let them cease their violations of the Constitution—let them faithfully execute the laws for your protection, or dissolution must ensue. The repeal of the Fugitive Bill or a refusal to execute it, will put an end to all division among the Southern people." Democrats also warned that if northerners did not return fugitives to the South, then the South would leave the Union.[51]

★

Although the parties agreed that northern failure to abide by the compromise would meet with resistance, they disagreed about the mode of resistance. Most Democrats accepted Congressman William Ashe's assertion that "unless some resource for protection is acknowledged to exist in the Sovereign States to shield them alike from wanton violations of the Federal compact—the destiny of the south is made up and sealed. That resource is the right of secession." Most Whigs, however, denied the right of secession and argued that southerners could only resist northern oppression through revolution. One party editor contended that "whenever that Government becomes destructive of those ends for which it was established, intolerably oppressive, and utterly regardless of the rights and happiness of the people of North Carolina, we shall be in favor of throwing off such government, and establishing new safe-guards for our future security and happiness. . . . We shall call [it] by its right name—we shall call it REVOLUTION and make up our minds to abide the consequences."[52]

Whigs believed that Democrats advocated the right of secession in order to prepare the people for disunion. They had suggested the same thing

51. Cooper, *Politics of Slavery*, 307–308; Potter, *Impending Crisis*, 128–29. For one historian who has recognized the ideological significance of the fugitive law issue, see J. Mills Thornton III, *Politics and Power in a Slave Society: Alabama, 1800–1860* (Baton Rouge: Louisiana State University Press, 1978), 448. Fayetteville *Observer*, October 22, 1850; Raleigh *Standard*, September 11, 1850.

52. William S. Ashe to Thomas D. McDowell, December 20, 1850, in Thomas D. McDowell Papers, SHC; Raleigh *Register*, December 14, 1850.

in the fight over the Nashville Convention and years earlier in the dispute over the annexation of Texas. The Fayetteville *Observer* declared that if the state endorsed the right of secession, "the next step . . . would be, to find some pretext, some real or imaginary grievance, to justify the right which, in an unguarded moment, and under false pretenses, had been claimed." The *Register* asserted that "their purpose is practical disunion! *They are aiming at a Southern Confederacy.*" Whig opposition to the right of secession precipitated a year-long debate over the subject. The debate itself focused on three specific problems: resolutions introduced into the state legislature asserting the right of secession, the real threat of secession posed by South Carolina, and the congressional elections of 1851.[53]

In November, 1850, after the new legislature assembled, William B. Shepard, one of the few Whigs in the state who supported the right of secession, introduced resolutions into the Senate that discussed the sectional dispute and declared "that the people of North Carolina, as an organized political community, have the right to secede or withdraw from the Union, whenever a majority of the people in Convention assembled, shall decide a withdrawal necessary to protect their property or persons from unconstitutional and oppressive legislation by the General Government." Democrats either supported Shepard's resolutions or offered others expressing similar sentiments. Whigs declared that no state had the constitutional right to secede, and they introduced resolutions which said that, in the face of intolerable oppression, North Carolinians would resist through revolution. The narrow Democratic majority lost a few Democratic votes every time it tried to pass a resolution in favor of the right of secession and could not carry one. The Whig minority was repeatedly rebuffed by a united Democratic party. In the end, the legislature failed to pass any resolutions on the subject.[54]

The debate took a practical turn as South Carolinians contemplated secession in 1851. Both parties in North Carolina agreed that the passage of the Compromise of 1850 was insufficient grounds for secession. Democrats frequently argued that South Carolina ought to wait for the other southern states, who "possess interests and feelings identical with her own." Secession would only be justified when "all reasonable hope for returning justice must depart, and dishonor and ruin must rise up before us as inevitable." Although the secession of South Carolina was unjustified, Democrats asserted, the federal government had no power to coerce a state back into the Union. This brought the debate back to the beginning: did a state have the right to secede? And if a state seceded, did the federal

53. Fayetteville *Observer*, December 24, 1850; Raleigh *Register*, June 18, 1851.
54. *SJ, 1850–51*, 210–11, 228–38; Sitterson, *Secession Movement*, 74–81.

government have the right to force that state back into the Union? We have seen the Democratic answer to those questions, but the Whig response bears further examination.[55]

Whigs, who by 1861 denied the right of the federal government to co-erce a state back into the Union, and who ardently supported separation from the Union when the Lincoln administration attempted coercion, in 1851 often supported the idea of using force. In September, the Raleigh *Register* declared that if, when a state seceded, "the other States, through the General Government, have no right to say a word against it, but must submit however destructive to those other State[s], . . . [that] will make our Government as but a 'tale told by an idiot'." The Whig congressional candidate in the mountain district, Burgess S. Gaither, declared that he would support the appropriation of money to keep South Carolina in the Union; another Whig candidate, Alfred Dockery, said that he would con-tribute his own money to prevent South Carolina from seceding. In July, 1851, the Fayetteville *Observer* summarized the position of many of the state's Whigs: "Some persons are, or affect to be, horror stricken at the bare thought of compulsion being used towards a State. 'What,' they cry, 'force a sovereign state!' We ask, why not? Are States not bound to perform their engagements? Have States a *right* to do wrong? . . . One sovereign may therefore compel another—and rightfully—to do justice, to perform his engagements, to maintain his plighted faith."[56]

The key to understanding the positions of the *Observer*, the *Register*, Gaither, and Dockery is the Whig party—or more specifically, the Whig ad-ministration in Washington. From the point of view of North Carolina's Whigs, Fillmore, whose administration had vigorously enforced the Fugi-tive Slave Act, proved himself a friend of the South. One Whig editor con-tended that secession was not justified because "the General Government has, throughout this struggle, *stood by the rights of the South*, and vindi-cated the supremacy of the laws." Raleigh leader John H. Bryan wrote that "we are all more and more pleased with the course of the President and he is daily growing into favour in the South. His course is noble and States-manlike and such as a Southern Patriot can sustain."[57] As Whigs, they be-lieved that a Whig administration posed no threat to slavery or to their own freedom. This would not be the case in 1861, when a Republican presi-dent, elected with no votes from North Carolinians, was in power. North

55. Raleigh *Standard*, March 5, May 28, 1851.

56. Raleigh *Register*, September 3, 1851; Raleigh *Standard*, May 28, 1851, June 18, 1851; Fayetteville *Observer*, July 29, 1851.

57. Raleigh *Register*, May 24, 1851; John H. Bryan to William A. Graham, May 29, 1851, in J. G. deRoulhac Hamilton and Max R. Williams (eds.), *The Papers of William Alexander Graham* (6 vols. to date; Raleigh: Department of Archives and History, 1957–), IV, 108.

Carolina Whigs in 1851 accepted the idea of coercing South Carolina because they believed that a satisfactory compromise had been reached in 1850 and, more important, because they trusted the administration only to use force against South Carolina and not also to threaten slavery or white liberty in the other southern states.

The debate over coercion and the right of secession continued through the congressional campaigns of 1851. Whigs claimed that a vote for a Democrat was a vote for the destruction of the Union, whereas a vote for the Whigs was a vote to preserve the Union. Democrats rejoined by arguing that, by asserting the right of secession, the Union would in fact be strengthened; therefore, Union-loving North Carolinians would vote for them. Moreover, a vote for a Whig was a betrayal of southern interests.

Throughout the campaign, Whigs were clearly on the offensive. They felt that they had the Democrats on the run and intended to press their advantage. Democrats were forced over and over again to defend their Unionism. Thomas Clingman, still a Whig but by then cooperating with the Democratic party in his district, was, charged one Whig, "deceiving a large portion of the voters by pretending to be for the Union and Whig policy" and by claiming that he was "a stronger Union man" than his opponent. After Clingman won the election, another Whig was incredulous "that Clingman could so far blind the eyes of our citizens, as to make them think that he was in favour of the Union!" Other advocates of the right of secession were placed in the same position. In their election postmortems, Democrats blamed the Whig victories in six of the nine districts on that party's charges that Democrats supported disunion. Historians have argued that during the crisis of 1850 southerners came to accept the right of secession. Although that may have been true for the Lower South, it was not the case in North Carolina.[58]

By the end of 1851, the pressure of the Whig onslaught had driven Democrats to declare themselves the best friends of the Union and of the compromise. The needs of the national party pushed them further in this direction. Since the presidential campaign of 1848, there had been no need for the party to assume a united position, and, as a result, North Carolina Democrats had taken a more extreme position on the secession issue than they would have otherwise. But as the new presidential election approached, they had to consider the views of their northern allies. William Holden, one of the state's most ardent advocates of southern rights, declared that he would support the compromise "for the sake of peace and

58. Raleigh *Register*, March 8, June 4, 18, July 16, 23, 30, 1851; Raleigh *Standard*, May 28, June 18, July 2, 30, August 27, 1851; Nicholas W. Woodfin to David L. Swain, July 28, 1851, quoted in Sitterson, *Secession Movement*, 88; A. R. Bryan to Thomas I. Lenoir, September 4, 1851, in Lenoir Family Papers, SHC. *Cf.* Potter, *Impending Crisis*, 143.

the Union, and I will stand by it in good faith and in silence." He then added, significantly: "I have no doubt we should gain, as a party, by passing Resolutions through the two Houses expressive of acquiescence in it." After all, he reminded Congressman Abraham W. Venable, "we all live, more or less, by party."[59]

The debate over the acceptance of the compromise, the Nashville Convention, and the right of secession was acted out in virtually every slave state, but what differentiated the experience of North Carolina and the rest of the upper South from that of the lower South was its partisan dimension. Whereas in the lower South, especially in Georgia, Alabama, and Mississippi, it eroded party lines, in North Carolina the debate was enmeshed in party politics. Whigs in much of the lower South had suffered from a chronic minority status, and they envisioned the new Union party, with its promise of attracting some Democrats, as a step toward victory. But, in the mixing of party lines, Whigs lost their own identity. When Union Democrats abandoned the party to return to the Democracy for the presidential election of 1852, not only was the Union party shattered but Whigs in the lower South were never again able to regroup. In North Carolina, Whigs had lost the governorship in 1850 for the first time since the advent of the second party system in 1836, but they remained highly competitive. For them, a Union party offered little other than a loss of their distinct partisan identity. They were willing to talk about a Union party or even to join one, but they clearly regarded it as no more than a Whig party vehicle. So did the Democrats. Union Democrats in parts of the lower South, who were a minority faction in their state parties and whose future prospects were therefore constrained, saw a path to promotion in the Union party. In North Carolina, after years as the minority party, Democrats had finally broken through and attained victory. They were only beginning to enjoy the luxuries of power and patronage, and, because they had won by such a narrow margin, it was imperative that the party remain united. The implications of the parties' decision to fight out the battle over the compromise on partisan grounds were profound. Although party lines in the lower South eroded during this time, in North Carolina the crisis actually strengthened partisan identities.[60]

★

In the presidential election campaign of 1852, both parties sought to prove their allegiance to the compromise and to affirm their devotion to south-

59. William W. Holden to Abraham W. Venable, December 24, 1851, and same to same, February [n.d.], 1851, both in Abraham Watkins Venable Papers, SHC.

60. Holt, *Political Crisis*, 118–19; Cooper, *Politics of Slavery*, 304–10; Thornton, *Politics and Power*, 186–89, 192–99, 353.

ern rights and the Union. Of the two parties, the Whigs clearly faced the greater problems. They had discovered to their delight that Millard Fillmore was committed to carrying out fully the terms of the compromise. For the same reason that southern Whigs liked him, northern Whigs despised him, so his nomination for a full term as president was anything but assured. Throughout 1851 and much of 1852, North Carolina Whigs, in their correspondence and their newspapers, called for Fillmore's nomination.

Even stronger than their desire for Fillmore's success was their concern that General Winfield Scott might be named their party's candidate. On the surface, one might have expected that Scott would have appealed to southern Whigs, since he was a Virginian who had actively supported the compromise effort in 1850. However, because they feared that Scott's most prominent backer, William H. Seward, the antislavery Whig senator from New York, would dominate a Scott administration, they vigorously opposed the general's cause. One of the state's leading Whigs, William A. Graham, prominently mentioned for the vice-presidential nomination, concluded that if Scott won the nomination and made no explicit commitment to the South on the compromise, "he will not get a single Southern State." It would be "ruinous to us at the South."[61]

Scott did receive the party's nomination, but the impact on North Carolina Whiggery was not as ruinous as Graham had feared. To the surprise of some observers, the convention quickly endorsed the compromise as a final settlement of the slavery controversy, so southern Whigs obtained the northern wing's crucial acquiescence in the compromise. Although the delegates from North Carolina stood faithfully behind Fillmore, a few border- and southern-state votes eventually pushed Scott over the top. North Carolinians were unhappy about Scott's nomination, but they delighted in the party's choice of William A. Graham as its vice-presidential candidate and its endorsement of the compromise.

If most North Carolina Whigs were pleased about Graham's nomination and the party platform, they remained leery of Scott. Party leader Henry W. Miller expressed their unease when he declared that if Scott "will place himself right . . . on the Compromise, . . . we can carry the State for him by a large majority." Miller continued:

> I must confess, however, that his silence is doing him injury where I have been, and the attacks of the Locofoco presses are forestalling public opinion and creating a prejudice against him, even amongst Whigs.

61. James W. Bryan to William A. Graham, March 24, 1852, James W. Osborne to Graham, March 25, 1852, John H. Bryan to Graham, April 5, 1852, Graham to James W. Bryan, March 22, 1852, all in Hamilton and Williams (eds.), *Graham Papers*, IV, 265–67, 281, 263.

. . . Unless he puts himself right of the Compromise, he will be beaten by thousands in our State, but *sound on that*, his military fame will give us a theme which will tell on the minds of the people. I cannot sustain any man who is unsound on the Compromise.

Scott never did put himself right on the compromise measures, yet Whigs like Miller supported him vigorously. For the most part, they relied upon William Graham's repeated assurances that Scott was "sound" and could be trusted. For example, two Whigs from Salisbury had decided not to vote for Scott, but they found a letter from Graham "so satisfactory, that they were determined not only to vote, but to use all their influence for Gen. Scott."[62]

The new confidence felt by Miller and most other Whigs was not shared by some. The Wilmington *Commercial* touched off a boomlet for a new Whig ticket headed by Daniel Webster, with Graham reprising his role as running mate. A sharp rebuke from Graham squelched that effort, but it did not change the sentiments of other dissatisfied Whigs. Longtime Whig leaders Kenneth Rayner and Congressman Thomas L. Clingman declined to support Scott, and Clingman came out for the Democratic candidate, Franklin Pierce, as a man safer for the South. The defections of these men and of a few others were important but should not be exaggerated because the overwhelming majority of Whigs ultimately rallied around Scott.[63]

Democrats had much less difficulty gathering support for Pierce. Never before concerned with the sectional origins of their presidential candidates, North Carolina Democrats were pleased that Pierce, as well as the other contenders for the nomination, were considered to be northern men with southern principles, men who would do nothing to injure the South.[64]

The campaign itself bore a striking resemblance to 1848. Once again, Whigs denounced the idea that any northern man could have southern principles; they quoted Pierce as saying that he opposed the fugitive-slave law and endlessly reminded voters that Martin Van Buren, the Free-Soil candidate in 1848, now supported Pierce. Whigs then asked "whether Franklin Pierce is a safe man for Southern people to put at the head of this Union," and they repeated the refrain that Scott was as sound on the compromise as any man.[65]

62. Henry W. Miller to William A. Graham, March 20, 1852, Robert G. Allison to Graham, August 18, 1852, both in *ibid.*, IV, 262, 375.

63. James R. Morrill, "The Presidential Election of 1852: Death Knell of the Whig Party in North Carolina," *NCHR*, XLIV (1967), 351, 355–56; William A. Graham to Thomas Loring, August 24, 1852, in Hamilton and Williams (eds), *Graham Papers*, IV, 377–79. On Clingman, see Raleigh *Standard*, October 8, 1852.

64. Morrill, "Presidential Election of 1852," 351–53.

65. Fayetteville *Observer*, August 10, 1852.

Democrats mirrored the Whig argument, though they claimed that it was Pierce who was the only true friend of the South—Pierce trumpeted his support for the compromise, whereas Scott spoke not at all about his views on it. Scott's candidacy, they said, endangered the South. If William Seward's "puppet Scott" were elected, the end result would be "the destruction of our institutions."[66]

Although the political rhetoric of 1852 differed little from that of 1848, the tone of the campaign contrasted sharply. Whereas North Carolina Whigs had been on the political offensive in 1848, they were definitely on the defensive in 1852. In 1848, they worried little about defections from their ranks, but four years later they struggled to keep their state coalition together. After denouncing Pierce for his supposedly antisouthern sentiments, the Fayetteville *Observer* marveled "that such is the man for whom *some* Southern Whigs profess an intention to vote because Gen. Scott is not good enough for them!" Such fears of defections never entered the minds of Whigs in 1848 as they gathered support for Zachary Taylor— then, they confidently assumed that it would be Democrats who would defect to Taylor.[67]

Whig indifference to Scott was to a surprising degree matched by Democratic indifference to Pierce. For all the apparent Whig disaffection with the Scott nomination, the platforms of the parties in support of the compromise were decidedly similar. It must have seemed to many, as Michael F. Holt has suggested, that the election was much ado about nothing. The compromise, both parties had declared, was the final settlement of the slavery dispute. And voters responded with a distinct lack of interest. Only 66 percent of those eligible turned out to vote, substantially fewer than in any presidential election since 1836 and some 13 percent fewer than had voted in August. Pierce won the election in the state by several hundred votes and in the nation by many thousands.[68]

Although Whigs in much of the lower South were smashed in the electoral contest, the race in North Carolina remained close. The presidential election solidified the Democrats' narrow majority in the state's politics, but more important, it reaffirmed the political consensus on the compromise, thus temporarily removing the slavery issue from partisan politics. In the congressional elections of 1853, unlike those of 1847, 1849, and 1851, which revolved around the issues of slavery, expansion, and the right of secession, politicians focused on the question of whether the federal government should distribute the proceeds from the sale of public lands.[69]

66. Tarboro *Southerner*, May 8, 1852.
67. Fayetteville *Observer*, July 20, 1852.
68. Holt, *Political Crisis*, 95–98, 128–30.
69. See chapter 3 above, p. 79.

The partisan discussion of the slavery issue in North Carolina resumed in a halfhearted way in 1854, when Stephen Douglas introduced a bill to organize the Nebraska Territory. In its final form, the bill established two territories, Kansas and Nebraska, and repealed the Missouri Compromise's prohibition on slavery in the parts of the Louisiana Purchase that lay north of the 36° 30′ line. For southerners, the repeal expressed well the southern desire for equality in the nation, since it offered them the right to take slaves into territory from which they had hitherto been excluded. Few southerners expected that Kansas would be hospitable to slavery, but they were satisfied that the bill acknowledged their rights and their equality in the nation. Democrats were especially happy with the bill. It was, they said, the logical extension of the Democratic doctrine that Congress should neither exclude nor establish slavery in the federal territories.[70]

North Carolina's Whigs were less enthusiastic. They attributed the bill to Douglas' political ambitions and argued that it would really provide no additional slave territory. Still, many of them felt the need to go along with it as an expression of their support for southern rights. The Raleigh *Register* declared that "since an issue *has* been or must be joined we see no other alternative left than to carry the measure through." Here, though, some of the state's Whig congressmen parted ways with the *Register* and other Whigs. Seeing little to be gained from the measure, they opposed it. In mid-May, Congressman Sion H. Rogers "doubt[ed] very much the propriety of repealing the Missouri Compromise, without effecting by it some practical good, to the South." Rogers believed that the failure to prohibit foreigners from voting in the territorial election ensured the exclusion of slavery from the new territories. Therefore, he concluded "that the South will actually be the loser by the bill . . . in it's [*sic*] practical operations." Rogers, along with Richard Puryear and John A. Gilmer, voted against the bill. The divisions in the Whig ranks revealed the party's inability to make slavery once again a party issue. If the parties had not actually forged a consensus on issues relating to slavery, party differences were at least no longer clear.[71]

★

Partisanship shaped the contours of North Carolina's response to the territorial crisis. It did so in three distinct but interrelated ways. In the 1840s, Whigs and Democrats both warned of dire threats to southern rights and

70. Cooper, *Politics of Slavery*, 352; Raleigh *Standard*, January 11, 18, February 8, 22, April 26, 1854.

71. Raleigh *Register*, February 15, 1854, quoted in Cooper, *Politics of Slavery*, 353; Sion H. Rogers to William A. Graham, May 1, 1854, and same to same, May 25, 1854, both in Hamilton and Williams (eds.), *Graham Papers*, IV, 514, 516.

slavery posed by antislavery men in the North. And each charged the other with subservience to those antislavery forces. Such charges impelled politicians to assert evermore strongly their devotion to southern rights and, as a result, made voters painfully aware of the antislavery threat. Hence, party competition tended to excite popular fears, but it also assuaged those fears. Elect us, politicians chimed, and your freedom and black slavery will be secure. In this respect, politicians treated the territorial crisis as they did other issues. In the early debate over the equal suffrage amendment, Democrats charged Whigs with faithlessness to the creed of white equality, and Whigs asserted that Democrats had betrayed the state's republican traditions. And each party offered safety from its opponents' iniquitous behavior, if only its candidates were elected.

The party system also influenced the state's response to the crisis of the late 1840s by preventing the parties from agreeing upon a plan of resistance. Because of the natural inclination of politicians to seek credit for preserving and defending southern rights and to deny it to their opponents, they proved unwilling to compromise. Whigs insisted that only Whigs and Whig policies could save the South, while Democrats said the same things about themselves and their policies. Therefore, although politicians in both parties believed that the South needed to be defended, they could not reach any common grounds about how to defend it.

The parties' unwillingness to support the bipartisan plan of action for the South, though, ironically enhanced popular devotion to southern rights. During the late 1840s and early 1850s, Democrats often chided Whigs for weakening the southern cause by refusing to endorse Democratic remedies for the crisis, and Whigs accused Democrats of doing the same. By criticizing the other party, Democrats and Whigs forced one another to assume a more aggressive southern rights stance. In that way, parties promoted a consensus on the need to defend the South. So while the partisan effort to outdo one another as the only true defender of southern rights may have dissuaded politicians from actually doing anything to protect those rights, it helped unify North Carolinians in their commitment to defend them.

Finally, because North Carolina's state parties were also cogs in national organizations, the national parties also influenced the state's response to the crisis. When the national party took a position on almost any issue, state politicians bent far to conform to it. The behavior of the state parties was not the expression of hypocrisy, but rather represented the political need to stay in line with the national party for the sake of party unity and party victory. Hence, the need to accommodate the northern wing of the party softened the sectional cries of the state party that was affected.

The state politician's need to keep his views fairly consonant with the national party's also reflected the fact that his personal political success was linked to a whole series of political relationships. He was elected as a Democrat or a Whig, and voters usually assumed that his views were consonant with those of the party, at the state and national levels. By implication, that politician assumed political responsibility for the behavior of the national organization and so tried to portray it in the most favorable light.

What North Carolina partisans ultimately came to agree upon was not a plan of action but rather acquiescence on the Compromise of 1850. It was a consensus based upon the worship of the two gods of the southern antebellum political religion, southern rights and the Union. Even the disagreement over the right of secession diminished as the crisis receded in 1851. By 1853, while each party continued to insist that they were the best southern party and that the party of their opponents was unsafe for the South, politicians had greater difficulty making that point because the parties no longer held distinctive views on the slavery issue. As with so many issues, by 1854 the differences between the parties seemed difficult to discern.

Six *The Politics of Continuity*

By 1855, North Carolina's parties had helped shape a consensus on issues ranging from social and economic policy making to constitutional revision to the defense of southern rights in the national government. As we have seen, in the 1830s and 1840s, partisan conflict over those issues had expressed the social, economic, and sectional cleavages in the state. Parties had offered voters the opportunity to obtain—or at least to believe that they could obtain—a redress for felt grievances. The parties in one way or another had expressed the fears and desires of different elements in white male society: property owners and the propertyless, merchants and farmers, easterners and westerners, non-slaveholders and slaveholders, men involved in the market economy and those who stood outside of it. Their interests and their very freedom, they believed, could be protected by their party's victory. Whether in legislative policy making, reforming the state constitution, or defending the South's interests, politicians identified the dragons that threatened the people's freedom and promised to slay them if elected. Both parties promised to kill the dragon, but they chose different weapons to do the deed. As Michael F. Holt has argued, partisan conflict over substantive issues convinced voters that their grievances *could* be redressed through political action. In fact, the party system did work to resolve many grievances: townsmen and others owning less than fifty acres of land were on the verge of obtaining the right to vote for state senators in 1855; the demands for internal improvements met with an increasingly favorable legislative response; and the parties deepened the consensus in favor of defending slavery as they jousted to prove their fidelity to southern rights.[1]

1. Michael F. Holt, *The Political Crisis of the 1850s* (New York: John Wiley & Sons, 1978).

However, voters demanded not only solutions, but conflict itself. Only then were they assured that the parties continued to be responsive to their concerns. But by late 1854 most of the outstanding issues had been settled. In this respect North Carolinians replicated the experience of people in other states. In those areas the disappearance of conflict undermined popular faith in the party system, but North Carolinians retained their belief in its efficacy. While the party system crumbled in the lower South and in the North in 1851 and 1853, it remained vital in North Carolina and much of the upper South.

The differences between North Carolina's political parties had emerged clearly in the economic issues raised by the depression of the 1830s and early 1840s. At the national and state levels, Democrats sought to remedy the depression by withdrawing government as much as possible from the economy and marketplace. Whigs, on the other hand, saw the need for a much more active role for the government in resolving the crisis. Indeed, this was the way the parties responded to the entire spectrum of issues. Whigs were much more likely to see the positive good that might come of government activity, Democrats to see the threat to liberty that increased government activity portended. This disparity of views was captured nicely in the long struggle to save the Raleigh and Gaston Railroad. Ambivalent about the project from the outset, Democrats had their worst fears confirmed by the railroad's difficulties. They saw only that the state was going deeper and deeper in debt to save the railroad. The government took care of private investors while citizens paid onerous taxes. And, they argued, anyone familiar with the history of republics knew that once a republic became indebted it lost its independence, and the loss of personal liberty would not be far behind. Whigs, though, tended to see the positive side of the issue. They were obviously embarrassed by the company's circumstances, but instead of bemoaning the loss of money, they appreciated what the money had bought—better transportation facilities for many, jobs and a market for goods and food stuffs for others.

To some degree, the partisan conflict over internal improvements and other kinds of government activism stemmed from eastern opposition to western demands for some expansion of government services. Easterners already paid the bulk of the state's taxes, so any increase in state expenditures was bound to drive up their taxes. In that sense, disagreement over internal improvements continued the state's historic sectional conflict. But it also expressed social conflict between those who, on the one hand, were either active participants in the market economy or who wanted to enter it, and those, on the other hand, who were satisfied with their limited access to markets or who feared being sucked into that economy. For all of them, the partisan conflict acted out the social drama. It became a surrogate means of resolving social, economic, and sectional conflict. In this way, party politics helped smooth the state economy's transition from relative self-sufficiency into the world of the market. In the late 1840s and early 1850s, interparty competition, along with the dramatic return of prosperity, drove Democrats into the Whigs' activist camp. That is not to say that everyone was satisfied with the new consensus by 1855. There were still wealthy easterners desperate to curb government expenditures and those who lived on the margins of the market economy and wanted to remain there. But it seems clear that the party system worked over the long run to create a social consensus.

The party system also provided a means of resolving grievances involving political power and political equality. Although there is no evidence of any popular demand for the removal of the fifty-acre property requirement for senatorial electors, by raising the issue Democrats channeled any underlying discontent over the evident maldistribution of political rights and power in the society into the equal-suffrage issue. Opposition to broad political change found its expression in the Whig party and its leadership. But given a constitutional structure that contained a property requirement excluding from senatorial elections half of those who voted for other officers, it was virtually inevitable that the equal-suffrage amendment would pass. Under the pressure of competition from the Democrats, and after seeking egalitarian grounds upon which to base their opposition to the measures, Whigs eventually capitulated and supported it.

The Whig party also provided an outlet for western grievances. It came to endorse a new constitutional convention, though it necessarily straddled the issue of what the convention should do. When Whigs eventually offered a limited convention that would not touch the basis for legislative apportionment, they retained western support by vigorously advocating the expansion of railroad construction in the west. Once again, party conflict acted out sectional and class conflict and by 1854 had done much to resolve that conflict. Of course, this did not mean that the parties were resolving the problems of society. Persons living in the west still were dissatisfied with the constitutional structure, but it seemed their grievances were being acted upon.

The parties also reinforced and deepened the society's commitment to the defense of southern rights. On the most basic level, white North Carolinians agreed that slavery and southern rights should be protected. But the parties contributed mightily to the popular sense that their region was endangered by northern attacks. By always seeking to outdo one another in their defense of the South, the parties kept ever present the northern threat.

For years Whigs and Democrats had perceived their own party as the only truly faithful defender of southern rights and slavery, and their opponents as faithless. Only in their hands, they said, could the cause of the South and the freedom of southern whites be safe. Likewise, they had viewed their party alone as the most virtuous defender of the Union, the palladium of their liberty. While the two parties offered different ways to protect southern rights and the Union, the avowed goals of each were the same. Hence, in this context, competition between the parties tended to strengthen the consensus on the question of southern rights, much as the parties differed about the way to protect those rights. If party competition did not encourage agreement about means, it certainly heightened southern sensitivity to northern attacks on slavery. Because of party competition southerners were clearly made more aware of the sectional threat than they otherwise might have been.

Party competition in the early 1850s also promoted a consensus over the means. While the parties continued to see safety for the South in their own victories and a threat to the South in their opponent's, both parties came to endorse the Compromise of 1850. And while North Carolina Whigs were clearly less receptive to the Kansas-Nebraska Act in 1854 than were Democrats, most felt compelled to fall into line and support the measure.

★

The development of a consensus on a whole range of issues in the early 1850s in North Carolina typified the political experience of most states, but whereas the decline in partisan conflict over issues in other states helped to destroy the party systems there, it had no similar effect in North Carolina or in most of the other states of the upper South. Although the Whig party in the lower South, most of the border states, and the North was dead by 1854, in North Carolina the party maintained its vitality through that year. Only after it became clear that the national party had disintegrated and the new American party had become well established did most Whigs abandon their old party banner for the American party.

Historians have devoted much attention to the supposed demise of the Whig party. In their search for an explanation for Whiggery's fate in North Carolina, they have pointed to the effects of the equal-suffrage issue, the sectional split within the party over constitutional reform, the sectional divisions in the national party over slavery, or to the reputedly more vigorous defense of southern rights offered by Democrats. Ultimately, though,

TABLE 20
Interparty Competitiveness in North Carolina, 1840–1854:
Percentage of Votes Needed to Win
Attained by Losing Party in Gubernatorial Elections

Election Year	Percent
1840	89.2
1842	93.8
1844	96.2
1846	90.0
1848	99.0
1850	96.8
1852	94.0
1854	97.8

these are explanations for a historical phenomenon that did not occur. The story of the Whig loss of power in North Carolina is not the story of the decline and death of a great party. Rather, it is the much smaller tale of the transition of the Whigs from a narrow majority to a narrow minority within the state.[2]

In the 1840s and the early 1850s, only several thousand votes separated one party from the other (see table 1, p. 43). When the Whigs won statewide elections in the late 1830s and through the 1840s, as they invariably did, they did so by slender margins. The only legislatures that they dominated totally were those of 1840 and 1846 (see table 12, p. 61). After 1848, the narrow Whig victories were replaced by narrow Whig defeats. Table 20 reveals that the party system remained extremely competitive between 1840 and 1854, whether Whigs were winning or losing. It becomes difficult to speak of great causes for the Whig party's demise when it is recognized that the Whig gubernatorial candidate in 1844 won the election with 51.9 percent of the vote, and ten years later the Democratic gubernatorial candidate won with a similar 51.1 percent. It is necessary to explain the Whig loss of power but also to explain why the party system in the state remained as vibrant as it did.

Party politicians recognized early on that the loyalties of voters to their parties became fixed once they made their attachments to a party. Since most voters did not regard such a commitment lightly, the task of the

2. J. G. deRoulhac Hamilton, *Party Politics in North Carolina, 1835–1860* (Durham: Seeman Printery, 1916), 124, 142; Clarence Clifford Norton, *The Democratic Party in Ante-Bellum North Carolina, 1835–1861* (Chapel Hill: University of North Carolina Press, 1930), 118, 136–37, 166; James R. Morrill, "The Presidential Election of 1852; Death Knell of the Whig Party of North Carolina," *NCHR*, XLIV (1967), 342–59; Thomas E. Jeffrey, "Thunder from the Mountains: Thomas Lanier Clingman and the End of Whig Supremacy in North Carolina," *NCHR*, LVI (1979), 366–95; William J. Cooper, Jr., *The South and the Politics of Slavery, 1828–1856* (Baton Rouge: Louisiana State University Press, 1978), 359.

party managers was not so much to convert voters as to get out the vote for their party's candidate. Therefore, Whig party managers played a crucial role in ensuring party victory in the 1840s. But their influence and success revived Whig misgivings about the value of political parties and the concomitant concentration of power in the hands of party leaders. In the late 1840s, in a fit of suicidal revenge for supposed past wrongs, Whigs destroyed much of the party machinery and helped precipitate their party's loss of power in the state.

Power in the Whig party in North Carolina, as in state parties throughout the Union, was centralized in the hands of men living in and around the state capital. As we have seen, North Carolina's miserable road system prevented people in outlying areas from playing a regular role in state party affairs, so men residing in proximity to Raleigh became the parties' powerbrokers. And Raleigh's location near the geographical center of the state gave added meaning to the term "centralization of power." These men converted their influence in the parties into power in government. In 1848, the governor, William A. Graham, both United States senators, Willie P. Mangum and George E. Badger, and two of the three state supreme court justices, Thomas Ruffin (a Democrat) and Frederick Nash (a Whig), all resided in Wake County or neighboring Orange.[3]

With Graham completing his second and constitutionally mandated final term in 1848, the state convention meeting that year would nominate a gubernatorial candidate. Since the last two governors, both Whigs, had come either from the west (John M. Morehead of Greensboro) or the center (Graham), eastern Whigs, and indeed Whigs throughout the state, expected the nomination to go to an easterner. By late 1847, Kenneth Rayner of northeastern Hertford County had emerged as the choice of the party leadership, but in December he declined to run. Therefore, unlike the custom of previous years, Whigs failed to reach a consensus on a candidate before the convention began. After Rayner blocked the nomination of front-runner Edward Stanly, a rival of his from coastal Washington County, the convention finally settled upon an innocuous compromise candidate, Charles Manly of Raleigh, an attorney, longtime member of the central committee, and trustee of the University of North Carolina.[4]

3. See chapter 2 above.

4. Fayetteville *Observer*, December 28, 1847; William A. Graham to James W. Bryan, January 11, 1848, Graham to James Graham, April 5, 1848, both in J. G. deRoulhac Hamilton and Max R. Williams (eds.), *The Papers of William Alexander Graham* (6 vols. to date; Raleigh: State Department of Archives and History, 1957–), III, 212–13, 218; Edward J. Hale to Daniel M. Barringer, January 21, 1848, in Daniel Moreau Barringer Papers, SHC; Charles Manly to Samuel F. Patterson, August 13, 1848, in Jones and Patterson Papers, SHC; Raleigh *Register*, February 26, 1848, February 27, 1850.

Whigs outside the convention, though, did not view Manly as a compromise choice. Even those who were not unhappy with his nomination believed that men from the center of the state had engineered it. One eastern Whig confided in his diary that "I cant help from thinking that his nomination was obtained by central influence." John H. Bryan, one of Raleigh's Whig leaders, felt compelled to write to his brother James, a prominent Whig in coastal Craven County, that "it is a great mistake to impute Manly's nomination to the Raleigh influence, as many seem disposed to do." Despite Bryan's plea, many Whigs reached precisely that conclusion.[5]

Intraparty dissatisfaction with Manly's nomination combined with his and the party's opposition to the equal-suffrage amendment to hurt him seriously, especially in the mountain region, where 54.8 percent of the farms contained less than fifty acres and nonlandowners were numerous. There, the Democratic vote surged 29.2 percent, while the Whig vote declined by 2.3 percent. The weakened Whig resolve was matched by the equal-suffrage-induced zeal of the Democrats. Manly, drawing his support from traditionally Whig areas, won the election, as had every Whig gubernatorial candidate before him, but with only 50.5 percent of the popular vote.[6]

Manly's narrow escape from defeat may have nurtured Whig hostility toward the "Raleigh influence," a feeling that was intensified by intraparty conflict over the appointment of a state supreme court justice. The death of Judge J. J. Daniel in the winter had created a vacancy on the supreme court, and the constitution obliged Governor Graham to appoint a judge who would sit until the legislature elected a permanent judge during its 1848–1849 session. Graham narrowed his choice to two men: Richmond M. Pearson from western Yadkin County, the longest-sitting superior court judge, and William Battle from Orange County, also a superior court judge. Prominent western Whigs like James T. Morehead, congressman from Greensboro, urged Graham to appoint Pearson. Morehead wrote: "Pearson is the older man & the older Judge, his location is more remote from the center—is further removed from that concentration of Judicial offices, which has given rise to so much dissatisfied [*i.e.*, dissatisfaction]."

5. William Valentine Diaries (MS in SHC), March 7, 1848; John H. Bryan to James W. Bryan, August 29, 1848, in Bryan Family Papers, SHC.

6. William A. Graham to James Graham, April 5, 1848, in Hamilton and Williams (eds.)., *Graham Papers*, III, 218; David Outlaw to Emily Outlaw, August 2, 1848, in David Outlaw Papers, SHC. Regional election results were computed from Thomas E. Jeffrey, "The Second Party System in North Carolina" (Ph.D. dissertation, Catholic University of America, 1976), 423–31. On the size of farms in the mountains, see Joseph Carlyle Sitterson, *The Secession Movement in North Carolina* (Chapel Hill: University of North Carolina Press, 1939), 19.

Another western attorney, Joseph Allison, put the matter more bluntly to Graham. "All your friends in the West are friends of Pearson," he claimed, "& are particularly in favour of his appointment as a man[,] the best qualified & who would be independent of that Raleigh Clique, to which the people are getting strongly opposed, for using power because they have it."[7]

Over these protests, Graham appointed his friend Battle to the judgeship and commissioned Battle's interim replacement. William Valentine, an eastern Whig, approved the latter appointment but was angered by Graham's designation of Battle. He believed Battle not as qualified as others, but he complained most bitterly that "all three of the Judges of the Supreme Court are residents of one County as though the Hawfields is the only place where are to be found men of sufficient talents for high office."[8]

Valentine correctly predicted that many Whigs would come to the legislature opposed to Battle's confirmation. J. M. Long, a commoner from the southwestern county of Cabarrus, reported to Whig congressman Daniel M. Barringer that "the great mass of the Whig party were for Pearson." A substantial majority of Whig legislators did favor Pearson, but because a minority insisted on voting for Battle at a time when Whigs held only a two-member majority on a joint ballot, Battle supporters prevented Pearson's immediate election. Ballot after ballot brought no decision, and Battle finally withdrew his name from consideration. Even then, several of his boosters continued to vote for him. Only after several Democrats cast their ballots for Pearson did he obtain the necessary majority. Democrats received in return the votes of several Whigs in the superior court election held to fill Pearson's vacancy; in the contest between Battle, who had given up his seat on the superior court to serve on the supreme court, and Democrat John W. Ellis, the votes of these Whigs quickly put Ellis over the top. Because of the obstinacy of Battle's supporters, Long claimed, "many Whigs are now *execrating* this so called central influence." J. Laurence Badger wrote to a friend on the day of the superior court election that "the words '*Raleigh Influence*,' and '*Orangemen*,' are becoming quite *unpopular*."[9]

The election of a U.S. senator by the same legislature provided Whigs

7. James T. Morehead to William A. Graham, April 1, 1848, in Governors' Papers, NCDAH; Joseph Allison to William A. Graham, March 5, 1848, in Hamilton and Williams (eds.), *Graham Papers*, III, 215.

8. Valentine Diaries, May 26, 1848.

9. J. M. Long to Daniel M. Barringer, December 16, 1848, J. Laurence Badger to Barringer, December 16, 1848, J.R. Hargrave to Barringer, December 13, 1848, all in Barringer Papers; *SJ, 1848–49*, 47, 49, 53, 61–65, 67–68, 81–82, 84, 111, 137, 186; *HJ, 1848–49*, 423, 426–27, 432, 439, 444, 446, 448, 450, 462, 464, 466, 507, 542, 625.

with further evidence of central control of the party organization. The Whigs, with their slight majority, needed a virtually unanimous party vote to reelect caucus candidate George Edmund Badger. Badger, a respected attorney and party leader from Raleigh, secretary of the navy in the Harrison-Tyler administration, and U.S. senator since 1846, was perceived by most Whigs as the leader of the state party; but he was a man of aristocratic demeanor who had difficulty mastering the give-and-take needed to keep the party machinery running smoothly. Congressman David Outlaw, who admired Badger's abilities as a senator, thought him "deficient, very in judgement [*sic*] as a party leader." Badger had confirmed Outlaw's opinion of him with his undiplomatic behavior at the state Whig convention, and many Whigs had blamed Badger's obstinate insistence on the nomination of his friend and cousin, Edward Stanly, for the convention's deadlock over the choice of a gubernatorial nominee.[10]

The legislative squabbling over the election of a supreme court justice caused further Whig dissatisfaction with Badger's leadership. Stanly, the senator's candidate for governor, was William Battle's prime defender in the General Assembly and one of the few to support Battle's candidacy to the very end. Some Whig legislators concluded that Stanly was following Badger's orders and blamed the senator for the intraparty dispute. By the time the judicial elections had been completed, "a good many" Whigs believed "that Mr. Badger is at the head of this central influence." This belief, legislator J. M. Long claimed, "is very injuriuosly operating against Mr. Badger."[11]

The difficulties faced by the Whigs in electing Badger were compounded by the ambition of Thomas Clingman, a Whig congressman from the mountain district. First elected to Congress in 1843, Clingman's subsequent support for the repeal of the "gag rule," which had prohibited the reading of antislavery petitions in Congress, upset many of his constituents and apparently caused his loss to another Whig in 1845. Reelected in 1847, he remained in the House until 1858, when the Democratic governor appointed him to the U.S. Senate. But Thomas Clingman harbored visions of a Senate seat for more than a decade before he attained it. In 1848 George Badger and the Raleigh leadership stood in the congressman's way. Clingman complained "that the middle portion of the State had *gormandized* every office and would continue to do so as long as the East & West would submit to it." When Attorney General Bartholemew F. Moore asked Clingman "if [he] was willing to break down the whig party by

10. David Outlaw to Emily Outlaw, February 18, 1848, in Outlaw Papers.
11. James. W. Osborne to Daniel M. Barringer, December 12, 1848, J. M. Long to Barringer, December 15, 1848, both in Barringer Papers.

being a candidate [for Badger's Senate seat] . . . he said that the distruction [*sic*] of the cormorant propensities of the middle part of the State was of much more importance than the preservation of any party." Consequently, Clingman permitted friends in the the legislature to nominate him.[12]

In the election, three Whigs, enough to prevent the senator's reelection, refused to support Badger: one easterner disturbed by Badger's conservative position on the slavery question and two westerners who supported Clingman. For a number of ballots, Democrats voted for Clingman; several more Whig votes might have given him the election, but those votes were not forthcoming. Finally, Clingman gave up and convinced one of his Whig supporters to switch to Badger, thereby securing the incumbent's reelection. Throughout the balloting, the vast majority of the party had supported Badger's reelection, but, as one Whig legislator asserted, "I assure you some of these votes are cast with reluctance."[13]

The conflicts over the senatorial and judicial elections and the gubernatorial nomination so enraged eastern and western Whigs that they demolished the central committee, which had been so instrumental in the party's success. In so doing, they expressed their lingering doubts about the virtues of political parties and party organizations. Although the Whig state convention renominated Charles Manly in 1850, it also appointed an executive committee to replace the central committee, altered the composition of the committee, and thereby rendered it impotent. The convention of 1848 had appointed eight Raleigh residents and a representative from each of the nine congressional districts to the central committee. Since only five men were needed to form a quorum, and since difficult traveling conditions prevented the whole committee from meeting, residents of the Raleigh area effectively controlled the committee. In 1850, the newly appointed executive committee was composed of three men from each district with no additional Raleigh members. The convention's failure to establish the number of men needed to make a quorum made formal committee actions almost impossible. The convention then made the question of the committee members' residence irrelevant by stripping the committee of all but one of the central committee's powers, entrusting to the executive committee only the power to establish the date and place for the next

12. Jeffrey, "Thunder from the Mountains," 366–95; Bartholemew F. Moore to Daniel M. Barringer, December 15, 1848, in Barringer Papers.

13. *SJ, 1848–49*, 90, 109, 125–27; *HJ, 1848–49*, 476, 505, 521, 523–25; Raleigh *Register*, December 16 and 23, 1848; Thomas L. Clingman, *Address of T. L. Clingman on the Recent Senatorial Election* (n.p., [1849]), in NCC; J. M. Long to Daniel M. Barringer, December 15, 1848, in Barringer Papers.

convention. This policy contrasted sharply with the central committee's mandate in 1848 to act to promote the party's interests.[14]

Because the Whigs had squeaked through the elections of 1848, they now needed an especially efficient organization, but just when they required the strength of the party's right arm—the central committee—they amputated it. In 1850, no committee raised funds for Charles Manly's reelection campaign, organized mass meetings for him, or coordinated his schedule of appearances or the efforts of county and local leaders on his behalf. Manly could hardly afford to be without the committee's help. A lackluster campaigner in a state where voters placed much value on a good stump speech, Manly was also identified with Whig opposition to the equal-suffrage amendment. During the campaign, moreover, he blundered by seeming to imply that the basis of representation for the state legislature should be apportioned according to the white basis. Democrats, as has been noted, linked Manly's supposed proposal to the ongoing congressional debates over the compromise measures and argued that it menaced the security of slavery.

There was one issue, however, upon which Manly seemed in command —the question of state aid to internal improvements. On the stump and in his message to the legislature, he had vigorously endorsed state aid for further railroad construction. At the same time, Democrats were deeply divided on the issue. Pro-improvement Democrats in fact had barely prevented the adoption of an anti-improvement plank in their party platform. However, Manly was unable to take advantage of the issue because of circumstances that lay largely beyond his control. During the legislative session of 1848–1849, western squabbling about the route of a proposed turnpike from Salisbury to the Georgia border had been bitter. Finally, the legislators were able to pass a bill aiding its construction only because the bill did not specify the actual route. Western legislators, whose votes were needed for passage, would not support any road that did not go through their county. The turnpike route was left to be determined by a committee appointed by the governor, and, as a result, Manly was bound to alienate the people of some county. The legislature might have been able to satisfy the losing counties with another transportation project, but Manly had no such fiscal balm to offer. When he appointed a committee whose members seemed to be leaning toward a route through Morganton and which then did choose that route, Manly, as we have seen, infuriated the citizens of the other main contender, Rutherfordton in Rutherford County. Thus in parts

14. Edward Stanly to David F. Caldwell, March 1, 1850 (typescript), in David F. Caldwell Papers, SHC; Raleigh *Register*, February 26, 1848, June 15, 1850.

of the west it became difficult for Manly to campaign as the friend of internal improvement.

In August, Manly became the first Whig candidate to lose a popular election, though only by three thousand votes. David Reid's meager margin of victory would have been even narrower but for the rebellion of Rutherford voters. This county, which gave Manly 74 percent of its votes in 1848, repudiated him in 1850 by giving him only 35 percent. The combination of Whig votes lost and Democratic votes gained added more than one thousand votes to the Democratic column. Since only three thousand votes separated the candidates, it is apparent that Rutherford County played a significant role in the election. Without Rutherford, Reid still would have won, but by an uncomfortably small margin—which undoubtedly would have been still smaller if the Whig party organization had been functioning. Without the help of his party, without Rutherford, and on the defensive because of his stand on constitutional revision, Manly lost the election.[15]

Historians have treated the gubernatorial election of 1850 as a revolutionary occurrence in North Carolina's political history. In fact, little had changed. If Rutherford County is excluded from one's calculations, then only about 2,600 votes changed between 1848 and 1850. The state had gone from a slight Whig majority to a slight Democratic majority. With a reconstituted central committee and a new candidate to replace Manly, Whigs could reasonably expect success in 1852.[16]

More significant for the future of the party system in North Carolina generally and of the Whig party specifically than the election of 1850 was the Whig response to the sectional compromise of that year. In the lower South states of Alabama, Georgia, and Mississippi, Whigs unknowingly participated in their own self-destruction when they helped establish the Union party, fusing with Unionist Democrats. In Alabama and Mississippi, at least, Whigs had long been a weak minority, and in Georgia they had begun to lose badly after years of victory. For them, the Unionist coalition seemed to offer victory, power, and patronage. But they were rudely awakened from their reveries of power when their erstwhile allies returned to the Democratic party in time for the presidential election of 1852. Bereft of their allies, the Whig parties never recovered, and soon the party system in those states became but a shadow of its former self.[17]

15. See chapter 3, pp. 74–75.

16. *Cf.* Cooper, *Politics of Slavery*, 311–12.

17. *Ibid.*, 304–10; J. Mills Thornton III, *Politics and Power in a Slave Society: Alabama, 1800–1860* (Baton Rouge: Louisiana State University Press, 1978), 186–89, 192–99, 353; Michael F. Holt, *The Political Crisis of the 1850s* (New York: John Wiley & Sons, 1978), 118–19.

In North Carolina, the idea of a Unionist coalition seemed preposterous. Whigs said that they would be happy to have Democrats join them and would not even mind calling themselves Unionists, but they made it very clear that they were Whigs and that any organization, be it named Whig or Union, would be a Whig organization run by Whigs. Although they had just lost the gubernatorial election, their unpopular candidate had fallen just short of victory, which they were certain lay waiting in 1852. In the nearer term, Whigs reasonably expected to do well in the congressional elections of 1851—and they did, winning six of the state's nine seats. So the continued strength of the Whig party in the state (and the similar strength of the Whig party in much of the upper South) made any bipartisan party-destroying coalition unattractive to Whigs.[18]

The party's ability to maintain its independence boded well for it in 1852, but Whigs did not recoup their state losses in that election, due in part to the continued bad feeling toward party leaders in Raleigh. Just before the meeting of the state convention that year, one member of the "Raleigh clique" wrote to a friend: "I have resolved to take no part in the deliberations of the Convention. The Whigs of the 'Central Clique,' as they are contemptuously designated, have been pretty effectually ostracized by both East & West." Another writer complained of the "insane jealousy of the Centre." Although distrustful of the Raleigh leadership, the convention delegates recognized that, by rendering the central committee impotent, they were burning down the entire Whig barn in order to kill the Raleigh mouse, so they appointed a nine-man executive committee "to act for the Whig party in the approaching campaign" and permitted three men to compose a quorum at committee meetings. But by placing only one man from Raleigh on the committee and choosing the rest from diverse parts of the state, they showed their distaste for the Raleigh leadership and also made it difficult for the committee to meet its increased responsibilities. As a result, the Whig gubernatorial nominee, John Kerr, set out on the campaign trail without a vigorous central body organizing his campaign.[19]

Kerr also faced problems because of his and his party's position on a state convention and because of the unpopularity of the national Whig party's presidential candidate, Winfield Scott. It will be recalled that westerners, pushing the question of constitutional reform beyond the equal-suffrage amendment, demanded a constitutional convention to re-

18. See chapter 5 above.
19. Henry W. Miller to William A. Graham, March 20, 1852, John H. Bryan to Graham, April 5, 1852, both in Hamilton and Williams (eds.), *Graham Papers*, IV, 262, 280–81. The committee did appoint assistant electors for the presidential campaign. Raleigh *Register*, September 8, 1852.

dress what they believed was the unequal distribution of power in the state. Because of the great significance of the west in the Whig coalition, the party felt compelled to confront this issue at the state party convention. The delegates' work did not please westerners since the platform straddled the issue and the gubernatorial candidate openly opposed a constitutional convention. Under those circumstances, it was not surprising that Kerr was well received in the east and that, when he arrived in the western counties where proconvention sentiment was strong, Whigs greeted him coolly. Kerr also carried the albatross of Winfield Scott's candidacy on his shoulders: Whigs unhappy with Scott might well take their dissatisfaction out on Kerr.

Kerr did lose; he was hurt especially in the mountains where, though he obtained 57.8 percent of the vote, his poll fell eight percentage points short of Manly's in 1850. Despite the fact that the Whigs lost the election, and despite the problems with the national campaign, they had not fared badly. Kerr won 47 percent of the vote, and several months later an unpopular Scott nevertheless garnered 49.5 percent. Whigs still remained quite competitive and could continue to count on a stable and reliable voter base. Men who had voted Whig in the past, it seems, generally voted Whig in 1852. Some may not have gone to the polls, but they did not bolt to the Democrats (see table 2, p. 44). Scott's candidacy, the divisive issues of constitutional reform, and the continuing weakness of the central committee had damaged the party, but these circumstances suggested that popular enthusiasm could be rekindled by new candidates and new issues. As the editor of the Fayetteville *Observer* remarked: "The Whig party, according to our opponents has died and been buried several times in the course of the last twenty years. But somehow it has managed to come to life again and thrash its opponents quite as often as it has been beaten."[20]

The Whig future looked even brighter because of the legislative elections. Although Democrats carried the Senate by a handy margin, Whigs controlled the House by several votes. The Whig majority was evidence that the party was not moribund, but, more important, that majority helped ensure the party's future. Upon the shoulders of the General Assembly in 1852 rested the chore of creating new congressional districts that would be set for a decade and new state senatorial districts for the next twenty years. Of course, in order for any redistricting legislation to pass, both houses would have to approve it. After interminable haggling over the redistricting, the parties approved compromise plans. Whigs, though, clearly felt they had gotten the best of the bargain since they voted much

20. Fayetteville *Observer*, September 12, 1853.

more heavily in favor of the plans than did the Democrats. Whigs thus prevented Democrats from reapportioning them out of existence. This would be important in helping Whigs to maintain their position vis-à-vis the Democrats in 1854 and would be crucial for the Whig revival in 1859 and 1860.[21]

Buoyed by the reapportionment, Whigs also found new life in an old issue—the distribution of the proceeds from the sale of public lands. The revival of the distribution issue came at an opportune time for North Carolina's Whigs. They, like Whigs elsewhere in the South, were being deprived by Democrats of their distinctive position on economic issues like state aid to internal improvements. Distribution offered them an opportunity to reestablish the fact in the voters' eyes that there was a difference between Whigs and Democrats. Moreover, because distribution had been a major element in the Whig creed since the beginning of the party system, it enabled Whigs to evoke the traditional ties of Whig voters to their party. And because the issue was now relevant to voters, it made those ties and those differences relevant as well. Finally, the distribution issue meant that the *national* Whig party, which on other issues looked little different from its opponents, continued to be ideologically relevant to North Carolina's voters.[22]

★

Although the party system in North Carolina remained vigorous, in 1854 it was threatened, as in many other states and localities, by the advent of cultural issues that cut across party lines. In North Carolina's case, the issue was temperance. But unlike the outcome in other states, where such issues disrupted traditional political patterns, in North Carolina party politicians repulsed the threat posed by the temperance effort and thereby revealed the persistent strength of the party system in their state.[23]

Temperance advocates had been active in North Carolina since the early days of the Republic, but support for the cause (following a nationwide trend) surged in the late 1840s and early 1850s. In 1846 the Sons of Temperance, the most important organization, had 4 local divisions and 139 contributing members. By 1849, it had grown to 44 divisions and 1,492 members, and two years later, after hiring a temperance lecturer to tour the state, the organization had 287 divisions and about 12,000 members.[24]

21. *HJ, 1852*, 491. Of the Whigs, 97.8 percent voted for the bill, whereas only 27.5 percent of the Democrats voted for it.
22. Raleigh *Register*, April 2, 1853.
23. Ronald P. Formisano, *The Birth of Mass Political Parties: Michigan, 1827–1861* (Princeton: Princeton University Press, 1971), 229–38; Holt, *Political Crisis*, 130–31.
24. Daniel J. Whitener, *Prohibition in North Carolina, 1715–1945* (Chapel Hill: University of North Carolina Press, 1945), 30.

Buoyed by its large contingent of members and by the success of temperance advocates in the North, the Sons of Temperance soon became embroiled in state and local politics. Its entrance into the political arena resulted logically from the organization's longstanding demand that politicians stop the traditional practice of treating citizens with food and drink in order to obtain votes and from its new advocacy of a general state prohibitory law. The movement for prohibition grew from the passage of similar laws in some northern states and from the inability of county and town governments to control the sale of liquor at the local level. County governments had long regulated the liquor trade through licensing, but when the Guilford County Court refused to grant any liquor licenses, the state supreme court in 1845 declared county prohibition of liquor sales unconstitutional. Therefore, the only avenue of recourse seemed to be the state legislature. In 1852 the newly strengthened Sons of Temperance led a statewide effort to petition the General Assembly for either outright prohibition or a requirement that a prospective liquor retailer obtain the approval of a majority of the citizens living in the area of his shop before he could obtain a license. By the time the statewide convention of the Sons of Temperance assembled in Raleigh in December, petitioners had gathered 18,000 signatures, about 13,000 of whom were voters. In a state where only a few thousand votes could tip an election, the presence of as many as 13,000 committed temperance men promised to wreak havoc with the politics of the state.[25]

The temperance convention itself became a matter of political controversy when a Whig member of the House of Commons offered a resolution permitting the convention to meet in the Commons hall. After a majority of Whigs, revealing their greater sympathies for the temperance movement, voted in favor of the resolution and most Democrats opposed it, the resolution was withdrawn. But the liquor issue quickly reappeared in the Senate when Walter L. Steele presented the gigantic petition in favor of prohibition. Again party lines hardened as Democrats tabled the petition over Whig opposition. Commoners accepted the petition but sent it to the judiciary committee, where it died. Although Whigs were more sympathetic to the temperance cause than Democrats, they evinced no desire to act on the petition's demands.[26]

After their setbacks in the legislature, temperance advocates decided to seek an outright prohibitory law. Although this decision drove off many supporters who only wanted to strengthen the existing laws, the prohibitionists worked hard in the legislative contests of 1854 in order to avoid a

25. *Ibid.*, 40–41.
26. *Ibid.*, 41.

repetition of earlier legislative defeats. In some counties they influenced local politics, but in others they had little effect.

In Orange County, the parties handled the issue with considerable skill. Responding to temperance pressure and recognizing their common stake in keeping the temperance issue out of politics, both parties agreed that the county should hold a referendum on liquor-law changes. The overwhelming defeat of the referendum boded ill for the temperance cause, but the referendum itself (upon which the parties assumed no official position) enabled the parties to keep the liquor issue out of Orange County politics.[27]

In other counties, the temperance issue became enmeshed in legislative elections and threatened to break down party lines. The tactics of the temperance men elicited as much opposition as they did support among voters. In Hamptonville, Yadkin County, after antiprohibitionists prevented a temperance lecturer from speaking, Josiah Cowles complained that his opponents in the legislative elections tried to identify him "with the 'Sons' knowing that the order is verry [sic] obnoxious in the county." He reported to his son: "I dont know how the thing will go but the question has swallowed up all others & there is a most intense excitement & the two extremes are driven as far apart as the Dales." Cowles lost the election and explained that the "'sons' operated against me also very much. I have never seen such excitement on any question." Cowles was not the only western Whig legislative candidate to confront problems because he was identified with the organization. Samuel Finley Patterson of Caldwell, one of the state's most prominent Whigs, faced an opponent who continually harped upon the active role Patterson had played in the Sons of Temperance in the 1840s and on his opposition to treating, but unlike Cowles, Patterson won.[28]

The divisions in Yadkin and Caldwell counties were replicated elsewhere. In Guilford County, an assemblage of temperance advocates warned legislative candidates that, if they did not support legislation designed to prevent the sale of alcoholic beverages in Guilford, it would not support their candidacy. Such demands prompted the Whig Greensboro *Patriot* to declare that the prohibition men were trying to cripple the Whig party in the overwhelmingly Whig county. In nearby Rowan County, the Whig party was temporarily disabled when temperance Whigs nominated a slate of candidates to oppose the one chosen by the regular Whig convention.[29]

27. *Ibid.*

28. Josiah Cowles to Calvin J. Cowles, July 9, August 4, 1854, both in Calvin J. Cowles Papers, NCDAH; Samuel F. Patterson to Rufus L. Patterson, July 11, 1854, in Samuel Finley Patterson Papers, Duke.

29. A. Netherly, *et al.*, to David F. Caldwell, July 4, 1854, in Caldwell Papers; Greensboro *Patriot*, July 22, 1854; Salisbury *Carolina Watchman*, May 24, 1854.

The Whig party was not the only one rent by the fight over temperance. The Democratic Raleigh *Standard* attributed the rare triumph of a Whig commoner in Wake County to the defections of temperance Democrats. Even in Edgecombe County, where Democrats regularly garnered 90 percent of the vote and where Primitive Baptist antagonism to any form of governmental coercion predominated, candidates hotly contested the temperance issue.[30]

Temperance activists also pressed their demands upon the parties' gubernatorial candidates. Both Democrat Thomas Bragg and Whig Alfred Dockery affirmed their personal support for temperance but declined to advocate or oppose the passage of a prohibitory law on the grounds that this task was the work of the legislature. Their contention that such legislation fell outside the governor's province was true, but that had stopped neither candidate from taking a stand on other legislative issues like constitutional reform or internal improvements. They simply wanted to keep the temperance issue out of the campaign, and they succeeded.[31]

Still, the impact of the prohibition issue on legislative races assured a debate over it in the next General Assembly. By the time the legislators gathered, though, temperance forces were divided between prohibitionists and supporters of a local option for the prohibition of liquor retailing. Even the Sons of Temperance rejected prohibition in favor of local option. Lawmakers took advantage of this division to defuse the threat that the temperance issue posed to the parties. While proclaiming their allegiance to the cause of temperance, they rejected another large petition in favor of prohibition; then, to appease temperance men, they established a new tax on capital invested in the liquor traffic. They also responded favorably to the call to allow towns to establish their own local policies on the sale of liquor. In the major piece of temperance legislation passed during the session, legislators set a precedent for other towns when they permitted the citizens of Salisbury, Rowan County, to hold a referendum on limiting the sale of liquor to purchases of over five gallons. They also permitted the local exclusion of grog shops. Over the next several years, towns and counties that demanded it were given the opportunity to keep their areas dry. In this way, politicians effectively turned temperance into a local question that sometimes divided citizens of towns and counties, but as far as the state's parties were concerned, the temperance issue was put into quarantine.[32]

---

30. Raleigh *Standard*, August 5, 1854; Tarboro *Southerner*, July 22, 1854.

31. Whitener, *Prohibition*, 45.

32. Hershal L. Macon, "A Fiscal History of North Carolina, 1776–1860" (Ph.D. dissertation, University of North Carolina, 1932), 417, 420; *HJ, 1854–55*, 64–65, 419–20. On the temperance issue in town politics, see Charlotte *Western Democrat*, December 11, 1855, January 15, 1856; Salisbury *Carolina Watchman*, February 8, 1855; Asheville *News*, June 9, 1859.

The parties had weathered the temperance storm, just as they had all other storms. Indeed, the North Carolina party system remained vibrant in 1854. Its strength was evident in areas other than temperance. Whigs, learning the hard lessons of 1850 and 1852, reconstituted the executive committee so that its members living near Raleigh could conduct the committee's business. They also wrote a platform and ran a state campaign that coupled moderate support for constitutional reform with ardent advocacy of state aid to internal improvements. Despite problems that arose from the temperance issue that year, the parties ran vigorously contested campaigns for governor and the General Assembly. Voters clearly felt that they had a great deal at stake. While turnout in other states under the second party system declined in the early 1850s, North Carolina voters in 1854 came out in greater numbers than they had since 1840 and divided their votes almost equally between Bragg and Dockery, the Democrat Bragg squeaking out a majority with only 51.1 percent of the vote. Whigs, it appeared, could look forward to challenging the Democratic candidate for governor two years later. But in 1856 no Whig opposed Governor Thomas Bragg; his opposition came from the newly formed nativist American party.[33]

33. Raleigh *Register*, February 25, 1854.

Seven *The Rise and Fall of the American Party*

Historians have given short shrift to the American party in North Carolina. J. G. deRoulhac Hamilton dismissed it as "nothing but the old Whig party in disguise." Henry M. Wagstaff declared that the party was a shelter for Whigs who refused to join the Democratic party. The conclusions of Hamilton, Wagstaff, and others contain a large kernel of truth, but they do not tell the whole story. An examination of the demise of the Whig party and the rise and fall of the American party in North Carolina reveals much about the nature of the second party system in the state. It shows the critical importance of the national party to the existence of a state party and shows the difficulties faced by a party trying to establish itself upon the ruins of another one. It also suggests that the establishment of the American party in North Carolina represented a phenomenon different from that which occurred in northern states.[1]

The creation of the American party in 1854 throughout much of the country elicited hostile responses from North Carolina's political press. The Know-Nothings, Democrats charged, planned to triumph "upon hatred to foreigners, intolerance in religious matters, and opposition to the rights of man." Whigs were just as vehement. The Salisbury *Carolina Watchman* said of the Know-Nothings:

1. J. G. deRoulhac Hamilton, *Party Politics in North Carolina, 1835–1860* (Durham: Seeman Printery, 1916), 73; Henry M. Wagstaff, *State Rights and Political Parties in North Carolina, 1776–1861* (Baltimore: Johns Hopkins University Press, 1906), 94; Michael F. Holt, *Forging a Majority: The Foundation of the Republican Party in Pittsburgh* (New Haven: Yale University Press, 1969); Michael F. Holt, "The Politics of Impatience: The Origins of Know-Nothingism," *JAH*, LX (1973), 309–31; Ronald P. Formisano, *The Birth of Mass Political Parties: Michigan, 1827–1861* (Princeton: Princeton University Press, 1971).

It is an institution of man, an institution which was brought forth in darkness and which is even yet shrouded from the glare of light—an institution which glides as the serpent or the shapeless ghost, and seeks to accomplish great measures of State by binding men in solemn oaths to secrecy, and to secret allegiance to the dictatorial powers of those who may stand at the head of the Order. . . . In other words, he sells himself to political bondage, and seals the bargain with the solemn appeal to God as a witness thereof. . . . Such a position in a free and enlightened country like ours, where every man should be a sovereign, is degrading.

The somewhat less hostile Raleigh *Register* agreed with the party's anti-Catholicism because there was an "antagonism between Romanism and Republicanism. Catholicity cannot live in an atmosphere of free thought." Nevertheless, it concluded "that the danger of an overshadowing Catholic ascendancy is not so imminent as it is by many represented to be."[2]

Despite obvious public opposition, the American party was apparently introduced in North Carolina in late 1854 by Kenneth Rayner, one of the state's leading Whigs. Rayner had been active in Whig politics since 1835, when he served as a member of the constitutional convention and as a member of the House of Commons. Over the next twenty years, Rayner, a wealthy slaveowner, could usually be found as a member of the Commons, the Senate, or the U.S. House of Representatives. In 1848 Whigs throughout the state assumed that he would be their gubernatorial candidate and were dismayed when he withdrew from the race. In 1852 Rayner's relations with the bulk of the Whig party were strained by his refusal to support the party's presidential nominee, Winfield Scott, whom he suspected of free-soil sympathies. Nevertheless, he remained within the party and played an active role in the state party convention in 1854. Yet his position in 1852 had revealed his unease with the direction in which the Whig party was drifting. Scott's candidacy seemed to Rayner to reveal southern Whigs' willingness to sacrifice southern rights for the filthy lucre of office. In the American party, Rayner found what he believed was a purer political movement, one that offered a chance to avoid the sectional politics that had vexed him and other southern Whigs in 1852. Rayner himself proposed the "third degree" or "Union degree" in the American party's oath. Inductees pledged allegiance to the Union and opposition to sectional conflict.[3]

2. Salisbury *Carolina Watchman*, November 16, 1854; Raleigh *Register*, November 16, 1854.
3. On Rayner's longstanding nativist sympathies, see *Speeches of Mr. Kenneth Rayner* (Washington, D.C.: n.p., 1845). On his opposition to Scott, see William Valentine Diaries (MS in SHC), July 21, 1852; Thomas Bragg to John Bragg, July 11, 1852, in John Bragg Papers, SHC. On

TABLE 21
Voting on Nativist Issues in the North Carolina General Assembly, 1854–1855

	Senate	*House*
Average Index of Disagreement	82.3	78.2
Average Percentage of Pronativist Votes		
Democrats	15.9	9.5
Whigs	98.2	87.7

Rayner returned to North Carolina in late November, 1854, from a national meeting of nativist leaders excited about the prospects of organizing the American party in the state. He concentrated his own efforts upon the state's legislators. In a letter to New York's American party leader, Daniel Ullmann, Rayner reported success: "Our legislature being in session many members *came in*, and from present appearances, I think we will have the greater portion of them in a few weeks." The success that Rayner reported was largely limited to Whig members of the legislature. When Democratic commoners tried to pass an anti-Know-Nothing resolution, 95.9 percent of the Whigs voted to table it. Table 21 reveals the extent to which Whigs endorsed the nativism of the American party. Within months, most Whigs had formally transferred their allegiance to the American party.[4]

Whig newspapers reflected this transition. The hostility toward the American party of the *Carolina Watchman* and the skepticism of the *Register* in late 1854 gave way to support in early 1855. In January, the *Register* said that "we do not hesitate for a moment to declare that, so far as the intentions of the 'new party' have been revealed, they are just and right." The *Watchman* altered its position even more dramatically. In early February, it claimed "that necessity forced the American people to adopt this mode [the American party] of attacking the stormy march of foreign influence—let the union of Whigs and Democrats and the rapidity with which thousands enrolled their names among the American party explain."[5]

At this time, the *Watchman* and the *Register* claimed to be Whig papers, but by May they were committed exponents of "Americanism." In

his continued ties to the Whig party, see Kenneth Rayner to David F. Caldwell, April 4, 1853, in David F. Caldwell Papers, SHC; Raleigh *Register*, February 25, 1854.

4. Kenneth Rayner to Daniel Ullmann, November 29, 1854, in Daniel Ullmann Papers, New York Historical Society, New York, New York.

5. Salisbury *Carolina Watchman*, February 1, 1855; Raleigh *Register*, January 13, 1855.

late May the editor of the *Watchman* declared: "The night of darkness has gathered in over the Union of these States; and while the Pope, and his colleagues are marching stealthily around the camp of Protestantism, it becomes our duty to place Americans on the watch towers of our political liberties. . . . The great battle between Popery and Protestantism has already begun in our beloved country." Not all of the Whig papers in the state entered the ranks of the American party. The prominent editor of the Fayetteville *Observer*, Edward J. Hale, refused to abandon the Whig party, but even he looked with some favor upon the Know-Nothings. Most Whig papers, in fact, made the switch.[6]

But why did they switch? The first and most important reason was the breakup of the national Whig organization. The state party, essentially, needed the national party in order to exist. In 1852, James Osborne, a prominent Charlotte Whig contemplating the dissension in the party, wrote to Edward Hale that "we have much power still remaining for the preservation of the true principles of the government." The impact that Whigs might have on the government "depends however on our national organization. If we break into fragments—or divide into mere sectional factions—we are impotent for good—and we surrender our institutions to the control of the worst passions and influences." A national party was therefore necessary in order to promulgate Whig principles in the national government. And, it should be remembered, the continued significance of the public-lands issue kept Whig principles relevant for North Carolinians.[7]

A national organization was also needed to get Whig politicians elected to positions in the national government so that they could implement those principles. John Kerr, Whig gubernatorial candidate in 1852, wrote to William A. Graham in 1854 that "questions of the greatest magnitude, connected both with our domestic and foreign relations are now, or will shortly be, presented, which it will require the purest hearts and wisest heads to comprehend and dispose of properly. We need the services of Statesmen, . . . of *Whig Statesmen* rather than democratic." Kerr concluded that, with the demise of the party, "we must have a new organization, whereby the true and genuine Whig materials of the Country can once more be made available."[8]

Whigs in the state were also bound to the national organization be-

6. Salisbury *Carolina Watchman*, May 31, 1855; Fayetteville *Observer*, May 7, 1855; Greensboro *Patriot*, January 6, May 5, 1855.

7. James W. Osborne to Edward J. Hale, May 29, 1852, in Edward Jones Hale Papers, NCDAH.

8. John Kerr to William A. Graham, July 4, 1854, in J. G. deRoulhac Hamilton and Max R. Williams (eds.), *The Papers of William Alexander Graham* (6 vols. to date; Raleigh: State Department of Archives and History, 1957–), IV, 50.

cause loyalty to the national party and national issues helped override intraparty conflict over divisive state issues. Whigs might disagree among themselves on issues such as constitutional reform, but they were united by adherence to the national Whig party and what it stood for. In 1852, the Raleigh *Register*, trying to avoid an intraparty schism over the calling of a constitutional convention, had contended that the only questions about which the state's Whigs were in complete agreement were those "great and fundamental principles connected with the National Government and its policy." The *Register* urged Whigs to keep the convention question out of the campaign and to "plant ourselves on the platform of the Whig Party, as a *National* Party." From the foregoing, it is evident that the national party served both as a campaign tool to avoid a divisive state issue and also as the glue that bound divergent factions of the state party together. Therefore, the national party—as the defender of Whig principles, the vehicle through which state politicians could influence national policy, the agency through which ambitious Whigs entered the national political arena, and as a force that united the state party—played a critical role in the survival and success of the state party.[9]

The disruption of the Whig party over the Kansas-Nebraska Act forced North Carolina's Whigs to admit reluctantly that the national party was dead. In early July, 1854, Congressman John Kerr wrote that "at present our old party is broken up. We are without nationality." Early the next year, Whig senator George E. Badger wrote to a colleague: "I believe what you say of the Whig party. I share in your regret at its dissolution."[10]

The death of the national Whig party did not put an immediate end to an individual's identification with that party. When the coowner of the Greensboro *Patriot* took over sole ownership of the paper in January, 1855, he declared: "I am, and ever have been a Whig, and expect, on all proper occasions, to advocate the doctrines of the Whig Party, without being acrimonious towards their opponents." As late as June, 1855, the editor of the Fayetteville *Argus* claimed that "we are not Know-Nothings, as we have before repeatedly said. We are Whigs." Yet both men eventually supported the American party. In large part, they were searching for another conservative party that would oppose the Democrats. The editor of the *Argus* explained his position when he wrote: "The Whig party . . . is at this time prostrated and powerless. Those who call themselves Democrats have the

9. Raleigh *Register*, March 3 and 31, 1852; Thomas E. Jeffrey, "The Second Party System in North Carolina" (Ph.D. dissertation, Catholic University of America, 1976), 227–28, 367.

10. John Kerr to William A. Graham, July 4, 1854, in Hamilton and Williams (eds.), *Graham Papers*, IV, 50; George E. Badger to James A. Pearce, March 29, 1855, in George Edmund Badger Papers, NCDAH.

government in their hands, and under their administration its honors and emoluments have been so dispensed and the patronage of the government has been so brought into conflict with the freedom of elections, as to disgust many good and conservative men of both the old parties." Under such circumstances, the American party appeared. The *Argus* contended that to "our native population . . . should be confided the sacred deposit of American nationality." Whigs, it is said, had initially stood aloof from the new party, but "the Whigs . . . are conservative, are ardently attached to the union and to the constitution honestly and fairly administered; and with them it matters not so much who governs the country as that it be well governed. Hence the disposition of the Whig press to give the American party a fair showing." The new party, for many Whigs, represented a solution for men who were partisans without a national party.[11]

The Whig attraction to the American party did not develop simply because the American party seemed like a potentially successful replacement for the Whig party; the Americans' antiparty views and nativism also comported well with Whig thinking. Throughout its life, the American party was a party that condemned party organization, and in so doing it built upon Whig beliefs in the evils of party. In late 1855, the *Register* denounced "the *incorrigible* devotee at the shrine of Party, who, forgetting country, patriotism, liberty, everything, goes for PARTY, *right or wrong.*" When American party members advocated the congressional candidacy of Edwin G. Reade, they claimed: "He is not a politician in the party sense of the term; by position and education, he is entirely free from the corrupting influences of party men, party schools, and party tactics."[12]

Parties, Americans charged, were deceitful organizations, saying one thing but doing another. One writer argued that Americans, coming from both of the old parties, "have . . . beheld these parties holding conventions, laying down platforms and regulations, by which their parties in future should be governed, and abandoning them when in power at their pleasure—a trick, a mere device to gull and deceive those who follow in their train." Henry W. Miller, former leader of the Whig party in Raleigh and in 1855 an American party leader, declared that "the two old parties met in National Conventions, in 1852, and adopted platforms of principles, and hardly had the ink dried on the paper before they were violated. Showing no regard for principle, but only a lust for office," both parties abandoned their principles. "Hence, in part, the formation of this great American party."[13]

11. Greensboro *Patriot*, January 6, 1855; Fayetteville *North Carolina Argus*, n.d., quoted in Greensboro *Patriot*, June 16, 1855.
12. Raleigh *Register*, November 28, 1855; Greensboro *Patriot*, May 19, 1855.
13. Greensboro *Patriot*, April 14, 1855; Raleigh *Register*, May 5, 1855.

The American party appealed not only to the antiparty sentiments of the Whigs but also to their nativism. Whig antiforeign and anti-Catholic rhetoric, for example, had been evident in the political discussions of 1854. Early in the year, when the papal nuncio visited the United States to resolve intra-Church disputes, the Fayetteville *Observer* contended that "the Catholic influence is surely now secure in the Administration." Whig nativism could also be seen in the party press's response to the passage of the Homestead Bill in the House of Representatives. The Raleigh *Register* complained that the enactment of that legislation would open up the public lands to settlement by the "scum" of Europe; soon after, it wrote that "there is not another nation on the face of the earth that would thus consent to be the receptacle of all foreign vagrants and vagabonds who may be discarded elsewhere." It went on to argue in words that would become commonplace a year later in American party rhetoric: "We are rapidly losing the national, distinctive character of Americans, by a mean and despicable subserviency to foreigners, whom we flatter and court for their votes and influence at elections; and it is from this cause that they are emboldened to combine to obtain public offices, and to put their hands into the public treasury, before they are acquainted with the nature of our institutions or even understood our language."[14]

Whigs also linked the foreign population to the rise of antislavery beliefs in the North. On the passage of the Homestead Act, the Raleigh *Register* said: "In a few years Oregon, Washington, Kansas, Nebraska, Minnesota, and a number of other territories, carved out of these, will be knocking at the door of Congress to be admitted as States—*free States, hostile to slavery[,] filled with a foreign population.*"[15]

Nativism and its close cousin anti-Catholicism appealed to more voters than Whigs alone. Historians of North Carolina have generally discounted the significance of anti-Catholicism in the state because there were so few Catholics or foreigners living there. In 1850, only 2,524 foreign-born persons lived in North Carolina, and of the state's 1,678 churches only 4 were Roman Catholic. However, it would be a mistake to ignore the attraction of anti-Catholicism to North Carolinians. People do not need to have much contact with another group in order to fear or hate it. In the 1830s, Alexis de Toqueville observed that in the United States racism was most pervasive in those northern states where few blacks lived. For many years colonial New Englanders, among whom there were few Catholics, held annual Pope Days to denounce the Pope and Catholicism.[16]

14. Fayetteville *Observer*, n.d., quoted in Raleigh *Standard*, February 4, 1854; Raleigh *Register*, March 11 and 18, 1854.
15. Raleigh *Register*, July 26, 1854.
16. *Cf.* Jeffrey, "Second Party System," 227–28; Alexis de Tocqueville, *Democracy in Amer-*

In fact, a strain of anti-Catholicism ran through North Carolina's history. For the first sixty years of statehood, North Carolina formally excluded non-Protestants from holding public office. The state removed the ambiguous ban on Catholics (though retaining it for non-Christians) only after lengthy debate in the convention of 1835 and then did so less out of a belief in religious tolerance than out of deference to Catholic delegate and justice of the state supreme court William Gaston. Thirteen years later, in 1848, many persons assumed that Episcopalian Charles Manly, the Whig candidate, lost votes because some citizens thought he was Catholic. Obviously, anti-Catholicism was not limited just to Whigs in its appeal, and there is little reason to believe that anti-Catholicism had abated by 1855, especially in light of the massive influx of Catholics into other parts of the country. Kenneth Rayner believed that "the strong Protestant element in our order [is] the strongest feature in it, with our rural population in the Country." Given the broad appeal of anti-Catholicism to both Democrats and Whigs, it is not surprising that in 1855 there was no simple transition from the Whig to the American party.[17]

Indicative both of the bipartisan attraction of the nativist Americans and of the predominance of Whigs in the new organization are membership lists from three local councils in Halifax County, near the Virginia border. One cannot assume that the lists are representative of the state, but they are nonetheless suggestive. Of the 108 members listed on July 31, 1855, 88 (81.5 percent) had been Whigs, 19 (17.5 percent) Democrats, and 1 had no stated previous partisan affiliation. The Americans were clearly a Whig-dominated organization with a substantial Democratic component. Unlike the situation in other states where the Know-Nothings drew many apolitical men into the order, Halifax Know-Nothings clearly drew their activists from men with definite past partisan identities.[18]

Those Know-Nothings who hoped their organization would draw support from Democrats as well as from Whigs would have been comforted by

---

ica, ed. Phillips Bradley (2 vols.; New York: Vintage Books, 1954), 359–60; David M. Potter, *The Impending Crisis, 1848–1861*, completed and edited by Don E. Fehrenbacher (New York: Harper and Row, 1976), 242. Also see Eugene Berwanger, *The Frontier Against Slavery: Western Anti-Negro Prejudice and the Slavery Extension Controversy* (Urbana: University of Illinois Press, 1967).

17. Harold J. Counihan, "The North Carolina Constitutional Convention of 1835: A Study in Jacksonian Democracy," *NCHR*, XLVI (1969), 335–64; Raleigh *Standard*, December 5, 1849; Kenneth Rayner to Daniel Ullmann, May 4, 1855, in Ullmann Papers.

18. The membership lists are located in J. H. Davis to John T. Gregory, July 31, 1855, R. H. Webb to Gregory, July 31, 1855, John T. Bishop to Gregory, July 28, 1855, all in the John T. Gregory Papers, NCDAH. Barbara Cain of the NCDAH staff kindly showed me the Gregory Papers. *Cf.* Dale Baum, "Know-Nothingism and the Republican Majority in Massachusetts: The Political Realignment of the 1850s," *JAH*, LXIV (1978), 959–86.

these lists. But next to Democrat James V. Allen's name was the notation that he had withdrawn from the group. We do not know whether the rest of the Democratic Know-Nothings in Halifax followed Allen's course, but if they behaved like many others in a similar position throughout the state, then they too eventually withdrew. The Know-Nothings also garnered the support of influential Democrats like William High, the sheriff of Wake County, and William T. Dortch, Democratic leader in Wayne County, but they stayed only a short while in the Know-Nothing organization and soon returned to the Democratic party.[19]

The experience of Democrat W. Rives of Chatham County suggests the reason many Democrats were initially attracted to the Know-Nothings but either left the order or never joined it. In response to a query from his children in early 1856, Rives conceded that at one time he planned to "join the K.N. as I was opposed to Foreignir [*sic*] paupers being sent here—also I have no faith at all in the Roman Catholic mode of Worship." Later he discovered to his dismay that the Know-Nothings were "a secret oath bound league." But the major reason Rives did not join the party was because he became convinced "that the originators of that league were only trying to do that which the Whigs so signally fail[ed] to do[,] to put down the Democrats." He went on to explain how he came to that conclusion: "The editor of the Fayetteville observer (as good a Whig as the state can boast of) said in his paper some time past that although he could not Join this oath bound party his sympathies were with them because they were calculated to do the Democratic party *harm* and we could not have a *worse party than that was*—who under these circumstances that had a drop of Democrat blood flowing in his veins could think of Joining such a party."[20]

If Democrats like Rives did not learn of the American party's Whiggishness from Whig papers like the *Observer*, they certainly learned of it from the Democratic press. Papers like the *Standard* told their readers that the Know-Nothings were little more than Whigs who had contracted "Popephobia." When the Know-Nothings claimed no attachment to either of the old parties, the Charlotte *Western Democrat* charged "that the great body of the Society are Whigs, and its influence is used for the benefit and promotion of the leading men of the Whig party. We look upon the organization as a Whig machine." Even if Democrats who joined the Know-Nothings ignored the Democratic press, they could not ignore the Whigs who ran the party meetings. As they became aware that they were in an

19. Raleigh *Standard*, August 1, 1855, June 25, 1856.
20. W. Rives to "Dear Children," February 8, 1856, in Rives-Dalton Family Papers, East Carolina Manuscript Collection, J. Y. Joyner Library, East Carolina University, Greenville, North Carolina.

anti-Democratic organization, they scurried out of that party and back to their old political home. Democrat Jesse Waugh had a common experience after he had debated a Know-Nothing politician in Stokes County. He reported that his "pride was flattered by seeing eight or ten unflinching democrats heretofore, recant and withdraw from that sink of pollution." Democratic papers filled their columns with endless declarations of Democrats who had withdrawn from the Know-Nothings.[21]

The early confusion of 1855 and the gradual clarification of party lines were evident too in the congressional races of that year. The American party sought congressional candidates from the ranks of discontented Democrats as well as from old Whigs. It did this in order to prove that it had no connection with the old parties and to broaden the popular support for the party beyond that of the minority Whigs. The experience of Democrat Abraham W. Venable provides a good example. Venable served in Congress from 1847 to 1853. Until 1853, he stood high in the state Democratic party hierarchy. In that year, he ran afoul of the Raleigh leadership, partly because he favored the distribution of the proceeds from the sale of the public lands—a stand that contradicted the position of the national party. The leadership ran a regular party candidate against Venable, and the resulting split in the party permitted a Whig victory. Two years later, the leadership defeated Venable's bid for the nomination in a district convention.[22]

Venable had never won favor among the state's Whigs—in fact, his virulent opposition to the Compromise of 1850 earned him the hostility of the Whig leadership. But this was the man whom the American party sought as its candidate in the Fourth District. Henry K. Nash wrote to Venable to ask him to run. "We do not ask you to desert your political principles," he said, "neither do we desire it." The American party just asked him to support the party's principles "in the canvass . . . and . . . on the floor of Congress."[23]

Venable decided to stay out of the race, but Americans did convince another unhappy Democrat, James B. Shepard, to run for Congress. Shepard had been a member of the Democratic party's central committee and ran as its gubernatorial candidate in 1846, but he rejected the party's embrace of state aid to railroads and engaged in what the party leadership

21. Charlotte *Western Democrat*, November 24, 1855; Jesse Waugh to Thomas Settle Jr., July 28, 1855, in Thomas Settle Papers, No. 2, SHC; Raleigh *Standard*, July 4, August 1, 1855.

22. Abraham W. Venable to Archibald H. Arrington, July 19, 1853, in Archibald H. Arrington Papers, SHC; Raleigh *Standard*, April 27, June 15, 22, July 20, 27, August 3, 10, 1853, April 25, 1855.

23. Henry K. Nash to Abraham W. Venable, April 26, 1855, in Abraham Watkins Venable Papers, SHC.

called disorganizing activities. In 1852 he led the successful floor opposition to the party caucus' candidate for the U.S. Senate and helped prevent the election of a senator. Shepard accepted the American party nomination and became one of four former Democrats to run as Americans in Democratic districts.[24]

By running former Democrats in Democratic districts and former Whigs in Whig districts, the American party indicated its desire to broaden the base of the party and belied its hostility to the compromises of party politics. As one opponent asked: "How . . . does it happen, that in Democratic Districts they have thus far in our State selected democrats, although Whigs belong to their party? If availability is no part of their creed, then why not nominate Know-Nothing Whigs in the Edgecombe and Wake Districts [two heavily Democratic districts]?" The Democratic Raleigh *Standard* commented that "the new party, though it preaches the doctrine of excluding from office old party hacks, seldom fails to bring them forward as candidates."[25]

Not only did the American party run into problems because of its nomination of former Democrats, but it also had difficulties with its Whig nominees. In early 1855, as candidates for Congress announced themselves, Whigs still tended to think of themselves as Whigs. Two such men were John Kerr, who had served as a Whig congressman in the Fifth District since 1853, and James A. Caldwell, a Whig leader in the Seventh District who sought the party's nomination in 1855. Caldwell announced his candidacy soon after General Atlas J. Dargan of Anson made a similar announcement. This led one Democrat to conclude that a Whig party district convention would be held and would nominate a third candidate. This Democrat was writing in early April; at that time he saw the Whig party as the district's primary anti-Democratic organization. Yet at the same time he recognized that "an element had entered into things. . . . To wit. Know Nothingism," although just what affect the new party would have he was not sure. The Know-Nothings did indeed affect the politics of the district. They were prominent enough for Caldwell to declare that "he was not the Know Nothing candidate, but was 'a Whig of the old line, a Henry Clay Whig,' and expected to be supported by that party." Then, responding to pressure to join the American party and run as its candidate, Caldwell gave it his halfhearted support; at the party's convention, he lost its nomination to former Democrat Samuel Stowe. Caldwell subsequently withdrew from the American party and the campaign and published a letter

24. Raleigh *Standard*, May 30, June 20, 27, July 25, 1855.
25. John Kerr to Editor of the Fayetteville *Observer*, May 29, 1855, quoted in Raleigh *Register*, June 9, 1855; Raleigh *Standard*, June 20, 1855.

claiming that Protestants were not threatened by the influx of Catholics and that the Know-Nothings were sympathetic to the abolitionists. He then came out in support of the Democratic candidate, Burton Craige.[26]

John Kerr took a somewhat different path to the Democratic party. In the summer of 1854, Kerr was seeking some way to revive the ailing Whig party: "We need the services of . . . *Whig Statesmen*. . . . We must have a new organization, whereby the true and genuine Whig materials of the Country can once more be made available." But Kerr's own political moorings had been loosened by his service in Congress, where his participation in the debates over the Kansas-Nebraska Act had convinced him that antislavery forces in the North posed a serious threat to the South.[27] When Kerr returned from Congress, the American party leadership apparently offered him an opportunity to run as its candidate, but Kerr refused and campaigned as a Whig. During the campaign he claimed, "I am *now, as ever*, a Whig, deeply convinced of the conservative tendency and influence of Whig principles."

Kerr's hostility to the American party developed not only from the slavery question but also from the way the party was organized and what it stood for. In an open letter to the editor of the Fayetteville *Observer*, Kerr wrote that "secret political oath-bound associations are always dangerous to liberty, and can never be justified in a free country." He declared his opposition "to the influx of foreign paupers and foreign criminals into our country. . . . But I will not consent to any system or policy which would exclude all foreigners from our shores." He concluded by saying that the worst thing about the Know-Nothings was that "they seek to inflame the worst passions of human nature, by connecting religion with politics."[28]

The American party, controlled by the old Whig leadership of the district and now the dominant force in the district's politics, ran Edwin G. Reade against Kerr. Kerr lost the election and soon afterward joined the Democratic party. Kerr's and Caldwell's experiences in 1854 and 1855 revealed the dilemma of lifelong Whigs as they contemplated membership in the American party. Their experiences also showed the confusion of partisan identities in early 1855 and the way in which party lines became firmly drawn later in the year.[29]

More suggestive of the continuities from Whiggery to Americanism

26. [?] to John F. Hoke, April 5, 1855, in John F. Hoke Papers, SHC; Fayetteville *Observer*, May 21, 1855; Charlotte *Western Democrat*, June 15, 1855.

27. John Kerr to William A. Graham, July 4, 1854, in Hamilton and Williams (eds.), *Graham Papers*, IV, 520.

28. John Kerr to the Editor of the Fayetteville *Observer*, May 29, 1855, quoted in Raleigh *Register*, June 9, 1855.

29. Fayetteville *Observer*, September 24, 1855.

was the candidacy of Richard C. Puryear, Whig congressman in the Sixth District. In early April, a Whig convention nominated Puryear for a second term. As a candidate, he continued to identify himself as a Whig, but one who accepted the principles of the Know-Nothing party. His opponent, Alfred M. Scales, complained to a friend that Puryear "is a slippery fellow, is now straining a point to make the impression that he cares nothing in the world about the K.N. that these are his principles if there were no such order & calls upon the people to assist him in carrying them out, not by taking the oath but as as [*sic*] he had done."[30]

Puryear won the election, as did two other American party candidates, four Democrats, and independent Thomas Clingman. The state's congressional delegation was thus little different from the delegation of 1853, when the state was represented by Clingman, three Whigs, and four Democrats. However, the First District, which had elected a Democrat in 1853 by a narrow margin (50.4 percent), in 1855 elected an American by a similar margin (51.7 percent). The Fourth District had elected a Whig in 1853 because two other candidates split the Democratic party vote; in 1855, this normally Democratic district easily elected a Democrat. Most significant, the elections revealed a persistence of older voting patterns: the correlation between the elections of 1853 and of 1855 in five competitive districts was .92.[31]

In 1856, the American party became even more exclusively a Whig organization. Its Whiggish orientation became evident at the party's convention in February, 1856, where, for all their antiparty claims, the Americans ran their convention in the usual Whig fashion. Delegates chose as their president Sion H. Rogers, Whig congressman from 1853 to 1855. Their candidate for governor was John A. Gilmer of Greensboro, a longtime Whig senator and a front-runner for the Whig gubernatorial nomination only four years before. The convention also established a state executive committee to coordinate the campaign; all ten of the men on the committee were former Whigs. The committee chairman had been the Whig executive-committee chairman in 1854, and four others had served at least once on the Whig committee since 1850. No one should have been astonished when delegate Alfred G. Foster accidentally praised Gilmer as the "Whig" nominee.[32]

30. Raleigh *Standard*, April 18, 1855; Greensboro *Patriot*, April 21, 1855; Alfred M. Scales to Thomas Settle, Jr., July 2, 1855, in Settle Papers.

31. The data were incomplete for the Kerr-Reade race. Therefore, the counties in that district were omitted from the calculations.

32. James W. Osborne to William A. Graham, January 12, 1852, in Hamilton and Williams (eds.), *Graham Papers*, IV, 233. The chairman was Henry W. Miller. The other former committeemen were John D. Hyman, John H. Haughton, Henry K. Nash, and Nicholas W. Woodfin. John W.

The platform that the American party adopted was a defanged version of the Whig platform of 1854. Like the Whigs (and the Democrats), the Americans endorsed state-aided internal improvements, but whereas the Whigs had given wholehearted support to the projects, Americans pulled back and endorsed only such expenditures "as will not burthen the people with oppressive taxation." They also revealed their Whig past when they called for the distribution of the proceeds of the public lands. Americans did take advantage of their new name and organization by jettisoning the issue of constitutional reform that had so damaged the Whig party in recent years. The platform declared that, because Whigs and Democrats in the party coalition differed over those issues, the American party refused to take a stand on constitutional revisions, except to state its opposition to a change in the basis of representation.[33]

Perhaps the best indication of the extent to which the Americans had become a weaker version of the Whig party is suggested by the minimal attention that the platform paid to foreigners and Catholics. The closest the party came to declaring its nativism was in its resolution on the public lands, in which it opposed "the policy of the General Government squandering the public lands to provide homesteads for foreign paupers and convicts." By this time, party leaders had clearly decided that for the state's citizens, among whom there were few foreigners, the foreign threat was not credible. This decision may have hurt the party because it removed one of the few issues upon which it and the Democrats disagreed. A firm nativist stance might have tempted nativist Democrats to support the American party, but during the campaign the American press gave little notice to the nativist issue.[34]

Americans were also vexed by the persistent identification of many North Carolinians with the Whig party. This was especially evident in the west. Calvin Cowles of Wilkes, when he requested documents from a congressman for use in the campaign, wrote that "there is much disafection [*sic*] amongst Whigs here." Later in the year, American editor John D. Hyman warned that "a very large majority of our people still profess to

---

Washington had served as an assistant elector in 1852. William H. Harrison was a delegate from Wake County to the convention of 1852. Ralph Gorrell was prominent in the Whig party in Guilford County. Richard A. Caldwell was chosen as a delegate from Anson County to the convention of 1852 and served as an assistant elector that year. The Whig ties of Thomas J. Wilson of Forsythe County are indicated in Jesse Waugh to Thomas Settle, Jr., July 28, 1855, in Settle Papers. The sources consulted for the other committeemen were Raleigh *Register*, June 16, 1850, April 28, September 8, 1852, February 25, 1854; Fayetteville *Observer*, April 20, September 14, 1852. The comment by Foster is quoted in Raleigh *Standard*, April 16, 1856.

33. Raleigh *Register*, April 16, 1856.
34. *Ibid.*

TABLE 22
Whig and American Vote for Governor, 1850–1856: Pearson Correlations

Election Year	1856
1850	.95
1852	.95
1854	.96

belong to the Whig party." In response, the American party leadership made a desperate effort to appeal to Whigs. They identified their principles with those of the Whig party and asked: "How could the great and patriotic men of the Old Whig party lend their aid to the election of such a politician as James Buchanan [Democratic presidential candidate], standing on a platform made . . . by that Party which denounced the men and principles of the Whigs, with a bitterness and violence unexampled in political warfare?" When a former Whig from Rowan County ran for the state senate as an anti-Know-Nothing who supported Democratic candidates, the Salisbury *Carolina Watchman* condemned him "because he has reversed his whole political history—deserted his old political friends and associates." [35]

The American party effort to identify itself with the Whigs acted as a self-fulfilling prophecy; by proclaiming their Whiggish origins, the Americans drove out the few Democrats remaining in the party. This helped make the party an exclusively Whiggish organization, but the fact that it was *not* the Whig party made it difficult for the Americans to attract all of the state's Whigs. As a result, the American party became little more than a weakened version of the Whig party.

The elections made this clear. Gilmer received 43.8 percent of the popular vote—more than 5 percent less than Alfred Dockery had won in 1854. Although Gilmer's vote was substantially lower than Dockery's, he drew his greatest strength from Whig areas (see table 22). Gilmer lost in every region of the state. He carried 39 percent of the vote in the coastal plain, 48.4 percent in the Piedmont, and 45.5 percent in the mountains. Although the coastal-plain percentage was similar to Dockery's 39.2 percent of the vote in 1854, the decline from 1854 was almost 5 percent in the Piedmont and more than 16 percent in the mountains. In both houses of the state legislature, Americans were relegated to weak minorities. Compared to the Whig delegation in the House in 1854, the Americans lost 26.3 percent

35. Calvin J. Cowles to Richard C. Puryear, July 4, 1856, in Calvin J. Cowles Papers, NCDAH; John D. Hyman to William A. Graham, October 8, 1856, in Hamilton and Williams (eds.), *Graham Papers*, IV, 665; Raleigh *Register*, July 23, 1856; Salisbury *Carolina Watchman*, July 22, 1856.

of the Whig seats from the coastal plain, 24.0 percent in the Piedmont, and 45.5 percent in the mountains. The elections were a disaster. As George Badger, a Whig who did not join the American party, wrote to John J. Crittenden: "Our election here day before yesterday has resulted in a most disastrous defeat to us and an amazing triumph to democracy. Our old line Whigs behaved like apes—have turned democrats [,] have ruined the state —Heaven help us!"[36]

★

As happened every four years, for several months after the state election the presidential election campaign continued and focused the attention of North Carolinians on national issues. From the advent of the American party in North Carolina, each party had claimed that only it could preserve slavery and the Republic. In so doing, the parties were continuing the old rhetorical battles of Whigs and Democrats.

Democrats charged that the Know-Nothings were a threat to the survival of the Republic. The Know-Nothings, Democrats claimed, had no right to call themselves Americans because they were antirepublican and anti-American. The editor of the Charlotte *Western Democrat* declared that the Know-Nothings' "existence smacks of something like treason, dire and dark." He opposed "all . . . secret political societies . . . because I believe they are unnecessary—repugnant to the genius of Republican Governments—and fraught with consequences that must end in the destruction of a free exercise of private judgment and wholesome enlightened public opinion."[37]

On the other hand, the American party argued that it alone could preserve republicanism in the country because it would end corruption in American politics and repel the threat to American liberty posed by foreigners and Catholics. When the American party abandoned its secrecy in the fall of 1855 and revealed its platform (Americans for government offices, religious freedom, and devotion to the Union), it declared that for the federal government "to be the Government that it was intended to be, those principles *must* be the springs of its action—PROSCRIPTION and CORRUPTION *must* be banished from its departments and political EQUALITY and TOLERATION made the order of the day." The alleged corruption of the Democratic party threatened the freedom of all native Americans. The *Register* warned its readers: "Let us not have our liberties taken away and subverted by being deluded, cajoled and deceived by empty professions, and

36. George E. Badger to John J. Crittenden, August 9, 1856 (typescript), in John Jordan Crittenden Papers, NCDAH.
37. Raleigh *Standard*, June 6, August 15, 1855; Charlotte *Western Democrat*, June 8, 1855.

under false pretences. The wost [*sic*] despotism on earth may be rocked in a Democratic cradle, and reared under a Democratic name. Tyranny and oppression has ever assumed a guise, and stolen upon the people like a masked thief at night."[38]

Not only would the American party put an end to the corruption that pervaded American society, but it claimed that it alone would be able to preserve the Union. Democrats, one party newspaper stated, had always catered to the abolitionists: "The truth is . . . that the worst and most dangerous abolitionists . . . have been democrats, and, at present, nearly all the leaders of the democracy at the North seem to be going over to the abolitionists." The American party, though, offered southerners protection by advocating congressional noninterference with the question of slavery's expansion into the territories. The *Carolina Watchman*, upon learning of the party's position in June, 1855, proudly announced that "a conservative platform on the slavery question has at last been secured by the American party—a consummation which neither Whigs nor Democrats have hitherto been able to effect." It went on to urge that "'Southern men' unite upon this platform—the only one in existence, upon which the South can place any reliance, or hope for any protection of her darling interests." The *Register* contended that "upon the American party, and on that alone, can the South rely for the preservation of its constitutional rights, against the current of abolitionist fanaticism,—pandered to as it is by the Foreign and Romish spoils hunters of party."[39]

Democrats responded in kind. They called the American party "an organization dangerous to the peculiar institutions of the Southern States." Repeatedly they pointed out that southern Know-Nothings were working together with northern abolitionists. Only the Democratic party, they insisted, could preserve the Union and slavery.[40]

The fear of northern antislavery sentiment became increasingly important in 1856, when the avowedly antislavery Republicans ran their first presidential candidate, John C. Frémont. The party's hostility to slavery and its support for congressional exclusion of slavery frightened many white southerners. This fear drove some former Whigs into the Democratic party and shaped the terms of political debate in the presidential campaign.

The plight of many southern Whigs in the election was a difficult one.

38. Raleigh *Register*, October 27, 1855, May 21, 1856. Also see Salisbury *Carolina Watchman*, February 1, May 31, 1855.
39. Raleigh *Register*, March 31, July 14, 1855; Salisbury *Carolina Watchman*, June 28, 1855.
40. Raleigh *Standard*, January 17, July 4, 1855; also see the report of the Warren Winslow-David Reid (not the governor) debate in the Fayetteville *Observer*, June 11, 1855, and of the John Kerr-Edwin Reade debate in the Greensboro *Patriot*, May 29, 1855.

James Buchanan ran as the Democratic candidate, and southern Know-Nothings nominated Millard Fillmore after much of the northern wing of the party bolted and eventually supported Frémont. Former and present southern Whigs certainly would not support Frémont. For those Whigs who had entered the American party, the choice was easy: they had supported Millard Fillmore when he had unsuccessfully sought the Whig presidential nomination in 1852 and were happy to support him again in 1856. Whigs who retained their Whig identity, like Edward J. Hale, former senator George E. Badger, and former senator and governor William A. Graham, tried to maintain their independence but found themselves co-opted by the American party. In February, a Whig political rally in Robeson County elicited an enthusiastic response from Hale's Fayetteville *Observer*. But the *Observer* was one of the few newspapers to offer any encouragement, and the Robeson effort to revive the Whig party died stillborn. The Whig revival aborted because the American party nominated popular former Whigs for president (Fillmore) and governor (Gilmer). A Whig national convention met in Baltimore in September, and many of the old Whig leaders in the state attended, but the convention merely ratified the nomination of Millard Fillmore.[41]

Other Whigs did not support Fillmore. The case of James Osborne, a Whig party leader from Charlotte and candidate for Congress in 1853, is particularly instructive. Osborn's move from the Whig to the Democratic party reveals much about the course that many others also took. It is likely that before 1856 few voters', ballots turned on the slavery issue. Whigs rarely voted Democratic or vice versa because they thought the opposition party was better at defending the slave interest. But 1856 was different because a candidate whom neither Whigs nor Democrats would vote for— Republican John Frémont—was running for president. Now Whigs and Democrats feared the election of a candidate in a way that they had never feared it before. And Whigs who were attracted to Fillmore thought twice about supporting him, because he did not appear to be the strongest anti-Republican candidate.

Osborne mulled the question over for several months. In March, before Fillmore's nomination, he asked William Graham: "What will the Whigs do? I am convinced that we cannot rally the Whig party under the Know-Nothing banner. . . . In the present aspect of the Country—when we are menaced with a Sectional contest under federal auspices . . . should not Southern Whigs consider before they go into the controversy at all, or if so, use their power so as to avert the evils of abolitionism?" At that time, Os-

41. Fayetteville *Observer*, February 14, 1856; Potter, *Impending Crisis*, 259–61.

borne recommended a stance of "masterly inactivity." Masterly inactivity seemed less than masterly by June. Osborne worried that "the organization of the Republican party, which is anti-slavery in fact, and altogether sectional in its theatre, is not an organization, of the South, even as a matter of necessity." He felt that fear of the Republican party would compel Whigs to abandon Fillmore because they expected him to lose. Osborne himself decided to support John Gilmer for governor ("his services to the State, and his thorough Whigism give him the claim on me"); however, he remained uncertain about whether he would vote for Fillmore.[42]

Osborne's uncertainty ended on September 19, when he penned an open letter in which he declared his support for James Buchanan. He preferred Fillmore, Osborne said, but "for the first time a mighty effort is being made to combine the free States in solid union against the slave States, and by force of numbers under the forms of the Constitution to deprive them of their equal rights to the common property, to abolish slavery at the capital . . . and to prostrate them before their oppressors." The only way "to meet the crisis," he wrote, was with "a united South" supporting Buchanan. Osborne and others saw themselves engaged in a contest with antislavery forces, embodied in Frémont's candidacy, and they believed that only Buchanan could defeat Frémont.[43]

The rationale that had led Osborne into the Democratic party also motivated the press of each party to argue that its candidate stood the better chance of defeating Frémont. Indeed, the presidential campaign in North Carolina evolved into a debate over which party had the stronger candidate vis-à-vis the Republicans. Western American editor John Hyman reported to William Graham that "if the people could be satisfied that Mr. Buchanan cannot be elected by the people, there would be a general stampede from his standard to that of Mr. Fillmore." And the Know-Nothing and Whig press tried to portray Buchanan in just that light. They argued that he could not win because free-soil Democrats would support Frémont, while conservative Democrats would back Fillmore. On the other hand, they said, Fillmore stood an excellent chance of winning.[44]

The Democrats replied in kind. Only Buchanan, they said, could thwart the abolitionist menace; Fillmore was a certain loser. The Democrats

42. James W. Osborne to William A. Graham, March 1, 1856, same to same, [July, 1856], both in Hamilton and Williams (eds.), *Graham Papers*, IV, 632–33, 642–43.

43. *Letters of James W. Osborne, Esq., Hon. D. M. Barringer and A. C. Williamson, Esq.: Old Line Whigs of North Carolina* (Charlotte: n.p., 1856), in NCC.

44. John D. Hyman to William A. Graham, October 8, 1856, William A. Graham, "Notes on a Speech," 1856, both in Hamilton and Williams (eds.), *Graham Papers*, IV, 664–65, 647–51; Raleigh *Register*, August 16, 20, 30, September 3, October 25, 1856; Fayetteville *Observer*, October 27, 1856.

TABLE 23
Whig and American Vote for President, 1848–1856: Pearson Correlations

Election Year	1856
1848	.95
1852	.96

proved good prophets. Fillmore finished third behind Buchanan in the national popular vote, and he received only 43.3 percent of North Carolina's vote—a smaller percentage than any major presidential candidate had obtained since the beginning of the second party system. Like Gilmer, Fillmore had run badly. He too received Whig votes, but not the entire strength of the Whig party (see table 23).[45]

By the standards of other states, the American party in North Carolina was competitive: it had won over 40 percent of the popular vote for its gubernatorial and presidential candidates. But by North Carolina's highly competitive standards, a vote under 45 percent was a disaster.

The American party now was but a bastardized and enervated version of the Whig party. Even before the presidential election, Americans had begun to shed their American-party identity and to link themselves increasingly to the Whig party. One Democrat reported in late September that "since the old line Whig Convention you can scarcely find a K N about here. We now have it that many of their most active men & even the President of one of their District meetings was not a member of the party." After the election, Know-Nothing partisans referred to themselves as "American-Whigs." By whatever name they called themselves, they faced the 1857 congressional elections with little enthusiasm. Congressman Richard C. Puryear lamented that "the glorious old whig banner trails in the dust and the American flag is drooping. Yet will I not surrender [,] I will not bow the knee to Baal or worship at the Shrine of Democracy." In the future, he vowed to hold on to "old whig principles." Some Whigs and Americans followed Puryear's example; in the coastal First District, an "American and Whig" convention in Edenton nominated as its candidate William N. H. Smith, a Whig who had never officially joined the American party.[46]

Most Americans, though, did "bow the knee to Baal." The Fayetteville *Observer* reported that, except in Smith's and Puryear's districts, "there are no indications of interest in the contest," and the party ran candidates

45. Raleigh *Standard*, September 10, 1856.
46. E. C. Hines to Henry M. Shaw, September 29, 1856, in Thomas Pittman Collection, NCDAH; *Speech of Hon. Kenneth Rayner in the Hall of the House of Commons, December 8, 1856* (n.p., n.d.), in NCC; Richard C. Puryear to Samuel F. Patterson, February 7, 1857, in Jones and Patterson Papers, SHC; Raleigh *Register*, April 25, 1857.

in only four of the eight districts. Only one of its candidates, John Gilmer, in the heavily Whig and American Fifth District, won election; Democrats captured all of the other races. The combination of American apathy and overwhelming Democratic victories virtually destroyed the American party. The Salisbury *Carolina Watchman* concluded that "the election is over, and the Whigs and Americans are beaten out of countenance. They are literally out of existence."[47]

The American party's rise and fall in North Carolina had been rapid. It had derived its support primarily from Whigs seeking a conservative national party to replace the shattered Whig organization, but it was unable to attract the full Whig vote. Nor was the party able to attract substantial numbers of Democrats, or to keep the Democrats it did attract. As a result, the party became a pale imitation of the Whig party. By 1857 the American party was moribund. The next year it held no convention and ran no gubernatorial candidate.

47. Fayetteville *Observer*, June 29, 1857; Salisbury *Carolina Watchman*, August 18, 1857.

Eight   *The Politics of Secession*

Southerners formed the Confederate States of America in two stages. In the first stage, the seven states of the lower South seceded from the Union between December 20, 1860, and February 4, 1861, and established the Confederacy. In the second stage, between April 17 and June 8, 1861, North Carolina, Virginia, Arkansas, and Tennessee joined their southern brethren. Both the persistence of Unionism in the upper South through mid-April and the subsequent secession of four states requires explanation.

Historians have accounted for the behavior of North Carolina and the rest of the upper South simply by pointing out, as David Potter has, that "the upper South was not as obsessively committed to slavery as the lower South." It is true that the proportion of slaves in the total North Carolina populace was smaller than in all of the lower South states except Texas. However, when it is recognized that the percentage of North Carolina's white families that owned slaves (29.1 percent) was greater than in Texas (28.5 percent), slightly less than in Louisiana (31.0 percent), and only 5 to 6 percent less than in Florida (34.5 percent) and Alabama (35.1 percent), and that there were more slaveowners in North Carolina than in every lower South state except Georgia, then it becomes apparent that white North Carolinians had as deep a personal interest in preserving slavery as did whites in much of the lower South. And, as we have seen, that popular commitment had been strengthened by party competition throughout the life of the second party system. During the secession winter, that sentiment was as strong as ever. One Unionist expressed this view well in November, 1860: "North-Carolina will never permit Mr. Lincoln or his party to touch the institution of domestic slavery. Her people are a unit on this point."[1]

North Carolina remained in the Union until May 20, 1861, not because its citizens were unconcerned about the fate of slavery or southern rights, but because of the persistence of the two-party system in the state. After the American party collapsed in 1858, its former leaders reorganized the Whig party. Successes in the congressional elections of 1859 and narrow losses in the gubernatorial and presidential elections of 1860 convinced Whigs that they would make further gains in the congressional elections of 1861 and win the state house and control of the General Assembly in 1862. They and other North Carolinians had learned that, although a party may be out of power, with effort it could regain power; so for them Lincoln's election was but a temporary setback, something that could be rectified four years hence. In states of the lower South without party systems, the people could see nothing but Republican victories in the foreseeable future. Nothing in their immediate experience suggested that the Republicans might be driven from power at some future date. But North Carolinians could see from their own experience that an opposition party might triumph.[2]

★

When the state legislature assembled in December, 1858, American party representatives recognized that their party was in shambles. Not since the founding of the second party system in the mid-1830s had a party been so poorly represented in the state legislature. Americans composed only 18 of the Senate's 50 members and only 38 of the House's 120. Those members took it upon themselves to revitalize the Whig party.[3]

They turned their attention first to the party organ at the state capital, the Raleigh *Register*. As the party's only Raleigh paper and its chief press spokesman, the *Register* exerted considerable power over party affairs. Its influence was evident in 1858, as the party reeled in the wake of its disastrous showing in the congressional elections of 1857. Only one American candidate, John Gilmer, had won election, and he had triumphed by a narrow margin in a district that Whigs had long dominated. As the state elec-

1. David M. Potter, *The Impending Crisis, 1848–1861*, completed and edited by Don E. Fehrenbacher (New York: Harper & Row, 1976), 505. On North Carolina, see Joseph Carlyle Sitterson, *The Secession Movement in North Carolina* (Chapel Hill: University of North Carolina Press, 1939), 22; Michael F. Holt, *The Political Crisis of the 1850s* (New York: John Wiley & Sons, 1978), 229; Raleigh *Standard*, November 14, 1860.
2. For an interpretation similar to the one offered here, see Holt, *Political Crisis*, 219–59.
3. Raleigh *Standard*, August 25, 1858.

tions of 1858 approached, the party's future appeared bleak. To the *Register*'s editor, John Syme, it seemed to have no future at all, and he concluded that the Democrats could be defeated only by encouraging the remnants of the American party to support an independent Democratic candidate, Duncan K. McRae. Syme hoped that a coalition of Americans and Democratic bolters might bring victory to the opponents of the regular Democratic party.[4]

If Syme had been editor of a paper in Fayetteville or Wilmington or Asheville, his proposal probably would have been received politely by other American papers and then ignored—but Syme edited the *Register*. When he announced his plan, most American party editors, who wanted to preserve the party and rebuild it, reacted adversely. However, those papers in the outlying areas had little statewide influence, since it was through the *Register* that the party would announce its next convention. Because the *Register* opposed the call for a convention and because the central committee chairman had abandoned the party, the Americans in other areas had no machinery by which they could call a convention. As a result, most of those members who wanted to retain the party's organization lamented the death of their party and then fell into line and supported McRae. Those who could not support him did nothing. John Pool, leader of the party in the northeast, complained to a friend that "he [Symes] has written us into the position of being obliged to have no candidate."[5]

Syme's plan proved disastrous. Democratic candidate John Ellis attained a larger victory than any candidate had enjoyed since North Carolinians first began to elect their governor in 1836. McRae gained the full support of neither group in his proposed coalition. His strongest support came from Whig or American counties, but many Americans would not support a renegade Democrat and stayed away from the polls (see table 24). As John Pool confided to another American party leader: "I will not vote for him. It is throwing away our principles, hauling down our flag, & surrendering to a body of deserters from the enemy's camp." Not only was McRae unable to bring out the full American vote, but he also failed to attract many Democratic voters.[6]

So when the American party legislators gathered to revive their party

4. See chapter 2; Raleigh *Register*, November 28, 1857.
5. Greensboro *Patriot*, n.d., quoted in Raleigh *Register*, December 9, 1857; John Pool to David F. Caldwell, March 30, 1858, in David F. Caldwell Papers, SHC.
6. Turnout was lower than in any gubernatorial election since 1840. See J. R. Pole, "Election Statistics in North Carolina, to 1861," *JSH*, XXIV (1958), 228; John Pool to David F. Caldwell, March 30, 1858, in Caldwell Papers. On McRae's inability to attract independent-leaning Democrats, see Archibald H. Arrington to Duncan K. McRae, May 1, 1858, and same to same, May 4, 1858, both in Archibald H. Arrington Papers, SHC.

TABLE 24

Democratic Vote for President (P) and Governor (G), and Vote for Secession (S), 1854–1861: Pearson Correlations

	1848G	1850G	1852P	1852G	1854G	1856P	1856G	1858G	1860P	1860G	1861S
1848P	.97	.96	.98	.96	.97	.95	.97	.91	.94	.95	.64
1848G		.96	.97	.97	.96	.95	.94	.90	.94	.94	.62
1850G			.97	.98	.96	.95	.94	.93	.93	.92	.63
1852P				.98	.99	.96	.96	.93	.95	.95	.66
1852G					.97	.95	.95	.93	.95	.94	.67
1854G						.96	.96	.92	.95	.95	.63
1856P							.99	.93	.95	.95	.67
1856G								.97	.97	.97	.67
1858G									.97	.96	.68
1860P*										.96	.70
1860G											.68

*Combined vote of John C. Breckinridge and Stephen A. Douglas

they recognized that their first major task was to gain control of the *Register* or to establish a new central organ. After changing the party name from American back to Whig and appointing an executive committee to coordinate party activities, they turned their sights on John Syme. The legislators realized that an effective central organ completely devoted to the party was a prerequisite for success. Although they failed to convince Syme to sell the *Register*, they attained their goal when he agreed to support the reorganized Whig party.[7]

Despite the pathetic condition of the party in the winter of 1858–1859, the leaders of the reorganization effort were remarkably enthusiastic. George Little, chairman of the executive committee, reported that "those who originated this movement are now perfecting . . . such general measures . . . as will insure in all probability the success of our party at the election next year [1860]." The optimism of Little and others was probably derived in part from efforts in Washington, D.C., to revive the Whig party. Under the guidance of John J. Crittenden, senator from Kentucky, conservatives from thirteen states met in Washington in December, 1858, to discuss a presidential ticket for 1860. It is surely no coincidence that North Carolina initiated efforts to revive the state Whig party that same month. The national party would provide the state organization with critically important national ties. McRae's showing in the gubernatorial election may also have inspired confidence among party leaders. Although he had fared poorly by the standards of other North Carolina gubernatorial candidates, he had still won over 40 percent of the vote—and that without the organizational efforts of a political party. Whigs, therefore, could count on a substantial anti-Democratic vote. A vigorous party organization might make Whigs competitive once again. A special congressional election held in the mountain district in August reinforced this sense of optimism. In the election, held to replace Democrat Thomas Clingman, whom the governor had appointed to a vacant seat in the U.S. Senate, American party candidate Zebulon Vance won an upset victory.[8]

Taking their cue from Vance's successful attack on massive Democratic expenditures, Whigs made the theme of their congressional election campaigns of 1859 the extravagant and corrupt behavior of the Democrats in

7. George Little to William A. Graham, January 26, 1859, same to same, September 14, 1859, both in J. G. deRoulhac Hamilton and Max R. Williams (eds.), *The Papers of William Alexander Graham* (6 vols. to date; Raleigh: State Department of Archives and History, 1957–), V, 86, 117; Raleigh *Register*, February 25, 1860.

8. Little to Graham, January 26, 1859, in Hamilton and Williams (eds.), *Graham Papers*, V, 86; Potter, *Impending Crisis*, 416–17; Albert D. Kirwan, *John J. Crittenden: The Struggle for the Union* (Lexington: University of Kentucky Press, 1962), 336–65; Raleigh *Standard*, August 25, 1858.

Washington, D.C. The Whigs were not manufacturing charges out of thin air. The Panic of 1857 had placed the federal treasury in a precarious position; expenditures remained high, while the depression caused revenues to decline dramatically. Buchanan, his secretary of the treasury, Howell Cobb, and the Democratic congressional leadership asked Congress to refrain from authorizing new expenditures, but the Democratic Congress ignored their recommendations. Various members attempted with little success to trim the appropriations bills for the army, navy, and postal system, and they also tried to reduce the Ways and Means Committee's $3,800,000 civil appropriations bill (which would provide money for local building and internal improvement projects). The final bill appropriated $2,000,000 more than the committee bill. "The battle for economy," historian Roy Nichols has concluded, "was a dismal failure."[9]

Democratic problems deepened as Republicans began to uncover evidence of congressional corruption. One investigation revealed corruption in the distribution of the public printing contracts, and another showed that one Massachusetts woolens company had hired a lobbyist who apparently tried to buy favorable votes for the Tariff of 1857. Still another indicated that there was much corruption in Secretary John Floyd's War Department. This series of investigations, which took place between 1858 and 1860, Nichols has written, "implant[ed] a general belief that the federal government was dishonest. Washington seemed to be a sink of graft and a den of shame."[10]

The most important document used by the Whigs in 1859 was a pamphlet entitled *What It Costs To Be Governed*, which purported to show how extravagant the Democratic party had been while it controlled the national government. The document concluded by calling the Buchanan administration "the most wasteful, extravagant and corrupt now in existence. Never has there been so shameless a prostitution of official power as is exhibited in the distribution of patronage and the uses of power by the Administration of James Buchanan."[11]

In the Fifth District, James M. Leach, prominent in the Whig revival, repeatedly attacked his opponent and the Democratic party because of the federal government's extravagance and corruption. The Fayetteville *Observer* reported that "the contest between Gen. Leach and Mr. Scales [the Democratic candidate] has turned mainly upon the extravagance of the Administration." Repeatedly Whigs asserted that they were "opposed to

9. Roy Franklin Nichols, *The Disruption of American Democracy* (New York: Macmillan, 1948), 191.

10. *Ibid.*, 195.

11. *What It Costs to Be Governed* (n.p., n.d.), in NCC.

the reckless extravagance, the open corruption, and the enormous expenditures of the present administration." When Scales tried to raise other issues, the Iredell *Express* called those issues "obsolete matters, most of them being dead and buried twenty years ago and more, and having not the least bearing upon or pertinency to, the issues involved in this canvass." The issues of the campaign, as far as the *Express* was concerned, revolved only around "Mr. Buchanan's spendthrift administration." [12]

Among the issues raised by Scales was the threat posed by the abolitionists. The *Express*'s reply to Scales reveals much about the campaign strategy of the Whigs in 1859. The *Express* asked: "What has Abolitionism (except that the President be an Abolitionist) to do with Mr. Buchanan's squandering the public moneys upon favorites and politicians?" As far as the Whigs were concerned, corruption and extravagance, not questions involving slavery and its preservation, were the major issues of the campaign. Other Whig papers charged that the Democrats had raised the specter of a Republican victory and the overthrow of slavery to divert attention from the real issues of the campaign. The Wadesboro *North Carolina Argus*, for example, argued that "it is the *decoy* cry which they hope will distract your attention from the *true issue*. What is the *true issue*? The true issue is *the corruptions of the Democratic party—the profligacy* of the Administration, the wasteful extravagance of the party." The Whig response to the issue of abolitionism said much about the ways that the state's two-party system influenced the sectional crisis. Believing that they had a popular issue, Whigs were determined not to allow the Democrats to obscure it with the abolition debate. In this instance, competition in the state encouraged Whigs to see less of a threat to the South from the Republicans and more from the state and national Democrats. [13]

By attacking the Buchanan administration and Democratic congressmen for extravagance and corruption, Whigs were arguing that with such men in power the survival of republican government was threatened. The death of republican government, in turn, prefigured the death of liberty. Democrats and Whigs had each frequently argued that only their own party could be trusted to preserve the Republic. In so doing, they spoke directly to popular fears for the survival of the Republic. In addition, the specific issues of 1859 had long been staples of Whig rhetoric. Whigs had based much of their presidential campaign of 1840 on the supposed corruption and extravagance of the Van Buren administration. So when Whigs claimed that the extravagance and corruption of the Democrats were antirepublican, they struck a responsive chord among voters.

12. Fayetteville *Observer*, July 11, 1859; Iredell *Express*, April 22, June 17, 1859.
13. Iredell *Express*, June 17, 1859; Wadesboro *North Carolina Argus*, May 12, 1859.

The Whig strategy succeeded. Of the five candidates they ran, four won. When Congress assembled in December, 1859, Whigs composed one-half of the North Carolina delegation. Democrats as well as Whigs attributed the Whig victories to the issue of government extravagance and corruption. One Democratic leader reported to a friend that "the opposition . . . as in 1840 raised the cry of corruption and extrava[ga]nce in the general government, and induced many to believe their statements true." In early 1860, Democratic editor William Walsh wrote to Congressman Lawrence Branch:

> The pamphlet, 'What it costs to be governed' damaged us severely last year, it certainly lost us two members of Congress and the same game will be played next fall. I was in Raleigh last [*sic*] and heard Dr. Henry of Bertie descant upon the extravagance of the federal government. He had just returned from Washington and bitterly denounced the anti-republican splendor'of the new additions to the Capitol, among other things he described the *Privees* as splendid rooms far superior to any dwelling in N. Carolina, furnished with splendid mirrors, and a marble table supplied with silver water pipes, china bowls, tooth brushes[,] combs, towels & c and a well paid Official in constant attendance. . . . Men whose democracy cannot be doubted, declare that there must be *retrenchment or a change of men*. There is a deep dissatisfaction at the enormous expenditure of the federal government, and in my opinion, nothing but the apprehension of the Black Republican Party stands between us and such another political overthrow as occured [*sic*] in 1840. Unless the democratic party in Congress, takes a *marked stand as a party*, in favor of retrenchment, we may as well put our house in order for the people will seek relief by supporting Opposition Candidates, so soon as the Presidential election is over.[14]

Little more than two months after the election, John Brown launched his ill-fated raid on the federal arsenal at Harper's Ferry, Virginia. The raid, the apparent complicity of Republicans in it, and the seeming support for it among many in the North horrified white North Carolinians. Brown raised for them the specter of servile insurrection that had always lain just beneath their consciousness, only to erupt in times of crisis. Because the people of North Carolina believed that their slaves were naturally docile and would only rebel at the instigation of outsiders like Brown, they formed vigilance committees throughout the state (not just in

14. Compiled Election Returns, in NCDAH; J. J. Martin to Jesse A. Waugh, September 2, 1859, in Jones and Patterson Papers, SHC; William Walsh to Lawrence O'Bryan Branch, March 1, 1860, in Lawrence O'Bryan Branch Papers, Duke.

areas with a high concentration of slaves) to root out men whom they deemed a threat, and the officers of moribund militia companies tried to infuse their units with new life. North Carolinians also set aside freedom of speech, at least as far as slavery was concerned. In the most publicized instance, they jailed the Reverend Daniel Worth for distributing Hinton Rowan Helper's antislavery book, *The Impending Crisis*. The apparent involvement of Republicans led some North Carolinians to think that the only way the South could protect itself was by leaving the Union. William Walsh, the Democratic editor of the Warrenton *News*, wrote that he had "always been a fervid Union man but I confess the endorsement of the Harpers Ferry outrage and Helper's infernal doctrine has shaken my fidelity and . . . I am willing to take the chances of every probable evil that may arise from disunion, sooner than submit any longer to Northern insolence and Northern outrage."[15]

Historians, following Walsh and others, have often seen John Brown's raid as bursting the fraternal bonds of the Union, but, considering the dangers that the raid and the North's apparent sympathy for it posed to a slaveholding society, the response of North Carolinians was measured. In neighboring South Carolina, the state legislature set in motion the political machinery that facilitated that state's secession from the Union, but the North Carolina state government responded hardly at all. The governor denounced the raid and unsuccessfully sought arms from the federal government, but nothing else.[16]

The state's inaction stemmed from the rhythms of the state's political year and its party system. The raid occurred during a traditionally fallow political season, after politicians had held their postmortems on the recent congressional elections and as they began to prepare for the campaigns ahead. If Brown had acted a few months sooner or later, he surely would have provoked a more spirited reaction from political leaders. The state's response was also minimized because the General Assembly was out of session and would not meet again until November, 1860. Given the weakness of the governor's office, only a special session of the legislature called by the governor could have offered a credible program of action for the

15. Victor B. Howard, "John Brown's Raid at Harpers Ferry and the Sectional Crisis in North Carolina," *NCHR*, LV (1978), 396–420; Noble J. Tolbert, "Daniel Worth: Tarheel Abolitionist," *NCHR*, XXXIX (1962), 284–304; Walsh to Branch, December 12, 1859, in Branch Papers.

16. Howard, "John Brown's Raid," 396–420; Sitterson, *Secession Movement*, 148–54; John W. Ellis to John B. Floyd, December 10, 1859, same to same, December 23, 1859, Floyd to Ellis, December 24, 1859, Henry K. Craig to Ellis, January 3, 1860, all in Noble J. Tolbert (ed.), *The Papers of John Willis Ellis* (2 vols.; Raleigh: State Department of Archives and History, 1964), I, 331, 337, 338–39, II, 342.

state. But Governor Ellis was loathe to take such a step. To Democrats like him, with strong ties to the national party, Democratic control of the national government seemed to offer protection enough for the South. Therefore, Ellis believed that it was more important for North Carolina Democrats to arm politically for the battles of the electoral campaigns ahead than to call the legislature together to buy arms for the militia or prepare for secession. Such attitudes reflected the broader bipartisan faith that the normal course of politics could avert the dangers posed by northern anti-slavery men. Ellis' decision was also apparently influenced by the presence of a reinvigorated Whig party, which would likely seek to impede an extraordinary response to the raid, much as it had resisted Democratic efforts in 1850. In addition, because the governor would soon be seeking reelection against a now-strong Whig foe, he had to be careful not to alienate supporters by taking an extreme position. Together these forces constrained his actions.[17]

★

The Democratic leadership, in fact, was much more concerned with the danger that Whigs posed to its continued hegemony in the state than it was with John Brown—and with good reason. For the first time in years, Whigs had assumed the political offensive, and at their state convention, held in Raleigh in February, they added a powerful issue to their arsenal. After much debate, delegates adopted a resolution urging that all property, including slaves, be taxed according to its value. Because the state constitution then provided that black slaves between the ages of twelve and fifty were subject to the poll tax at the same rate as free males between twenty-one and forty-five years, the *ad valorem* taxation of slaves would require a constitutional amendment. Following the conservative argument advanced by Whigs during their days of opposition to the equal-suffrage amendment, the party sought to amend the constitution through a convention, not by the legislative method that Democrats had followed. The *ad valorem* proposal would change the tax status of slaves from polls to property and place the state's increasing tax burden more squarely on the shoulders of slaveholders.[18]

Throughout the 1850s, as the state's role in the economy grew, its debt

17. Nathan H. Street, Peter G. Evans, and John N. Washington to Ellis, January 9, 1859 [1860], and Ellis to Hugh Waddell, Joseph J. Jackson, and Nathan A. Ramsay, January 10, 1860, both in Tolbert (ed.), *Ellis Papers*, II, 345–50.

18. Raleigh *Register*, February 25, 1860; Francis Newton Thorpe (comp.), *The Federal and State Constitutions, Colonial Charters, and Other Organic Laws of the States, Territories, and Colonies Now or Heretofore Forming the United States* (7 vols.; Washington, D.C.: Government Printing Office, 1909), V, 2799.

mounted. From 3.3 million dollars in 1850, the state debt almost tripled to 9.1 million in 1860. Taxes kept pace. Between 1851 and 1859, the tax on real estate jumped from 6 cents per hundred dollars of property to 20 cents, a 333-percent increase. Landowners were actually subjected to a greater increase in taxes because the reevaluation of property during the prosperous 1850s drove up property values. From 1855 to 1859, the value of North Carolina's real estate rose 29.6 percent. Professional men and artisans also faced greater taxation. Barely taxed at all at the beginning of the decade, they paid an income tax of roughly 1 percent by 1859. The poll tax for whites and slaves also soared from 20 cents in 1851 to 80 cents in 1859, a rise of 400 percent.[19]

Although the increase in the tax on slaves was substantial, it satisfied few of those who thought that slaveowners should bear a heavier tax burden. Such people were unhappy because the slave tax increase had been limited by the increase in the white poll tax. Despite an absolute increase in the taxation of slaves (along with land, the state's most valuable property), the slave tax provided a relatively small proportion of the state's tax revenue. Unlike lower South states such as Alabama, where the tax on slaves accounted for 32 percent of the state's tax revenue in 1860, North Carolina derived only 18.4 percent of its revenues from the taxation of slave property in 1859. Of course, slaveowners were also paying a large share of the taxes on land and luxuries, but the limits on the slave tax placed those whose wealth was relatively more in land than in slaves at a disadvantage and thereby left many people with a sense that slaveowners did not pay their fair share of the state's taxes and that generally the system of taxation was inequitable.[20]

By taxing all property, including slaves, according to its value, the Whig proposal offered a way of meeting the growing demands of the state treasury in an equitable manner. The idea was not new in the state. In 1852, Democratic governor David S. Reid had recommended that the leg-

19. "Treasurer's Report for the Two Fiscal Years Ending September 30th, 1850," in *Executive and Legislative Documents, Session of 1850–1851* (Raleigh: State Printer, 1851), 19–20; "Treasurer's Report for the Two Fiscal Years Ending September 30, 1860," in *Executive and Legislative Documents, Session of 1860–1861* (Raleigh: State Printer, 1861), No. 6, p. 47; Hershal L. Macon, "A Fiscal History of North Carolina, 1776–1860" (Ph.D. dissertation, University of North Carolina, 1932), 416.

20. The North Carolina figures were calculated from "Comptroller's Report for the Fiscal Year Ending September 30th, 1860," in *Executive and Legislative Documents, Session of 1860–1861*, No. 8, pp. 147–55. For Alabama, see J. Mills Thornton III, *Politics and Power in a Slave Society: Alabama, 1800–1860* (Baton Rouge: Louisiana State University Press, 1978), 103. Also see Donald Cleveland Butts, "A Challenge to Planter Rule: The Controversy over the Ad Valorem Taxation of Slaves in North Carolina, 1858–1862" (Ph.D. dissertation, Duke University, 1978), 30–31.

islature tax all property except slaves according to value, and two years later some Whigs urged that *ad valorem* taxation should apply to slaves as well. However, until the late 1850s the chief suggestion for meeting the state's debts was the Whig call for a distribution of the proceeds of the public lands. Only in 1858 did the legislature give serious consideration to the new tax proposal. Then, though partisanship was at its lowest ebb in more than two decades and party discipline was minimal, consistent supporters of the *ad valorem* taxation came largely from Whig-American ranks and consistent opponents from the Democrats (see table 25). Although the parties were often not as united on the question as they had been on some issues contested in the 1840s, given the weakened state of the party system the extent of interparty disagreement was considerable.[21]

The roll call of votes on the *ad valorem* proposal, however, revealed another trend. While nonslaveholding legislators and those owning fewer than ten slaves divided evenly on the issues, those who owned ten or more slaves voted overwhelmingly (80.6 percent) against it. The potential for an intensification of class conflict in North Carolina over *ad valorem* taxation was apparent.[22]

Whatever possibility existed that the *ad valorem* issue would array large slaveholders against the other white North Carolinians was largely removed by the Whig endorsement of it. That support helped turn a class issue into a partisan one. As with other political issues like suffrage reform, the party system turned potentially explosive social conflict into much less disruptive political channels.

Throughout their campaign for *ad valorem* taxation, Whigs abided by the political requirement that parties and candidates prove their fidelity to white equality and freedom. They had learned a hard lesson in their battle against equal suffrage, but in 1860 it was apparent that they had learned their lesson well. Just as the Democrats had called their plan for suffrage reform "equal suffrage," Whigs called their plan for tax reform "equal taxation." And just as Democrats had argued that equal suffrage would promote white equality at the ballot box, Whigs argued that equal taxation would promote white equality before the tax collector. A Whig spokesman contended that the *ad valorem* proposal was "a scheme of perfect equality [which] would compel every man and every class of men and every section of the state to contribute a fair and just proportion of the public burdens." Another Whig, former congressman Sion Rogers, who was running for a seat in the House of Commons, told listeners that if they "wanted a Gover-

21. Butts, "Challenge," 14–16.
22. Calculated from *ibid.*, 162. Butts emphasizes the class component in the roll-call votes but discounts the role of partisanship. See *ibid.*, 39–50.

TABLE 25
Roll-Call Votes on Economic Issues and Constitutional Reform, 1858–1861, by Party

	Senate	House
AVERAGE INDEX OF PARTISAN DISAGREEMENT		
Ad Valorem Taxation		
1858–1859	58.0	49.1
1860–1861	53.0	88.3
Distribution of Public-Lands Proceeds		
1860–1861	—	98.1
Permit Jews to Hold Office		
1860–1861	59.0	37.5
Internal Improvements		
1860–1861	15.1	13.7
Probanking Legislation		
1860–1861	25.4	18.5

	Senate		House	
	Democrats	Whigs	Democrats	Whigs
PERCENT AFFIRMATIVE				
Ad Valorem Taxation				
1858–1859	8.7	66.7	28.5	77.8
1860–1861	29.4	82.4	8.7	97.0
Distribution of Public-Lands Proceeds				
1860–1861	—	—	1.9	100
Permit Jews to Hold Office				
1860–1861	84.0	25.0	53.1	13.6
Internal Improvements				
1860–1861	58.0	68.4	50.3	62.3
Probanking Legislation				
1860–1861	57.9	74.8	47.9	66.4

SOURCES: For 1858–1859, see Butts, "Challenge to Planter Rule," 163; for 1860–1861, see *SJ, 1860–1861*, 173, 270–71, 275–76, 286, 293, 295, 304–305, 319–20, 324–26, 347, 371, 384, 386–87, 404–405; *HJ, 1860–1861*, 391–92, 423–24, 437–38, 466–67, 471–72, 595–97, 605, 615–16, 627–28, 630, 640, 645, 648, 654–55, 657–58, 695–97, 713–14, 721–22, 730–31, 750–52.

nor who would . . . put the poor man on an equal footing with the rich man at the taxbox, to vote for John Pool, the equal taxation candidate."[23]

The Whigs argued further that the resulting equality would strengthen the popular commitment to the preservation of slavery. John Hays, a Whig candidate for the legislature, pointed out that, if a war broke out between North and South, the nonslaveholding whites would compose the bulk of the South's fighting force. In light of that, he asked: "Is it fair, then,—is it politic to burthen them with a larger proportion of taxes than other persons? Should the State discriminate against such a large and devoted body of her people, when so much depends upon wedding them to her institutions?" Whig gubernatorial candidate John Pool argued that "the best mode of strengthening slavery was for the slave owner to be willing to submit to an equality of taxation." Such arguments placed Whigs in the mainstream of southerners who argued that the democratization of southern state constitutions would enhance the devotion of all white men to society's institutions, including slavery. They also represented a response to Democratic charges that the *ad valorem* proposal divided slaveholders and nonslaveholders at a time that unity was imperative.[24]

The Democrats, after much behind-the-scenes debate, came out in opposition to *ad valorem* taxation. That stance ensured that North Carolinians would view the issue largely through partisan rather than class lenses. Following the political script that had been written by both parties in the 1830s, Democrats asserted their primacy as the state's defender of slavery. They claimed that, whereas Democrats sought to unite North Carolinians in defense of slavery against the Republican onslaught, Whigs tried "to excite and array the prejudices of . . . the non-slaveholder against the slaveholder," so that North Carolinians would be divided at a time when northern attacks on slavery made unity imperative.[25]

Although Democrats decried the class appeals of the Whigs, they made some of their own. First, they contended that the *ad valorem* method would not bring equal taxation but would actually lead to more oppressive taxes for the yeoman farmer. Governor John W. Ellis, after being renominated, told the Democratic convention that the adoption of *ad valorem* taxation would mean that

> the land of the hard working man, upon which he makes a subsistence for his family, the growing citizens of the State, should be taxed just as high as the gold and silver plate that decorates the abodes of the luxu-

23. Raleigh *Register*, June 16, May 19, 1860.
24. *Ibid.*, May 23 and 30, 1860.
25. Wilmington *Journal*, July 19, 1860; Salisbury *Banner*, May 22, 1860, quoted in *Little Adder*, July 27, 1860, in NCC.

rious; that the plough horse that tills the crop of the man who eats his bread 'in the sweat of his face,' shall be taxed as much as the racer of the man of pleasure; that the pleasure carriage and the road wagon; the billiard table and the threshing machine; the spirits that make drunk the inebriate, and the medicine administered to the sick, shall be taxed alike under one equal horizontal and unbending rule of ad valorem.

Democrats went further to argue that *ad valorem* taxation would reach into the homes of all and tax even the poor man's tin cups and his farm implements. Moreover, because the Whig proposal suggested that *all* property would be taxed, Democrats contended that it meant that an army of tax-gatherers would roam the land infringing on the privacy and liberty of free men. Ellis charged that Whigs "would send the tax-gatherer into every house, with inquisitorial powers, exacting with a relentless hand, a tax upon every species of property great and small; everything that we eat, drink and wear, from the time we come into the world until we go out of it, from the cradle to the grave." From the Democratic perspective, Whigs would put government into every home in order to exact oppressive taxes and thus create "grinding oppression" for the state's citizens, especially the poor.[26]

Democrats also opposed the tax amendment because, they argued, it would upset the compromises of the convention of 1835. They pointed out accurately that easterners thought of the linkage of the slave and white poll tax as a means of limiting the taxation of slaves and therefore as a partial quid pro quo for increasing the representation of the west in the legislature, since easterners believed linkage would offer protection against westerners' imposing an unfair tax burden on the east. Ellis argued that the compromises had to be honored. Precisely because the state now needed more funds, it was especially important that such a solemn agreement not be breeched. It was with just such a time in mind, he said, that easterners had demanded the constitutional provision on slave taxation. And he went further, to link the compromises of the state constitution with those of the U.S. Constitution and to argue that to break one would encourage breaking the other. Implied in this argument was a threat to the constitutional position of slaveholders generally. "The same reasoning sustains both," he said. "If the one falls, upon what ground shall we uphold the other?" So Ellis' opposition to *ad valorem* taxation became a fight to preserve the U.S.

26. "Speech of John W. Ellis, Delivered Before the Democratic State Convention, in Raleigh, March 9, 1860," in Tolbert (ed.), *Ellis Papers*, II, 400–401; Salem *Press*, n.d., quoted in *Little Adder*, June 1, 1860.

Constitution, "that Temple of Liberty under whose protecting arches three generations of contented and happy men have lived, and prospered, and enjoyed a civil liberty without a parallel in the annals of free peoples." He, in common with all antebellum North Carolina politicians, was fighting to preserve white freedom and black slavery.[27]

The *ad valorem* debate sparked intense popular interest in the campaign. Abram Martin reported to a friend that "our county and State Elections has bin the Topics of the day ever cince May court as the Whigs cam out in favor of Taxing the negro as property and not as persons as they allway Hav bin." E. R. Piles, a Whig living in Anson, a major cotton-planting county, wrote editor Edward Hale that "the action of our Convention gives universal satisfaction among Anson Whigs. Not for a good many years past have I seen them so enthusiastic and sanguine of success as at present." The enthusiasm expressed at one Whig mass meeting was so great, another writer said, that it "reminded me of the Log Cabin times. . . . We were well nigh deafened with cheers for Ad valorem & Bell & Everitt [*sic*]."[28]

Just as in "the Log Cabin times" of 1840, Whigs thought they could win, despite the fact that they had not won a statewide election since 1848. William Graham wrote John J. Crittenden in late February that "local policy of deep interest will enter into the canvass, with the most propitious influences in our favor." Even more optimistic was George Badger's letter to Crittenden: "Every thing is going on here beautifully—*Equal taxation* is overruling everything and every body opposed to it and we have a cheering prospect of electing a Whig Governor, though Ellis was elected two years ago by a majority of 16,000."[29]

The allusions to the elections of 1840 proved appropriate in one respect. Not since 1840 had so many North Carolinians turned out to vote in a state election. For the first time since then, more than 80 percent of North Carolina's white adult male population cast ballots. In another respect, however, the analogy to the Log Cabin campaign was inaccurate, since the Whigs, who had won in 1840, did not attain victory this time. They lost the gubernatorial election and obtained only a minority of seats in the General Assembly. But the Whigs had made enormous gains. Whereas the Democrats had a joint ballot majority of fifty-eight in the legislature in

27. "Speech of John W. Ellis," in Tolbert (ed.), *Ellis Papers*, II, 398.
28. Abram Martin to John D. Dunn, August 3, 1860, in John D. Dunn Papers, Duke; E. R. Piles to Edward J. Hale & Sons, March 27, 1860, in Edward Jones Hale Papers, NCDAH; H. H. Buxton to Ralph P. Buxton, July 21, 1860, in Ralph Potts Buxton Papers, SHC.
29. William A. Graham to John J. Crittenden, February 27, 1860, in Hamilton and Williams (eds.), *Graham Papers*, V, 143–44; George E. Badger to John J. Crittenden, May 6, 1860 (typescript), in John Jordan Crittenden Papers, NCDAH.

1858, it was reduced to sixteen in 1860. Even more important to the Whigs was John Pool's good showing in the gubernatorial race; he received 47.2 percent of the vote. Whigs had built their moral triumph on the backs of traditional Whig voters. Voting throughout the state bore out John Ellis' prediction for the east: "As a general thing the party lines will be drawn as usual." Indeed, table 24 reveals that Pool drew his greatest support from Whig counties and Ellis from Democratic ones.[30]

It was apparent to most Whigs that victory in the next couple of years was well within their reach. They had come close in 1860 and might easily gain control of the governor's mansion and the legislature two years hence. The moral victory of 1860 might well be the electoral victory of 1862. Oliver H. Dockery, son of the Whig gubernatorial candidate in 1854, rejoiced when he learned of the results: "We have lost Pool by a small vote— but yet all the prestige of success is ours. One more such a day & they are ruined. So may it be."[31]

★

Since 1855, North Carolina Whigs had searched for an anti-Democratic national party to replace the Whig party. They thought they had found it in the American party, but their hopes for that party's future were dashed by its sectional divisions. In 1858, evidence that national political leaders were planning to establish a new party and to run a candidate for president had apparently encouraged state leaders to reorganize the Whig party at the state level. When William Graham told delegates to the state party convention in 1860 that former Whigs were establishing the Constitutional Union party and planned to hold a national convention later that year, the delegates responded enthusiastically. Graham reported to John J. Crittenden that at the convention he had "already enlisted every man of the opposition [Whig party] of whom I have heard any expression of opinion."[32]

The national convention met in Baltimore in June and nominated former Whigs John Bell of Tennessee for president and Edward Everett of Massachusetts for vice-president on the Constitutional Union ticket. Bell faced three other men in the presidential contest. Party ballots for Republican Abraham Lincoln did not appear in North Carolina, but Bell vied for the votes of North Carolinians with two Democratic candidates, Stephen A. Douglas and John C. Breckinridge. At the Democratic national conven-

30. Pole, "Election Statistics," 228; Raleigh *Register*, August 15, 1860.
31. Oliver H. Dockery to Edward J. Hale, August 11, 1860, in Hale Papers.
32. William A. Graham to John J. Crittenden, February 27, 1860, in Hamilton and Williams (eds.), *Graham Papers*, V, 143–44.

tion held in Charleston in April, delegates from the lower South had walked out because of a conflict over the party platform. The remainder of the convention, including the entire North Carolina delegation, failed to agree upon a candidate, so it adjourned to Baltimore several weeks later. When the Baltimore convention refused to seat some of the Charleston seceders, the rest of the lower South delegations and most of the upper South delegations left the convention; three North Carolina delegates remained. The portion of the Baltimore convention who had stayed then nominated Douglas, and the bolters, meeting nearby, chose Breckinridge.[33]

Encouraged by Democratic divisions, Whigs adopted several different kinds of appeals to get their supporters to the polls. They continued their attacks on the extravagance of the Democratic administration, but generally the party downplayed that issue and confronted the Democrats on questions involving the Union and slavery.

They first attacked as unnecessary and inflammatory the Breckinridge Democrats' demand that the federal government protect slave property in the territories. The Whigs argued that slavery had already been excluded from the territories because of hostile geography and climate, so one could only conclude that the Democrats were exploiting the issue for partisan gain, despite the fact that the debate over that issue weakened the bonds that tied the Union together. Placing the Union in jeopardy for political gain was inexcusable. Similarly, John Pool, during the gubernatorial campaign, claimed that Democratic "agitation of the slavery question had begun to stink in the nostrils of the people of North Carolina."[34]

The Democratic sins relating to slavery, the Whigs charged, were nothing compared to their ill-concealed desire to destroy the Union. They argued that, if the Breckinridge ticket won, its supporters would happily abide by the results, but if Lincoln were elected, "they will not await any act of Lincoln's violative of the Constitution, and aggressive upon Southern Constitutional Rights, but at once declare the Union to be at an end." Again and again Whigs contended that, although all Democrats were not disunionists, all disunionists were Democrats. The *Register* declared: "A disunionist cannot be found at the South *outside the Democratic party.*" Whig denunciations represented a new formulation of an old political theme. Ever since 1844, when Whigs charged that Democratic plans to annex Texas would lead to disunion, they had denounced their opponents as traitorous disunionists. Now, Whigs contrasted Democratic disunionism with the Unionism of their own party: "The Whigs at the South are to a

33. Nichols, *Disruption*, 288–320; Sitterson, *Secession Movement*, 162–68.
34. Raleigh *Register*, February 22, 25, July 25, 1860.

man for defending the Union 'at all hazards and to the last extremity.'"[35]

On the eve of the election, Whigs still hoped for a Bell victory but would "oppose every attempt to break up the Union, founded on the *bare fact* of Abraham Lincoln's election." This stance they contrasted with the behavior they expected of Breckinridge supporters: "How mean, then, as well as wicked, is the conduct of those who avail themselves of all the means provided by the Constitution to elect the man of their choice, and failing to do so, refuse to abide by the result of the election!!" Whigs, who had found the state political system so responsive in 1859 and 1860, could see no reason to abandon that system just because an opponent was elected.[36]

The disruption of the national Democratic party at Charleston and Baltimore created some confusion in the state Democratic party. Many of North Carolina's leaders, including Governor Ellis, supported the candidacy of Stephen Douglas and were unenthusiastic about the southern demand for federal protection of slavery in the territories. The leadership's support for Douglas was also derived from intraparty factional feuding. William W. Holden, editor of the *Standard* and a longtime supporter of James Buchanan's political pretensions, was the administration's chief spokesman in North Carolina and hence Douglas' chief critic. Two years earlier, Holden had lost bids for the party's gubernatorial and senatorial nominations. In 1860 he endorsed the *ad valorem* tax proposal and offered only lukewarm support to Ellis' reelection campaign. It was no wonder that Holden's rivals, like Ellis and Congressman Lawrence O'Bryan Branch (who believed that Holden had designs on his Wake District seat), aligned themselves with Douglas in his dispute with Buchanan.[37]

So party leaders went to the Charleston and Baltimore conventions supporting different candidates, and they returned still supporting different candidates, only now Ellis and other Douglasites endorsed Buchanan's candidate, his vice-president, John C. Breckinridge, while Holden rallied to support Douglas. Ellis had concluded unhappily "that the sympathies of the people are with B[reckinridge] & L[ane]," and so he decided to follow his constituents. Holden came to support Douglas because he thought he spied at the conventions a deliberate effort by some southern radicals to break up the Union. Surely, however, factional disputes within the state

35. *Ibid.*, September 15, July 14, 1860.

36. *Ibid.*, November 3, 1860.

37. Chaplain W. Morrison, *Democratic Politics and Sectionalism: The Wilmot Proviso Controversy* (Chapel Hill: University of North Carolina Press, 1967), 118–19, 216n.; Raleigh *Standard*, December 23, 1857, April 21, 1858; Brian G. Walton, "Elections to the United States Senate in North Carolina, 1835–1861," *NCHR*, LIII (1976), 189–90; Lawrence O'Bryan Branch to his wife, February 6, 1859, and same to same, May 29, 1859, both in Mrs. Lawrence O'Bryan Branch Papers, NCDAH.

party had much to do with the political version of musical chairs that Ellis and Holden were playing.[38]

Holden's support for Douglas, however, remained an ill-kept secret. Because he too recognized that Douglas' candidacy elicited little popular enthusiasm and because he hoped to keep the party together, Holden encouraged Douglas in his private correspondence, but his *Standard* endorsed Breckinridge and advocated the vice-president's claims. The closest the powerful editor came to public support for the Illinoisan was through repeated assertions that the Douglas men were acting in good faith and that factional leaders should seek a reconciliation for the sake of the party. Without Holden's open support, though, Douglas Democrats never lit a fire under their man's campaign, and the race in North Carolina boiled down to Bell and Breckinridge.[39]

One of the most difficult problems the Breckinridge men faced was answering the accusation that Breckinridge was the candidate of the disunionists. The response of the Breckinridge supporters reveals the moderating effect that close competition between two organized political parties could have on an election campaign. The pressure from the Whigs caused Breckinridge supporters to mute the more radical sentiments they held and to emphasize their commitment to the preservation of the Union. Thus, throughout the campaign, they asserted that, because they were the strongest defenders of southern rights, they were therefore the best defenders of the Union.[40]

As had become typical of voter turnout in North Carolina elections, fewer people voted in the presidential election than had cast ballots in August. Only 70 percent of the white adult males in the state cast ballots in November, whereas more than 82 percent had voted in August. Those who voted apparently cast their ballots in much the same way that they had in the gubernatorial election—the coefficient of correlation between voting in the two elections was a high .90. The counties that gave Pool the greatest support in August gave Bell and Everett the greatest support in November (see table 24, p. 183).[41]

Breckinridge won the state's electoral votes, but the contest was a narrow one. Of the 96,230 ballots cast, he received 48,539—a majority of only 848 and 50.4 percent of the votes cast. Bell finished second with 44,990

38. John W. Ellis to Daniel M. Barringer, July 15, 1860, in Daniel Moreau Barringer Papers, SHC; William W. Holden to Stephen A. Douglas, June 1, 1860, in Stephen A. Douglas Papers, Manuscripts Room, University of Chicago Library, Chicago, Illinois.

39. Raleigh *Standard*, July 4 and 18, 1860.

40. Wilmington *Journal*, October 18, 1860.

41. Pole, "Election Statistics," 228.

votes—46.7 percent of those cast. Stephen Douglas won only 2.8 percent of the vote.

The close race in the presidential election, after a similar one for the governorship a few months earlier, convinced most North Carolina politicians and voters that the two-party system had returned to the state with all its vigor. The results of the election certainly convinced the state's Whigs that a future victory was not far off. The presidential and gubernatorial elections taught the Whigs that the political system could work for them and showed that a party could come back from defeat and attain victory. This understanding would have an enormous impact on their perception of the political situation in the nation after the presidential election of 1860.

★

Soon after the election was over, North Carolinians learned that Abraham Lincoln had won. Lincoln's victory certainly alarmed most North Carolinians; the fears of the recent past had become realities. Yet virtually all Whigs and many Democrats opposed any move toward secession.

Most North Carolinians believed that Lincoln's election was an insufficient cause for secession. They felt that the political system could benefit them and not only northerners. Whigs, at least, had seen the political tide turn in the state. Why could not the same thing happen at the national level? Unionists admitted that the Republicans had won the day but argued that it was a victory for one day only. In the near future, conservatives would drive the Republicans from power. A month before the election, the Greensboro *Patriot* had remarked that "it would be a nice piece of folly to dissolve the great and glorious Union simply because" the intraparty quarrels of the Democrats had "permitted a minority to gain *temporary* ascendancy." William Graham argued that "Lincoln failed by five hundred thousand votes of having a majority of the people vote for him. He was elected because his opponents were divided. This would not occur again."[42]

Not only was the Republican triumph expected to be short-lived, but during Lincoln's four years in office many North Carolinians believed that the Congress and Supreme Court would prevent him from taking any rash actions. "The President," Graham wrote, "is not a sovereign to whom we owe our allegiance." Rather, "he is but the chief servant among those of the national household, whom the people from time to time call to the perfor-

42. Greensboro *Patriot*, October 4, 1860, quoted in Sitterson, *Secession Movement*, 174 (emphasis added); William A. Graham, "Notes for a Speech," February, 1861, in Hamilton and Williams (eds.), *Graham Papers*, V, 219.

mance of duties limited and defined by the Constitution and Laws." A meeting in Hillsboro declared that the authority of a president was "defined and restricted by the Constitution and laws, liable to be checked and restrained within his legitimate powers by Congress and by the Judiciary."[43]

Believing that Lincoln's victory was but a momentary triumph for the Republicans and that while in office Lincoln could be restrained, Unionists saw no reason for disrupting the Union. William Graham asked: "Who can prepare for a declaration of independence . . . upon the ground that we have been out-voted in an election in which we took the chances of success?" Graham and other Unionists were telling North Carolinians to abide by the rules of the political game: it had been played fairly and had been won by the Republicans; four years hence, conservative men would drive them out of power. In the meantime, other branches of government would restrain the new president. If Lincoln broke the rules (*e.g.*, attempted to coerce the lower South back into the Union), North Carolina would leave the Union. Nothing less would justify disunion. Unionists repeatedly advised the people to wait until Lincoln had taken overt hostile steps before acting.[44]

Secessionists had a much different interpretation of what might justify secession and what the future course of American politics would be. They believed that Lincoln's election was sufficient cause for secession. This belief rested in part on their perception of the political future. Obviously, if they accepted the Unionist contentions that an anti-Republican coalition would win in 1864 and that Lincoln would be shackled until that time, there would be no reason for secession. But secessionists saw no way to reverse the Republican tide. It would roll on inexorably and inevitably toward its destination—the deprivation of southern rights in the national government and the ultimate abolition of slavery. The recent breakup of the Democratic party, in which North Carolina Democratic leaders had played such an intimate role, had apparently left them with little sense that the Democratic party could soon offer viable opposition to the Republicans.[45]

★

Three weeks after Lincoln's election, Governor Ellis sent his biennial message to the General Assembly, which was meeting for its regularly scheduled session. In the message, he lamented the state of public affairs and recommended that the legislature appoint delegates to a convention of all

43. William A. Graham to A. M. Waddell, February 5, 1861, in Hamilton and Williams (eds.), *Graham Papers*, V, 223.
44. "Extract from Graham's Salisbury Speech on October 12, 1860," in *ibid.*, V, 178–79.
45. Wilmington *Journal*, October 25, 1860.

the southern states. He also urged the assembly to call a state convention that would meet after the adjournment of the regional meeting. In the meantime, he wrote, the General Assembly should strengthen the state's militia and authorize the purchase of munitions.

The legislature responded by passing a bill that reorganized the militia and appropriated $300,000 for weapons. Then, ignoring the idea of a southern conference, they appointed a joint committee to consider Ellis' and the secessionists' call for a state convention that might take North Carolina out of the Union. Secessionists eventually obtained part of what they wanted, but only after weeks of haggling; they certainly did not get the kind of bill they desired. While the states of the lower South seceded from the Union, North Carolina legislators talked. Their conservative response to the events of the winter stemmed not from any lack of commitment to slavery but from the persistence of party conflict in the state.[46]

North Carolina's legislators were men of means with a deep financial interest in the preservation of slavery. The proportion of slaveholders among them was higher than in any other southern state, and the percentage of planters ranked the state fourth in the entire South. Of those southerners who made most of the political decisions during the secession crisis, the legislators had as much at risk as any.[47]

Patterns of slaveownership in the General Assembly, although similar to those found in 1850, were not an exact replica. As was the case a decade earlier, more than 80 percent of the legislators owned slaves, and about 35 percent owned 20 or more. The median slaveholding was also similar to 1850: 12 in the House and 25.5 in the Senate. Whig and Democratic commoners continued to own roughly the same number of slaves, but unlike the situation in 1850, when the slaveholdings of Whig and Democratic senators were also similar in size, in 1860 the median Democratic slaveholding (33) was almost twice that of the Whigs. The Whig stance on *ad valorem* taxation or on secession may have alienated some of the party's wealthier

46. John W. Ellis, Governor's Message, November 20, 1860, in Tolbert (ed.), *Ellis Papers*, II, 489–515; Sitterson, *Secession Movement*, 183–87.

47. Data was gathered on 163 of the state's 170 legislators, 110 of 120 commoners and 48 of 50 senators. The major sources of the data are: Schedule No. 1, Free Inhabitants, and No. 2, Slave Inhabitants, of the Eighth Census of the United States, 1860, copies in NCDAH and microfilm copies in the Detroit Public Library. I have also depended upon the research notes of Professor Ralph A. Wooster. My own research in the census confirmed the accuracy of Professor Wooster's data for 1860. See my comments on 1850, p. 46, n. 38, above. On slaveholdings in other state legislatures, see Ralph A. Wooster, *The People in Power: Courthouse and Statehouse in the Lower South* (Knoxville: University of Tennessee Press, 1969), 41; Wooster, *Politicians, Planters, and Plain Folk: Courthouse and Statehouse in the Upper South, 1850–1860* (Knoxville: University of Tennessee Press, 1975), 40.

potential candidates, whereas the Democratic position on those issues may have encouraged their wealthier politicians to seek public office. But it should be pointed out that the parties' positions on particular issues had not influenced the relative economic status of Whig and Democratic commoners. The difference in the partisan distribution of slaveholding also affected two wealthy and competitive eastern senatorial districts, which had elected Whigs in 1850 and narrowly elected Democrats in 1860. In any case, too much emphasis should not be placed upon the differences in Whig and Democratic senatorial slaveownership. The large slaveholdings of Democratic senators may have enhanced their commitment to secession, but, as we shall see, the poorer Democratic commoners had the same commitment. Whigs, with a median slaveholding of 17, were substantial slaveowners by any standards. Their slaveholdings, for example, compared favorably with the median slaveholdings of Alabama's senators in the legislature of 1859–1860 (19.5). It would be reasonable to assume that North Carolina's Whig senators were as interested in preserving slavery as the Alabamians, but Alabama's senators unanimously endorsed the summoning of a convention in the event of a Republican's election, whereas North Carolina's Whig senators opposed it. The Whigs' behavior was influenced by party ties, not by class. The wealthiest Whigs voted as Whigs, the poorest Democrats as Democrats. And, as we shall see, when members of either party broke ranks to vote with the other side on specific issues, the bolters were not exclusively wealthy Whigs or poor Democrats.[48]

The persistence of partisanship surprised few politicians, who recognized that continued party conflict made concert unlikely on the question of secession or Union. As Governor Ellis had observed before the presidential election; "Political differences and party strife have run so high in this state for some years past and particularly during the past nine months that anything like unanimity upon any question of a public nature could scarcely be expected; and such is the case with the one under consideration [*i.e.*, secession]. Our people are very far from being agreed as to what action the state should take." Democratic Speaker of the Senate Henry T. Clark had the same thing in mind when he complained that Whig leaders would "adhere to the old Hulk as long as a plank floats."[49]

48. The two eastern districts were Halifax and Craven. If those two districts had elected Whigs with slaveholdings equal to those of the elected Democrats, then the Whig median would have risen to 22 and the Democratic median would have dropped to 29. On Alabama, see J. Mills Thornton III, *Politics and Power in a Slave Society: Alabama, 1800–1860* (Baton Rouge: Louisiana State University Press, 1978), 297.

49. John W. Ellis to William H. Gist, October 19, 1860, in Tolbert (ed.), *Ellis Papers*, II, 469–70; Henry T. Clark, to Lawrence O'Bryan Branch, January, 1861, in Branch Papers.

Early in the session, party lines appeared shaky, but ultimately they held. William Holden's *Standard*, the state party organ, stridently asserted its Unionism and denounced the governor's message. Democratic legislators responded by refusing Holden admission to the party caucus and depriving him of the office of state printer. Outside the pale of the Democratic party, Holden became an invaluable ally of the Union Whigs. Over the years, Holden had acquired a loyal readership, so that his presence in the Unionist coalition was bound to attract a number of Democrats. But he drew few Democratic legislators with him. Indeed, on votes relating to secession, party lines remained strikingly firm, as firm as they had been in the 1840s. When members of the House of Commons or the Senate voted on whether to raise the United States flag over the state capitol or on whether or not the United States government owned Fort Sumter, or on a series of similar questions, Democrats could be found supporting the pro-secession position and Whigs the pro-Union side (see table 26).[50]

Partisanship on the secession question was galvanized by differences over other issues. Although parties were no longer divided over questions like state aid to internal improvements, they continued to differ over *ad valorem* taxation, the propriety of distributing the proceeds from the sale of the public lands, and over a constitutional amendment to allow Jews to hold public office. Introduced by a commoner from Wilmington, where most of the state's Jewish population resided, the proposed amendment received most of its support from Democrats, who remained true to their traditional acceptance of religious diversity, and most of its opposition from Whigs, who also followed their own traditional desire for a homogeneous Protestant political community. Just as conflict over a variety of issues in 1850 made bipartisan unity untenable during the territorial crisis, disagreements over other issues made such unity difficult during the secession crisis (see table 25, p. 192).

The most crucial question that lawmakers debated was whether to call a state convention to discuss North Carolina's relations with the rest of the Union. Such a convention might take the state out of the Union, just as conventions were doing throughout the lower South. Early in the session, the legislature appointed a committee to decide whether a convention should be called. On December 12, the committee's secessionist Democratic majority suggested that the national situation was so critical that a convention should be summoned as soon as possible, while the Unionist Whig minority belittled the need for a convention. Democrats tried to ram

50. Raleigh *Standard*, November 28, 1860.

TABLE 26
Roll-Call Votes on Prosecession Measures in the North Carolina
General Assembly, 1860–1861, by Party

	For a State Convention	
	Senate	House
AVERAGE INDEX OF PARTISAN DISAGREEMENT	70.3	72.0
PERCENT AFFIRMATIVE		
Democrats	95.6	92.6
Whigs	25.4	19.9
	Prosecession Measures	
	Senate	House
AVERAGE INDEX OF PARTISAN DISAGREEMENT	73.6	75.3
PERCENT AFFIRMATIVE		
Democrats	90.6	94.5
Whigs	12.4	19.1

SOURCES: *SJ, 1860–1861*, 92, 147–48, 158, 186–87, 193–94, 224–25, 232, 242–43; *HJ, 1860–1861*, 157–58, 204, 262, 302, 310, 330, 343–44, 348–49, 352–54, 356–57, 364–67, 374, 384–85, 454–55, 456–57.

the convention bill through the General Assembly, but their effort was doomed because the state constitution required a two-thirds majority in both houses in order to call a convention. In 1858, with a joint majority of fifty-eight, Democrats might have pushed through the bill with ease, but in 1860, after the Whig party had rebounded, the Democratic majority stood at only sixteen. If Democrats hoped to pass a convention bill, they would have to shape it according to the wishes of the Whig minority.[51]

Whigs ultimately delayed the bill's passage for more than six weeks, thereby destroying any momentum for secession that might have been accumulating because of the rapid succession of lower South states leaving the Union. After receiving major concessions from the Democrats, enough Whigs finally voted for the bill, and on January 29 it became law. The bill provided that on February 28 enfranchised North Carolinians would vote for or against a convention. Concurrently, each county would elect a number of delegates that would be equal to the county's representation in the House of Commons. If approved by a popular majority, the convention could be summoned by the governor any time after March 10. The act then

51. *HJ, 1860–61*, 163–69.

restricted the convention to a discussion of federal affairs and provided that any action it took would have to be ratified by the voters. Democrats had hoped to take advantage of the crisis atmosphere by holding the convention quickly and by avoiding popular ratification of secession, in keeping with the precedents of the lower South. What they finally got was a law that did not even assure the meeting of a convention. And the action of a convention, if it met, would be constrained by the requirement that voters ratify its work. The combination of a conservative constitution and partisanship had thus shaped the legislature's response to the secession crisis.[52]

The vote of Senate Whigs on the final bill is particularly interesting because of the disparity in slaveholdings among Whigs and Democrats, which was noted above. The seven Whigs who voted for a convention held a median of 3 slaves; the nine die-hard Unionist Whigs owned 19.5. Whatever other motives prompted some Whigs to vote with the Democratic majority, a deep personal involvement in the slave system was not among them.[53]

The effects of the Whig delays must be seen in the larger context of the secession winter. When the election was held in February, the public mood was vastly different from the mood that had prevailed in January, the date for which the secessionists had wished. In January, state after state in the lower South was abandoning the Union and preparing to join the Confederacy. But in late February a peace convention was meeting in Washington, and Virginia, Tennessee, and several border states had already rejected secession. Viewed in this light, Whig delays gave Union sentiment in North Carolina a chance to jell.[54]

Nevertheless, Democrats had finally won the chance to obtain a convention, and, given their majority in the state, they could view the upcoming election with confidence. However, one roll-call vote late in the legislative session should have made them wary. When Whigs proposed that the General Assembly send representatives to the assemblage of southern states at Montgomery, Alabama, and to the peace meeting in Washington, D.C., Democrats who were intent on secession opposed it. They wanted to send a delegation only to Montgomery. In the balloting, about 30 percent of the Democratic commoners voted in favor of the Whig bill, and it passed. This minority, while casting repeated votes in favor of secessionist proposals, was still willing to give the Union another chance. Those dissenting Democrats owned just as many slaves as other Democratic commoners and often came from counties where slaveholding was widespread. If a

52. *Public Laws of North Carolina, 1860–1861* (Raleigh: John Spelman, 1861), 27–30.
53. *SJ, 1860–61,* 207.
54. Potter, *Impending Crisis,* 505–506, 545–47.

comparable proportion of Democrats in the convention election proved similarly inclined, then the secessionists would fail.[55]

★

Secessionist concerns grew as Whigs and Union Democrats led by William Holden increasingly identified themselves as members of a Unionist coalition with no ties to past party affiliations. Holden declared: "We know no party, and we neither cherish nor remember any personal differences in this great struggle for the Union. We are for the country without regard to men or party." Edward J. Hale, editor of the Whig Fayetteville *Observer*, wrote that "old party lines are forgotten, as if they had never existed." He reported that among the seventy-six delegates at a Union meeting in his home county, Cumberland, forty-five were Democrats, twenty-seven Whigs, and there were four whose partisan affiliation was unknown.[56]

Although the events of the winter had altered somewhat the shape of state politics, there were still significant continuities. Except for a few prominent dissidents like Holden, the Democratic party leadership worked actively for secession, while Whig party leaders strongly favored the Union cause. Whig Tod Caldwell reported that in his mountain county, Burke, "the democratic leaders [are] all secessionists, [while] our Whig friends [are] generally firm for the Union and conservatism." Many Whigs, in fact, felt that they were on the popular side of the issue and hoped to use the election campaign as an opportunity to convert Democrats to Whiggery. One Whig said of his Democratic neighbors: "I believe that Democracy can be driven out of them . . . now is the time to work on them." The optimism of that Whig was mirrored by the pessimism of Democrat William J. Yates, a member of the Council of State and editor of the Charlotte *Western Democrat*, who worried that the Democratic leadership's advocacy of immediate secession had hurt the party irreparably. "I fear," he wrote, "the 'old democracy' have lost power in the state."[57]

During the campaign for the election of delegates and, indeed, throughout the entire secession crisis, the Unionists argued that secession and North Carolina's membership in a southern government would affect the state adversely. Contrary to what the secessionists were claiming, the Unionists contended, slavery would be injured, not benefited, as a result of

55. *HJ, 1860–61*, 384–85.

56. Raleigh *Standard*, February 13, 1861; Fayetteville *Observer*, February 25, 1861.

57. Tod R. Caldwell to William A. Graham, February 11, 1861, in Hamilton and Williams (eds.), *Graham Papers*, V, 233; William A. [Lash?] to John F. Poindexter, November 27, 1860, in John F. Poindexter Papers, Duke; William J. Yates to Lawrence O'Bryan Branch, February 26, 1861, in Branch Papers.

secession. They believed that war was certain to follow secession and that the abolition of slavery would be the certain result of war. Bartholemew F. Moore lamented to a friend that "slavery is mad and running on to its own destruction." John H. Bryan wrote his brother in a similar vein: "The dissolution of the union would be the end of slavery."[58]

If secession did not cause the death of slavery in the entire South, Unionists said, it would certainly destroy the institution in North Carolina. They agreed that the upper and lower South were both committed to the preservation of slavery, but since the upper South was selling slaves to the lower South, the former desired higher prices for slaves, while the latter wished for lower ones. Unionists, therefore, perceived the movement to reopen the African slave trade as a direct threat to the upper South. The Raleigh *Register* warned North Carolinians that the reopening of the trade would bring to "utter ruin . . . the slavery property of this State."[59]

The Unionists also appealed to the local pride and independence of their fellow citizens. The Wilmington *Herald* asked North Carolinians: "Do they wish, will they *submit*, to be dragged into revolution and anarchy, and all to please the State of South Carolina, who by her insufferable arrogance, and conceited self-importance, has been a constant source of annoyance and disquietude to the whole country, North and South, for the last thirty years? Will our people so far forget their independence, and their manhood, as blindly to follow the lead of that State into civil war?" North Carolinians, the paper answered, would act as the independent free men they were and reject South Carolina's plans.[60]

Unionists argued further that secession would lead to war and to the establishment of a strong military government that would tax the people heavily and would threaten their personal liberties. John H. Bryan wrote to his brother that "the mass of the people are not disposed to give up the union[,] still less to pay heavy taxes & do the fighting that may occur." In late February, the Fayetteville *Observer* summed up most of the Unionist arguments. It pointed out that the central government had little direct impact on the lives of its citizens, but if the Union were destroyed "*war must follow*. . . . With it come visits of the tax-gatherer . . . with heavier demands and on our part less ability to meet them; bloodshed; all the horrors of civil war; and eventual destruction of that great interest [slavery]

58. Bartholemew F. Moore to James W. Bryan, February 12, 1861, John H. Bryan to James W. Bryan, December 13, 1860, both in Bryan Family Papers, SHC.

59. John Menningham to Bedford Brown, December 20, 1860, in Bedford Brown Papers, SHC; *Speech of T. N. Crumpler, Ashe, on Federal Relations, Delivered in the House of Commons, January 10, 1861* (n.p., [1861]), in NCC; Raleigh *Register*, February 6, 1861.

60. Wilmington *Daily Herald*, November 9, 1860, in Dwight L. Dumond (ed.), *Southern Editorials on Secession* (New York: American Historical Association, 1931), 227–28.

whose safety is made the pretext for destroying the Government which protects it."[61]

The secessionists, rather than trying to assuage popular fears concerning the future southern confederacy, dwelt upon the evils that would result from remaining in the Union. From the time they learned of Lincoln's election, a large portion of Breckinridge's supporters began to call for the secession of the state. Republicans, they claimed, would ultimately abolish slavery in the South, and abolition would bring disaster for the region. One secessionist asserted that "we must either be freemen or submit to have our homes made desolate by the snares of the No[r]thern Fanatic or what is worse to be destroyed by the indolent race we now hold as Slaves." The Wilmington *Journal* warned that abolition would lead to the equality of the freed blacks and those whites who had not the money to flee. "Wealth would fly the community; deprived of capital, impoverished by his worthless free negro neighbors, the position of the white man forced to remain, would be a most deplorable one." The *Journal* went on to argue that "the negro race we shall always have with us." But whites would have some choice: "Shall we have it as an ungovernable, unprofitable, lawless and vicious element, driving out wealth and asserting its equality with all who are compelled to stay, or shall we have it in its proper place, as a subordinate race—its subordination being natural, founded upon race, elevating the position of the poorest man of the dominant race, and adding to the wealth and comfort of the whole community."[62]

The only solution was for North Carolina to secede. Once the secessionists had delineated that bleak picture of North Carolina's future in the Union, they still had to answer charges that they were "lawless men" who sought "secession for the sake of secession." They replied by portraying themselves as defenders of "our rights and our equality." They were men who would accept secession "as a means to secure those rights which we feel to be no longer safe in the Union." Then the secessionists argued that "our rights are *not* safe in the Union," nor was there any evidence to indicate that any sectional compromise could be reached. For those reasons, "not the love of secession," they concluded that secession was the only remedy."[63]

Critical to the secessionists' contention that they were not "lawless

61. Raleigh *Standard*, December 5, 1860, February 6, 1861; John H. Bryan to James W. Bryan, December 18, 1860, in Bryan Family Papers, SHC; Fayetteville *Observer*, February 18, 1861.

62. Nash County Southern Rights Meeting, January 17, 1861, quoted in Raleigh *State Journal*, February 20, 1861; J. Bryce to Samuel F. Patterson, January 5, 1861, in Jones and Patterson Papers; Wilmington *Journal*, February 21, 1861.

63. Wilmington *Journal*, February 21, 1861.

men" was their argument that a satisfactory solution could not be attained in the Union and that therefore North Carolina had to choose between the North or the South. In late February, the Wilmington *Journal* argued that "it is too late in the day to talk about compromises. None can be effected, and the border Southern States must decide to which Confederacy they will attach themselves."[64]

The secessionist belief that no compromise could be attained was made debatable by Virginia's invitation to all of the states to meet in Washington on February 4 to work out a compromise on the slavery question. Because the peace conference met from the fourth to the twenty-eighth—the day of the North Carolina convention election—it was difficult for the secessionists to claim that a compromise was impossible. On the other hand, Unionists continually harped upon the fact that a peace conference was in session and that the people of the state ought to give the delegates an opportunity to reach a compromise. To prove their point, the Unionists flooded the state's newspapers with telegrams saying that compromise was near. The secessionists countered with telegrams and letters from Washington denying that compromise was possible.[65]

Apparently the secessionists had considerable difficulty convincing voters of their moderation. One Democratic editor and supporter of secession, William Yates, wrote Congressman Lawrence Branch that the secession Democrats had "pursued a suicidal policy." The fact that "some of our friends in the Legislature . . . proclaimed *secession* as the object for which they wanted a Convention" alienated many voters. As a result, Yates believed, the vote would "go largely against secession."[66]

The election results proved Yates a good prophet. A slight majority of North Carolina voters (50.3 percent) rejected the call for a convention; of 93,995 votes cast, the anticonvention majority was only 661. Because many Unionist leaders had supported the call for a convention, the vote did not reflect Union sentiment in the state. A more accurate reflection of popular sentiment was the position of the delegates. My own analysis indicates that 81 of the 120 delegates chosen were Unionists and 39 were secessionists.[67]

But the position of the winners in the contest is only useful for delineating broad patterns of Union and secession sentiment, for there was, of

64. Raleigh *State Journal*, February 27, 1861; Wilmington *Journal*, February 21, 1861.

65. Sitterson, *Secession Movement*, 223; David S. Reid to Thomas W. Kean, *et al.*, February 18, 1861, in William Holland Thomas Papers, Duke.

66. William J. Yates to Lawrence O'Bryan Branch, February 26, 1861, in Branch Papers.

67. I found it impossible to distinguish unconditional from conditional Unionists, as J. Carlyle Sitterson did. Sitterson found 42 secessionists, 28 conditional Unionists, and 50 unconditional Unionists (Sitterson, *Secession Movement*, 223). For my analysis of the delegates, see Appendix B.

course, much difference between a county where voters cast 90 percent of their ballots for a Unionist candidate and one where they cast 51 percent. In order to clarify such differences, the actual votes for the delegates must be examined. An analysis of the returns indicates that 60.1 percent of the voters cast Union ballots in the February election. Despite the fact that most of the dominant Democratic leadership supported secession, the secessionist vote was less than 40 percent.[68]

Historians, in their attempt to explain patterns of support for Union or secession, have tried to relate it to the proportion of slaves in the total population. However, the low positive coefficient of correlation (.42) between the proportion of slaves in a county and that county's vote on secession suggests that there was little general relationship beween the two. It should also be pointed out that this correlation was similar to correlations found when comparing the proportion of slaves to the Democratic vote in earlier elections (see Appendix A, table 29). A closer look at these patterns, though, suggests that there was some relationship. Of the eighteen counties where slaves composed less than 15 percent of the total population in 1860, all voted Unionist in 1861, and of the twenty-nine counties where slaves made up less than a fourth of the population, twenty-five voted Unionist. The forty-six counties with greater than 25 percent of their population enslaved were almost evenly split on the question. While twenty-two voted Unionist, the remaining twenty-four gave secessionist majorities. Stated another way, twenty-four of the twenty-five secessionist counties had a quarter or more of their population enslaved. As J. Carlyle Sitterson has concluded, "a secession county was likely to be a slaveholding county, but a slaveholding county might not necessarily be a secession county." Somewhat similar results are found when one compares the density of slaveholders in a county with a secession sentiment in that county. The coefficient of correlation between the percentage of free families owning slaves and the secession vote was .43.[69]

Historians have argued further that there were clear geographic bases for secession sentiment and that secessionists received most of their popular support in the slaveholding counties of the coastal plain, while the strongest support for the Union came from the mountainous Appalachian counties. Although it is true that the main area of secession strength was the coastal plain, the region of most intense Unionism was the central and

68. See Appendix B for a discussion of the vote and for the figures upon which this analysis is based.

69. Sitterson, *Secession Movement*, 224. When the Breckinridge vote is held constant, the partial coefficient of correlation between the proportion of slaves and the prosecession vote drops to .296.

upper Piedmont, not the mountain counties. Support for the Union was strong in the mountain counties, but it was not as intense as Unionism in the Piedmont.

More striking than the relationship of geography or slaveholding patterns to secession and Union sentiment was the close relationship between the vote in the February election and voting patterns in elections held in the 1840s and 1850s. The fact that the Democratic party had been the majority party through the 1850s, while the secessionists had lost badly, indicated that there was no one-to-one relationship between the Democratic vote and the secession vote. However, there was a continuity in voting patterns from antebellum gubernatorial and presidential elections to the convention election. The strongest Whig counties in the state tended to be the strongest Unionist counties; the strongest Democratic counties were usually the strongest secessionist counties. The coefficient of correlation between the county-level Democratic vote in the 1840s and the county-level secession vote in 1861 was about .67; between the Breckinridge vote and the secession vote it was .70 (see table 24, p. 183).

The relationship between prewar and convention-election voting patterns may also be examined in a different way. Of the twenty-five secession counties identified, twenty-three had voted for Democrat John Ellis in the 1860 gubernatorial race. And of the twenty-seven counties that voted heavily for Ellis (over 60 percent), nineteen voted secessionist. On the other hand, of twenty-nine counties casting majorities for Whig John Pool, twenty-seven voted Unionist in 1861.

A comparison of the secession vote and the vote for John C. Breckinridge reveals that twenty-one of the twenty-five secession counties had given Breckinridge a majority, and eighteen of the twenty-one voted more than 60 percent for him. Not all Breckinridge counties in 1860 were secession counties, however. Although he received majorities in thirty-two counties, only twenty-one of them supported secession. The anti-Breckinridge vote (which was almost entirely the vote for John Bell, since Stephen Douglas received so few votes) bore a close resemblance to the Unionist vote. Of forty-one anti-Breckinridge counties, thirty-seven voted Unionist in 1861. The persistence of the party system and of party organization had clearly carried over to the vote on secession.

Even so, the relationship between voting in the secession election and in previous state elections was weaker than similar comparisons made between the antebellum elections themselves (see table 24, p. 183). A number of counties did political somersaults. There were several Democratic counties that voted Unionist and some strong Whig counties that either voted for secessionists or barely elected Unionists. These dramatic changes were not a reflection of the proportion of slaves in a county. It is true that wealthy rice-planting Whig Brunswick County voted secessionist, but wealthy tobacco-planting Democratic Caswell County voted Unionist. An examination of figure 4 and table 31 reveals that most of the Democratic counties that voted Unionist sat along the border with Virginia, whereas most of the Whig counties that leaned toward secession bordered South Carolina. It would appear that social and economic intercourse across state lines influenced the way people in these counties responded to the secession crisis.

★

The election indicated that North Carolinians remained staunch supporters of the Union. Some of the elation was lost because the peace conference failed. But in early March Unionists and secessionists alike were not so much concerned with compromising the sectional difficulties as they were with whether the new president, to be inaugurated on March 4, would try to force the seceded states back into the Union. Both Unionists and secessionists had long opposed any attempt to "coerce" the seceded states. They warned the North that any attempt to compel the return of those states to the Union would cause North Carolina's secession. In January, the Raleigh *Register* stated: "To the plan of coercion we are utterly opposed, and when an attempt is made to carry it into execution, it will meet the united resistance of fifteen States, and be the commencement of the bloodiest era in the annals of time." In early February, U.S. District judge Asa Biggs, a secessionist, wrote to a friend that he would abide by any decision of the people to remain in the Union "*provided* she does not, by her decision, require me to be a party to a civil war, to coerce by the sword, seceding States."[70]

The act of coercion implied several things to North Carolinians. First, they saw that by it Lincoln would precipitate a war, and North Carolinians, obliged to choose sides, would unite with their brethren of the South, with whom they had common interests—especially the ownership of slaves—and feelings. Second, they viewed coercion as the first attack on the institution of slavery. In a letter to Secretary of State William Seward, Whig Unionist John Gilmer explained that "the only thing now that gives the secessionists the advantage of the conservatives is the cry of coercion—that the whipping of a slave state, is the whipping of slavery." Third, North Carolinians rejected the use of force by the North because they perceived it as an attempt to subjugate the South, to suppress the liberties of free men,

70. Raleigh *Register*, January 19, 1861; Asa Biggs to Lawrence O'Bryan Branch, February 5, 1861, in Branch Papers.

to deny men the right to govern themselves. If the federal government could force a restoration of the Union, could it not compel North Carolinians to accede to other kinds of demands? As one secessionist put it, coercion changed "the issue . . . from the Negro to that of a question of popular liberty."[71]

So it was with great anxiety that North Carolinians awaited the new president's inaugural address. After reading the address, secessionists and Unionists interpreted it in ways most congruent with their own expectations. Secessionist David Schenk perceived the address as nothing less than a war message, while Unionist editor William Holden declared that the address showed the new administration's pacific intentions.[72]

Some Unionists were left uneasy by the president's speech. Methodist minister T. Page Ricaud lamented: "'Lincoln's Inaugural,' and the partial failure of the 'Peace Congress,' with the evident indifference of Congress to the whole subject, had discouraged many prominent truehearted Union men . . . and I fear every day's influence in strengthening the Secession ranks." Hamilton Jones complained to Stephen Douglas that "the ambiguous character of his inaugural . . . has hurt us some in this State."[73]

Basing their analysis on plaintive remarks like those of Ricaud and Jones, historians have argued that, in the weeks following the convention election, the failed peace conference, and the inaugural address, Unionism in North Carolina, with no positive plans or program, declined rapidly in the face of the vigorous onslaught of the well-organized secessionists. The fear of inaction did, in fact, bother some Unionists. Quentin Busbee argued that, if the Unionists failed to establish a line of policy, "I fear, we shall from inaction, be drifted by our Governor and others into the mailstrom [*sic*] of the Montgomery Concern."

It is also true that the secessionists were better organized than before and that, in secession, they had a positive and simple plan to offer the people. On March 22, for example, they met in Goldsboro to establish a State Rights party whose goal was to convince the people of the state to "reconsider their action" of February 28 and to call for a convention. The Golds-

71. C. Q. Lemmonds, *Speech of C. Q. Lemmonds, Esq. on the Convention Bill, Delivered in the House of Commons, January 17, 1861* (Raleigh: John Spelman, 1861), in NCC; Raleigh *Register*, January 19, March 6, April 10, 1861; Raleigh *Standard*, February 27, 1861; John A. Gilmer to William H. Seward, March 8, 1861, in Frederic Bancroft, *The Life of William H. Seward* (2 vols.; 1899; reprint ed., Gloucester, Mass.: Peter Smith, 1967), II, 547; C.B. Harrison to Lawrence O'Bryan Branch, December 2, 1860, in Branch Papers.

72. David Schenck Diaries (typescript in SHC), March 18, 1861; Raleigh *Standard*, March 13, 1861.

73. T. Page Ricaud to Jones Fuller, March 13, 1861, in Fuller-Thomas Papers, Fuller Division, Duke; Hamilton C. Jones to Stephen A. Douglas. March 10, 1861, in Douglas Papers.

boro convention appointed an executive committee to coordinate party activity and resolved that "all efforts to obtain any . . . guarantees for the safety of the Southern States . . . have failed." Therefore, it determined that North Carolina ought to secede and join the Confederacy.[74]

But, although some Unionists were discouraged because of their own inaction and the activity of the secessionists, most remained optimistic about keeping the state in the Union and about solving the nation's crisis. Unionists advocated what they often called the "let alone" policy. The federal government was to allow the lower South to leave in peace, then the remaining states would gather together in a harmonious atmosphere to compromise differences on the question of slavery. Meanwhile, the seven states of the Confederacy would find that they could not prosper as a nation and would soon petition for readmission to the Union.

George Badger stated the basics of the plan in a letter to James W. Bryan. Badger recommended that Congress pass two laws: it would first recognize the independence of the seceded states, then it would pass "a joint resolution offering the plan of the peace conference or something equivalent to the states as amendments of the constitution." Then, he continued, "we shall have peace & quiet—and in three years the 'confederation' will bust up and all its members (but S. C.) will be asking for readmission."[75]

Central to Badger's thinking—and to the thinking of most advocates of the "let alone" policy—was the assumption that the seven states of the lower South could not form an effective national government. Left on their own, the states would break up the new nation as they had broken up the old. Bartholemew F. Moore declared that "a Southern Republic will be worse than a rope of sand." Moore, Badger, and others underestimated the Deep South's commitment to independence, but they realized that only if the southern Unionists could convince northerners who were committed to the preservation of the Union that the Union would be whole again in a few years could they convince Republicans to adopt the "let alone" policy.[76]

Another significant aspect of the policy was the way in which Unionists virtually ignored the actual question of slavery. While they talked about the need to reach a compromise if North Carolina was to stay in the Union, the Unionists clung as strongly as ever to the Union, despite the repeated

---

74. Quentin Busbee to Stephen A. Douglas, March 11, 1861, in Douglas Papers; Wilmington *Journal*, March 28, 1861. On the supposed decline of Unionism, see Sitterson, *Secession Movement*, 232–38; Robert W. Johannsen, *Stephen A. Douglas* (New York: Oxford University Press, 1973), 851–52. A major exception to this general interpretation is Daniel W. Crofts, "The Union Party of 1861 and the Secession Crisis," *Perspectives in American History*, IX (1978–79), 327–76.

75. George E. Badger to James W. Bryan, March 8, 1861, in Bryan Family Papers.

76. Bartholemew F. Moore to his daughter, December, 1860 (typescript), in Bartholemew F. Moore Letters, NCDAH.

defeats suffered by the advocates of compromise. To be sure, they continued to talk about compromise, but the talk was permeated with vagueness. George Badger might talk about the adoption of the peace conference's recommendations, but he had no intention of advocating secession if those recommendations were rejected. North Carolina Unionists certainly hoped that some compromise on the question of slavery might be reached, but most of them would stick with the Union come what might. The major goal of the "let alone" policy was to keep the states of the upper South in the Union by preventing violent conflict between the federal government and the seceded states.

Throughout March and early April, Unionists believed that the "let alone" policy had been adopted by the Lincoln administration and that North Carolina would remain in the Union for the indefinite future. On March 30, the Raleigh *Register* declared that nothing had happened since February 28 "to induce the people . . . to reverse the verdict rendered that day. . . . On the contrary, there is a feeling of greater security in the country now than existed when the vote was taken." The next day, one of Raleigh's leading Unionists wrote to Stephen Douglas that "if its [the Lincoln administration's] policy is peace, & that policy is promptly carried out, we can overwhelm the secessionists in this state." Hamilton Jones expressed similar optimism in a letter in which he asked Stephen Douglas to persuade Lincoln not to use force against the seceded states. If the seceded states were left alone, all would be well. "The administration," he pleaded, "has no right to destroy the only party [North Carolina Unionists] that can put down the secessionists. We can do it[,] we are doing it[,] and if left alone we will do it." Allen T. Davidson, who was traveling south from his home in western North Carolina, wrote to his wife that "if old Abe behaves himself, [Unionists would] yet save the country from the damnation and misrule of this irresponsible mob."[77]

Even if the "let alone" policy were to be implemented by the Lincoln administration, Unionists still would not have resolved the basic problem of Republican antagonism to the South and slavery. Granted that the Lincoln administration might be checked for four years, or that it would act in a conciliatory manner toward the South for those years, yet what would happen after Lincoln had served his term? What if a more radical Republican were elected four years hence? North Carolina Unionists thought carefully about those and other related questions, and they came up with different but overlapping plans of action.

One group suggested that the Republican victory resulted from divi-

77. Henry W. Miller to Stephen A. Douglas, March 31, 1861, Hamilton C. Jones to Douglas, March 3, 1861, both in Douglas Papers; Allen T. Davidson to his wife, April 7, 1861, in Allen Turner Davidson Papers, SHC.

sions in conservative ranks and that conservatives had learned their lesson and would not fight among themselves in 1864. William Graham, preparing notes for a speech, wrote that Lincoln "was elected because his opponents were divided. This would not occur again." He and others like him trusted that the chastening experience of having a Republican in the White House for four years would unite all opponents of that party. Graham's plans for 1864, though, were ultimately dependent on providing a viable alternative to Lincoln and the Republicans. The most likely person to rally the opposition was Stephen Douglas, who since the election campaign had established himself as a staunch Unionist and conciliator. Although Douglas would not have been the first choice of Whigs like Graham, he did represent the hopes of the small group of Democrats who had supported him in 1860. They had backed him then because they wanted, in the words of Robert P. Dick, "to preserve the *seed* of a National Democracy," not because they thought he could carry the state. Although Douglas' poor showing in November indicated that Dick and others had barely preserved the seed of a national party, Dick's faith in the future of the party showed a persistent belief in the viability of the party system.[78]

After the election, Douglas Democrats began to see the possibility of Douglas' emerging as the leader of a broad coalition opposed to the Republicans. North Carolinians wrote to Douglas in the winter and spring of 1861 that many of their neighbors regretted their decision to vote against him. Given another chance, they would cast their ballots for him, and they hoped to get that chance in 1864. Douglas supporter Henry Miller had earlier foreseen such a political coalition emerging. "I am thoroughly convinced," he wrote to Douglas, "the opposition, the *entire* opposition look to *you* as the only man who can defeat Black Republicanism at the next election. I hope yet to see you President of the *United* States." Enoch Jones wrote Douglas that the people of North Carolina looked to him "as being the man that will, at no distant day, hasten the overthrow of the now dominant party, and come out victorious over the enemies of our domestic institutions at the North, and the common disturbers of our National peace at the South." Jones and Miller, of course, skimmed over the fact that Douglas had run poorly in the South and had won few electoral votes in the North in November. Whether Douglas would be any more effective in 1864 remained to be seen, but his Unionist activities during the secession winter may well have broadened his base of support.[79]

78. William A. Graham, "Notes for a Speech," February, 1861, in Hamilton and Williams (eds.), *Graham Papers*, V, 219; Robert P. Dick to Thomas Settle, Jr., July 11, 1860, in Thomas Settle Papers, No. 2, SHC.

79. Henry W. Miller to Stephen A. Douglas, November 28, 1860, Enoch Jones to Douglas, March 25, 1861, both in Douglas Papers.

A smaller third group of Unionists considered the possibility of establishing a coalition of southern Unionists and conservative Republicans. The most important advocate of such a coalition was one of the state's most conservative Whigs, John A. Gilmer. Gilmer was seeking the kind of conservative national party that many southern Whigs had sought ever since the death of the national Whig party. Men like him had hoped in the mid-1850s to find that political salvation in the American party, which had run Gilmer for governor in 1856, and in the Constitutional Union party later in the decade. Now Gilmer saw the possibility of establishing a party of southern Whigs and conservative northern Republicans. In late December, Gilmer pleaded with Lincoln to pursue a conservative southern policy. "You may divide from your many party friends," he wrote, "but by the preservation of the peace of the country you will nationalize yourself and your party." Lincoln and Seward may have had such a goal in mind, for during March and early April they adopted a conciliatory policy toward the South. To southern Unionists, it appeared that the "let alone" policy had been adopted by the administration.[80]

Assuming that things were going well in Washington, Unionists in the state busily organized the Union party. The presidential election of 1864 was still far off. Of more immediate concern were the contests for congressional seats in 1861. Whig Zebulon Vance announced that he was a candidate for reelection in the mountain district. The Charlotte *Western Democrat* reported that Whigs in the Sixth District had announced plans to hold a party convention in late April and complained that "many of the old political enemies of the democratic party (assisted by some who have acted with the democratic party) intend to make an effort to get into office by huzzaing for the Union." The Union party was most active in the organizing in the Raleigh district under the direction of William Holden. Holden's first choice for candidate was Henry W. Miller, who had been active in the Whig and American party organizations. Miller had joined the Democrats in 1858 because he felt that theirs was the only organization that could protect the South, and in 1860 he had supported Stephen Douglas.[81]

Before declaring his candidacy, Miller wanted to be "brought forward by a mass meeting of the District, in a convention." Only an organized effort would enable him to defeat the popular secessionist Lawrence Branch

80. John A. Gilmer to Abraham Lincoln, December 29, 1860, in Robert Todd Lincoln Papers, LC, (microfilm copy in Wayne State University Library, Detroit, Michigan). I would like to thank Professor Daniel W. Crofts for bringing this letter to my attention. Daniel W. Crofts, "A Reluctant Unionist: John A. Gilmer and Lincoln's Cabinet," *Civil War History*, XXIV (1978), 225–49; David M. Potter, *Lincoln and His Party in the Secession Crisis* (New Haven: Yale University Press, 1942), 318–32; Crofts, "Union Party."

81. Charlotte *Western Democrat*, April 16, March 26, 1861.

in the heavily Democratic district. Not only was it necessary for there to be a well-organized party behind him, but he wanted to make sure that the national government planned no attempt to coerce a seceded state. If coercion were planned, he would certainly refuse to run, but "if its policy is peace, & that policy is promptly carried out, we can overwhelm the Secessionists in this State."[82]

The firing on Fort Sumter on April 12 shattered the optimism of Unionists like Henry Miller, and Lincoln's proclamation calling for troops to suppress the rebellion turned those men from Unionists into secessionists. W. N. H. Smith, a Whig member of Congress and a strong Unionist, wrote to his colleague Zebulon Vance: "The Union feeling *was strong* up to the recent proclamation. This War Manifest Extinguishes it, and resistance is now on every mans lips and throbs in every bosom. . . . Union men are now such no longer." Several weeks after Lincoln called for the troops, Josiah Cowles, a Yadkin County Whig politician and a substantial slaveholder, explained to his son why his views had changed: "I was as strong a union man as any in the state up to the time of Lincolns proclamation calling for 75000 volunteers. I then saw that the south had either to submit to abject vassallage or assert her rights at the point of the Sword." He had opposed coercion, he said, "believing it to be virtually a distruction to liberty."[83]

The change in Josiah Cowle's attitude toward the Union mirrored the changes of thousands of other North Carolinians. The press and politicians proclaimed that the incipient war was to be fought in the name of popular liberty. William Holden wrote in his Raleigh *Standard* that "the proclamation of Mr. Lincoln has left no alternative but resistance or unconditional submission. The Southern man who would quietly submit to the doctrines enunciated in that document, is fit only for a slave."[84]

Governor Ellis called the General Assembly into a special session. The legislators, in turn, provided for the election of delegates to a convention that would meet in Raleigh on May 20. Although delegates came to the convention virtually unanimous in their support for separation, some of the old demarcations of partisan difference remained. Since 1850, Whigs had argued that secession was illegal and therefore revolution was the only proper response to intolerable oppression. Democrats had defended the legitimacy of secession. In 1861, Whig Unionist William A. Graham sought election as the convention president as a "revolutionist," but he

82. Henry W. Miller to Stephen A. Douglas, March 31, 1861, in Douglas Papers.

83. William N. H. Smith to Zebulon B. Vance, April 26, 1861, in Frontis W. Johnston (ed.), *The Papers of Zebulon Baird Vance* (Raleigh: State Department of Archives and History, 1963–), 99; Josiah Cowles to Calvin J. Cowles, June 3, 1861, in Calvin J. Cowles Papers, NCDAH.

84. Raleigh *Standard*, May 8, 1861.

lost to Democratic secessionist Weldon N. Edwards. After the election, the delegates passed an ordinance of secession rather than a declaration of revolution, as old Unionists desired. The convention then ratified the permanent Constitution of the Confederate States of America.[85]

During the rest of the session, the delegates confronted a number of other constitutional questions, and their decisions on those matters resolved some of the outstanding issues of the late 1850s and reconfirmed the consensus in favor of the positive state. Because North Carolina was now on a war footing, they agreed that the state would have to raise taxes, and because the war was going to be fought to defend slavery, they amended the constitution to tax slaves by the *ad valorem* method. They also permitted Jews to hold office. And they defeated repeated eastern efforts to amend the constitution in order to limit the size of the state debt and to impede passage of appropriation bills in the General Assembly.[86]

★

When North Carolina left the Union on May 20, almost all North Carolinians supported that decision. Yet little more than a month before, Unionist sentiment had dominated the state. Between February 28, when they voted overwhelmingly for the Union, and April 15, the Unionism of most North Carolinians endured. In March and early April, North Carolina did not drift toward secession. During this time, Unionists looked to the future with a feeling of optimism tinged with some foreboding. If Lincoln would only pursue the "let alone" policy that he had supposedly adopted, the Unionists would triumph in the state. North Carolina and the rest of the upper South would stay in the Union. Meanwhile, the seceded states would find that they were unable to establish a nation and would see that Lincoln posed no threat to them. They would then apply for readmission to the United States. The nation would thus be reunited.

The Unionist perception of a soon-to-be reunited nation resulted directly from the persistence of the two-party system in the state. The fact that Whigs had come close to victory after years of defeat convinced many North Carolinians that the hated Republican party could be driven out of power in 1864 and that in the meantime the political system would prevent the Lincoln administration from taking actions hostile to southern interests.

85. John W. Ellis, "Governor's Proclamation," April 17, 1861, "Governor's Message," [May 1, 1861], "Governor's Proclamation," May 1, 1861, all in Tolbert (ed.), *Ellis Papers*, II, 621–22, 697–706; *SJ, 1860–61, 1st Extra Session*, 19; *HJ, 1860–61, 1st Extra Session*, 18; *Journal of the Convention of the People of North Carolina Held on the 20th Day of May, A.D. 1861* (Raleigh: Jno. W. Syme, 1862), 5–6, 10–16, 72–73.

86. *Convention Journal*, 171–72, 92–93, 43, 166–68.

If the strong Unionism of the Whigs had been the cause of their revival, it would be a circular argument to contend that the existence of a vital two-party system strengthened the cause of Unionism in North Carolina. Then, one would be arguing that Unionism caused the revival of the two-party system, which in turn caused the persistence of Unionism in the state. But the Whig revival occurred, and the party system was thus revitalized, because of national and state issues unrelated to the secession crisis. Yet the presence of that party system helps to explain why North Carolinians clung with such tenacity to the Union.

North Carolinians recognized that partisan conflict had divided them during the secession crisis. Now that secession was accomplished, politicians declared for the sake of wartime unity they would refrain from partisan activity. But party politics and the party system were too strong to be stilled by the guns of Fort Sumter. Less than a year after the state seceded, partisan activity was as intense as ever before.

Nine *The Continuity of Politics 1861–1862*

The secession of North Carolina created a flood tide of antiparty sentiment in the state. Indeed, throughout the South, editors and politicians proclaimed a cessation of old political differences and asserted the need for unity in the face of northern invasion. Although it may be, as David M. Potter and Eric L. McKitrick have argued, that the presence of a two-party system aided the northern war effort and its absence weakened the South, this notion never would have convinced southerners.[1]

Antiparty attitudes generally reflected an absence of party politics in the Confederacy. Confederate congressmen, for example, did not vote along party lines. It appears that the same was true in most of the Confederate states, though historians have generally ignored political developments there. The lack of parties in the lower South during the war was nothing new; that region had not had a competitive party system for some years. In much of the upper South, where party competition had persisted through that decade, the war turned most of the region into a battlefield and put an end to politics-as-usual. In North Carolina, however, isolated from most military action, older political patterns persisted, though modified by the state's experience in the secession crisis and the war.[2]

1. David M. Potter, "Jefferson Davis and the Political Factors in Confederate Defeat," in David Donald (ed.), *Why the North Won the Civil War* (Baton Rouge: Louisiana State University Press, 1960), 90–114; Eric L. McKitrick, "Party Politics and the Union and Confederate War Efforts," in William Nisbet Chambers and Walter Dean Burnham (eds.), *The American Party Systems: Stages of Political Development* (New York: Oxford University Press, 1967), 117–51.

2. Thomas B. Alexander and Richard E. Beringer, *The Anatomy of the Confederate Congress: A Study of the Influences of Member Characteristics on Legislative Behavior, 1861–1865* (Nashville:

As North Carolinians learned of Lincoln's proclamation of April 15 and prepared for their state to leave the Union, editors and politicians proclaimed the advent of an era of good feelings in state politics. The partisanship that had divided North Carolinians for so many years would cease, and words that stood as symbols of that division—Democrat, Whig, Secessionist, Unionist—would disappear from the political vocabulary. North Carolina would be a unit, unanimous in its determination to repel the northern invader. The Democratic Wilmington *Journal* proclaimed: "Wilmington is a unit! We know no party but the party of the South! We bury past contests and their recollections. We cease to quarrel over names." The Union Whig Raleigh *Register* wrote that "the 'edict has gone forth' from the people that all the old parties and party animosities should be 'deep in the bosom of the ocean buried.'" [3]

An attack on politicians accompanied the denunciation of political parties. Before the congressional elections of 1861, the Fayetteville *Observer* warned voters to "preserve the country from ignoramuses, from demagogues, from professional politicians, and from the merely selfish office hunter." Running for reelection to the Confederate Congress in 1863, Thomas S. Ashe wrote modestly to a friend: "You are a statesman. I am not. I am not even a *politician*, and God forbid I ever should be." [4]

The opposition to politicians and political parties derived from several sources, chiefly the belief that partisan activity would divide the people at a time when unity was imperative. In December, 1861, the Wilmington *Journal* extolled the virtues of the two-party system and insisted that "parties have always existed and always will exist." Nevertheless, the paper contended, partisan organizations should not be tolerated while the South fought for its independence. The *Journal* believed that parties disappeared when "some controlling necessity, or impending danger" compelled the unity of the people. Under such circumstances, partisan competition would only cause discord, "bickerings . . . heartburnings . . . [and] jealousies," and ultimately would diminish the people's ability to mount a vigorous war effort. The Raleigh *Register*'s editor, John Syme, agreed with the *Journal*'s assessment. Discussing the election of delegates to the secession convention of May, 1861, Syme urged that something be done quickly "to allay that fell spirit of discord which will inevitably be awakened if aspiring politicians are allowed to go before the people." [5]

Vanderbilt University Press, 1972); Thomas B. Alexander, "Persistent Whiggery in the Confederate South, 1860–1877," *JSH*, XXVII (1961), 305–29.

    3. Wilmington *Journal*, April 18, 1861; Raleigh *Register*, May 8, 1861.

    4. Fayetteville *Observer*, September 23, 1861; Thomas S. Ashe to Edward J. Hale, August 5, 1863, in Edward Jones Hale Papers, NCDAH.

    5. Wilmington *Journal*, December 5, 1861; Raleigh *Register*, May 8, 1861.

Antiparty sentiment received further support from those who felt that partisan competition would encourage the North. Partisan bickerings, they argued, would make northerners think that southerners were divided in their support of the war effort and therefore could be defeated easily. "If we indulge in dissensions among ourselves," the Fayetteville *Observer* wrote, "we encourage the enemy to continue and renew and redouble his efforts to conquer and subjugate us."[6]

The opposition of North Carolinians to partisan organizations was grounded not only in the pressures of the war, but also in their experiences of the preceding years. Misunderstanding the ways in which partisanship had encouraged North Carolina to stay in the Union, many observers saw antebellum political practices as a major cause for the dissolution of the Union. The Greensboro *Patriot* argued that "political jugglers distracted and divided the people in the old Government, and contributed much to bring us into the condition we now find ourselves." Thomas I. Faison, a candidate for Congress in 1861, believed "conventions were one of the main causes that helped break up the old government." The Raleigh *Standard* contended that "party spirit was largely instrumental in destroying the old government, and in involving the two sections in war." If "blind party spirit" were indulged in, it would "destroy the new, as it has destroyed the old government."[7]

A minority of North Carolinians found more elemental evils emanating from the antebellum political system. Parties, they argued, perverted true democracy by destroying the purpose of the franchise. The Salisbury *Watchman* contended that "the very object of the ballot is, that every man may vote for whom he pleases. But where conventions and meetings set up opinions and arrange parties, the original intention of the ballot is defeated, and the election becomes the result of party management." In the summer of 1862, the Wilmington *Journal* complained that an attempt "is now making to remove the coming [gubernatorial] election from the arena of free choice and untrammelled judgment into that of bitter partisanship."[8]

The evils that resulted from partisan strife led politicians to question whether parties would be necessary after the war. Some, like the editor of the Salisbury *Watchman*, wished that parties would never be revived. He wrote hopefully: "We are all free from *party* now, and so far as elections are concerned it would be a Heaven's blessing if we would remain so." More prevalent was the belief that political parties would inevitably be restored

6. Fayetteville *Observer*, August 3, 1863.

7. Greensboro *Patriot*, June 26, 1862; Fayetteville *Observer*, October 21, 1861; Raleigh *Standard*, September 4, 1861.

8. Salisbury *Carolina Watchman*, May 26, 1862; Wilmington *Journal*, October 10, 1861.

after the South achieved independence. Most politicians agreed with the Fayetteville *Observer* when it contended that it would "know no party, till this war is ended, save the great party opposed to the vile yankee government and people."[9]

Thus, early in the war, most North Carolinians thought that political parties were a nuisance and ought to be discountenanced for the duration of the conflict. These sentiments, derived mostly from the exigencies of the war, along with other problems involved in the secession crisis and in mounting a war effort, altered a party system that had remained viable and stable since the late 1830s. Yet a party system that had survived the stresses of the 1850s could not be destroyed overnight. The popular election in November, 1861, of members to the first permanent Confederate Congress and of electors for the presidency and vice-presidency indicated the difficulty of translating abstract antiparty sentiment into practice.

★

Newspaper editors, reflecting antiparty ideas, adopted new policies regarding the endorsement of congressional candidates. As in the 1850s, newspapers urged voters to cast their ballots for the best man, but unlike in the 1850s, they refrained from telling them who that best man was. The Salisbury *Watchman*, though a partisan Whig paper before the war, declared: "As regards the Congressional election, let each man vote for the gentleman of his choice, whether he is a candidate or not." The Democratic Wilmington *Journal* hoped that "men of good sense and some experience will be sent from all the districts. We do not want mere partizans—we do not want party politics to rule in this matter." Papers like the *Journal* and *Watchman* remained true to their word; rarely did a newspaper endorse the candidacy of any one man.[10]

In response to antiparty rhetoric and sentiment, the candidates also disregarded much of the traditional paraphernalia associated with congressional campaigns. Foregoing the usual district convention, most of the candidates entered the field "on their own hook" or in response to the published solicitation of friends. For instance, William N. H. Smith, a Whig congressman during the secession crisis and a member of the Confederate Provisional Congress, announced his candidacy for a seat in the first permanent Congress in a public letter to voters in the First Congressional District. He noted approvingly that "the instrumentality of conventions . . . seems to have disappeared before the generous and patriotic impulses

9. Salisbury *Carolina Watchman*, November 4, 1861; Fayetteville *Observer*, June 23, 1862.
10. Salisbury *Carolina Watchman*, November 11, 1861; Wilmington *Journal*, October 31, 1861.

which the presence of a common danger has inspired." He therefore took the opportunity to announce his candidacy. Once announced as candidates, the congressmen-to-be often shunned public speaking. This was especially true in the uncontested districts. When Thomas D. McDowell announced his candidacy in the Fourth District, he expressed an unwillingness to canvass the district: "I do not believe that the people desire [a canvass], as divisions might result therefrom." But in some closely contested districts, like the Piedmont Fifth and Sixth, candidates published calendars of their joint speaking engagements and made a thorough canvass of their districts."[11]

The number of candidates in the districts indicated the changes wrought by the war and the organizational confusion that beset the state's political parties. In most districts before the war, two candidates, representing the major parties, normally sought office. In 1861, only two of the state's ten districts had such a "normal" two-man race, and in one of those districts, the Sixth, two Democrats opposed one another. In the other districts, voters faced either the feast of choosing between many candidates or the famine of having to vote for a single man. Four candidates appealed to voters in the Third and Seventh districts and three in the Fifth. In the other five districts, candidates ran without opposition. Only in the congressional elections of 1857, in which the moribund American party opposed Democrats in four of the eight contests, had so many candidates run unopposed.[12]

In late 1861, much of the antebellum political system was in disarray, but the election of a congressman in the Fourth or Cape Fear District suggests that the form of antebellum politics often carried over into the war. In early October, Thomas D. McDowell, the district's delegate to the Provisional Congress, announced his candidacy for a seat in the permanent Congress. Unopposed in the election, he took his seat in February, 1862.[13]

In light of the political practices of the district in the 1850s, McDowell appeared to people in his district as the obvious person to represent them in Congress. A wealthy planter, lawyer, and merchant in rural Bladen County, well connected with the local Democratic party leadership, Thomas McDowell had entered politics in the late 1840s. In 1850 he ran successfully for a seat in the state senate, where he served until 1855. Bored with the day-to-day business of the General Assembly, the ambitious McDowell sought a seat in Congress, but at the Democratic district convention in 1855, Warren Winslow of Fayetteville defeated his bid for the party's nomination. In 1857 and 1859 McDowell made abortive attempts to replace

11. Raleigh *Register*, October 26 and 12, 1861; Wilmington *Journal*, October 10, 1861.
12. Compiled Election Returns, in NCDAH.
13. Wilmington *Journal*, October 10, 1861.

Winslow as the regular party nominee. At the beginning of the war, Democrats in the district recognized him as second only to Winslow in the party. When Winslow became an adviser to the governor, the state convention elected McDowell as a delegate to the Provisional Congress. So when McDowell decided to run for Congress, most Democrats agreed with A. J. Galloway, who wrote to McDowell that the congressional seat "was due to you."[14]

The procedure by which McDowell obtained his seat in Congress, though unlike antebellum practices in other districts, conformed with methods used in his district. The failure to hold a convention was hardly an innovation in the Fourth District, since in the previous decade Democrats had convened only one district convention (1855) to nominate a congressional candidate. Nor was it unusual that McDowell had no opponent in the race, for throughout the 1850s the opposition to the regular Democratic party candidate in the overwhelmingly Democratic Cape Fear District was either nominal or nonexistent.

The methods of antebellum politics also continued in the eastern Third Congressional District and the mountainous Ninth. In the Ninth, Burgess S. Gaither and Leander Q. Sharpe, Whig party leaders of Burke and Iredell counties, after announcing their candidacies, settled their differences by submitting their claims to a convention. The convention nominated Gaither, who was elected without further opposition. In the Third District Democrats held an informal convention in Goldsboro, despite criticism by local newspapers, and nominated for Congress Owen R. Kenan, a former Democratic legislator from Duplin County, who won a plurality of the votes cast.[15]

The results of the election suggested that other facets of antebellum politics had continued as well. The delegation to the first permanent Confederate Congress was composed of six former Democrats and four former Whigs, similar in composition to North Carolina's delegation to the last U.S. Congress. In every district, the elected congressman was affiliated with what had been the majority party in his district before the war. The four Whigs represented districts that had voted Whig in the 1859 congressional elections, and the six Democrats came from districts voting Democratic in 1859.[16]

14. A. J. Galloway to Thomas D. McDowell, September 20, 1861, in Thomas D. McDowell Papers, SHC. McDowell's career may be followed in the McDowell Papers and in the C. B. Heller Collection, NCDAH.

15. Raleigh *Standard*, October 23, 1861; Wilmington *Journal*, October 31, 1861.

16. Wilfred B. Yearns states erroneously that the Fifth and Sixth districts, both of which elected secession Democrats, were Whig districts. See Yearns, "North Carolina in the Confederate Congress," *NCHR*, XXIX (1952), 365–66.

These continuities may be seen also in the Fifth and Sixth districts, where voters had a clear choice between secession Democrats and former Unionists (one a Whig and one a Democrat), and from which election returns are available. It appears that they voted in much the same way as they had when confronted by a choice between a Whig and a Democrat before the war. The strongest Democratic counties in the congressional elections of 1859 were the strongest secession Democratic counties in the congressional contests of 1861. The secessionists won in both districts.[17]

Although the congressional elections revealed substantial continuities in the political system, the election of a congressman in the Piedmont Sixth District and the statewide balloting for presidential electors signified a shift in the state's political nomenclature and, indeed, in much of the orientation of the state's politics. Before the war, politicians and voters distinguished between two major political groups: Democrats on one side and Whigs or Americans on the other. From the secession crisis forward, men increasingly came to identify themselves and their opponents based on their attitudes toward the Union during that crisis. They saw themselves either as "original secessionists" (secessionists before Lincoln's proclamation) or "old Unionists" (Unionists before the proclamation). In one sense, the transition meant little because there was a strong correlation between Whiggery and Unionism, between Democracy and secessionism. Yet the change in names provided an umbrella under which the large number of Union Democrats could stand without feeling that they had betrayed the Democratic party and converted to Whiggery. As the war dragged on, the change assumed greater importance, for the people began to blame their sufferings on the men who had encouraged the dissolution of the Union.

The change in nomenclature was illustrated in the congressional race in the Sixth District, located in the north central part of the state, where two former Democrats, Robert P. Dick and James R. McLean, sought election. It was not unusual for a district whose counties had voted predominantly Democratic during the 1850s to run two Democratic candidates. But the question upon which the two men differentiated themselves was unusual. There was no disagreement over present policy, for both candidates pledged firm adherence to the cause of southern independence. Their difference lay in the opposite positions that each had assumed during the secession crisis. In 1860 Dick had refused to leave the Baltimore convention when most of the state's delegation had departed, and in the

17. A comparison of the Democratic vote in 1859 and the secession Democratic vote in 1861 reveals a coefficient of correlation of .93.

ensuing presidential campaign he became the state's foremost supporter of Stephen A. Douglas. From Lincoln's election to the middle of April, 1861, Dick and William Holden led the Union Democrats. McLean, prominent in district party politics, had been an early supporter of secession.[18]

The importance of the "original secessionist"–"old Unionist" division in the state became more apparent in the presidential election of 1861. Throughout the Confederacy, Jefferson Davis and Alexander Stephens ran unopposed for president and vice–president, but in North Carolina voters had a choice between two electoral tickets, both pledged to support Davis and Stephens. Although some politicians intended the formation of the two tickets as a test of strength between secessionist Democrats and former Unionists, they chose a peculiar way to distinguish the tickets. The tickets had four names in common and contained men representing a broad spectrum of political antecedents, from secession Democrat to Union Whig. The composition of the two tickets differed, however, with the secessionist ticket including eight secession Democrats and four Union Whigs, and the "old Unionist" ticket including four secession Democrats, three Union Democrats, and five Union Whigs. But the main difference between the two was the symbolic distinction imparted to them by the political press. Supporters of the secessionist ticket argued that the election of their ticket would reaffirm North Carolina's commitment to eternal separation from the North. The Wilmington *Journal* pointed out that many northerners believed there would be a resurgence of Union sentiment in the state. In order to disabuse them of this notion, the *Journal* argued: "We really do think that sound policy requires that we should vote for no electoral ticket that does not, by its antecedents and otherwise, carry with it the full expression of an idea—the full endorsement of a policy—the policy of definite, final, irrevocable separation." Advocates of the "old Unionist" or People's ticket could only protest that the old Union men were just as faithful to the Confederacy as the original secessionists. They added to this an appeal to antiparty sentiment. "This is a fair, just, no party ticket," the Raleigh *Standard* proclaimed, one that would "put down the hydrahead of party now raised for selfish purposes in our midst."[19]

Voters, unaroused by the lack of choice and more concerned about the war than politics, turned out in small numbers. The 46,000 voters represented a turnout of about half the number registered in the February secession convention vote. Of those who voted, about 58 percent cast ballots for the secessionist ticket. This constituted an enormous gain for the se-

18. Wilmington *Journal*, November 21, 1861.
19. *Ibid.*, October 31, 1861; Raleigh *Standard*, November 6, 1861.

cession Democrats, who received less than 40 percent of the votes cast in the February election. The euphoria created by the onset of the war had benefited them immensely, and the problems that the war would create were only beginning to be felt in November, 1861. With some validity, the Wilmington *Journal* stated that the vote represented an endorsement of the secession Democrats and their policy. The supporters of the People's ticket interpreted the results differently. Editors like William Holden of the Raleigh *Standard* attributed the ticket's defeat to the low turnout in areas that had been strongly Unionist in February. Holden was apparently correct. In the Fifth and Sixth districts, where comparisons can be made, there was a strong correlation between the decline in turnout from February and secessionist gains since then (.90). But that still indicated an unwillingness on the part of the old Unionists to contest the supremacy of the secession Democrats.[20]

★

The logic of Holden's explanation for the defeat of the People's ticket impelled him to argue that the only way for former Unionists in the state to attain victory was with a strong organization. On December 11, 1861, Holden proclaimed: "Proscribed, crowded out and crowded down, suspected, maligned, and almost crushed, the old Union men are determined *now* to take a stand, and to appeal to the people." They would make that appeal, he said, as the Conservative party.

Editor since 1844 of the Raleigh *Standard*, the Democratic party's central organ, Holden had been instrumental in revitalizing the party in the late 1840s and maintained considerable influence over the party's organization through the 1850s. After unsuccessful attempts to obtain the Democratic nominations for governor or senator in 1858, however, he began to drift away from the mainstream of the party. Holden's refusal to join the state delegation's bolt of the Baltimore convention in 1860 and his subsequent lukewarm support for the Breckinridge-Lane ticket alienated other Democratic leaders. His Unionist position after Lincoln's elections caused the final rupture. Therefore, until Lincoln's proclamation, Holden, as leader of the Union Democrats, cooperated with Union Whigs in an effort to keep North Carolina in the Union. After Lincoln's proclamation turned Holden into a supporter of separation, Wake County voters elected him and two former Union Whigs to the secession convention.[21]

20. A. J. Galloway to Thomas D. McDowell, September 20, 1861, in McDowell Papers; Wilmington *Journal*, November 21, 1861; Raleigh *Standard*, November 13, 1861.
21. Holden's career is treated adequately in Edgar E. Folk, "William Woods Holden, Political Journalist" (Ph.D. dissertation, George Peabody College for Teachers, 1937). On Holden during the secession crisis, see the Raleigh *Standard*.

Only a few weeks after North Carolina seceded, Holden initiated criticism of the state administrations of John W. Ellis and his successor, Henry T. Clark, for their policies regarding coastal defense, taxation, and the recruitment of troops for the state militia. But most of all he attacked the governors' appointment policies, claiming they were partisan and discriminated against men who had been Unionists until Lincoln's proclamation. So when Holden announced his determination to form an opposition party, he surprised few North Carolinians.[22]

Holden's major allies in the proposed Conservative party coalition were to be the Union Whigs, who had contributed the bulk of the Unionist vote in February. From the earliest days of the war, Union Whigs had been committed to the idea of a war in which party would be ignored and committed, as well, to obtaining a share of the offices. As a result, they were appalled by what seemed to them the partisan and proscriptive policies of the state administrations. The day before North Carolina formally seceded from the Union, Jonathan Worth, a staunch Unionist and long-time Whig, wrote: "Democracy is only simulating harmony with Union men. It was never more malignant toward its old opponents." Former Whig congressman Zebulon B. Vance complained to his wife: "I see a pretty determined purpose there to carry on affairs under a strict party regime; none but Locos and Secessionists will be appointed to the Offices: the old Union Men will be made to take back Seats and do most of the hard work and make bricks without straw."[23]

Yet, at the same time, Union Whigs felt themselves unable to maintain their old organization, partly because they believed that partisan organizations should be discountenanced during the war. More important in their calculations was the realization that their opposition to the state administration would elicit Democratic charges that they were destroying the existing political harmony and encouraging the enemy. But the situation began to change in November. The election taught them that the only way to victory was through organization. As the winter progressed, prices began to rise and casualties continued to mount. Federal troops, who had taken Cape Hatteras in July, 1861, launched an attack on North Carolina's coast in February, 1862. By early April, they occupied much of the coast. In April, too, President Davis asked Congress to enact a conscription bill, thus raising the specter of a strong military government. Amid all of this, Whigs charged that the governor continued his proscriptive policies. The

22. Raleigh *Standard*, May–December, 1861.
23. Jonathan Worth to John B. Troy, May 21, 1861, in J. G. deRoulhac Hamilton (ed.), *The Correspondence of Jonathan Worth* (2 vols.; Raleigh: Broughton, 1909), I, 150; Zebulon B. Vance to Harriet Vance, May 18, 1861, in Frontis W. Johnston (ed.), *The Papers of Zebulon Baird Vance* (Raleigh: State Department of Archives and History, 1963), 100.

reestablishment of a well-organized loyal opposition seemed justifiable, indeed necessary, to many of them.[24]

An alliance with Holden appealed to many of these Whigs. While working with him during the secession crisis and in the secession convention, they apparently had come to trust him. They recognized that they needed a central party newspaper in Raleigh in order to establish an effective organization; after discarding the idea of setting up a new paper, they came to rely on Holden's *Standard* to fill that need. The Whigs, a minority through the 1850s, must have also seen that an alliance with Holden, leader of the Union Democrats during the secession crisis, could gain them the support of enough Democrats to form a majority coalition.[25]

The first test of the alliance's viability came during the nomination of candidates for governor. The Democrats, who often referred to themselves as Confederates in an effort to broaden their appeal, had nominated their candidate—William Johnston of Charlotte—in February. Johnston announced his candidacy in response to his nomination by a bipartisan meeting in his home town. A lifelong Whig active in local politics, Johnston had supported secession after Lincoln's election. He ran successfully in the convention elections of February and May, 1861, and served as a member of the secession convention. At the time of his nomination, he was a colonel in the commissary department and president of the Charlotte and South Carolina Railroad.[26]

Two months after Johnston announced his candidacy, and while local Conservative party meetings were being held throughout the state to nominate local candidates and to suggest suitable gubernatorial candidates, about thirty Conservatives from all parts of the state met in Raleigh to nominate their party's candidate for governor. The composition of the caucus suggested the Whiggish nature of the Conservative party. Of eleven participants identified, ten had been leaders in the Whig party; Holden was the exception. When the caucus discussed the available candidates, they further revealed their Whiggish proclivities. The first name suggested was William A. Graham, Whig party leader, former governor, and former U.S. senator. After declining to run for personal reasons, Graham proposed John Pool, Whig candidate for governor in 1860 and therefore closely identified in the public mind with the Whig party. Graham's support for Pool reflected his own belief that little had changed in the political system; Whigs would still oppose Democrats.

24. Edwin G. Reade to William A. Graham, July 2, 1861, Augustus S. Merrimon to Graham, December 20, 1861, both in J. G. deRoulhac Hamilton and Max R. Williams (eds.), *The Papers of William Alexander Graham* (6 vols. to date; Raleigh: State Department of Archives and History, 1957–), V, 281–82, 347–51.

25. Edwin G. Reade to William A. Graham, July 2, 1861, in *ibid.*, V, 282.

26. Charlotte *Western Democrat*, March 11, 1862.

Other members of the caucus recognized the need to nominate a man who would enable Conservatives to appeal to former Democrats as well as former Whigs. James M. Leach and John A. Gilmer, Whig congressmen in the last U.S. Congress, suggested their former colleague in the House, Zebulon B. Vance. A Whig from Buncombe County, nestled in the Blue Ridge Mountains, Vance had served in the House of Commons in 1854 but had been defeated two years later when he had sought election to the state senate. In 1858 he had won a special congressional election and had been reelected for a full term in 1859. A Unionist until mid-April, 1861, Vance had joined the army as a private upon learning of Lincoln's proclamation and thereafter had risen quickly to the rank of colonel. His service in the army probably led his supporters in the caucus to argue that he would have an appeal beyond his identification with the Whig party. After some discussion, the caucus nominated Vance as the Conservative candidate. As in the 1850s, Conservatives then held local meetings to ratify the choice of Vance.[27]

The gubernatorial campaigns run by Vance and Johnston differed markedly from those of the antebellum period. Since 1840, gubernatorial candidates had stumped the state in search of votes, but in 1862 neither candidate made a speech or, after publishing a letter of acceptance, uttered a public word about the campaign. The two men allowed the newspapers to conduct the campaign for them, and many of the papers assumed their task with fervor. Yet 1862 was not like 1854 or 1860. Some prominent editors, partisans in the 1850s, refused to do more than indicate their support for a particular candidate. Others switched sides; Holden's Democratic *Standard* served as the Conservative party's central paper, while the antebellum Whig organ, the Raleigh *Register*, advocated the Democratic cause. More important, the issues of the campaigns had changed. No longer did participants discuss the virtues of railroads and plank roads, or the democratization of suffrage requirements, or the equalization of taxation. Instead, politicians sought to prove that their party and candidate were the more loyal to the Confederacy, would bring the more efficient administration to the state government, and were the more opposed to political parties.

The adherents of both parties denounced the existence of parties and argued that their candidate would rid the state of that evil. The Conserva-

27. On the number of men at the caucus and on Leach's and Gilmer's advocacy of Vance, see James M. Leach to Zebulon B. Vance, March 5 and September 22, 1864, both in Zebulon Baird Vance Papers, NCDAH. For most of the identified participants, see Daniel G. Fowle to William A. Graham, April 9, 1862, in Hamilton and Williams (eds.), *Graham Papers*, V, 381–82. For the identification of another participant, Graham's refusal to run, and Graham's suggestion of Pool, see George Little to Edward J. Hale, April 9, 1862, in Hale Papers; Raleigh *Standard*, June 21, July 5, 12, and 16, 1862.

tives, Holden wrote, "are not party men, but they are opposed to party." With an army officer as their candidate, the Conservatives could contend plausibly that Vance was running as a patriotic southerner rather than as a representative of a political party. In late June, Holden wrote: "He [Vance] is not a party, but the peoples' [sic] candidate." To reinforce this claim, he placed Vance's name on the *Standard*'s masthead as the candidate of the People's party—the same name he had used to describe their electoral slate in 1861.[28]

Vance, too, perceived the gains to be made by portraying himself and the Conservative party as opponents of political partisanship. In early June, he wrote to a friend: "As sure as you live, moderation, nopartyism, harmony and deprecation of strife constitute our true tactics." Thus, in his public letter of June 15, in which he announced his candidacy, he "deprecat[ed] the growing tendency towards party strife amongst our people." Vance's depiction of how he became a candidate reinforced the image of himself as a man who disapproved of political parties. Although he had agreed to run in response to the nomination of the party caucus in Raleigh, in his letter he claimed that he was merely responding to a spontaneous call from the people.[29]

Conservatives carried this strategy further in their attacks on Vance's opponent, William Johnston. The *Standard* claimed that Johnston was "the candidate of the spoils party office holders, and the ultra partizan papers of the State." Moreover, Johnston's voting behavior as a member of the secession convention "showed that he *was a party man*."[30]

The picture of Johnston as a partisan contrasted sharply with the Democratic party's view of him. Their choice of Johnston and their subsequent representation of him suggested that they too sought to appeal to the antiparty sentiments of the electorate. His Whig background allowed them to argue that in nominating him they had transcended petty partisanship. Since few people outside the boundaries of Mecklenburg County thought of Johnston as a politician and since he was a railroad executive, Democrats could describe him as a successful businessman without ties to any party, who would administer the governor's office efficiently. The Charlotte *North Carolina Whig* proclaimed: "Col. Johnston is, par exellence the man for the crisis, and being free, and untrammelled and uncontrolled by party cliques and office seeking demagogues, he can and will be exactly what the Governor of a great Commonwealth ought to be—the unbiased Executive

28. Raleigh *Standard*, June 25, 1862.
29. Zebulon B. Vance to George Little, June 1, 1862, in Little-Mordecai Papers, NCDAH; Raleigh *Standard*, June 25, 1862.
30. Raleigh *Standard*, July 16, 1862.

Officer of a great, enlightened, and free people." The Charlotte *Western Democrat* claimed that the state needed a good businessman like Johnston for its governor, "no politician and no political trickster."[31]

Democrats contrasted Johnston's nonpartisanship and business experience to his opponent's career as a professional politician. The *Western Democrat* complained that Vance was a man of "strong partizan prejudices." Moreover, "he has been a whig candidate for office in his county and District ever since he was 21 years old, and in consequence of his partizan course, is odious to a respectable number of people."[32]

After paying homage at the altar of antiparty, the Democrats revived the tactics that they had utilized successfully the year before. They contended that they and their candidate were the more loyal and the more fully committed to Confederate independence. Their platform suggested the totality of that commitment. It pledged "an unremitting prosecution of the war to the last extremity; complete independence; eternal separation from the North; no abridgement of Southern boundaries; no compromise with enemies, traitors, and tories." Their commitment would include support for measures like conscription that aroused popular dissatisfaction. Papers supporting the Democrats, like the Raleigh *Register*, after expressing some reservations about the conscription law, came to regard it as "the only measure which will give us enough men" to defeat the North. The election of Johnston would therefore affirm North Carolina's complete support for an independent South and for the Davis administration. It would prove to the North that Unionism no longer existed in North Carolina.[33]

Democrats contrasted their attitudes with what they believed to be the Conservatives' lukewarm adherence to the southern cause. The Democratic press complained that the Conservatives always criticized the state and national administrations, never praised either, and never justified the righteousness of the cause for which all were fighting. Conservative attacks on "secessionists," Democrats charged, encouraged the North. The Yankees, Democrats claimed, perceived such Conservative attacks as assertions "that secession is an *evil* which ought to be cured by the reconstruction of the Union, and the election of Mr. Vance would be regarded by the North as a declaration by the people of North Carolina in favor of the reconstruction of the Union."[34]

Conservatives replied by arguing that the Democrats were the ones

31. Charlotte *Western Democrat*, June 10, July 29, 1862; Charlotte *North Carolina Whig*, August 5, 1862.
32. Charlotte *Western Democrat*, July 29, 1862.
33. Raleigh *Register*, June 21, July 30, 1862; Charlotte *Western Democrat*, April 15, 1862.
34. Raleigh *Register*, July 19, 1862.

who were really encouraging the enemy. In the heat of the campaign, the Democrats sought "to create the impression that a large portion of our people are untrue to their State, their country, and themselves." This led northerners "to believe that instead of waging a war to subjugate us, they are actually engaged in a war for our liberation from a despotism." [35]

The Conservatives had another ready-made answer in the person of their gubernatorial nominee, who was a colonel in the army. Vance himself pointed out that "if I have any strength more than other men it consists in my record on the war question, and the absence of any room for the favorite slanders of disloyalty, aid & comfort to the enemy &c." George E. Badger, formerly prominent in the Whig party and a Conservative leader in the secession convention, allayed most remaining fears of Conservative disloyalty. In July, 1862, he wrote a public letter to a friend in New York City in which he asserted that all North Carolinians favored the continued independence of the South. [36]

Although demanding the "prosecution of the war at all hazards," the Conservatives insisted that independence be obtained while upholding state and Confederate constitutions, thus leaving civil liberties unimpaired and military power subordinate to civilian power. They expressed the popular fear that during time of war the military power might supersede the civil and portrayed themselves as the best defenders of the supremacy of civil power. Local party meetings throughout the state proclaimed in their resolutions that "the military power should always be subordinate to the civil power." These resolutions were apparently passed in response to the recently enacted conscription law, which, as we shall see, aroused fears that the Confederate government was taking the initial step toward a strong military government. On the stump, local candidates made more direct attacks on the law. The Wilmington *Journal* complained that "the local candidates running as 'conservatives,' very generally had a fling at the 'Conscription law.'" [37]

Conservatives pictured their opponents as "destructives"—men who had destroyed the good old government but lacked the foresight, wisdom, or ability to build a new society in the South—and they argued that the Democrats had been unprepared to meet the exigencies created by the war. The state administration, they charged, established a weak and porous coastal defense, armed the state's troops inadequately, and squan-

35. Fayetteville *Observer*, July 28, 1862.

36. Zebulon B. Vance to George Little, June 1, 1862, in Little-Mordecai Papers; Raleigh *Standard*, July 23, 1862.

37. Raleigh *Standard*, June 4, 1862; Wilmington *Journal*, August 21, 1862. See chapter 10 below.

dered public funds. Unable to stabilize the state's finances at the beginning of the war, Democrats had to raise taxes when treasury funds ran low.

In sum, Conservatives created an image of the Democrats as inept men, unable to administer the affairs of state, and blamed them for the evils that had befallen the state since the war began. The Democrats had brought these problems upon the people but were unable to solve them. Such men had to be replaced by Conservatives, who were better equipped to cope with these difficulties. Conservatives portrayed themselves as moderate and thoughtful men, the type of men who build societies rather than destroy them. They were men who never would have left North Carolina's coast defenseless, her troops without arms, her treasury without gold. They were prudent, careful men, who would adhere rigidly to the constitution and would maintain the supremacy of civil power. Indeed, they were the only men people could trust during such tumultuous times.[38]

The Whiggish Conservatives directed their appeals to voters who had been Unionists in February, 1861. Even the staunchest Whig partisans must have realized that the Conservatives could not attain victory with only Whig votes, since that party had been in a minority through the 1850s. In the campaign, the Conservatives tried to establish continuities between the secession crisis and wartime politics. Men who had supported the Union up to Lincoln's proclamation, they argued, ought to vote Conservative. Much of this argument was based on the supposedly discriminatory appointment policy of the Confederate and state administrations, and Conservatives complained repeatedly that those governments refused to appoint old Union men to offices. Although this theme conveyed to Democrats the impression that Conservatives were merely grumbling about their own inability to obtain offices, in fact Conservatives were seeking to appeal to an audience larger than a few disgruntled office seekers. They contended that, by discriminating against old Union men when making appointments, the governments discriminated against all old Union men. The only way for former Unionists to rectify the situation was to elect Conservative candidates.[39]

On July 28, North Carolina's soldiers cast their ballots. Of the 11,683 soldiers who voted, 65.8 percent cast their votes for Vance. The soldier vote foreshadowed the results of the entire election. Vance received 74 percent of the votes cast in the civilian election held on August 4. Winning

38. See the June and July, 1862, issues of Fayetteville *Observer*, Raleigh *Standard*, Salem *People's Press*, and Salisbury *Carolina Watchman*. For a summary of Conservative perceptions of the opposition, see Augustus S. Merrimon to William A. Graham, December 20, 1861, in Hamilton and Williams (eds.), *Graham Papers*, V, 347.

39. Greensboro *Patriot*, August 7, 1862.

majorities in all but twelve counties, he won 72.7 percent of the combined vote. By far the largest margin of victory in any gubernatorial election to that date, it represented a dramatic popular repudiation of the Democratic leadership that had controlled the state for more than a decade.

However, voter participation had declined by one-third from the 1860 gubernatorial election. The low turnout was probably caused by several factors. The Federal army's occupation of a portion of the coast eliminated occupied counties from participation and drastically reduced the turnout in neighboring counties. In addition, the war had absorbed the entire interest of many people, to the exclusion of politics. Finally, Democrats may have stayed away from the polls because they were dissatisfied with the administration of Governor Henry T. Clark (who had become governor after John Ellis' death in July, 1861) but were unwilling to vote for Vance, or because they were unwilling to vote for a man of Whig antecedents like Johnston.

Although the large margin of victory and the small voter turnout were unusual by antebellum standards, the patterns of voting bore a remarkable similarity to those of the antebellum period. The fairly high correlation of the 1862 vote with the gubernatorial elections in the 1840s and 1850s suggests that voting patterns established in the late 1830s and early 1840s remained firm in North Carolina through 1862 (see table 27). Areas of Whig voting strength before the war were the Conservative strongholds in 1862. Of thirty-one counties giving a majority to the Whig gubernatorial candidate in 1860, twenty-seven gave Vance at least 75 percent of their vote. Since Johnston won only 27.3 percent of the vote, counties that gave him at least 30 percent of their vote may be considered his areas of greatest strength. Johnston received such a vote in thirty-one counties; twenty-eight of them had voted for Democrat John Ellis in 1860.[40]

Yet the first year and a half of the war had altered antebellum voting patterns. Correlations between the county-level Democratic vote in 1862 and the Democratic vote in antebellum elections were not as high as the correlations among the antebellum elections themselves. The coefficient of correlation between the 1862 and 1850 Democratic vote was a high .70, but between the 1860 and 1850 vote it was a higher .92 (see tables 27 and 24, pp. 239 and 183).

More closely related to the voting patterns in the 1862 gubernatorial election than the antebellum elections was the secession convention election of February, 1861. Although there had been a strong relationship between Whig voting and Unionism, the convention election nevertheless

40. This analysis is based on counties for which both 1860 and 1862 data are available. Counties occupied by Union forces were, of course, excluded.

TABLE 27
Coefficients of Correlation Between Democratic Vote in the 1862
Gubernatorial Election, and the Democratic Vote in Antebellum
Gubernatorial Elections and the Prosecession Vote
in the Secession Convention Election of February, 1861

Election Year	1862
1844	.72
1848	.70
1850	.70
1852	.70
1854	.72
1856	.69
1858	.68
1860	.69
1861	.82

had represented some weakening of traditional voting patterns. These changes clearly carried over to the gubernatorial election. The coefficient of correlation between Unionism and the Vance vote at the county level was .82, higher than the latter's correlation with the antebellum Whig vote and comparable to the high correlations of voting patterns in the antebellum elections. The strongest Union counties in 1861 tended to be the strongest Vance counties in 1862. This suggests that the coalitions formed during the secession crisis altered somewhat the persistent voting patterns of the antebellum period.

The close relationship between the voting patterns in 1862 and 1861 and between those in 1862 and the antebellum period should not obscure substantial changes in voting behavior that had taken place. Although the strongest Democratic counties in 1860 had tended to be the strongest Johnston counties in 1862, the overwhelming Vance victory indicated that in most counties support for Johnston was much lower than it had been for Democratic and secession candidates. Catawba County, at the foot of the Blue Ridge, as one example, had voted over 70 percent Democratic before the war and cast more than 85 percent of its votes in favor of secession in February, 1861. Although it was one of the leading Johnston counties in 1862, it gave him less than 48 percent of its vote.

The election was more than a triumph for Vance, because Conservatives also captured a large majority of the seats in the state legislature. Acting much like the political partisans that they were, Conservatives replaced Democratic officeholders with members of their own party. They elected William Graham as Confederate senator, William Holden as state printer, and Jonathan Worth as state treasurer, and they appointed a Conservative state auditor and Conservative solicitors and judges. The extent of the Conservatives' political housecleaning was suggested by the pressures placed upon Worth while he was making clerical appointments in the treasury. "Many of our friends here, if not all," Worth wrote to William Graham, "demand the decapitation of *all* the destructives. I think I shall not yield to the demand. . . . I think I ought to retain one or two of our political opponents." One Democratic legislator complained that Conservatives sought "to proscribe every original secessionist for all time to come, . . . I have never witnessed so much thirst for office."[41]

Amid the intense antiparty sentiment that pervaded the thinking of politically minded North Carolinians, two vigorous political parties existed in the state during 1862. The Conservatives, especially, had all the attributes of a political party. Led mostly by former Whigs, the Conservatives were more than a bastardization of the Whig party but less than a brand new political organization. The party's method of nominating a gubernatorial candidate by caucus was unlike antebellum state-party conventions but was clearly the action of a political party. More like the practice before the war, the Conservatives held local party meetings to suggest gubernatorial candidates and, once Vance was in the field, held meetings to endorse the choice. The two candidates did not participate in the campaign that followed, but the newspapers of both parties, though discussing issues different from those of earlier years, conducted a typically vigorous campaign. When the votes were counted, they revealed that both Democrats and Conservatives distributed patronage as any political party would—indeed, in just the way that the Conservatives had attacked the Democrats for doing in their campaign. Thus, while the antebellum party system had been revolutionized in the northern states during the early 1850s and had collapsed in the lower South at about the same time, it persisted, though, with substantial changes, in North Carolina through 1862.

41. Francis E. Shober to Mary Wheat Shober, November 28, 1862, in Wheat-Shober Papers, SHC; Jonathan Worth to William A. Graham, December 31, 1862, in Hamilton and Williams (eds.), *Graham Papers*, V, 438; J. W. Russ to Thomas D. McDowell, November 21, 1862, in McDowell Papers.

Ten *"The Last Vestige of Freedom Is Departing From Us" The Politics of Liberty 1863–1865*

The massive triumph of the Conservatives in 1862 represented a dramatic repudiation of the party that had led North Carolina out of the Union and into war and reflected a growing popular discontent with the Confederate government that soon erupted into fear and hatred. In 1863, citizens held public meetings throughout the state to denounce Confederate policies and to call for peace negotiations, and they elected Conservatives to nine of the state's ten congressional seats. By 1864, popular rejection had so devastated the old secessionist Democratic leadership that both gubernatorial candidates came from the Conservative ranks. In light of the virtual unanimity with which North Carolinians had endorsed secession, their hostility to the Confederate government was remarkable. But just as North Carolinians had seceded to protect their liberty from the tyrannical Lincoln administration, so too did they fear the tyrannical intentions of the Davis administration. And just as the existence of a competitive two-party system during the antebellum years and the secession crisis had influenced the political attitudes of North Carolinians, now its absence had equally profound effects.

Historians have long been aware of widespread discontent in the Confederacy but have disagreed about its causes. In 1925, Frank L. Owsley attributed it to bickering between the Confederate and state governments over states' rights. Other scholars have offered an array of different explanations: persistent unionism, the conscription law, impressment, the tax-in-kind, alleged class legislation like the exemption from the draft of a man to oversee twenty or more slaves, and the economic hardships of yeoman farmers.[1]

But students of the Civil War have generally ignored one cause for opposition to the Confederate government that contemporaries often gave as an explanation for their own dissatisfaction. Antagonists of the Confederate government feared that the central government intended to rob the people of their liberties and that the Confederacy was becoming a "central military despotism." Several historians have noted the expression of those fears but have generally dismissed them as exaggerated political propaganda or as the result of the workings of insane minds. But those fears were expressed too frequently in private correspondence to be disregarded as propaganda and were enunciated by too many men who were without political ambition to conclude that they were prompted by political motives. And too many men of undoubted sanity feared for their liberty to dismiss the fears as the ravings of the deranged. It is therefore necessary to explain the nature of those fears, how and why they grew, and how they were expressed and ultimately resolved.[2]

From the time of Lincoln's call for troops until the end of the war, southern politicians and private citizens contrasted the loss of liberty in the North with the preservation of it in the South. They sneered at northerners who supinely gave up their liberties—such men, they said, were fit subjects for slavery. Lincoln revealed his tyrannical designs when he decided unilaterally to levy war on the South and when, in April, 1861, he suspended the writ of habeas corpus. Liberty, southerners maintained, no longer existed in the North. North Carolinians agreed with the editor of the Raleigh *Standard* when he contended: "All that is left on this continent of Constitutional liberty must be looked for in the Confederate States."[3]

1. Frank L. Owsley, *State Rights in the Confederacy* (Chicago: University of Chicago Press, 1925); Albert Burton Moore, *Conscription and Conflict in the Confederacy* (New York: Macmillan Company, 1924); Georgia Lee Tatum, *Disloyalty in the Confederacy* (Chapel Hill: University of North Carolina Press, 1934), 3–23; Bell I. Wiley, *The Plain People of the Confederacy* (Baton Rouge: Louisiana State University Press, 1943), 36–39; Paul D. Escott, *After Secession: Jefferson Davis and the Failure of Confederate Nationalism* (Baton Rouge: Louisiana State University Press, 1978), 54–134.

2. For typical examples, see E. Merton Coulter, *The Confederate States of America, 1861–1865* (Baton Rouge: Louisiana State University Press, 1950), 386, 389–90, 393. Three historians have taken these fears seriously: John B. Robbins, "The Confederacy and the Writ of *Habeas Corpus*," *Georgia Historical Quarterly*, LV (1971), 83–101; David Donald, "Died of Democracy," in David Donald (ed.), *Why the North Won the Civil War* (Baton Rouge: Louisiana State University Press, 1960), 79–90; John C. Schwab, *The Confederate States of America, 1861–1865* (New York: Charles Scribner's Sons, 1901), 186–228.

3. Fayetteville *Observer*, June 3, September 2, 1861; Raleigh *Standard*, September 4, 1861.

The simple juxtaposition of despotism in the North with liberty in the South was short-lived. After it became apparent that the war would last more than a few months, some southerners came to appreciate the need for a centralization of the war effort and for a government that would be strong enough to curb disloyalty. But the central government in Washington had always had little impact on the lives of North Carolinians. Would they now accept a stronger, more centralized Confederate government, one that would almost inevitably infringe on popular liberties? Ought they to surrender some of their cherished liberties, they asked themselves, in order to obtain independence from the northern despots? And if they gave up some of their liberties for the duration of the war, would they be able to regain them after the war? The victorious Conservatives answered these questions to the satisfaction of most North Carolinians.[4]

★

Conservatives, adhering closely to the ideas of their revolutionary ancestors and of antebellum politics, defined liberty as freedom from an arbitrary government. Governments had to act within the limits set by freedom's "chosen instruments—the constitution and the laws." A free man would be protected from arbitrary arrest and imprisonment and from unduly heavy taxation, and, within the bounds of law, he would be able to express himself freely and to own property unmolested.[5]

A man who was not free was a slave. Slavery meant more to white North Carolinians than a system of forced labor for blacks: it was a social and political concept indicating a person's submission to the arbitrary will of another. They believed that the white man who was deprived of his liberties was just as much a slave as the black bondsman. Black slavery was only the most extreme example of the condition of slavery, but the presence of black slaves was important because it constantly reminded white North Carolinians of just what it meant to be enslaved. Black slavery also reinforced for white men a belief in the fragility of their own liberty, a belief that white North Carolinians inherited from their revolutionary ancestors. Unless liberty was protected constantly and carefully, it would be destroyed. "We must retain our self-possession, and our liberties, too, in the progress of this war," wrote one Conservative, "or we will look in vain for them at its close."[6]

4. Fayetteville *Observer*, February 18, 1861.

5. Governor's Message, November 17, 1862, in *The War of the Rebellion: A Compilation of the Official Records of the Union and Confederate Armies* (130 vols.; Washington, D.C.: Government Printing Office, 1880–1901), Ser. IV, Vol. II, 188, hereinafter cited as *Official Records*.

6. See chapter 5 above; James C. Johnston to Zebulon B. Vance, March 10, 1863, in Governors' Papers, NCDAH; William A. Graham's speech before the secession convention opposing

Conservative sensitivity to threats against popular liberty reflected not only a response to actions of the Confederate government, but also a persistence of antebellum beliefs. As we have seen, antebellum political dialogue revolved around the promotion and protection of the freedom and equality of North Carolina white men. The major political issue in the state from 1848 until the mid-1850s was the Democratic party's advocacy of the elimination of the fifty-acre requirement for senatorial electors—a measure that the party called "equal suffrage." In response to the Democratic proposal, Whigs from the underrepresented western part of the state argued that only increased western representation in the state legislature, through the adoption of the "white basis," would make white North Carolinians truly free and equal. Later, the entire Whig party claimed that the same benefits could be derived from taxing slaves on an *ad valorem* basis. The promotion of white equality and freedom was also the goal of politicians in both parties when they defended the right of southerners to settle with their slaves in federal territories. And politicians based their defense of slavery on the grounds that the debasement of black people promoted equality and freedom among whites. On such issues, politicians spoke to the white North Carolinian's fear of having his equality and freedom abridged.

The threat to liberty, equality, and the republican government that protected them came from the aggressive, expansive power of government officials. "All encroachments [on liberty]," warned one Conservative editor, "are sure to begin with and eminate [*sic*] from our rulers." If checks were not placed on the power of rulers, they would concentrate power in their hands and use it to destroy the liberties of the people. Therefore, the people needed specific safeguards for their liberties. First they demanded that civil power always be supreme over military power. This axiom of English and political thought had particular relevance to southerners at war. Because the strength of the military necessarily increased during wartime, it seemed possible that the military power would become supreme, and therefore Conservatives argued that it was "necessary to hold in check that propensity which war is always likely to bring fourth [*sic*]—a military rule to override the civil power." For this reason, Conservatives were especially sensitive to any encroachments of the military on the civil power.[7]

---

the enactment of a test oath, in J. G. deRoulhac Hamilton and Max R. Williams (eds.), *The Papers of William Alexander Graham* (6 vols. to date; Raleigh: State Department of Archives and History, 1957–), V, 311–40; Fayetteville *Observer*, April 7, 1862; Bernard Bailyn, *The Ideological Origins of the American Revolution* (Cambridge, Mass.: Harvard University Press, 1967); J. Mills Thornton III, *Policies and Power in a Slave Society: Alabama, 1800–1860* (Baton Rouge: Louisiana State University Press, 1978).

7. James J. Philips to Zebulon B. Vance, October 29, 1863, in Governors' Papers. For a few

A strong state government was the second safeguard of the people's liberties, since it could serve as a buffer between the people and the arbitrary will of the central government. Because they considered the state as the major defender of their freedom, North Carolinians were acutely aware of all the central government's infringements on the power and rights of the states.[8]

Jefferson Davis first raised the specter of a strong military government in March, 1862, when he asked Congress to enact a law permitting the conscription of white men between the ages of eighteen and thirty-five. Since most soldiers in the Confederate army had volunteered for one year, their time would be up that April, and Davis argued that conscription was needed to prevent the army's collapse and to maintain some continuity in its membership. Although the bill passed easily in the Confederate Congress, men of all political persuasions in North Carolina reluctantly accepted the need for conscription. Their state had provided more than its quota of soldiers, so why, North Carolinians asked, should they have to contribute more men when other states were not meeting their requirements? If many more men were drafted, the few remaining men in nonslaveholding areas of the state would be unable to cultivate sufficient crops to feed the people.[9]

More important than those complaints was the fear that conscription represented the first step toward military despotism. If the central government and the military alone decided when and how many troops were needed and then took sole responsibility for recruiting them, it would be but a small step for the military to attain complete ascendancy in the South. Upon hearing of Davis' request for a conscription law, Congressman Thomas S. Ashe wrote to a friend: "It is said by [its] friends . . . to be the only means of saving the country, but I must confess I fear [it] will be the inauguration of a strong military government."[10]

By assuming complete control over recruitment, the Confederate government infringed on the powers of the states. Richard Puryear, who had been a member of the Confederate Provisional Congress, worried that states' rights are "repudiated and trodden under foot and germs of consolidation is already springing up on its ruins. Consolidation leads to despo-

---

examples of the repeated demands that the civil power remain supreme over the military power, see Raleigh *Standard*, September 17, 1862, April 22, August 26, October 21, 1863; S. S. Bingham to James G. Ramsay, September 8, 1863, in James Graham Ramsay Papers, SHC; Nathaniel Boyden to Zebulon B. Vance, March, 1863, James M. Leach to Vance, March 5, 1864, both in Zebulon Baird Vance Papers, NCDAH.

8. Richard C. Puryear to Henry T. Clark, April 23, 1862, in Henry Toole Clark Papers, Duke.
9. Moore, *Conscription and Conflict*, 13–14; Fayetteville *Observer*, May 19, 1862.
10. Thomas S. Ashe to Kemp P. Battle, April 1, 1862, in Battle Family Papers, SHC.

tism—and further than this I would not lift the veil." Because conscription strengthened the military and weakened the state government, Puryear continued, it threatened the people's liberty. "The people are jealous of their rights and many begin to fear that their rulers have designs upon their liberty. Amidst the difficulties which surround us and the dangers which threaten us nothing should be done to increase their fears and apprehensions. And what is better calculated to do this than this conscription?"[11]

Despite the Conservatives' apprehension over the loss of civil liberty, as the need for the conscription law became evident they grudgingly acquiesced in it. But they warned that "we are in the very midst of perils, no not only from the common enemy, but also from those whom we have delegated to transact our public business."[12]

Similar fears were aroused by the suspension of the writ of habeas corpus. The Confederate Congress first authorized the president to suspend the writ in threatened areas from February 27 to October 13, 1862, and then extended authorization to February 13, 1863. Davis used that authority in Salisbury, North Carolina, site of a Confederate prison. Those actions excited fears of arbitrary arrests by military authorities. Conservative Governor Vance, in his message to the General Assembly in November, 1862, feared that once the writ was suspended "no man is safe from the power of one individual. He could at pleasure seize any citizen of the State, with or without excuse, throw him into prison, and permit him to languish there without relief—a power that I am unwilling to see intrusted to any living man." The possibility of arbitrary arrests became a reality in the fall of 1862, when Confederate authorities arrested the Reverend R. J. Graves on grounds of disloyalty and removed him to Richmond's Confederate prison, Castle Thunder. Upon learning of his case, the General Assembly passed a resolution instructing the governor to demand Graves's release. Although Vance complied with the legislature's resolution and obtained the prisoner's freedom, Graves's arrest had frightened persons like the editor of the Raleigh *Standard*, who worried that it "is a gross violation of the Constitution and Bill of Rights of this State, and of the first principles of liberty." The military arrests of men like Graves impelled Tod R. Caldwell, attorney and Conservative party leader, to write that "no man, even tho he is clothed with a little brief military authority should be allowed to trample the laws under his feet and set himself up as superior to law & the law making power." He warned that "if something is not done to crush out this tyranny, we had as well confess ourselves slaves, for we are truly no better than slaves."[13]

11. Richard C. Puryear to Henry T. Clark, April 23, 1862, in Clark Papers.
12. Salisbury *Carolina Watchman*, April 28, 1862.
13. Thomas B. Alexander and Richard E. Beringer, *The Anatomy of the Confederate Congress:*

The suspension of the writ of habeas corpus and the subsequent arrests of North Carolina citizens also aroused apprehension about the independence of the state's judiciary. Conservatives regarded an independent judiciary as critical to the protection of liberty, since only judges neither bound to the authorities nor indebted to them for favors could check governmental encroachments on liberty. The independence of the state's judiciary seemed threatened in mid-1863 when Secretary of War James A. Seddon attempted to obstruct the judicial process. Seddon blamed the desertion of North Carolina troops on the general belief that the state courts had declared the conscription law unconstitutional, and he asked the governor to use his influence to restrain the judges. Vance, who considered an independent judiciary "the only hope of freedom in times of passion & of violence," indignantly refused. "An upright judge," he wrote, "must deliver the law as he conceives it to be, whether it should happen to comport with the received notions of the military authorities or not. I must therefore most respectfully decline to use my influence in restraining or controlling that coordinate branch of the government which [is] . . . in great danger of being overlapped and destroyed by the tendency of the times."[14]

The controversies surrounding several cases before the state supreme court in the spring and summer of 1863 confirmed fears of central government subversion of the judiciary's independence. In October, 1862, Congress had passed a second conscription act, which extended the eligibility of white males to age forty-five. Under the first act, John W. Irwin had hired as a substitute a man between the ages of thirty-five and forty-five. The War Department determined that Irwin's substitute could now be conscripted, leaving Irwin without a representative in the army and therefore liable to conscription himself. Military authorities arrested Irwin for draft evasion. Upon Irwin's request, state supreme court Chief Justice Richmond Pearson, who maintained that the second law did not pertain to substitutes, granted a writ of habeas corpus and ordered Irwin freed.

Believing Pearson's decision erroneous, Secretary Seddon refused to release the prisoner. This action led to a heated exchange of letters between the secretary and the governor and eventually to Vance's order that the state militia prevent Confederate authorities from rearresting men released on writs of habeas corpus. In the interest of military efficiency,

A Study of the Influences of Member Characteristics on Legislative Behavior, 1861–1865 (Nashville: Vanderbilt University Press, 1972), 169–71; Governor's Message, November 17, 1862, in *Official Records*, Ser. IV, Vol. II, 188; Raleigh *Standard*, December 17, 1862; Tod R. Caldwell to James G. Ramsay, November 30, 1863, in Ramsay Papers.

14. Zebulon B. Vance to John H. Haughton, August 17, 1863 (draft), in Vance Papers; James A. Seddon to Zebulon B. Vance, May 23, 1863, Vance to Seddon, May 25, 1863, both in *Official Records*, Ser. I, Vol. 51, Pt. 2, pp. 714–15.

Vance and Seddon eventually reached a compromise regarding such men, but the conflict itself indicated to North Carolinians that the Confederate authorities were undermining judicial independence. In August, 1863, the chief justice cautioned Vance "that the independence of the judiciary cannot be maintained, unless all encroachments are met with firmness."[15]

By mid-1863, the threats to the state's judiciary, the arbitrary arrests, the suspension of the writ of habeas corpus, and the conscription laws had convinced many North Carolinians that the Confederate government was becoming what Congressman Burgess S. Gaither called "a consolidated military despotism." Their fears were increased by the apparently arbitrary impressment of goods by the army and by the implementation of a 10-percent tax-in-kind for farmers, many of whom were just barely subsisting on their harvests. The appointment of a nonresident to administer the tax-in-kind seemed further evidence of the central government's intentions. North Carolinians also registered other complaints that have seemed silly to some historians. For example, Vance and others repeatedly accused President Davis and his administration of purposely ignoring North Carolinians when appointing generals. Such accusations could be dismissed as the complaints of hypersensitive men, but they actually were yet another political defense of the equality and freedom of North Carolinians. Vance was demanding that North Carolina's soldiers be treated as the equals of soldiers from other states, just as North Carolinians had asserted their equality with northerners before the war.[16]

North Carolinians expressed their discontent at almost one hundred meetings held in all parts of the state in July and August of 1863. At these meetings, they urged their fellow citizens to unite to "declare whether they shall be freemen or slaves," and they complained of the central government's unfair treatment of North Carolina. They also praised the independence of the state judiciary and Vance's defense of it. Judicial decisions, said the participants at one meeting, "will be disrespected by none but oligarchs, tyrants, despots, and haters of republican liberty." The meetings also lauded the state's soldiers for their sacrifices and bravery. "But," participants added, "if the civil law is not maintained, and if civil liberty is not to be the great result of this contest, then will these services have been offered in vain." They also called for the initiation of peace negotia-

15. The Irwin case is discussed in J. G. deRoulhac Hamilton, "The North Carolina Courts and the Confederacy," *NCHR*, IV (1927), 369–72, and in Richard E. Yates, *The Confederacy and Zeb Vance* (Tuscaloosa, Ala.: Confederate Publishing Company, 1958), 53–56; Richmond M. Pearson to Zebulon B. Vance, August 11, 1863, in Governors' Papers.

16. Burgess S. Gaither to Zebulon B. Vance, April 24, 1863, in Vance Papers; Horace W. Raper, "William W. Holden and the Peace Movement in North Carolina," *NCHR*, XXXI (1954), 499. *Cf.* Owsley, *State Rights*, 94–95.

tions with the North. With the congressional elections only a few months off, the participants at most meetings either nominated candidates or proclaimed their refusal to support anyone not committed to the commencement of peace negotiations. After an appeal from Governor Vance on September 7, no additional protest meetings were held, but the discontent persisted and deepened.[17]

★

The peace meetings precipitated a split in the Conservative party between editor William Holden and Governor Vance that eventually culminated in their opposing campaigns for the governorship in 1864. Historians have generally concluded that their dispute resulted from Holden's desire for reunion and Vance's opposition to it, and that as a result the election campaign became a contest for the loyalties of North Carolinians. This analysis accepts Vance's interpretation of the campaign and ignores the similarity of Vance's and Holden's views on most questions. It also ignores the collapse of the party system in 1863 and 1864 and the effect of that collapse on the state's politics.[18]

In the gubernatorial election of 1862, North Carolina voters repudiated the party that had dominated the state's politics for more than a decade. The defeat suffered by the Democrats was worse than any party had suffered over the previous two decades. It was a devastating defeat, one from which they never recovered. Although composing a small minority in the legislature of 1862–1863, Democrats made plans to revitalize party organization. They established a central committee and a committee of correspondence—organizational devices reminiscent of antebellum political practices. Legislator Eli Hall of New Hanover County hoped that, because of such organizational efforts, Democrats would "never have such a snap judgment taken upon us—as we submitted to last summer." Hall's hopes never materialized. The establishment of those committees, rather than reviving party fortunes, signaled the last gasp of a dying party. After a brief flurry of activity among leaders and the press, nothing more was said about the committees or the party's organization.[19]

It is in the context of the demise of the Democratic party that the growing divisions in the Conservative party must be viewed. Until the summer

17. Raleigh *Standard*, August 5 and 12, July 29, August 19, 1863; Frank Moore (ed.), *The Rebellion Record: A Diary of American Events, with Documents, Narratives, Illustrative Events, Poetry, Etc.* (11 vols. and supplement; New York: G. Putnam, 1861–68), VII, 497–98.

18. Richard E. Yates, "Governor Vance and the Peace Movement," *NCHR*, XVII (1940), 1–25, 89–113; Raper, "William W. Holden," 493–516.

19. Eli W. Hall to Thomas D. McDowell, February 13, 1863, in Thomas D. McDowell Papers, SHC; Fayetteville *Observer*, February 19, March 9, 1863.

of 1863, Conservatives generally agreed with Holden's declaration that the party's "great object is to preserve liberty among ourselves while we are struggling for it against the common enemy. Conservatives are not willing to exchange one despotism for another, or one tattered Constitution for another." Holden also expressed the party's view of how peace could be obtained: "We shall obtain this great blessing only when we shall have thoroughly defeated the enemy at all points, and endured the privations, the losses, and the sufferings of war until that enemy shall have despaired of success."[20]

But as discontent with the war grew, Holden reflected and encouraged it with a shift in his position toward the attainment of peace. "We verily believe," he wrote in June, "that a large majority of the *people* in the two sections prefer peace to war, but they are so committed and hampered that even negotiations looking to peace seem to be impossible." Later in June he proposed a specific plan: "A Convention of all the States might lead to peace. The North would enter such a body in favor of restoration, and the South would enter it in favor of separation, but both would be for peace. If they could not agree, they could disagree and separate forever." Of course, if the negotiations deadlocked and the parties agreed to disagree and separate, then the South would attain exactly what it desired—independence with peace. Southerners would have no incentive to compromise, and there was little evidence that suggested that northerners would be any more willing to accept southern independence after negotiations had failed than they had been in 1861. But the weakness of Holden's plan did not deter him from advocating it, nor others from supporting it.[21]

Holden's support for a peace plan caused his contemporaries—and has caused historians since—to speculate about his motives. Democrats and many Conservatives concluded—and most historians have agreed—that Holden intended the peace movement to end in the reconstruction of the United States. Holden's own editorials give credence to this view. In his editorial on June 24, he alluded to the differences between the two sections, not the two countries. In early August, he wrote that the *Standard* supported "no peace which will not preserve the rights of the sovereign States and the institutions of the South," but he omitted any mention that peace must be accompanied by the Confederate independence.[22]

At the same time, Holden denied that he supported reconstruction. In early October, 1862, he declared that for months he had advocated, "as I advocate now, resistance to Mr. Lincoln." He asserted that peace might be

20. Raleigh *Standard*, December 3, 1862, March 4, 1863.
21. *Ibid.*, June 10 and 24, 1863.
22. Yates, "Governor Vance"; Raper, "William W. Holden"; Raleigh *Standard*, August 5, 1863.

gained if the South gave up its claims to Maryland, Kentucky, and West Virginia. If those terms

> or some terms should be offered to the North and rejected, and the answer should be, lay down your arms ye rebels—submit to a territorial condition, or return to the old government deprived of your slave property, with your slaves set loose in your midst, with the loss of all your currency and your bonds, to be saddled with the payment of the federal war debt, and yourselves the inferiors of the Northern States in the federal government. What would be the effect of this? It would *reunite* our people as one man.

Even in asserting his opposition to reconstruction, Holden was leaving the door ajar to the possibility of reunion under circumstances not as degrading as those discussed in the editorial. Holden was not a Unionist; he opposed reconstruction but was willing to accept it if there was no alternative. He expressed this view well when he declared that the *Standard* to choose between the two evils, we would rather live with than under the Northern people." [23]

Governor Vance wanted peace, too, but only peace with independence. He viewed Holden's plea for negotiations as a step toward reconstruction. Realizing in early June that his and Holden's views diverged, Vance sought advice from leading Conservatives in the state. Several of them met with Vance and Holden later in the summer to try to convince the editor to discountenance the peace meetings that were being held throughout the state. Holden claimed that he was only reporting the proceedings of the meetings, not encouraging them, and refused to change his position. Vance concluded that he did not "see much help for a split. I fear it must come." He asked Holden to point out publicly that the *Standard* did not speak for the governor and that Vance disagreed with the paper's position on peace negotiations. Vance tried again in early September to effect a reconciliation, but that meeting produced the same results. Holden refused to try to dissuade citizens from holding the peace meetings. Vance thereupon put an end to the meetings with a proclamation. [24]

Despite their differences of opinion over the peace meetings, a public quarrel between Vance and Holden did not emerge. This was due in part to the fact that the two men agreed on most issues. The *Standard* delineated those areas of agreement in late July: "Both of us hold that we cannot cease to fight as long as we are invaded; and both of us hold that liberty

23. Raleigh *Standard*, October 7, August 26, 1863.

24. Zebulon B. Vance to Edward J. Hale, June 10, July 26, September 7, 1863, all in Edward Jones Hale Papers, NCDAH; Raleigh *Standard*, July 29, 1863.

among ourselves must be maintained while we are fighting for it against a common enemy, and that the rights and interests of North Carolina as one of the Confederate States, must be upheld and respected at all hazards." Although no open split occurred, the governor promoted the division privately when he urged editor Edward Hale to "pitch into him [Holden]— cry aloud and spare not." For the next several months, the Fayetteville *Observer's* attacks upon Holden and the *Standard* were the only signs of disagreement between Holden and the governor, and then only the few who knew that the *Observer* was speaking as the governor's unofficial organ understood the import of the *Observer's* treatment of the Raleigh editor.[25]

On the surface, at least, all appeared well with the Conservative party; yet a few months later, during the winter of 1863–1864, the party was ruptured by division over the calling of a state convention and by a Vance-Holden contest for the governorship. The split in the party might simply be attributed to a difference of opinion between Conservative supporters of peace negotiations and Conservative opponents of them. That difference certainly existed. Nevertheless, there was a large common ground upon which Vance and Holden and their supporters agreed. Why did they move in the direction of intraparty contention and controversy instead of in the direction of compromise?

★

The absence of a Democratic opposition accounted for the direction that intraparty affairs took. If the Democrats had remained a viable opposition, the only way the Conservatives could have attained success would have been through unity. With the Democrats dead at the state level and in most parts of the state, Conservatives could afford intraparty squabbling and division. The congressional campaigns of 1863 revealed how the presence or absence of a competitive opponent influenced the Conservatives.

The Eighth Congressional District had been largely Democratic before the war and had supported secessionist candidates in the election of February, 1861. Later in 1861, it had elected William Lander to Congress without opposition. But after the congressional elections of 1861, the tide had turned against the Democratic party and its leaders. Lander, a leading Democrat, came in for his share of the criticism. Conservative R. D. Whitley claimed that "Mr. Lander is objected to on various points; one of which is his last man and last dollar doctrin [*sic*] while he and his son wants [*sic*] to be that last man and have that last dollar." Another Conservative claimed that Lander was now so heartily disliked that many former secessionists would not vote for him. Lander had obviously aroused the hostility of at

25. Raleigh *Standard*, July 29, 1863; Zebulon B. Vance to Edward J. Hale, August 11, 1863, in Hale Papers; Fayetteville *Observer*, August 17, 1863.

least the Conservatives in the district, but this did not prevent him from announcing his bid for reelection in August, 1863, or from campaigning throughout the district.[26]

Conservatives had no intention of allowing the election to go uncontested as they had in 1861, but the party's choice of a candidate did not become certain until October—less than a month before the election. The confusion among Conservatives revealed the absence of thorough party organization in the district. Despite the weakness of party organization, Conservatives recognized that they could only attain victory by running one candidate. From midsummer forward, they concentrated on choosing one of two prominent former Union Whigs—Judge William Preston Bynum of Lincoln County and Dr. James Graham Ramsay, state senator from Rowan County. Bynum was apparently the first choice of many, including Ramsay, but when Ramsay asked him in mid-August if he would run, Bynum equivocated. He told Ramsay that he had no interest in becoming a candidate, but he showed a poorly hidden desire to run: "I have been kept under by the Democracy in this & surrounding counties, so long & with such triumphant satisfaction to their leaders, that I confess that my carnal mind is enmity against them, & I have an inward uprising when I have a prospect of putting *them* where they have so long kept me."[27]

Antebellum partisan warfare had not yet ended, at least not in the minds of men like Bynum. Nevertheless, for personal reasons, he decided that he could not run an effective race and urged Ramsay to take the field. He told Ramsay that either of them could defeat Lander: "I predicate my success upon the cause & Landers great loss of popularity, & the same reasoning would apply to you, augmented by your personal popularity in Rowan."[28]

After Bynum decided not to run, Conservatives turned to Ramsay. These men wanted a Conservative victory, and they would not quibble much about Ramsay's opinions on public policy. J. S. Maxwell expressed the feelings of most Conservatives when he wrote to Ramsay that "I trust there will be but one conservative candidate out—otherwise there would be a division; and unless we could compromise, we would loose [*sic*] all." Not wanting above all to lose the election to the much-hated Lander, Conservatives with very different attitudes toward the peace movement expressed a willingness to support Ramsay. For example, in mid-September, twelve Conservatives petitioned Ramsay to run. They declared: "We are in favor of a vigorous prosecution of the war as the only safe 'avenue to a

26. R. D. Whitley to James G. Ramsay, September 14, 1863, J. S. Maxwell to Ramsay, September 12, 1863, both in Ramsay Papers.
27. William P. Bynum to James G. Ramsay, August 24, 1863, in *ibid.*
28. William P. Bynum to James G. Ramsay, October 5, 1863, in *ibid.*

speedy & lasting peace.' We are therefore opposed to reconstruction as impracticable & impossible." Ramsay was also supported by men like J. H. King of Lincoln County, who told Ramsay that "the people of this county want a conservative, who will favor all honorable means to stop the strife and desolation and horible [*sic*] slaughter of human life that must follow a continuation of this dreadful civil war, to represent them in congress, who approves negotiations for an amicable and honorable settlement of our present national troubles." Clearly, the views of King and those of the twelve petitioners were dramatically different, yet in order to defeat Lander they were willing to ignore their differences on the peace question.[29]

Ramsay, who was not bound to any faction of the party in the district, finally decided to run. After he announced his candidacy, Conservatives rallied around him. Although his campaign was limited by the lack of time before the election and by his time-consuming work as a physician, voters elected him by a narrow margin. No intraparty factionalism had plagued the Conservatives, and that alone permitted Ramsay's victory. The absence of factionalism represented the party's response to William Lander's candidacy.[30]

In the neighboring Tenth District, Conservatives did not have the benefit of an opponent like Lander, and, as a result, they divided their support among three candidates. The two Democratic candidates (one of whom soon withdrew) posed no threat to the success of the Conservative candidate, and this created an environment conducive to factionalism in the Conservative ranks; three Conservatives announced their candidacies—incumbent Allen T. Davidson, George Logan, and John Hyman. With no serious opposition, the Conservatives could afford the luxury of an intraparty dispute. Whereas the men urging James Ramsay to run in the Eighth District made few demands on him concerning his position on the peace question, sharp ideological disputes developed among Conservatives in the Tenth District. The major division lay between Davidson and Hyman on the one hand and Logan on the other. Davidson and Hyman expressed the mainstream Conservative position of hostility to the encroachments of the Confederate government and to the original secessionists, yet they disliked the peace meetings because they saw them as the first step toward reconstruction. Logan was nominated by a Conservative party convention that had evolved from the peace meetings, and he endorsed the sentiments expressed at those meetings. Logan viewed Hyman and Davidson as politi-

29. J. S. Maxwell to James G. Ramsay, September 12, 1863, S. S. Bingham, *et al.*, to Ramsay, September 15, 1863, J. H. King to Ramsay, September 22, 1863, all in *ibid*.

30. James G. Ramsay to "Friend Shober," October 9, 1863 (draft), in *ibid*. For the vote, see Compiled Election Returns, in NCDAH. A third candidate ran, but he received only a scattering of votes. See J. F. Stansill to Ramsay, October 22, 1863, in Ramsay Papers.

cians who would prosecute the war endlessly, until devastation was complete. The other two believed Logan and his supporters "would be willing to reconstruct the union with slavery abolished."[31]

In addition to this ideological conflict, there was a clash of ambition between Hyman and Davidson, and neither man showed a willingness to compromise. When Governor Vance asked Hyman to effect a reconciliation with Davidson in order to prevent the election of Logan or a Democrat, Hyman replied with a host of reasons why methods of compromise like a convention or a caucus were unacceptable. In the end, both men ran; so did Logan and Democrat Marcus Erwin. Logan won convincingly.[32]

Conservatives in the Eighth and Tenth districts had approached the campaigns in markedly different ways. When competition with a strong Democratic candidate existed, the Conservatives managed to mute their ideological differences and settle upon one candidate. When they faced little or no competition, they quarreled among themselves.

One might argue that circumstances in the two districts differed because of the different personalities of the Conservative leaders in each district, but this contention is refuted by the repetition of the same pattern in other districts in the state. In the Ninth District, where Democrats could rarely be found, Conservative Burgess Gaither, who disapproved of the peace meetings, found himself opposed by a Conservative supporter of the meetings, S. P. Smith. Another opponent of the peace meetings, Conservative incumbent John A. Gilmer from the overwhelmingly Whig Unionist Greensboro district, faced similar opposition from peace-movement supporter Bedford Brown. On the other hand, in the Second District, where the Democratic party had dominated the antebellum political scene and where William Johnston ran well in 1862, E. C. Yellowly ran as the only Conservative candidate. Similarly, in the Democratic Fourth District, Conservatives concentrated their strength on Thomas C. Fuller. Conservatives in those Democratic districts simply could not afford the intraparty factionalism in which Conservatives elsewhere could indulge.[33]

★

Conservatives captured nine of the state's ten congressional seats and lost the tenth by a mere seventeen votes. With nothing but victories behind them, it seemed that Conservatives could revel in their enhanced power. But with such a preponderance of popular support—with, indeed, the

31. William L. Love to Zebulon B. Vance, April 3, 1863, in Vance Papers; Leander S. Gash to Vance, September 7 and 23, 1863, in Governors' Papers; John D. Hyman to Edward J. Hale, December 4, 1863, in Hale Papers.
32. John D. Hyman to Zebulon B. Vance, April 30, 1863, in Vance Papers; Compiled Election Returns.
33. Compiled Election Returns.

establishment of virtually a one-party system in the state—the Conservatives became increasingly vulnerable to schism. During the months following the elections, new measures of the Confederate government increasingly convinced North Carolinians that their freedom was in jeopardy, and intraparty disagreement over the appropriate state response to this danger precipitated the disruption of the Conservative party.[34]

In December, 1863, Congress abolished the substitute law, which had permitted men liable to conscription to hire substitutes, and explicitly subjected those principals to conscription. The law itself aroused opposition because it seemed a repudiation of the government's "contract" with the principals, and it engendered another round of conflict between the state supreme court and the War Department.[35]

The law apparently affected few men in North Carolina; thus it was not the pervasiveness of its impact that caused complaint. Those men who had bought their way out of fighting elicited little sympathy. But many Conservatives objected to the government's repudiation of its obligations, for if the government could ignore one agreement with its citizens it could ignore others. Congressman James M. Leach wrote to Governor Vance that, although the people had no immediate interest in the substitute law, "the fear with them is that if the Government rides over this law it will over others, & that civil rights & civil & personal liberty will depart the land."[36]

The substitute law also renewed the Confederate government's conflict with the judiciary. Chief Justice Pearson, believing the new law unconstitutional, granted writs of habeas corpus to all principals who requested them. Partly in response to decisions like Pearson's, Congress once again empowered President Davis to suspend the writ, whereupon Pearson declared that the suspension of the writ was inapplicable to the principals. Vance warned Secretary Seddon that if the Confederate government attempted to rearrest men free on writs, he would call out the militia to protect them. Seddon replied that those already discharged would be allowed to remain free, but all further writs would be ignored.[37]

While the state and Confederate governments were arguing over Pearson's decisions, in February, 1864, Congress passed a new conscription law. The act extended the conscription age from eighteen to seventeen and from forty-five to fifty. The new conscripts, organized under control of the Confederate government for local defense, would free reserved state troops for conscription into the general army.[38]

34. *Ibid.*
35. Coulter, *Confederate States*, 319.
36. James M. Leach to Zebulon B. Vance, March 8, 1864, in Vance Papers.
37. Hamilton, "North Carolina Courts," 389–99; Yates, *The Confederacy*, 56–62.
38. Alexander and Beringer, *Anatomy of the Confederate Congress*, 112.

This act seemingly contravened the right of a sovereign state to maintain "troops for war." Without such troops, the states and their citizens would be wholly dependent for their protection on the central government. Vance worried that the implementation of the act would leave "this State . . . powerless, without the shadow of military organization to enforce obedience to law." It would be "contrary to the genius of our new government," he wrote to Secretary Seddon, "to reduce a Sovereign State to [a] dangerous and humiliating condition." Attorney and Conservative leader Augustus Merrimon warned Vance not to give up the troops to the central government: "If you allow the whole fighting population of the state to be taken, you will be a mere formal officer and the state a formal organization, without power, subject to the insults and tyranny of President Davis and his subordinates." One member of the state's home guard lamented: "If what few troops the State claims are given up, we will be reduced to a '*miserable Dependency.*' You can see, no doubt, that we are all fast approaching a central military Despotism." [39]

The most ominous of all the central government's actions was Congress's renewed authorization of the suspension of the writ of habeas corpus from February 15 to August 1, 1864. North Carolinians believed, with some justification, that the act was aimed at them. Davis had advocated the suspension because of the need to suppress disloyal meetings (like those held in North Carolina) and to overcome the objections of local judges (like Chief Justice Pearson) to the substitute law. [40]

The power that Davis would amass from the suspension of the writ troubled North Carolina Conservatives. In a private meeting between the state's congressional delegation and the president, Senator Edwin Reade told Davis that North Carolinians disapproved of the suspension because it clothed Davis with dictatorial power. When Davis said that he would not abuse the power, Reade replied: "I had not intimated that he would, but that the people of North Carolina were unwilling to trust anyone with the power." Upon learning of the passage of the suspension law, Governor Vance warned Davis that, if the bill "be strictly within the limits of the Constitution, I imagine the people of this state will submit to it, so great is their regard for law. If it be adjudged, on the contrary, to be in violation of that instrument and revolutionary in itself, it will be resisted." [41]

The suspension impelled some Conservatives to ask just what the

39. Zebulon B. Vance to James A. Seddon, April 4, 1864, in Governors' Papers; Augustus S. Merrimon to Zebulon B. Vance, February 22, 1864, in Vance Papers; S. E. Westry to Kemp P. Battle, March 3, 1864, in Battle Family Papers.

40. Alexander and Beringer, *Anatomy of the Confederate Congress,* 171–72.

41. Edwin G. Reade to Zebulon B. Vance, February 10, 1864, in Vance Papers; Zebulon B. Vance to Jefferson Davis, February 9, 1864, in Governors' Papers.

South was fighting for. In a letter to Senator William Graham, Richard Puryear pleaded: "I hope you will never adjourn until you have restored the writ of habeas corpus, and placed our lives, our property and our liberties beyond the reach of Despots." If North Carolinians were to lose their liberties, it would not matter who won the war, he maintained: "The people of this state—all loyal, all true to the South, willing to fight and die for liberty, . . . never will wear the chains of a foreign or Domestic tyrant. . . . We shall have first to forget the deeds of our forefathers, and lose all appreciation of the blessings they bequeathed to us. Then we shall be fit subjects for Slavery, and it matters not whether our Master be a Northern or a Southern tyrant." Conservative R. D. Whitley agreed that the attainment of Confederate independence would be a pyrrhic victory without the writ to protect personal freedom. In a letter to his congressman, he wrote that "the Habeas Corpus Suspension act that unbounded Streach of Power unknown to Republican Governments all seem to agree will soon leave nothing worth fighting for."[42]

The suspension of the writ of habeas corpus, combined with the substitute and conscript laws and Confederate defiance of the decisions of the chief justice of the state supreme court, convinced North Carolina Conservatives that they faced an impending military dictatorship. The central government had repudiated its obligations by abolishing substitution, had subverted the state's judiciary by ignoring the chief justice's decisions regarding the law, and threatened the sovereignty of the state with its new conscription law. Then Congress authorized the president to suspend the writ of habeas corpus, subjecting personal liberties to arbitrary abuse.

The future of liberty seemed bleak. In late February, Augustus Merrimon reported from Asheville "that the people are really alarmed, greatly alarmed for the safety of their liberties under our forms of government. They are indeed alarmed, and I confess there is cause for the alarm, and believe me when I tell you, this very alarm, but too well founded, is going far towards precipitating the South upon a fearful doom." In January, Congressman James T. Leach asked Senator William Graham: "What shall we do to stay the hand of a military despotism more to be dreaded than death itself; is not the priceless gem of civil and religious liberty worth the risk of rescueing [sic] it from the hands of the wicked dynasty that is now shaping our ruin?" In April, 1864, the president of the Council of State, Fenner B. Satterthwaite, urged the governor to speak out against the suspension of the writ of habeas corpus. "It may," he wrote, "be instrumental in saving

42. Richard C. Puryear to William A. Graham, May 10, 1864, in Hamilton and Williams (eds.), *Graham Papers*, VI, 101–102; R. D. Whitley to James G. Ramsay, April 18, 1864, in Ramsay Papers.

civil liberty, for I confess that I am alarmed myself at the rapid strides which have been made towards a Military Despotism."[43]

★

Some alarmed Conservatives argued that North Carolina should take formal steps to protect herself and her citizens from that threat. They determined that the legislature should call a state convention so that the state could act in her sovereign capacity to defend herself. According to Conservative editor William W. Holden, such a convention would seek an armistice with the North and, at the same time, would "protect the State against the encroachment of arbitrary power. It would see to it that the proud head of the State was bowed to no despot. It would insist that the civil law should prevail in all cases." A convention would also "demand that the Congress and the military shall respect that civil law and the inalienable rights of our people." Petitioners throughout the state pleaded with Governor Vance to convene the legislature so that it could call a convention, because they viewed "with indignation & alarm the encroachments of Congress & the executive on the Sovereignty of the State & the constitutional rights of the citizens, which neither plighted faith, the sanctity of contracts nor the guaranties of the constitution serve to restrain. . . . The inevitable tendency . . . unless speedily checked is the overthrow of civil liberty, & the establishment of a military despotism." Another leader of the convention movement, Thomas Settle, a former Democratic speaker of the state senate and a Douglas Democrat in 1860, charged that "the Confederate government is completely controlled by bad, desperate men, who in violation of plain laws and the Constitution are usurping to themselves powers by which they can destroy not only private rights but States rights, and finally clothe Jefferson Davis with more power than is now possessed by any crowned head in Europe." Writing in January, 1864, Settle cautioned that if the recently proposed legislation regarding taxation, the currency, conscription, and the suspension of the writ of habeas corpus were adopted (and they were), then "the rights of persons and property will be completely destroyed & we will all find ourselves at the mercy of tyrants." Political decisions, he said, had reached the most basic level. North Carolinians would have to determine whether "white men will remain free." Conservatives like Settle and Holden thought that North Carolinians could preserve their freedom only by calling a convention.[44]

43. Augustus S. Merrimon to William A. Graham, February 22, 1864, James T. Leach to William A. Graham, January 6, 1864, both in Hamilton and Williams (eds.), *Graham Papers*, VI, 28, 3; Fenner B. Satterthwaite to Zebulon B. Vance, April 18, 1864, in Governors' Papers.
44. Raleigh *Standard*, January 19, 1864, quoted in Raper, "William W. Holden," 506–507. A

Historians who have examined the purposes of the convention movement have agreed with the assessment of Governor Vance and have seen it as a major step toward reconstruction. It is true that reconstructionists supported the proposal and that if a convention had been called to defend the rights of the state and its people, it may have found no defense against the encroachments of the Confederate government except through reunion with the North. But just because reconstruction was a logical culmination of the convention movement does not mean that it was the goal of convention advocates. On the contrary, the evidence cited above suggests that many Conservatives were trying to extricate themselves from an almost inextricable situation. They wanted to protect their freedom and seek an honorable peace, but in the Confederacy. State Treasurer Jonathan Worth advised Vance not to attack convention supporters as reconstructionists "*intending* to withdraw the State from the Confederacy. I presume very few favor a convention for this purpose." Other convention supporters declared that a convention would be able to seek an honorable peace. If those efforts failed, "it can in no case injure, but would greatly strengthen the cause, for in that event, we would fall back united, upon the Cannon & the sword with redoubled courage & energy, as the last & only alternative."[45]

Other Conservatives, led by Governor Vance, rejected the idea of calling a convention because they believed it would lead to reconstruction rather than to an honorable peace. Men like Vance persisted in their effort to preserve the rights and liberties of North Carolinians but opposed anything that seemed to hint at reconstruction. State legislator C. D. Smith expressed those Conservatives' fears of reunion: "All we who have battle[d] nobly for Habeas corpus in N Carolina, must naturally feel great trepidation in regard to linking our destiny with a government [Lincoln's] that has made a clean breast of it. Moreover, I am strongly inclined to the believe that our return at this juncture would be a voluntary submission to the worst of slavery."[46]

The split in the Conservative party over the convention question broadened into open political warfare in March, 1864, when William Holden announced himself as a gubernatorial candidate opposed to the reelection of Governor Vance. Holden argued that Vance had inadequately protected

copy of the petition may be found in M. Masten, *et al.*, to Thomas Settle, Jr., January 7, 1864, Thomas Settle, Jr., to M. Masten, *et al.*, January 14, 1864, both in Thomas Settle Papers, No. 2, SHC.

45. Raper, "William W. Holden"; Jonathan Worth to Zebulon B. Vance, May 1, 1864, in Vance Papers; proceedings of a public meeting, Caldwell County, February 8, 1864, in Governors' Papers.

46. Zebulon B. Vance to Edward J. Hale, January 22, 1864, in Hale Papers; C. D. Smith to James G. Ramsay, November 17, 1863, in Ramsay Papers.

popular liberty in North Carolina and had only a lukewarm commitment to its protection. Only a state convention, he maintained, could protect the state and its citizens from the overweening power of the Confederate government, and he denied that the calling of a convention would lead to reconstruction. Hence, for Vance to oppose the convention was for him to oppose the establishment of safeguards for the threatened liberty of the people. In all of his attacks on Vance, Holden sought to identify the governor with the discredited Democratic secessionists. Vance, in turn, argued that his record proved him an ardent defender of popular liberty. Furthermore, he contended that his opposition to the convention had nothing to do with the question of liberty but rather reflected his opposition to reconstruction. He denied that he was allied with the secessionists and went out of his way to abuse them.[47]

Vance based his campaign strategy upon the assumption that secessionists would not be strong enough to run a candidate and so would have to support him. When editor Edward Hale urged Vance to court the secessionists or face the prospect of a Democrat's entering the race, Vance replied: "I dont agree with you about the the [sic] secessionists running the third man. They are as dead as a door nail—they will be obliged to vote for me, and the danger is in pushing off too big a slise [sic] of the old union men with Holden." Therefore, he focused his attention on retaining the votes of the old Unionists.[48]

Vance began his reelection campaign on Washington's Birthday in a speech to the citizens of Wilkesboro, in the mountainous northwest corner of the state. The speech provided the basis for political debate throughout the campaign, which Vance waged on the stump and Holden from the editorial chair. In an effort to conciliate convention supporters, many of whom were in his audience, Vance declared that their intentions were good, but that they did not realize that a convention would lead the state back to the Union and therefore had to be prevented. Because Vance assumed that secession Democrats would support him regardless of what he said, he felt no compunctions about attacking them. Assuming the accepted Conservative position, he blamed them for the evils that had befallen the state since 1861. This stance enabled Vance to dissociate himself from them. The governor also offered some mild criticism of the recent suspension of the writ of habeas corpus.[49]

Vance's attack on the secessionists at Wilkesboro and elsewhere aroused

47. Raleigh *Standard*, May 25, 1864.
48. Edward J. Hale to Zebulon B. Vance, February 8, 1864 (draft), Zebulon B. Vance to Edward J. Hale, February 11, 1864, both in Hale Papers.
49. Raleigh *Conservative*, April 20, 1864.

their ire. William Robinson, editor of the Goldsboro *Republican and Patriot*, warned Vance that if he continued to attack the secessionists, they would run a third-party candidate. Such a candidate, he said, would throw the election to Holden. But Robinson's threat and similar public threats from other Democrats left Vance unfazed. After his Wilkesboro speech, a self-satisfied Vance declared that "the Secessionists . . . are as well satisfied with it [the speech] as I desire them to be."[50]

As Vance had forecast, despite their bluster, the secessionists were too weak to run a viable candidate. Gradually secessionist leaders joined the Vance camp. Abhorring Holden, who had abandoned them during the secession crisis and whom they suspected of reconstructionist sentiments, they were left with little choice but to support Vance. Leading Democratic spokesmen like Thomas Clingman and former Confederate Attorney General Thomas Bragg, the Wilmington *Journal*, and the Raleigh *Confederate*, all fell into line.[51]

Democratic support for the governor led Holden to charge that Vance had gone over to the "destructives." Vance's Wilkesboro speech and the fact that men like Clingman and Bragg supported him proved that contention. Vance's task during the campaign was to refute Holden's charges. If Conservatives were convinced that Vance had allied himself with the Democratic secessionists, it is likely that they would have abandoned him. William P. Bynum summarized popular attitudes when he wrote to Vance that "the people . . . , when they find that leading Democrats whom they formerly idolized, are going to vote such a way, they will vote the opposite. Such is their inveterate hatred of their former Gods, whom they regard as the authors of all their calamities." He advised Vance to create as much political distance from the secessionists as possible.[52]

The governor responded by publishing correspondence in which he urged the president to initiate peace negotiations with the North. He had written to Davis originally in order to prove his commitment to peace, "except at the expense of the country's ruin and dishonor." In his letter, he told Davis that if he made "some effort at negotiations with the enemy," it would "rally all classes to a more cordial support of the government." Although the president had turned him down and although Vance had never really expected such an initiative to bear fruit, he had proven his desire for peace. He reiterated his position throughout the campaign, and in so do-

50. William Robinson to Zebulon B. Vance, May 30, 1864, in Vance Papers; Vance to Edward J. Hale, March 6, 1864, in Hale Papers.
51. Wilmington *Journal*, March 10, 1864; Thomas L. Clingman to Zebulon B. Vance, February 18, 1864, Walter L. Steele to Vance, March 21, 1864, both in Vance Papers; John M. Tate to J. L. Brown, April 10, 1864, in Nancy Brown Young Papers, SHC; William W. Holden to Calvin J. Cowles, March 18, 1864, in William Woods Holden Papers, NCDAH.
52. William P. Bynum to Zebulon B. Vance, May 7, 1864, in Vance Papers.

ing he distinguished himself from the president and his supporters and from Holden.[53]

Vance needed not only to escape the close embrace of the secessionists, but also to prove to his supporters that he was a stout defender of civil liberty. His Wilkesboro speech had upset many Conservatives because he seemed to apologize for the suspension of the writ of habeas corpus. Holden charged that the speech exposed the hollowness of Vance's commitment to the preservation of the freedom of North Carolinians. John H. Haughton, one of the governor's political confidants, advised him to answer the serious charge that he had endorsed "that justly odious law suspending the great writ of Habeas Corpus." Council President Satterthwaite informed Vance that "the *only* ground of complaint against you is the *fear* of some of your friends that . . . you are yielding too much to the Richmond administration, and have not taken that *decided* opposition to the serious encroachments, which has been made upon the *rights* and *liberties* of the people. That is the ground upon which Mr. Holden and his friends assale you." He suggested that Vance "take the very highest ground in favour of 'Constitutional liberty.' Express your opinion boldly upon the policy of the suspension of the writ of habeas corpus." Satterthwaite assured Vance that "it would remove every ground of suspicion and Complaint against you! it would take 'all the wind out [of] Mr. Holden['s] sale' and he would be compelled to withdraw, and give you his support or be so badly beaten in the race as never to raise his head again."[54]

Accepting the advice of Haughton, Satterthwaite, and others, Vance "boldly" defended the sacred writ of habeas corpus in a major speech delivered before three thousand people in Fayetteville on April 22, in his message to the General Assembly on May 17, and thereafter on the stump. In his message, which occupied four and one-half columns of the Fayetteville *Observer*, Vance's denunciation of the suspension of the writ of habeas corpus covered two full columns. His new tactic succeeded. The Reverend A. W. Cummings reported to Vance that while traveling his circuit in the mountains he had talked with many people about the election. "Two weeks ago Holden would have received a majority of votes within my bounds." In one precinct, Cummings had found all but one man supporting Holden. "I am from that country to day," he wrote in early May, "I am happy to find a great change going on among the people all in your favor. It arises from what they learn to be your opinions and action upon the Habeas Corpus,

53. Zebulon B. Vance to Edward J. Hale, December 30, 1863, in Hale Papers; Vance to Jefferson Davis, December 31, 1863, Davis to Vance, January 8, 1864, both in Vance Papers; Fayetteville *Observer*, April 25, 1864.

54. Raleigh *Standard*, May 25, 1864; John H. Haughton to Zebulon B. Vance, April 23, 1864, Fenner B. Satterthwaite to Vance, April 18, 1864, both in Governors' Papers.

and the continuance of the war." After Vance's message was delivered to the General Assembly, Jonathan Worth, who sympathized with Holden, declared: "I see no cause to H[olden] for continuing in the field, and I think V[ance]'s friends who were becoming alienated have generally expressed their satisfaction."[55]

While Vance portrayed himself as a friend of liberty and of peace, he also argued that the convention would produce neither. A state convention, he declared, could do nothing that the legislature could not do, except take the state out of the Confederacy. That would lead North Carolina into a war with the Confederacy and ultimately back into the Union. A return to the Union would not mean a restoration of freedom, Vance declared, but rather "the destruction of *everything*." A vote for Holden, Vance and his supporters argued, was a vote for continued war and for a return to northern despotism.[56]

Underlying Vance's attack on Holden was the charge that Holden was disloyal to the Confederacy. Only a month before the election, Vance Conservatives discovered the existence of a secret Unionist organization, the Heroes of America. The organization existed, to be sure, as did Unionism in parts of the state, but its exposure just weeks before the election was surely no coincidence. Vance's supporters widely publicized the existence of the Heroes during July, the month before the election, and though most of them did not charge Holden with being a member of the organization, they did try to associate him with it and with Unionist sentiment in North Carolina.[57]

Vance ran a masterful campaign. Between February and May he changed the issues of debate in the campaign. In February he had been on the defensive because of his apparently lukewarm defense of the liberties of North Carolinians. Vance eliminated that issue by coming out vigorously in defense of the writ of habeas corpus. By early summer, the issue had become the loyalty of William Holden and the aims of the convention movement. By the end of July, Holden spent much of his time denying that he was a member of the Heroes of America or that he wanted North Carolina to make a separate peace with the Lincoln administration.[58]

Vance, in effect, gave the electorate what it desired. He defended the liberties of the state's citizens while demanding that southerners continue their armed struggle for independence. And he contended that the conven-

55. Fayetteville *Observer*, April 25, May 23, 1864; James M. Leach to Zebulon B. Vance, April 27, 1864, A. W. Cummings to Vance, May 9, 1864, both in Vance Papers; Jonathan Worth to J. J. Jackson, May 30, 1864, in J. G. deRoulhac Hamilton (ed.), *The Correspondence of Jonathan Worth* (2 vols.: Raleigh: Broughton, 1909), I, 309.

56. Fayetteville *Observer*, April 25, May 23, 1864.

57. *Ibid.*, July 4, 11, 18, August 1, 1864.

58. Raleigh *Standard*, July 27, 1864.

tion would do nothing to protect liberty or promote peace but, instead, would lead to a bloody war with the other Confederate states and to submission to the despotic North.

Soldiers and civilians came to the polls and gave Vance a massive victory. He won 80 percent of the total vote, 87.9 percent of the soldiers' vote, and 77.2 percent of the civilian vote. Holden obtained a majority in only three of the state's counties; in twenty of the counties unoccupied by the Union army, he received less than fifty votes.

Voting patterns in the state bore little relationship to patterns in previous elections. It would be illogical to compare the Holden vote in 1864 with the Johnston vote in 1862, since Democratic secessionists could hardly be expected to have voted for Holden. It would be almost as illogical to compare Vance's vote in 1864 to the vote of his own opponent in 1862. The difficulty with making comparisons between the election of 1864 and past elections suggests just how much the politics of North Carolina had changed since 1862.

The lack of any relationship between the 1864 gubernatorial election and any previous gubernatorial election symbolized the end of a political era in North Carolina. No longer was there competition between Democrats and Whigs or Americans or Whiggish Conservatives. Repudiated in 1862, Democrats offered little opposition to Conservatives in the congressional elections of 1863 and none in the gubernatorial election of 1864. The Democratic party as North Carolinians had known it would never rise again.

Vance's victory also represented a popular commitment to a position that ultimately proved untenable. The intense opposition to conscription, to the suspension of the writ of habeas corpus, and to other acts indicated the unwillingness of North Carolinians to accept the centralization of government operations necessary for an effective war effort or to allow any incursions on their rights. But they rejected the alternative of returning to the old Union, where the Lincoln administration had, as they saw it, snuffed out all liberty. In the end, they could only assume a negative stance and fight to preserve civil liberty in the South.

★

The fears for liberty excited by the Confederate government among North Carolinians and other white southerners rested upon a firm historical foundation. Inheriting many of the political beliefs and fears of the American revolutionaries, southerners were prepared to divine the worst of motives in the government's actions. Those fears were exacerbated further because the war brought a central government in contact with most people for the first time. Before the war, the vast majority dealt with the federal government only through the postmaster. The war brought conscription, "arbitrary" arrests of civilians, central government "subversion" of the judiciary, the impressment of private property, heavy taxes, and the suspension of the writ of habeas corpus. Many southerners viewed these drastic actions with horror and asked themselves whether the government had designs on their liberty.[59]

The anxieties of North Carolinians and other white southerners were paralleled in the North, yet the contours of dissent in the two sections differed. Northern popular discontent with the Lincoln administration was limited by the existence of a two-party system in that section. The partisan desire to defeat the Democratic party helped to unite even discontented Republicans behind Lincoln's policies. And the existence of a strong Republican organization, ready to denounce even a hint of Democratic disloyalty, moderated Democratic actions.[60]

The Democratic party played an additional role in shaping and moderating dissent in the North. Just as North Carolina Conservatives attacked and distrusted the apparently despotic Davis administration, so too did northern Democrats respond to the Lincoln administration. But the Democrats, with an effective national organization, could hope to oust Lincoln in 1864. They offered northerners the traditional means by which Americans protected their liberty—voting for the opposition party. Voters in North Carolina and other Confederate states were offered no such alternative. Because North Carolina Conservatives had ties with no national party, they could not hope to neutralize Davis, and because he was serving one six-year term, they could not remove him. Conservatives saw no way to rid themselves of the threat of despotism through the ballot box. While northern discontent was channeled into and moderated by the Democratic party, North Carolina Conservatives were left with two unsatisfying choices. A small portion moved unwittingly in the direction of disloyalty to the Confederacy and reconstruction of the Union; the larger portion was left to complain bitterly and impotently of the threat to its freedom.[61]

The absence of a national two-party system shaped the attitudes of North Carolinians toward the Confederate government; so too did the presence of a statewide two-party system. While North Carolinians had rejected the exercise of power by the Confederate government, they had ac-

59. Fayetteville *Observer*, February 18, 1861.
60. David M. Potter, "Jefferson Davis and the Political Factors in Confederate Defeat," in Donald (ed.), *Why the North Won the Civil War*, 91–112; Eric L. McKitrick, "Party Politics and the Union and Confederate War Efforts," in William Nisbet Chambers and Walter Dean Burnham (eds.), *The American Party Systems: Stages of Political Development* (New York: Oxford University Press, 1967), 117–52.
61. On Democratic fears, see Joel H. Silbey, *A Respectable Minority: The Democratic Party in the Civil War Era, 1860–1868* (New York: W. W. Norton, 1977), 62–88.

cepted the exercise of considerable power by the state government. Under Governor Vance, for example, the state engaged in blockade running, clothed its troops, and effectively enforced the conscription laws. The acceptance of state power derived less from an ideological commitment to states' rights than from the state's party system. The party system provided an effective mechanism for removing from power those rulers who threatened popular liberty. After all, the voters had overwhelmingly elected Conservative Zebulon Vance in 1862 and thereby rebuked the Democratic party which had ruled state politics since 1850.[62]

Although the structure of politics shaped the ways in which North Carolinians responded to the Confederate government, that response was also influenced by a nonpolitical factor—the state's geographic location. Although the enemy occupied part of the state's coastline and threatened the mountain counties on the Tennessee border, North Carolina was one of the southern states most isolated from military action. As an interior state, North Carolina was more susceptible to the demands of the Confederate government than other states. For example, North Carolina and two other states paid about two-thirds of the total produce collected under the tax-in-kind. At the same time, the need for measures like conscription and the suspension of the writ of habeas corpus were not readily apparent to North Carolinians because the enemy posed no immediate threat. Thus, North Carolinians were called upon to make more sacrifices than were people in other states at a time when they least perceived the need for such efforts.[63]

Those geographic and political factors combined to make North Carolinians especially alert to any incursions on their liberty. By 1864, most of them had come to feel that the Confederate government was seeking to establish a military despotism and rob them of their liberty. They agreed with merchant Leander S. Gash when he wrote to Governor Vance: "Gradually the last vestige of freedom is departing from us, We all feel it. None of us feel that we have the manhood we once had. It is humiliating yet it is so."[64]

★

Times of crisis often reveal and reshape the inner workings of societies, and in this respect Confederate North Carolina was typical. The war exposed the nature of the state's antebellum political world and presided over its unraveling. It uncovered the relationship of politics and liberty, as

62. Yates, *The Confederacy*, 34–35, 68–84.
63. This interpretation was influenced by Alexander and Beringer, *Anatomy of the Confederate Congress*, 320–22, 336–37, and by Professor William L. Barney's comments on my essay, "The Rise of Opposition to the Confederate Government in North Carolina" (Paper delivered at the Annual Meeting of the Southern Historical Association, Atlanta, Georgia, 1976).
64. Leander S. Gash to Zebulon B. Vance, September 7, 1863, in Governors' Papers.

mid-nineteenth-century white North Carolinians understood that relationship. Yet the experience of war also brought an end to the party system that North Carolinians had known since Jackson's time.

The men who participated in politics—and most white men did—had absorbed the revolutionary fear that republican government, and hence liberty, were in constant, imminent jeopardy. But where the revolutionaries and their children had relied largely upon constitutions to defend the Republic, the antebellum and wartime generations placed their faith in the party system as the conservator of their freedom.

Throughout the life of the second party system, at the heart of political conflict lay the dispute over the best way to preserve republicanism. On a whole host of issues, ranging from economic and social policy making to constitutional change to the defense of slavery and southern rights, Democrats and Whigs in North Carolina battled to prove themselves the best defenders of republican government. In their disagreements over these issues, politicians consciously intensified anxieties about the dangers to republican government, but then presented their own programs and candidates as the best means of averting those dangers. Trooping to the polling place, citizens participated, at least symbolically, in the struggle to save republican government.

In the issues discussed and in the goals ostensibly sought, the political system in North Carolina resembled that of other states throughout the country. But in the structure of its politics and the course of its political development, North Carolina often departed from the national norm. And those differences profoundly influenced the ways in which North Carolinians viewed the political system of the state and the Union. Throughout the antebellum years, North Carolina, like much of the upper South but unlike the rest of the states, enjoyed a remarkably competitive and persistent two-party system. Because the elections were so close and the party loyalties of voters so deep, the parties were more concerned about bringing out loyal voters than with converting the supporters of their opponents, much less luring independents, of whom there were few. Therefore, it was crucial that party leaders maintain efficient organizations and that the parties present to voters coherent and distinct positions on the important issues of the day. The politician's impulse to distinguish himself from his competitor was intensified by the citizenry's expectation that parties would offer genuine alternatives on issues of immediate concern to them. The political conflicts of the 1840s expressed and often intensified the social, economic, and sectional (both within the state and between the states) conflicts in society. In so doing, politicians conveyed to voters a sense that the political system was responsive and that therefore republican government was safe.

By the late 1840s and 1850s, however, the political conflicts of earlier years were disappearing or at least becoming neutralized. Whereas in the 1840s the parties had differed sharply about the role of government in society and the role of citizens in the governing process, by the mid-1850s the party system had shaped a political consensus in favor of a positive liberal state. By this time, too, partisan conflict had also intensified the popular commitment to the defense of southern rights and eroded the partisan differences over how best to protect those rights.

The disappearance in North Carolina of party conflict on a variety of issues replicated the experience of other states in the mid-1850s, but whereas the newfound consensus undermined the party system elsewhere, it had no similar effects on North Carolina. The state's political stability was largely attributable to the electoral strength of the state Whig party in the early 1850s, to the Whigs' ability to protect themselves during the reapportionment of legislative seats in 1852, and to the continued relevance of the traditional issue of distributing the proceeds of federal public land sales. Even the nativist American party, which in the North differed so much from the Whigs and Democrats, became in North Carolina but a continuation of the Whig party and laid the groundwork for the Whig party revival of 1859–1860. In 1860, North Carolina continued to enjoy a vibrant, competitive party system. Whigs, who had been out of power since 1850, had come near victory in 1860. They learned that, although defeated, a party could regain power in the next election. Therefore, although they abhorred Abraham Lincoln's election to the presidency, they did not regard it with the same alarm of people in the lower South. Their own continuing experience with competitive party politics led them to believe that Lincoln could be curbed during his term in office and that, with redoubled efforts, the Republicans could be ousted in 1864. But when Lincoln called for troops to suppress the rebellion of the seceded states in mid-April, 1861, white North Carolinians saw what they believed to be the beginnings of despotic government in the United States. Almost unanimously they supported secession. Their longstanding fears for the survival of republican government had suddenly found a frightful confirmation.

These people who were so sensitive in 1861 to apparent threats to their liberty could not readily accept the centralization of government power necessitated by war. Confederate government demands aroused the fear that the Davis administration was seeking to destroy the liberties of the people. The dimension of this fear was shaped by and in turn influenced the state party system. The persistence of party politics through 1862 had heightened popular awareness of the Confederate government's incursions on popular liberty, but it also encouraged the parties to reaffirm repeatedly their allegiance to the Confederacy and to moderate attacks on the

Confederate government. But the demise of the Democratic party placed power within the state in the hands of the Conservatives for the foreseeable future. Without the need for party unity to obtain victory, the Conservative party splintered. In the gubernatorial campaign of 1864, there was no active defender of the Davis administration; indeed, each candidate devoted much of his campaign to proving that he was the better champion of peace and freedom and the most ardent opponent of the president.

While party politics molded the way North Carolinians perceived the Confederate government and the war, the conditions brought about by the war profoundly altered the state's party system. Growing fears for their freedom led North Carolinians to repudiate and render impotent the Democratic party that had run the state since 1850. The demise of the Democratic party during the war marked the end of the long-lived, stable, and competitive second party system in North Carolina.

Appendix A

Percentage Slaves and Slaveholders in Total Population, 1850 and 1860, and Democratic Votes for President and Governor, 1840–1862

TABLE 28

Percentage Slaves in Total Population (1850), and Democratic Vote for President (P) and Governor (G), 1840–1852: Pearson Correlations

Election Year	Percent Slave, 1850
1840P	.40
1840G	.42
1842G	.34
1844P	.36
1844G	.37
1846G	.38
1848P	.40
1848G	.39
1850G	.42
1852P	.43
1852G	.39

TABLE 29

Percentage Slaves in Total Population (1860), and Democratic Vote for President (P) and Governor (G), 1854–1862: Pearson Correlations

Election Year	Percent Slave, 1860
1854G	.49
1856P	.44
1856G	.43
1860P*	.33
1860G	.50
1862G	.43

*Combined vote of John C. Breckinridge and Stephen A. Douglas

TABLE 30
Percentage Slaveholders in Total Population (1860), and Democratic Vote
for President (P) and Governor (G), 1848–1862: Pearson Correlations

Election Year	Percent Slaveholders, 1860
1848P	.38
1848G	.38
1850G	.35
1852P	.42
1852G	.36
1854G	.41
1856P	.39
1856G	.38
1860P*	.22
1860G	.43
1862G	.40

*Combined vote of John C. Breckinridge and Stephen A. Douglas

Appendix B
The Secession Convention Election of
February, 1861

Historians have long debated the extent of popular support of southerners for secession during the winter of 1860–1861. They have often supported their arguments with analyses of voting returns for delegates to a state's secession convention and, in some cases, for referenda on whether or not their state should hold a convention. But historians have had particular difficulty analyzing the extent of secession sentiment in North Carolina based on its convention election of February 28, 1861. On that day, North Carolinians voted by a narrow majority against assembling a state convention and, at the same time, elected delegates to the convention that was never held. The vote for or against a convention often did not reflect popular attitudes toward the Union, because Unionists in some parts of the state supported the call for a convention. A better measure was the votes for delegates, who usually assumed clear positions on the question of secession. Once the convention question had been decided, however, contemporaries saw little need to gather the returns for the delegate election in a central place. In order to obtain a clearer picture of secessionist sentiment in North Carolina, I gathered many of these returns from legislative papers, county records, and extant newspapers. Since some of the delegate returns are missing and since the returns for the convention question sometimes reflected more accurately popular attitudes toward the Union than did the delegate returns, I have merged the two sets of data to provide an estimate of secession sentiment in the state.

In my identification and classification of the candidates, I have followed several rules. If there is an extant newspaper for a candidate's locality, I

FIGURE 4.
The Secession Convention Election of February, 1861

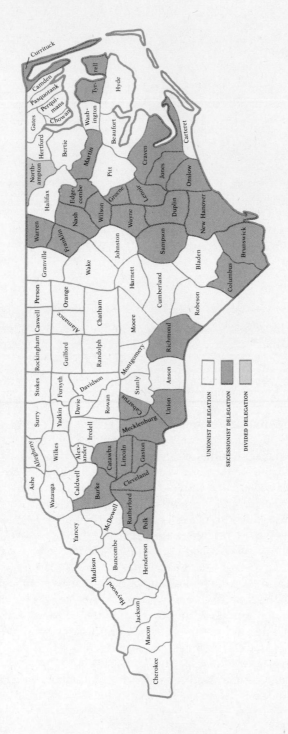

UNIONIST DELEGATION
SECESSIONIST DELEGATION
DIVIDED DELEGATION

From *The Secession Movement in North Carolina* by J. Carlyle Sitterson. Copyright 1939 by the University of North Carolina Press. Published for The James Sprunt Studies in History and Political Science.

have relied primarily on its assessment for identification. Whether or not such existed, I crosschecked candidate identification in as many newspapers as possible. Although the assessments of the various newspapers were occasionally at odds, in most cases they reached a consensus. Even in cases where they disagreed, the correct choice usually became obvious.

Although the delegate returns provide the best estimate of Union and secession sentiment, they must be used with caution. Sometimes, for instance, the distinction between Unionist and secessionist candidates was blurred. When newspapers in the state analyzed the vote in coastal Craven County, they identified W. B. Wadsworth as the leading Unionist vote-getter. The local paper, the New Bern *Daily Progress*, contended on March 6 that Wadsworth was not a Unionist, but it admitted that a Union meeting had nominated him. Since it appears that Unionist voters perceived Wadsworth as the Unionist candidate, I concluded to treat him as such.

At times it was advisable to use the vote for or against the convention instead of the delegate vote. This was often true when a delegate ran unopposed. In northeastern Camden County, for example, Union Whig Daniel D. Ferebee ran without any formal opposition. He received all but 7 of the 309 votes cast for the delegate. It seemed more accurate to use the convention vote, in which secessionists had a better opportunity to register their sentiments. Camden's voters cast 290 votes against a convention and 41 for it. As a rule, if a county with an unopposed Union slate voted against a convention or one with an unopposed secession slate voted for a convention, the convention vote was substituted. Otherwise, the county's vote was deleted from the analysis.

The convention vote was substituted under other circumstances as well. When the delegate vote was unavailable, I used the convention vote if certain conditions were met. If a county voted for a convention and elected a secession delegation or against a convention and elected a Union delegation, the convention vote was usually included (for exceptions, see the notes to table 31).

Thus, columns 5 and 6 of table 31 contain estimates of Union and secession strength by county. Because of various problems alluded to above, eight counties have been eliminated from the analysis.

TABLE 31

The Secession Convention Election of February, 1861

County	Opposed Convention	For Convention	Highest Union Delegate	Highest Secession Candidate	Union Vote	Secession Vote	Delegate Position*
Alamance	1101	293	967	480	967	480	2U
Alexander	598	246	—	—	598	246	U
Allegheny	255	115	—	—	255	115	U
(Ashe)	758	144	—	—	758	144	
Anson	461	520	613	449	613	449	2U
Beaufort[1]	653	590	935	—[3]	—	—	2U
Bertie	632	138	666	—	632	138	2U
Bladen	460	480	539	415	539	415	U
Brunswick	61	627	339	363	339	363	S
Buncombe	389	1219	1095	531	1095	531	U
Burke	273	718	547	584	547	584	S
Cabarrus	306	898	535[2]	670[2]	535	670	S
Caldwell	651	186	711	129	711	129	U
Camden	290	41	302	—[4]	290	41	U
Carteret	394	415	505[2]	305[2]	505	305	2U
Caswell	137	692	821	269	821	269	S
Catawba	158	918	—	924	158	918	2S
Chatham	1795	283	1854	175	1854	175	3U
Cherokee	901	149	—	—	901	149	U
Chowan	222	204	367	79	367	79	U
Cleveland	117	1270	425	1016	425	1016	2S
Columbus	183	620	199	609	199	609	S
Craven	362	891	568	855	568	855	2S
Cumberland (& Harnett)	959	1038	1612	484	1612	484	3U
Currituck	86	447	86	432	86	432	S
Davidson	1806	366	1726	382	1726	382	2U
Davie	734	262	718	269	718	269	U
Duplin	71	1252	—	—	71	1252	2S
Edgecombe	17	1588	—	1524	17	1588	2S
Forsyth	1409	286	1519	483	1409	286	2U
Franklin	79	794	—	—	79	794	S
Gaston	166	864	177	861	177	861	S
Gates	508	367	354[2]	154[2]	354	154	U
Granville	743	1056	1057	822	1057	822	3U
Greene	106	457	—	—	106	457	S

County							Class.*
Guilford	2771	113	2508	—	2771	113	3U
Halifax	39	1049	574	538	574	538	2U
Haywood	307	504	437	399	437	399	U
Henderson	647	573	1041	279	1041	279	U
Hertford	292	239	302	230[5]	302	230	U
Hyde	161	476	496	172	496	172	2U
Iredell	1818	191	1823	176	1823	176	U
Jackson[1]	83	435	—	—	—	—	2U
Johnston	621	741	1142	198[3]	1142	198	S
Jones	71	259	104[2]	227[2]	104	227	S
Lenoir	195	447	174	429[6]	174	429	U
Macon	359	250	—	—	359	250	S
Lincoln	86	708	87[2]	707[2]	87	707	U
Madison	532	345	565	318	565	318	S
Martin	22	662	—	642	22	662	U
McDowell	217	638	469	389	469	389	2S
Mecklenburg	252	1448	306	1318	306	1318	U
Montgomery	870	81	807	—[7]	807	81	S
Moore	1257	135	877	—[8]	1257	135	U
Nash	93	989	—	922	93	989	S
New Hanover	210	1781	517	1516	517	1516	2S
Northampton[1]	327	576	—	—	—	—	S,U
Onslow	89	631	97	583[9]	97	583	S
Orange	1436	458	1537	356	1537	356	2U
Pasquotank	426	159	485	128	485	128	U
Perquimans[1]	182	299	244[2]	—[10]	—	—	U
Person[1]	167	593	—	—	—	—	U
Pitt	177	986	952	506	952	506	2U
Randolph	2466	45	2434	321	2466	45	2U
Richmond	251	383	307	321	307	321	S
Robeson	871	490	957	413	957	413	2U
Rockingham	570	808	852	685	852	685	2U
Rowan	1150	882	1218	837	1218	837	2U
Rutherford (and Polk)	308 / 123	970 / 362	—	—	—	—	2S
Sampson	530	972	577	926	577	926	2S
Stanly	763	85	—	—	763	85	U
Stokes	890	204	915	151	915	151	U
Surry	1136	207	1085	218	1085	218	U

*U = Union; S = Secession

County	Opposed Convention	For Convention	Highest Union Delegate	Highest Secession Candidate	Union Vote	Secession Vote	Delegate Position*
Tyrrell[1]	158	134	—	—	—	—	S
Union	483	548	—[11]	583	483	548	S
Wake	1246	1406	1932	758	1932	758	3U
Warren	33	774	75	720	75	720	2S
Washington	418	238	396	276	396	276	U
Watauga	536	72	275[12]	28	536	72	U
Wayne	242	1250	254	1207	245	1207	2S
Wilkes	1895	51	1798	—	1895	51	2U
Yadkin	1490	34	1296	—[13]	1490	34	U
Yancey	598	556	652[2]	502[2]	652	502	U
TOTAL	47338	46671			54781	36341	

*U = Union; S = Secession

[1] Deleted from analysis because there was a difference between the position of the delegate elected and the convention vote. (In Beaufort, although the county voted against a convention and elected Union delegates, the closeness of the convention vote and the inability of the secessionists even to run a candidate, suggests that the convention vote vastly overstates the extent of secession sentiment in the county.)

[2] Figures calculated from majorities given in newspapers. These figures are a close approximation of the actual vote.

[3] Scattering of 27 votes.

[4] Scattering of 7 votes.

[5] Scattering of 3 votes.

[6] Scattering of 22 votes.

[7] The Unionist opponent was also a Unionist. The loser received 441 votes.

[8] The Unionist opponent was also a Unionist. He received 114 votes.

[9] Scattering of 10 votes.

[10] Unionist opponent was a Unionist. Estimated from majority figures, the loser received 238 votes.

[11] Scattering of 270 votes among six candidates.

[12] Unionist victor was a Union and anticonvention candidate. In addition to a secession candidate, there was a second Union and anticonvention candidate who received 145 votes, and a Union and proconvention candidate who received 128 votes.

[13] Scattering of 9 votes.

SOURCES: The votes for and against the convention were taken from Compiled Election Returns, NCDAH. The delegate election results in Legislative Papers, NCDAH, were used whenever possible. Frequently, the results were not reported to the legislature. Moreover, the Legislative Papers did not identify a candidate's position on secession. Therefore, in order to obtain other election results and to identify the position of a candidate on secession, I consulted the following newspapers for the issues published within several weeks before and after the election: Charlotte *Western Democrat*, Fayetteville *Observer*, Greensboro *Patriot*, Hillsboro *Recorder*, Newbern *Daily Progress*, Newbern *Weekly Progress*, Raleigh *Register*, Raleigh *Standard*, Raleigh *State Journal*, Salem *People's Press*, Salisbury *Carolina Watchman*, Wadesboro *North Carolina Argus*, Wilmington *Herald*, and Wilmington *Journal*. All the newspapers are available on microfilm. Of the newspapers, I found the Fayetteville *Observer* the most reliable.

Appendix C
A Note on Data and Statistical Methods

VOTING DATA

North Carolina voting data poses significant problems for historians seeking to examine changes in voting patterns over time. Between 1836 and 1861, the General Assembly created a veritable flood of new counties. That made it difficult to make the data consistent from one year to the next. I initially consolidated adjacent counties involved in county formations between 1840 and 1865 and thus created a number of "counties" for statistical purposes. This method gave me uniform categories for the data, but it also forced me to lump together too many counties and therefore distorted somewhat the patterns of voting. The results of this method may be found in Marc Wayne Kruman, "Parties and Politics in North Carolina, 1846–1865" (Ph.D. dissertation, Yale University, 1978), 30.

I ultimately decided to adopt the method of Professor Thomas B. Alexander, which eliminates a county if it was involved in a county formation in either of the two elections being compared. Coefficients of correlation and regressions were calculated with data weighted and unweighted for population, and I have presented the weighted results. But whether the data was weighted or not, or whether counties were lumped together or not, the end result proved to be the same—a very strong positive correlation of voting patterns from 1840 to 1860.

For a discussion of the statistical methods used to analyze the voting data, see Charles M. Dollar and Richard J. Jensen, *Historian's Guide to Statistics: Quantitative Analysis and Historical Research* (New York: Holt, Rinehart, and Winston, 1971), 61–71, 87–94. Scatter diagrams confirmed the fact that there was a strong linear association between the antebellum elections.

LEGISLATIVE ROLL-CALL VOTES

As a general rule, I tried to examine all votes on significant policies. Because only voting members were considered, I tried to eliminate votes taken late in the session when many legislators had already left for home. The party affiliations of legislators were determined by examining newspaper reports and the votes for speakers of the House of Commons and the Senate.

The methodologies used for examining the roll-call votes are simple. The percent affirmative refers to the percent of the voting members of a party who voted "yes" on a particular issue. The index of disagreement is the difference between the percent affirmative votes of the two parties. See Michael F. Holt, *The Political Crisis of the 1850s* (New York: John Wiley & Sons, 1978), 26–27.

There is some apparent, though not real, inconsistency in the percent affirmative tables and the index of disagreement tables. However, the difference between the two parties' percent affirmative votes on an issue involving more than one roll-call vote need not equal the index of disagreement on that issue. For example, if on three roll-call votes on one issue, Democrats voted 40, 50, and 70 percent affirmative, while Whigs voted 35, 55, and 75 percent affirmative, the mean disagreement would be 5. But the mean Democratic affirmative would be 55 and the mean Whig percent affirmative would be 53.3, leaving a difference of 1.7.

Bibliographical Essay

PRIMARY SOURCES

Manuscript Collections

The manuscript collections of Whig, Democratic, American, and Conservative party leaders provided much of the evidence upon which this study was based. Nevertheless, there are some problems with them. Most collections contain only incoming correspondence; rarely did a politician retain copies of his own letters. There were a few exceptions, like the Bryan Family Papers, SHC, which include the letterbooks of James W. Bryan, and the Calvin J. Cowles Papers, NCDAH, which include Cowles's letterbooks, but even in those cases most of the letters pertain only to personal business matters. Therefore, historians seeking information about a particular individual must find letters in other collections. A second drawback to the use of manuscript collections is their incompleteness. Only portions of most men's papers are still extant.

Even more disappointing was the paucity of papers of several significant individuals. The William Woods Holden Papers, NCDAH, contain only a few letters pertaining to the antebellum period and to the war. The minuscule George Edmund Badger Papers, in SHC, NCDAH, and Duke, although they provide some insights into that prominent Whig's attitudes, were too slight to be of much use.

Despite those drawbacks, the information provided by manuscript collections proved invaluable for this study. The most important collections relating to the Whig party are the papers of Daniel Moreau Barringer, the Battle Family, the Bryan Family, David F. Caldwell, the Clingman-Puryear Family, and David F. Outlaw, all in SHC, and of John H. Bryan, in NCDAH and the East Carolina University Library, Greenville, North Carolina. The

Barringer Papers are especially useful for the correspondence of western Whigs and for insight into Whig patronage policy in the late 1840s. The Battle Papers contain a scattering of letters relating to the Whig party, to the Bell-Everett campaign in North Carolina, and to wartime politics. (Kemp P. Battle helped manage the party's campaign in 1860 and served as Vance's private secretary during the war.) The Bryan collections reveal the inner workings of the Whig party and the attitudes of a prominent eastern Whig, James W. Bryan, and his brother, John H. Bryan, long active in the central committee. The Caldwell Papers contain significant correspondence relating to the sectional divisions in the party over the calling of an unrestricted state constitutional convention. The Clingman-Puryear Papers are important for the information they provide about Thomas Clingman's break with the Whig party. The Outlaw Papers show how one Whig congressman viewed state politics from his vantage point in Washington; the collection is especially useful for Outlaw's detailed letters to his wife about the sectional crisis of the late 1840s and about the Compromise of 1850. Other collections relating to the Whig party that proved useful include the Edmund Deberry Papers, the Jarratt-Puryear Papers, the Jones and Patterson Papers, the Lenoir Family Papers, and the William Valentine Diaries, all in SHC.

A number of manuscript collections helped illuminate the workings of the Democratic party. The David Settle Reid Papers, NCDAH, provide considerable information about Reid's three gubernatorial campaigns, the issues of constitutional reform, and the Democratic party's position on governmental aid to internal improvements. Although there is no collection of Governor Thomas Bragg's papers, an important diary of his, kept during 1861 (typescript in SHC), letters by him in the John Bragg Papers, SHC, and some of his correspondence in the Thomas Pittman Collection, NCDAH, were all helpful. The John W. Cunningham Papers, Jones and Patterson Papers (which contain the papers of Democrats Jesse A. Waugh and Rufus L. Patterson), the Thomas D. McDowell Papers, all in SHC, and the C. B. Heller Collection (which contains more McDowell papers), NCDAH, provide insights into local party affairs in the southeastern and northwestern parts of the state. The Henry T. Clark Papers, Duke, and the Abraham Watkins Venable Papers, SHC, are valuable for letters from William Holden on the sectional crisis and the Compromise of 1850. Clark's papers also contain significant material on the secession crisis and his brief term as governor from 1861 to 1862, while Venable's papers allow one to explore the relationship of dissident Democrats to their party and to the American party. The most important source of information about dissident Democrats, especially Duncan K. McRae's independent candidacy in 1858, is the

Archibald H. Arrington Papers, SHC. The Lawrence O'Bryan Branch Papers, Duke, and the Mrs. Lawrence O'Bryan Branch Papers, NCDAH, are also extremely valuable.

On the question of state aid to internal improvements, the Lenoir Family Papers, SHC, and the Thomas I. Lenoir Papers, Duke, include the papers of western internal-improvements advocate and propagandist William A. Lenoir. The William Holland Thomas Papers, Duke, contain information about western support for government aid and about the Democratic party in the extreme western part of the state. Other interesting letters relating to internal improvements may be found in the Hugh McRae Papers, Duke, and scattered throughout the Governors' Papers, NCDAH.

On the American party, see the collections of Whig party leaders and also the William Lafayette Scott Papers, Duke. They include letters from Commoner Levi Scott to his brother written during his service in the state legislature in 1856–1857. The letters furnish unusually good, detailed information on the American party's organization in the legislature. Valuable American party membership lists may be found in the John W. Gregory Papers, NCDAH. Important letters by American party leaders, Kenneth Rayner and Henry W. Miller may be found in the Daniel Ullmann Papers, New York Historical Society.

On the secession crisis, the views of a Union Democrat are presented in the James L. Harrington Papers, while the sentiments of many secession Democrats may be found in the Lawrence O'Bryan Branch Papers, both at Duke. North Carolina Unionists expressed their sentiments to Benjamin Sherwood Hedrick, driven out of his professorship at the University of North Carolina after supporting Republican John C. Frémont in 1856. Hedrick's papers (at Duke) also supply information about the unstudied but significant Quaker migration to Indiana during the secession crisis and through the war. Invaluable for the secession crisis are numerous letters from North Carolina Unionists to Stephen A. Douglas, many of whose papers are deposited in the Manuscripts Room, University of Chicago Library, Chicago, Illinois. Also useful are the Bartholemew F. Moore Papers, NCDAH, and the Allen Turner Davidson Papers, SHC.

The most important collections for a study of wartime politics are the Zebulon Baird Vance Papers and the portion of the Governors' Papers relating to Vance's governorship, both in NCDAH. Matters of political and personal significance may be found in the ostensibly official Governors' Papers, while official matters are discussed in Vance's private papers. Taken together, the two collections provide a vivid source of information about Vance's administration, his relations with the Confederate government and William Holden, and about the development of dissent in the state. Two extremely important letters written by Vance on his gubernatorial campaign of 1862 are in the Little-Mordecai Papers, NCDAH.

Vance frequently wrote to Edward Jones Hale, editor of the Fayetteville *Observer*, whose papers are deposited in NCDAH. The Hale Papers are also valuable for other wartime correspondence and for information on Duncan K. McRae's independent candidacy. The papers are disappointingly thin on the period before 1858.

The James Graham Ramsay Papers, SHC, are excellent for studying Ramsay's campaign for Congress in 1863 and contain significant letters about legislative debates during the secession crisis. The Thomas Settle Papers, Series 1 and 2, the James T. Leach papers, both in SHC, and the Calvin J. Cowles Papers, NCDAH, furnish information about wartime dissent and about the supporters of William Holden. Also helpful were the Katherine C. P. Conway Papers, the William Woods Holden Papers, both in NCDAH, and the Edward C. Yellowly Papers, SHC.

Published Correspondence

The most important published correspondence is J. G. deRoulhac Hamilton and Max R. Williams, eds., *The Papers of William Alexander Graham* (6 vols. to date; Raleigh: State Department of Archives and History, 1957–). These volumes are among the first sources one should consult for a study of the Whig or Conservative parties, but they must be used with care. The first four volumes, edited by Professor Hamilton, often present severely edited letters. What seemed unimportant to the editor might be important to another historian. Also missing are significant letters to Graham located in the Bryan Family Papers, SHC, and in the Governors' Papers, NCDAH. The volumes coedited by Max R. Williams are well done. Henry T. Shanks, ed., *The Papers of Willie Person Mangum* (6 vols.; Raleigh: State Department of Archives and History, 1950–56), contain important letters concerning the Whig party in the 1830s and early 1840s. J. G. deRoulhac Hamilton, ed., *The Correspondence of Jonathan Worth* (2 vols.; Raleigh; Broughton, 1909), provides important information about the Whig party revival of 1859, the Unionist Whig response to the secession crisis, and wartime dissent. A portion of the papers of Zebulon Vance are also in print. Frontis W. Johnston, ed., *The Papers of Zebulon Baird Vance* (Raleigh: State Department of Archives and History, 1963), only includes Vance's correspondence through 1862. Therefore, the bulk of the valuable material about Vance must be sought in the Vance Papers and the Governors' Papers, discussed above.

Noble J. Tolbert, ed., *The Papers of John Willis Ellis* (2 vols.; Raleigh:

State Department of Archives and History, 1964), contains the correspondence of the Democratic governor from 1859 to 1861 and supplies information about party affairs in the 1840s and 1850s and about the secession
crisis. The *Papers*, though, are incomplete. Tolbert failed to publish important letters by Ellis in the Lawrence O'Bryan Branch Papers, Duke,
and in the Thomas Pittman Collection, NCDAH. J. G. deRoulhac Hamilton, ed., *The Papers of Thomas Ruffin* (4 vols.; Raleigh: Edwards and
Broughton, 1918–1920), contain occasionally useful letters.

Newspapers

Newspapers were the most important sources of information for this
study. When read carefully, they illuminate party ideology, strategy, and
organization. The most important papers consulted were the Democratic
organ, the Raleigh *North Carolina Standard* (referred to throughout this
study as the Raleigh *Standard*), and the Whig organ, the Raleigh *Register*.
They expressed their party's views on issues, candidates, and party organization. They are also a good source for studying the state legislature, since
they published reports on the Senate and House proceedings (from a partisan point of view) and frequently published speeches of their fellow partisans. The newspapers are also an excellent source for official documents
like the governor's biennial message.

In order to understand the attitudes of Whig and Democratic partisans, one must go beyond the confines of the capital city. Newspapers
published in other parts of the state illuminate intraparty disputes and local politics and provide a different perspective on issues, strategies, and
organization than is to be found in the Raleigh papers. The Fayetteville
Observer and the Greensboro *Patriot* informed my understanding about
eastern and western Whig attitudes, as did the Salisbury *Carolina Watchman*, the Wadesboro *North Carolina Argus*, the Asheville *Highland Messenger*, the Statesville *Iredell Express*, the Charlotte *Journal*, and the Wilmington *Herald*. Western Whig unhappiness with the party may be seen in
scattered issues of the Rutherfordton *Mountain Banner* and the Asheville
News. The *News* became a Democratic paper in 1854.

The Democrats suffered from a paucity of newspapers. In addition to
the *Standard*, the most useful Democratic newspapers were the Charlotte
Western Democrat, the Fayetteville *North Carolinian*, the Wilmington *Journal*, and the Tarboro *Press*, which changed its name to the Tarboro *Southerner* during the crisis of 1850. The Tarboro paper was especially valuable
for understanding eastern opposition to an activist state. Very useful for
the *ad valorem* campaign of 1860 was the Democratic campaign news-

paper, the *Little Adder* (published by the Salisbury *Banner*), which is located in NCC.

I consulted other newspapers at specific points and for statistical information. They include the Charlotte *North Carolina Whig*, the Elizabeth City *Sentinel*, the Goldsboro *Patriot and Republican*, the Hillsboro *Democrat*, the Hillsboro *Recorder*, the Milton *Chronicle*, the New Bern *Progress*, the Raleigh *Star*, the Salem *People's Press*, and the Warrenton *News*.

For the war years, the Raleigh *Confederate* superseded the *State Journal* and spoke for much of the old Democratic leadership. The Raleigh *Conservative*, which began publication in 1864, served as Vance's campaign organ during that year. All of the newspapers cited, except for the *Little Adder*, are available on microfilm.

SECONDARY SOURCES

General Studies

The following discussion does not pretend to be comprehensive, only to describe the historical studies that I have found most helpful and to show where my study of North Carolina fits into the historiography of antebellum and Civil War American politics.

At the outset, I should mention two of the most valuable books for this study: J. Mills Thornton III, *Politics and Power in a Slave Society: Alabama, 1800–1860* (Baton Rouge: Louisiana State University Press, 1978); and Michael F. Holt, *The Political Crisis of the 1850s* (New York: John Wiley & Sons, 1978). Thornton's contention that the goal of antebellum Alabama politics was the preservation of the freedom and equality of white Alabamians deeply influenced my thinking about antebellum politics in general. However, North Carolina was a very different place from Alabama, and Thornton's study enabled me to make more effective comparisons between the upper and lower South. Holt's similar argument that the heart of party conflict in antebellum America was over different ways to preserve republicanism and his emphasis on the importance of party conflict over issues enhanced my understanding of how the party system functioned and why North Carolina's persisted for as long as it did.

On the republican ideology and the fears for the survival of republican government that underlay antebellum politics, I have found the following most helpful: Bernard Bailyn, *The Ideological Origins of the American Revolution* (Cambridge, Mass.: Harvard University Press, 1967); Gordon S. Wood, *The Creation of the American Republic, 1776–1787* (Chapel Hill: University of North Carolina Press, 1969); John R. Howe, "Republican

Thought and the Political Violence of the 1790s," *American Quarterly*, XIV (1967), 147–65; Roger H. Brown, *The Republic in Peril: 1812* (New York: Columbian University Press, 1964); Richard Buel, Jr., *Securing the Revolution: Ideology in American Politics, 1789–1815* (Ithaca, N.Y.: Cornell University Press, 1972); and Richard B. Latner, "The Nullification Crisis and Republican Subversion," *JSH*, XLIV (1977), 19–38.

The most important study of the origins of the second party system is Richard P. McCormick, *The Second American Party System: Party Formation in the Jacksonian Era* (Chapel Hill: University of North Carolina Press, 1966), which relates party formation to the contest for the presidency. He shows clearly the importance of a viable national party to the life of the state parties, but he overstates the pragmatic nature of the emerging party system. His contention that the regional ties of presidential candidates accounted for the different timing of party formation in the states is developed further for the South in William J. Cooper, Jr., *The South and the Politics of Slavery, 1828–1856* (Baton Rouge: Louisiana State University Press, 1978). Cooper argues that the southern Whig party was formed in response to what some politicians perceived as Van Buren's affinity for the antislavery movement. Charles G. Sellers, Jr., "Who Were the Southern Whigs?" *AHR*, LIX (1954), 335–46, links party formation to disagreements over banking and shows the relationship between Whiggery and the world of commerce.

As politicians shaped the party system in the 1830s, party lines became clarified. Joel H. Silbey, "The Election of 1836," in Arthur M. Schlesinger, Jr., and Fred Israel, eds., *History of American Presidential Elections* (4 vols.; New York: Chelsea House, 1971), I, 577–600, shows that voters established their party loyalties in the South in 1836—a pattern followed in North Carolina. Ideological differences also became apparent. See Holt, *Political Crisis*; Robert Remini, *Andrew Jackson and the Bank War* (New York: W. W. Norton, 1967); David J. Russo, "The Major Political Issues of the Jacksonian Period and the Development of Party Loyalty in Congress, 1830–1840," *Transactions of the American Philosophical Society*, LXII (1972); James Roger Sharp, *The Jacksonians Versus the Banks: Politics in the States After the Panic of 1837* (New York: Columbia University Press, 1970).

In recent years, historians have paid appropriate attention to the political beliefs of the parties. The best analysis at the national level is William R. Brock, *Parties and Political Conscience, 1840–1850* (Millwood, N.Y.: KTO Press, 1979), though it overstates the significance of national politics. Brock also offers an illuminating analysis of the Whig party during the Tyler administration. Another more broadly focused study is Rush Welter, *The Mind of America, 1820–1860* (New York: Columbia University Press,

1975), which shows that party conflict revolved around the best means of preserving freedom and republican government. He shows how conservative Whigs accommodated themselves to the democratic age, but he is unsuccessful in linking them to the Federalists. There are two excellent studies of the ideologies of the major parties: Marvin Meyers, *The Jacksonian Persuasion: Politics and Belief* (Stanford: Stanford University Press, 1957), and Daniel Walker Howe, *The Political Culture of the American Whigs* (Chicago: University of Chicago Press, 1979), which stresses the Whig debt to the "country party" ideology of the eighteenth century. Howe's assessment of the political practices of Whig politicians is less satisfactory. So is his treatment of southern Whigs, who were much more like their northern counterparts than he admits, and who, in the upper South, were a more potent political force in the 1850s than he avers.

That Whigs and Democrats acted on their beliefs in the nation and the state is evident from a number of studies: Thomas B. Alexander, *Sectional Stress and Party Strength: A Computer Analysis of Roll-Call Voting Patterns in the United States House of Representatives, 1836–1860* (Nashville: Vanderbilt University Press, 1967); Joel H. Silbey, *The Shrine of Party: Congressional Voting Behavior, 1841–1852* (Pittsburgh: University of Pittsburgh Press, 1967); Lee Benson, *The Concept of Jacksonian Democracy: New York as a Test Case* (Princeton: Princeton University Press, 1961); Herbert Ershkowitz and William Shade, "Consensus or Conflict? Political Behavior in the State Legislatures During the Jacksonian Era," *JAH*, LVIII (1971), 591–622; Ronald P. Formisano, *The Birth of Mass Political Parties: Michigan, 1827–1861* (Princeton: Princeton University Press, 1971); Peter Levine, *State Legislative Parties During the Jacksonian Era: New Jersey, 1829–1844* (Cranbury, N.J.: Fairleigh Dickinson University Press, 1977); William G. Shade, *Banks or No Banks: The Money Issue in Western Politics, 1832–1865* (Detroit: Wayne State University Press, 1972); and the studies of Holt, Sharp, and Thornton, cited above.

Although antebellum Americans bowed at the shrine of party, they did so with some reluctance. Several studies helped me place antiparty thought in North Carolina in its proper context: Richard Hofstadter, *The Idea of a Party System: The Rise of Legitimate Opposition in the United States, 1780–1840* (Berkeley: University of California Press, 1969); Lynn L. Marshall, "The Strange Stillbirth of the Whig Party," *AHR*, LXXII (1967), 445–68; Ronald Formisano, "Political Character, Antipartyism, and the Second Party System," *American Quarterly*, XXI (1969), 683–709; and Howe, cited above.

On constitutional reform, the best studies are: Fletcher M. Green, *Constitutional Development in the South Atlantic States, 1776–1860: A Study in the Evolution of Democracy* (Chapel Hill: University of North Carolina Press, 1930); Green, "Democracy in the Old South," *JSH*, XII (1946), 3–23; Chilton Williamson, *American Suffrage: From Property to Democracy, 1760–1860* (Princeton: Princeton University Press, 1960). Constitutional change in the southern states still requires further study.

On the relationship of party politics and policymaking, I have found James Willard Hurst, *Law and the Conditions of Freedom in the Nineteenth-Century United States* (Madison: University of Wisconsin Press, 1956); and Richard L. McCormick, "The Party Period and Public Policy: An Exploratory Hypothesis," *JAH*, LXVI (1979), 279–98, particularly suggestive. However, their contention that both parties accepted the virtues of governmental promotion is inaccurate for North Carolina in the 1840s but well describes attitudes from the mid-1850s onward.

Good overviews of the South generally are: Charles S. Sydnor, *The Development of Southern Sectionalism, 1819–1848* (Baton Rouge: Louisiana State University Press, 1948), and Avery Craven, *The Growth of Southern Nationalism, 1848–1861* (Baton Rouge: Louisiana State University Press, 1951). Although Sydnor offers a fine general account of the period, his contention that "party conflict . . . had the hollow sound of a stage duel with tin swords" does not ring true. Craven's book, though it focuses too much on the lower South and on the significance of national issues, offers important insights on the ties that bound southern politicians to their national parties during the late 1840s and early 1850s.

William J. Cooper's *The South and the Politics of Slavery* helped me place North Carolina politics within the context of the entire South. Cooper's focus on the slavery issue is the source of both his book's greatest strengths and its weaknesses. By examining one aspect of southern politics, he is able to illuminate the variety of ways in which slavery as a political issue influenced southern political development. However, his insistence that all political issues became wrapped in the politics of slavery ultimately distorts the nature of southern politics, because politicians and voters were concerned about more than the slavery issue. In addition, Cooper's acute perception of the ways in which political parties exacerbated sectional tensions needs modification because it minimizes the ways in which the party system also curbed conflict.

The present study offers an ironic partial confirmation of Eugene Genovese, *The Political Economy of Slavery: Studies in the Economy and Society of the Slave South* (New York: Pantheon Books, 1965), and *The World the Slaveholders Made: Two Essays in Interpretation* (New York: Pantheon Books, 1969), neither of which deal directly with politics but portray a planter-dominated South driven out of the Union by the slave economy's voracious demand for more land. Wealthy slaveowners certainly dominated North Carolina politics, but as a class these slaveowner-politicians were enthused about neither landed expansion nor secession. Moreover, Genovese's belief that planters imposed their political will on the society in general is belied by the profoundly democratic style of North Carolina politics. On these points, George M. Fredrickson, *The Black Image in the White Mind: The Debate on Afro-American Character and Destiny, 1817–1914* (New York: Harper & Row, 1971), is perceptive.

Fredrickson's study, an excellent account of racial thought in nineteenth-century America, also influenced my thinking about the commitment of white North Carolinians to the preservation of slavery. So did Edmund S. Morgan, *American Slavery, American Freedom* (New York: W. W. Norton, 1975); Morgan, "Slavery and Freedom: The American Paradox," *JAH*, LIX (1972), 5–29.

Regarding the issue of slavery's expansion, North Carolinians were more concerned with the right to take their slaves into the territories and less with the actual expansion of slavery. The contention that southerners were demanding the actual expansion of slavery is most forcefully stated in Genovese, *Political Economy*, cited above, and William L. Barney, *The Road to Secession: A New Perspective on the Old South* (New York: Praeger, 1972). More persuasive interpretations are advanced by Cooper, Holt, and Thornton, all cited above, and Chaplain W. Morrison, *Democratic Politics and Sectionalism: The Wilmot Proviso Controversy* (Chapel Hill: University of North Carolina Press, 1967).

The best study of the sectional conflict by far is David M. Potter, *The Impending Crisis, 1848–1861*, completed and edited by Don E. Fehrenbacher (New York: Harper & Row, 1976). Potter's analysis of the white southerner's loyalty to the South and to the Union informed my chapters on slavery and secession. He places that subject in a larger context in his "The Historian's Use of Nationalism and Vice Versa," in David M. Potter, *The South and the Sectional Conflict* (Baton Rouge: Louisiana State University Press, 1967), 34–83. More specialized studies of the sectional conflict that I found particularly useful were: Morrison, *Democratic Politics and Sectionalism*, and Holman Hamilton, *Prologue to Conflict: The Crisis and Compromise of 1850* (Lexington: University of Kentucky Press, 1964), which should be read in conjunction with Holt, *Political Crisis*, and Don E. Fehrenbacher, *The Dred Scott Case: Its Significance in American Law and Politics* (New York: Oxford University Press, 1978). The Scott case itself had little impact on North Carolina politics.

Historians of American politics in the 1850s have rightly emphasized the dramatic changes that took place at the national, state, and local levels. As such, they offer a valuable counterpoint to the continuities evident in North Carolina. The most helpful include: Formisano, *Birth of Mass Political Parties*; Michael F. Holt, *Forging a Majority: The Formation of the Republican Party in Pittsburgh* (New Haven: Yale University Press, 1969); Holt, *Political Crisis*; Joel H. Silbey, *The Transformation of American Politics, 1840–1860* (Englewood Cliffs, N.J.: Prentice-Hall, 1967); and Thornton, *Politics and Power*. Two studies have emphasized the continuities in voting behavior: Thomas B. Alexander, "The Civil War as Institutional Fulfillment," *JSH*, XLVII (1981), 3–32; and Joel H. Silbey, *A Respectable Minority: The Democratic Party in the Civil War Era, 1860–1868* (New York: W. W. Norton, 1977).

On the Know-Nothing party, Michael F. Holt provides a provocative analysis in his "The Politics of Impatience: The Origins of Know-Nothingism," *JAH*, LX (1973), 309–331; and in his *Political Crisis*. North Carolina Know-Nothings expressed the same discontent with the old parties that Holt has found elsewhere, but few North Carolinians expressed those sentiments before the breakup of the national Whig party. The best study of the nativist party in a slave state is Jean H. Baker, *Ambivalent Americans* (Baltimore: Johns Hopkins University Press, 1978), but the ethnic diversity of and substantial immigration into Maryland made Know-Nothingism in that state different from that in more homogeneous states like North Carolina. The most complete study of the party in the South is W. Darrell Overdyke, *The Know-Nothing Party in the South* (Baton Rouge: Louisiana State University Press, 1950). Also useful is James H. Broussard, "Some Determinants of Know-Nothing Electoral Strength in the South, 1856," *Louisiana History*, VII (1966), 5–20, which points out that southern Know-Nothings derived most of their electoral support from old Whigs.

On the election of 1860, Ollinger Crenshaw, *The Slave States in the Presidential Election of 1860* (Baltimore: Johns Hopkins University Press, 1945), is helpful. John V. Mering, "The Slave-State Constitutional Unionists and the Politics of Consensus," *JSH*, XLIII (1977), 395–410, understates the differences that existed between the Constitutional Unionists and the Democrats in the election campaign. Roy Franklin Nichols, *The Disruption of American Democracy* (New York: Macmillan, 1948), helped me to place the problems of North Carolina's Democrats in a broader political context.

The most helpful general study of the secession crisis is Potter, *Impending Crisis*, though I disagree with his conclusions about the motives of the upper South. Don E. Fehrenbacher, *The South and Three Sectional Crises* (Baton Rouge: Louisiana State University Press, 1978), asserts that southern secession was an assertion of regional and personal self-respect. North Carolinians and others in the upper South were equally committed to the preservation of southern honor, but they did not perceive the threat in the same way as people did in the lower South.

In recent years, historians have offered a variety of thoughtful interpretations of the secession of the southern states. They include: Thornton, *Politics and Power*, discussed above; Steven Channing, *Crisis of Fear: Secession in South Carolina* (New York: Simon & Schuster, 1970), which emphasizes the racial fears of South Carolinians; William L. Barney, *The Secessionist Impulse: Alabama and Mississippi in 1860* (Princeton: Princeton University Press, 1974), which emphasizes the expansionist desires of slaveholders; and Michael P. Johnson, *Toward a Patriarchal Republic: The Secession of Georgia* (Baton Rouge: Louisiana State University Press, 1977), which argues that slaveholders sought to cement their hegemony in a divided South. The arguments of each helped to clarify my thinking about secession, but because all but Thornton's study of Alabama focus almost exclusively on the secession crisis, they fail to place secession into a broader political context. North Carolinians were as afraid of a servile insurrection as South Carolinians, but they did not move quickly toward secession. And the position of North Carolina's slaveholders was certainly threatened by the implications of the *ad valorem* taxation campaign, but they were divided by party over secession. As to the Southwest, Thornton's study of Alabama shows that Alabamians seceded in order to preserve their freedom, not to expand slavery. Thornton, though, links the intensification of the fears of Alabamians to their response to the dramatic economic changes of the 1850s. North Carolinians faced a similar spurt of economic development as railroads, turnpikes, and banks proliferated and state expenditures and taxes soared, but these upheavals left North Carolinians with little of the sense of crisis that Alabamians felt. It would appear that the absence of a viable, competitive party system gave people in the lower South much less of a sense that they could thwart impending dangers—in the form of racial fears, threats from nonslaveholders, or the economic changes of the previous decade. My own emphasis on the role of political parties is similar to that offered by Holt, *Political Crisis*.

An excellent study of secession in the upper South is Daniel W. Crofts, "The Union Party of 1861 and the Secession Crisis," *Perspectives in American History*, IX (1978–79), 327–76, which argues persuasively that Unionism maintained its strength in that region up until Lincoln's call for troops in mid-April. Whereas Crofts emphasizes the upheaval in southern politics during the secession crisis, I am most impressed by the continuities. Also helpful for understanding the nature of upper South Unionism is David M. Potter, *Lincoln and His Party in the Secession Crisis* (New Haven: Yale University Press, 1942).

Emory M. Thomas, *The Confederate Nation, 1861–1865* (New York: Harper & Row, 1978), is the best overview of the South's experience as an independent nation, though his interpretation of the antebellum South and of secession is unpersuasive and though he virtually ignores popular discontent with the Davis administration. The most important study of Confederate politics and of the Confederate Congress is Thomas B. Alexander and Richard E. Beringer, *The Anatomy of the Confederate Congress: A Study of the Influences of Member Characteristics on Legislative Behavior, 1861–1865* (Nashville: Vanderbilt University Press, 1972). Studies of politics in the Confederate states are desperately needed.

Although I disagree with Frank L. Owsley's interpretation of the rise of opposition to the Confederate government, his *State Rights in the Confederacy* (Chicago: University of Chicago Press, 1925), is still the place to begin any study of political conflict between the Confederate and state governments. Also useful for an understanding of Confederate dissent are: Albert Burton Moore, *Conscription and Conflict in the Confederacy* (New York: Macmillan, 1924); Georgia Lee Tatum, *Disloyalty in the Confederacy* (Chapel Hill: University of North Carolina Press, 1934); and Bell I. Wiley, *The Plain People of the Confederacy* (Baton Rouge: Louisiana State University Press, 1943). Paul D. Escott, *After Secession: Jefferson Davis and the Failure of Confederate Nationalism* (Baton Rouge: Louisiana State University Press, 1978), offers a valuable portrait of the suffering endured by the southern yeomanry and a thoughtful analysis of popular discontent, but he ignores the ideological dimension of that discontent. More sensitive to popular fears of Confederate despotism are: David Donald, "Died of Democracy," in David Donald, ed., *Why the North Won the Civil War* (Baton Rouge: Louisiana State University Press, 1960), 79–90; and John B. Robbins, "The Confederacy and the Writ of *Habeas Corpus*," *Georgia Historical Quarterly*, LV (1971), 83–101.

Historians often treat the Confederacy in a vacuum; rarely do they relate wartime developments to the 1850s or to Reconstruction. Two exceptions are Thomas B. Alexander, "Persistent Whiggery in the Confederate South, 1860–1877," *JSH*, XXVII (1961), 305–29; and Alexander and Beringer, *Anatomy of the Confederate Congress*. But also see John V. Mering's skeptical, though unpersuasive, response to the idea of persistent Whiggery in his "Persistent Whiggery in the Confederate South: A Reconsideration," *South Atlantic Quarterly*, LXIX (1970), 124–43. One excellent study that links the political worlds of the antebellum period, wartime, and Reconstruction in a non-Confederate slave state is Jean H. Baker, *The Politics of Continuity: Maryland Political Parties from 1858 to 1870* (Baltimore: Johns Hopkins University Press, 1973). The war had a deeper impact on the politics of Confederate states like North Carolina than it did on Maryland. Joel H. Silbey, *A Respectable Minority*, a fine study of the Democratic party, allowed me to make comparisons between politics in North Carolina and in the Union. On this point, I have also benefited enormously from Eric L. McKitrick, "Party Politics and the Union and Confederate War Efforts," in William Nisbet Chambers and Walter Dean Burnham, eds., *The American Party Systems: Stages of Political Development* (New York: Oxford University Press, 1967), which argues that the presence of a two-party system in the North and its absence in the South strengthened the northern and weakened the southern war efforts. Although my conclusions often differ from McKitrick's, the influence of his essay is apparent in my chapters on Civil War politics. In the same collection, essays by William Nisbet Chambers, Paul Goodman, Richard P. McCormick, Frank Sorauf, and Theodore Lowi all influenced my thinking about political parties.

North Carolina Politics

The standard study of antebellum North Carolina politics is J. G. deRoulhac Hamilton, *Party Politics in North Carolina, 1835–1860* (Durham: Seeman Printery, 1916), which unpersuasively argues that the preoccupation of North Carolinians with national politics prevented them from confronting state problems. The study is also marred by numerous factual errors.

Three studies of North Carolina aided my understanding of the state's politics before 1840. One should begin a study of Jacksonian politics in the state with William S. Hoffmann, *Andrew Jackson and North Carolina Politics* (Chapel Hill: University of North Carolina Press, 1958), which examines the interrelationship of state and national politics. Even better are: Harry L. Watson, *Jacksonian Politics and Community Conflict: The Emergence of the Second American Party System in Cumberland County, North Carolina* (Baton Rouge: Louisiana State University Press, 1981), which the author kindly allowed me to read in manuscript form; and Harold Joseph Counihan, "North Carolina Politics, 1815–1836: State and Local Perspectives on the Age of Jackson" (Ph.D. dissertation, University of North Carolina at Chapel Hill, 1971). Watson's study has implications that reach well beyond one county or one state, and I relied heavily on it for my understanding of North Carolina politics in the 1830s. He deftly shows how politicians linked local, state, and national issues into a coherent whole. A fruitful comparison may be made between his book and Paul E. Johnson, *A Shopkeeper's Millenium: Society and Revivals in Rochester, 1815–1837* (New York: Hill & Wang, 1978). Counihan offers a fine analysis of party formation at the state level.

A recent dissertation, Thomas Edward Jeffrey, "The Second Party System in North Carolina" (Ph.D. dissertation, Catholic University of America, 1976), overlaps with the present study. His analysis of party organization is illuminating and proved helpful. However, his emphasis on the significance of local issues and on the pragmatic nature of the party system contrasts sharply with my conclusions. He has published some of his findings in "Political Parties and Internal Improvements, 1835–1861," *NCHR*, LV (1978), 111–56, which argues that legislators were divided on the question of internal improvements in the late 1830s and 1840s by section, not by party, but his conclusions are not borne out by his data; and in "Thunder from the Mountains: Thomas Lanier Clingman and the End of Whig Supremacy in North Carolina," *NCHR*, LVI (1979), 366–95, which is the fullest account of that politician's career and which emphasizes how Clingman exploited issues involving intrastate sectionalism to weaken the Whig party in the mountains. James R. Morrill, "The Presidential Election of 1852: Death Knell of the Whig Party of North Carolina," *NCHR*, XXXIV (1967), 342–59, also gives Clingman credit for bringing about the demise of the Whig party but stresses how Clingman utilized the southern rights issue. Both Morrill and Jeffrey, though, overstate Clingman's role and exaggerate the extent of the Whig party's decline.

Clarence Clifford Norton, *The Democratic Party in Ante-Bellum North Carolina 1835–1861* (Chapel Hill: University of North Carolina Press, 1930), and Herbert Dale Pegg, *The Whig Party in North Carolina*, (Chapel Hill: Colonial Press [1968?]), offer useful accounts of the two parties but lack interpretive focus. The best study of the government's role in the antebellum economy is Cecil K. Brown, *A State Movement in Railroad Development: The Story of North Carolina's First Effort to Establish an East and West Trunk Line Railroad* (Chapel Hill: University of North Carolina Press, 1928). On plank roads, see Robert B. Starling, "The Plank Road Movement in North Carolina," *NCHR*, XVI (1939), 1–23, 147–74. The most complete study of the *ad valorem* taxation issue is Donald Cleveland Butts, "A Challenge to Planter Rule: The Controversy over *Ad Valorem* Taxation of Slaves in North Carolina" (Ph.D. dissertation, Duke University, 1978).

The standard account of the secession movement is Joseph Carlyle Sitterson, *The Secession Movement in North Carolina* (Chapel Hill: University of North Carolina Press, 1939). Although it is weakened by a failure to examine secession within the broader context of the state's political history, it still provides a good introduction to the secession of North Carolina.

The most valuable studies of wartime politics are: Richard E. Yates, *The Confederacy and Zeb Vance* (Tuscaloosa, Ala.: Confederate Publishing Company, 1958); Richard E. Yates, "Governor Vance and the Peace Movement," *NCHR*, XVII (1940), 1–25, 89–113; Richard E. Yates, "Zebulon B.

Vance as War Governor of North Carolina, 1863–1865," *JSH*, III (1937), 43–75; and Horace W. Raper, "William W. Holden and the Peace Movement in North Carolina," *NCHR*, XXXI (1954), 493–516. Biographical studies that are useful for understanding wartime politics are Glenn Tucker, *Zeb Vance: Champion of Personal Freedom* (Indianapolis: Bobbs-Merrill, 1965); and Richard L. Zuber, *Jonathan Worth: Biography of a Southern Unionist* (Chapel Hill: University of North Carolina Press, 1965).

Two other studies are filled with numerous nuggets of information: Guion Griffis Johnson, *Ante-Bellum North Carolina: A Social History* (Chapel Hill: University of North Carolina Press, 1937); and Hershal L. Macon, "A Fiscal History of North Carolina, 1776–1860" (Ph.D. dissertation, University of North Carolina, 1932).

Index

to legislative representation, 94; popular ratification of, 102; as an expression of social conflict, 142; mentioned, 45, 138, 191, 244
Erwin, Marcus, 76, 255
Expansion, territorial, 108–13
Expenditures, government, 78, 189–90

Fayetteville, 8, 17, 66
Fayetteville *North Carolina Argus*, 88, 163
Fayetteville *Observer*, 64, 129, 131, 153, 162, 170, 176, 178, 208, 225, 252, 263
Fillmore, Millard, 131–32, 134, 176–78
Florida, 180
Floyd, John, 185
Foreign-born, 15, 165
Fort Sumter, 219, 221
Franklin County, 7
Free-Soil party, 105, 135
Frémont, John C., 175, 176, 177
French Broad River, 10
Fugitive-slave law, 124, 128–29, 131
Fuller, Thomas, 255
Fulton, James, 69

Gaither, Burgess, 131, 227, 248, 255
Gales, Joseph, 42
Gales, Seaton, 42
Gales, Weston, 42
Galloway, A. J., 227
Gash, Leander S., 267
Gaston, William, 166
General Assembly. *See* Legislature
Georgia, 10, 64, 106, 133, 151
Georgia Platform, 128
Gilmer, John A., 171, 173, 177, 179, 181, 213, 218, 233, 255
Goldsboro, 67
Goldsboro *Republican and Patriot*, 262
Governor: power of, 11, 43–45; popular election of, 12, 20; attraction of office, 33; significance to parties, 45
Graham, James, 74–75, 113
Graham, William A.: nomination for governor, 30–33; reluctance to accept gubernatorial nomination, 33; on internal improvements, 45, 62, 65; election as U.S. senator, 53; gubernatorial canvass of, 62–63; as vice-presidential candidate, 134–35; appoints supreme court justice, 146; identification with Whig party, 176; on Constitutional Union party, 196; interprets Lincoln's election, 200–201, 217; candidate for secession convention presidency, 219–20; in Conservative party cau-

cus, 232; elected Confederate senator, 239; mentioned, 74, 98, 145, 162, 196, 240
Granville County, 7
Graves, Calvin, 67–69
Graves, R. J., 246
Greensboro, 67, 74
Greensboro *Patriot*, 89–90, 95, 126, 128, 163, 200, 224
Guilford County, 16, 105, 156

Habeas corpus, writ of: suspension of, 246–47, 248, 256, 257–59, 260, 263, 265, 266, 267
Hale, Edward J., 161, 162, 176, 195, 207, 252, 261
Halifax County, 7, 166, 203n
Hall, Eli, 249
Hamilton, J. G. deRoulhac, 159
Hamptonville, 156
Harrison, William Henry, 3–4, 108
Hartford Convention, 127
Haughton, John H., 263
Hearstfield, William, 70
Helper, Hinton Rowan, 188
Henry, Louis D., 28, 34
Herding, 10
Herrenvolk democracy, 107
Heroes of America, 264
Hertford County, 145
High, William, 167
Hillsboro, 67, 201
Hoke, Michael, 41
Holden, William W.: loses gubernatorial nomination, 32; as editor, 42; supports internal improvements, 65–66, 72; on equal-suffrage amendment, 90; on legislative representation, 93; and election of 1850, p. 72; and gubernatorial election of 1852, p. 97; and Compromise of 1850, pp. 132–33; and presidential election of 1860, pp. 198–99; Unionism of, 204; as leader of Union Democrats, 206–207, 229; on Lincoln's inaugural address, 214; and Union party, 218; endorses disunion, 219; and presidential election of 1861, p. 230; career of, 230; and Conservative party alliance, 232; in Conservative party caucus, 232; on Vance, 234; elected state printer, 239; splits with Vance, 249; and reconstruction, 250–51; peace plan of, 250; expresses Conservative party views, 250; views compared to Vance's, 251–52; on state convention, 259; and campaign of 1864, pp. 260–61, 263, 264; and Heroes of America, 264